D1630104

Richard Bradford

The Odd Couple

The Curious Friendship between Kingsley Amis and Philip Larkin

The Robson Press

First published in Great Britain in 2012 by
The Robson Press (an imprint of Biteback Publishing Ltd)
Westminster Tower
3 Albert Embankment
London SE1 7SP
Copyright © Richard Bradford 2012

Plates: pages 1, 4, 6, 7 (bottom left and right) ©Society of Authors on behalf of the estate
of Philip Larkin/Hull University Archives at Hull History Centre;
pages 2, 3, 5, 7 (top), 8 © Getty Images Ltd

Every reasonable effort has been made to trace copyright holders of material reproduced in
this book, but if any have been inadvertently overlooked the publishers would be glad to
hear from them.

ISBN 978-1-84954-375-0

10 9 8 7 6 5 4 3 2 1

A CIP catalogue record for this book is available from the British Library.

Set in Garamond.

Printed and bound in Great Britain by
CPI Group (UK) Ltd, Croydon CR0 4YY

For Amy

And for Helen and Gerard Burns

Contents

Introduction and Acknowledgements

During a thirty-year period between the mid-1950s and the 1980s, Kingsley Amis and Philip Larkin produced, respectively, the finest fiction and poetry of the era.

In *Stanley and the Women* Amis contemplates the enclosed, impenetrable condition of insanity as the worst form of human misery, and through Nash, the common-sense psychoanalyst, he allows us a glimpse into his own most essential literary, and, I suppose philosophical, precept: 'The rewards for being sane may not be very many but knowing what's funny is one of them. And that's an end of the matter' (Kingsley Amis, *Stanley and the Women*, p. 183).

Amis is too often second-graded as a novelist because he knew what was funny. The only comic mode now granted respect by the literati is the kind of surreal speculation on the absurdities of the intellect that finds its way into the work of Joyce, Beckett, Pinter and their successors. It is acceptable because it detaches comedy from anything remotely realistic and because it has more to do with smug elitism than laughter. In Amis's novels we are continuously aware of a presence that hovers behind and around the narrator, always ready to pounce and never willing to allow a piece of dialogue or solemn proclamation of intent to get past without first puncturing whatever pretentions to absolute validity it might carry with it. His work restores to English a brand of comedy lost since the eighteenth century. It is certainly difficult to find a set of beliefs or a code of existence in Amis's work that is actively promoted rather than systematically demolished, but the same could be said of the writings of Jonathan Swift. Amis does not write parables, or submit disguised solutions to personal, intellectual or political problems. Instead, he allows his characters and his own powerfully intolerant intellect to roam through a finely crafted version of the world we know. His work is serious *because* it is funny.

This same tendency to perceive most human beings as by degrees preposterous and infuriating is what cemented the friendship between Amis and Philip Larkin within weeks of their first encounter in Oxford. For Larkin, however, humour was the flip side of a mordant, depressive state of mind. He began as an able practitioner of fiction but the very nature of the genre, involving as it does an obligation to transplant vast tracts of experience into narrative, was at variance with his temperament. For him, life in general was tiresome enough, and having to endure it yet again in lengthy passages of prose was more than he could stand. Instead, he found in verse a means of shifting between private and public registers without spending too much time with either. His stepping stones were the minutiae of ordinary existence. In 'Vers de Société', for example, he has been asked round to dinner by a distinguished university colleague, and he alters the wording of the letter in accordance with his feelings about the prospect.

> *My wife and I have asked a crowd of craps*
> *To come and waste their time and ours: perhaps*
> *You'd care to join us?* In a pig's arse, friend.

Thereafter, the poem becomes the occasion for reflections on how such gatherings prompt him to perceive life as largely a catalogue of equally pointless routines, variously customised to reinforce the assumption that something might matter. As an exercise in depressive loneliness, verging upon nihilism, it matches anything by Kafka. The state of mind rehearsed by the words is unenviable but we are not asked to share it; far more powerful is our feeling of admiration for a work of art. In his verse, Larkin appears to relish the tedious, the ordinary, often the distasteful. What makes his work superior to that of his contemporaries is his ability to graft such material on to poems of seemingly incongruous elegance. For this reason he is loathed. Academics hate him because he is not self-indulgent. He makes his language work for him and the reader, not for them: 'There's not much to *say* about my work. When you've read a poem, that's it, it's all quite clear what it means' (Philip Larkin, *Required Writing: Miscellaneous Pieces, 1955–82*, pp. 53–4). Academics and other members of the literary establishment dislike writing that is self-evidently beautiful but which does not, like modernism, demand their services as explicators.

Here too, Larkin and Amis have much in common. Both undermine the longstanding injunction of the literary and university hierarchy that, without innovation, writing is intellectually hidebound, indebted to nothing but the past. Each of them disproves this formula by demonstrating that formal conservatism can coexist with urgent questionings of the way we think and live. Moreover, they show that the successful command of traditional techniques requires far more skill and intellectual investment than the tired and predictable practices of experiment.

In the latter half of the twentieth century they were the torchbearers for writing that tested the intellect and sensibility of its readers without resorting to the self-obsessed preoccupations of modernism. The fact that they also maintained an intimate, often difficult, friendship for nearly forty-five years involves another insight into their effect upon literary history. 'What if' hypotheses are generally the hobbyhorses of historians but it is fascinating to wonder about what would have happened if Larkin had not met Amis in the Front Quad of St John's, Oxford, that day in May 1941, if their encounters during the subsequent year had been merely brief and cursory until Amis departed for military service. They would certainly have become writers but their work would have been very different from what they have bequeathed us. Their continued relationship energised, sometimes even shaped, much of their finest writing. *Lucky Jim*, the novel that launched Amis's career, could not have been written without Larkin. It was not simply a matter of him offering advice and encouragement to his friend. Their exchanges had by the early 1950s become a site for exclusive disclosures, observations, confessions; the sort of things routinely thought to lie too deep for discussion or exchange. This was the impetus for Amis's debut novel, and indeed their ongoing friendship was the foundation for much of Amis's work of the 1950s. Larkin came to life as a poet with *The Less Deceived* and *The Whitsun Weddings*, and Amis's influence was significant for both collections. But while Amis exploited their intimacy for his writing, Larkin's mature poetry was largely a reaction against it. In 1961 Larkin felt so drained, even humiliated, by his connection with Amis that he ceased communications with him. Within a decade, amicable relations had been restored. It was not simply that Larkin now felt sufficiently secure with his own literary achievements to allow Amis back. He knew he was an exceptional poet but he knew also that even if he continued to keep Amis at arm's length his presence would, until death, be an unrelenting feature of his existence, and would by implication continue to cast a shadow across him as a poet. So with commendable, if wary, resignation, he resumed their friendship.

Aside from its effect on their work, their relationship demonstrates how easy it is to mistake intimacy for exploitation and misapprehension. It would not be inaccurate to state that they knew each other better than anyone else knew either of them, yet quite often it seemed that Amis's perception of Larkin was a convenient simplification of who he really was. Sometimes the latter felt that he had become like a character in one of Amis's novels: authentically engaging and querulous but nonetheless someone else's creation. Conversely, Larkin frequently detected idiosyncracies and preoccupations in Amis to which his friend had blinded himself.

It is a fascinating story, and while a good deal of the material that charts it is in the public realm, notably in collections of letters, my work has benefited greatly from unpublished documents still in library archives. With regard to this, I am particularly grateful to the Hull History Centre (referred to below as 'Hull'), the Henry E. Huntington Library, San Marino, California (referred to below as 'Hunt'), and the Bodleian Library, Oxford (referred to as 'Bod'). If none of these abbreviations is used, the letter or book from which the quotation comes appears in one of the published collections listed in the Bibliography. In bracketed references to correspondence, Larkin is 'L', Amis 'A', and all other correspondents are referred to by either their surname or first name.

Sarah Chestnutt and Rosemary Savage deserve thanks for their assistance, and Hollie Teague and Olivia Beattie laboured heroically during the production period.

Dr Amy Burns has played a vital part in the work for this book.

Thanks are due to Faber & Faber Ltd and to the estate of Philip Larkin for granting permission to quote from the work of Philip Larkin, and thanks are due to Orion and the estate of Kingsley Amis for permission to quote from Kingsley Amis's work.

The following have provided useful information in interviews, some conducted with specific reference to this book and others for my earlier work on Amis and Larkin: Martin Amis, Elizabeth Jane Howard, Colin Howard, Esmond Cleary, Eric Jacobs, Sam Dawson, Mavis Nicholson and Christopher Hitchens.

1

Before They Met

Amis's account in his *Memoirs* of his life in suburban Norbury blends disbelief with black comedy. It seemed to him, aged sixty, that his early years were too preposterous to be taken seriously. First, he offers the reader a tour of his satellite relatives, as if keen to postpone for as long as possible a visit to 16 Buckingham Gardens, home of his father, William, mother, Rosa ('Peggy') and himself, their only child. He introduces us to Mater and Dadda, his paternal grandparents, with a deadpan account of their ghastly existence in their Victorian manor house, 'Borchester', in Purley, where Amis would be taken for meals at Christmas and for family birthdays.

Amis can never recall Dadda addressing him directly, but he remembers being obliged to kiss both of his grandparents, who apparently had an almost equal preponderance of facial hair. He also remembers how Dadda would sit at the head of the table, napkin stuffed into his shirt collar, and, between savage bouts of eating and drinking, tell jokes which combined the vulgar with the surreal. The actual presence of Dadda would have been disturbing enough, but this was later supplemented by William's account to the teenaged Kingsley of how Dadda had effectively ruined the family business. J. J. Amis & Co. were glassware wholesalers, and Dadda had become convinced that he had access to a brand of unbreakable plates, glasses and related domestic paraphernalia. To test this thesis, or perhaps just to entertain the family, Dadda once crept into the drawing-room and hurled one of the items at the stone fireplace, a performance he repeated for potential clients in the company office. He was on all occasions apparently both surprised and disappointed when these products disintegrated. Mater was equally peculiar but far more disagreeable. Her legendary meanness involved the leaving out of only two matches for the maids to light the gas in the morning, and the substitution of grocer's bags for lavatory paper.

Amis's aunt, Dora, his mother's sister, went mad, officially. Amis remembers, aged about eleven, sitting with her in his parents' kitchen. She kept asking him to move his chair away from the window so that she could 'see if there's anyone out there'. This sense of anticipating something dreadful, apocalyptic but never clearly specified, attended Dora's entire existence, and eventually, in 1941, she was committed to a mental hospital. Apparently she flourished in this environment, virtually taking over the running of the kitchen from the employees. On the day she heard of her mother's death, her neurotic symptoms, already in abeyance, disappeared for good, and within a year she was taken on as a middle-rank administrator in the same hospital.

Amis's uncle, Leslie, his father's brother, replaced Dadda as manager of the ailing J. J. Amis & Co. Glassware, and after Dadda's death was responsible for the increasingly unpleasant Mater. Amis liked Leslie and was saddened by 'his horrible life' (*Memoirs*, p. 4). In his late teens, Amis was approached by his father with some apparently disturbing news. Leslie had told his brother that he wanted to go to bed with men, and William had advised him to 'see a doctor'. No one knew if Leslie's homosexual instincts were real or hypothetical, but in any event, when Mater died, everything changed. Leslie sold the business premises and invested his inherited capital in a world cruise, during which he 'fucked every female in sight' (*Memoirs*, pp. 4–5). Two years later he was dead.

Freudians would no doubt have a field day with all of this, but we can leave its effect upon Amis to common sense. His aunt on his mother's side and his uncle on his father's side had reconciled themselves to their own identity only after the death of their last parent. Amis, by the time he left home, would know that he had already embarked upon a very effective strategy of independence. 'As I came to sense the image in which my father was trying to mould my character and future I began to resist him, and we quarrelled violently at least every week or two for years' (*Memoirs*, p. 14). In the *Memoirs* Amis concedes, if only implicitly, that his father *did* play a vital role in the shaping of his tastes and character. He operated as a foil, a testing ground, for enthusiasms and inclinations that Kingsley would acquire independently.

William was once a Liberal who turned into an arch-Tory after the Great

War, and his affiliation was strengthened by the General Strike and the emergence of the Labour Party as a serious contender for power. Amis himself, summarising his father's view of him, became a 'bloody little fool of a leftie' and an avid supporter of Joseph Stalin. Unlike his love of music, which was transparent and unflagging, Amis's political opinions were always reactive, shifting, often self-contradictory, a condition that owed something to his early instinct to rebel against anything his father espoused.

Their arguments were on Kingsley's part rooted in a level of self-willed alienation. 'What my father wanted me to be was, of course, a version of William Robert Amis, a more successful version...' (ibid., p. 17). After war service spent tending airships in Scotland, William Amis had joined Colman's, the mustard manufacturers, as a junior clerk, where he stayed, gradually acquiring seniority, until retirement. Kingsley never regarded his father as a failure, but he hated the idea that success involved, at least for people of his own lower middle-class origins, a future in the higher regions of banking or commerce.

Amis's early life was an assembly of adult narratives, stories of a potential future, all of which he strenuously avoided and rejected. But what was their alternative?

At St Hilda's Primary School, Amis was introduced to literature by a Miss Barr, a 'tall, Eton-cropped figure of improbable elegance' (Memoirs, pp. 24–5). He cannot recall the texts promoted by Miss Barr, but after moving to Norbury College, a local state school with ambitions, he encountered Mr Ashley, who employed what was in those days a radical method of teaching English. Ashley made them read Shakespeare, and then had them contrast this with almost-contemporary poetry, mostly the verse of the Georgians. He also believed that for his pupils properly to understand and appreciate literature, they should attempt to write it. Aged ten, Amis had written ninety-nine lines of blank verse and a 300-word short story, published in the school magazine, on Captain Hartly, a 'veteran hunter' of rhino.

In 1934, aged twelve, Amis went to the City of London School, an institution of solid academic reputation that took boys of various backgrounds. His father and his uncle Leslie had been pupils. William paid for his first year there, gambling on Kingsley's securing a scholarship, which he did in his next year. At the school, middle-class fee-payers mixed with a large number of scholarship boys, and for Amis his six years there were like university, and often better. He was taught Latin and Greek poetry in a way that encouraged him to enjoy its distant beauty and to recognise that poetry per se transcended linguistic difference. He discovered A. E. Housman, whose verse he would treasure, even more than that of his friend Larkin, for the rest of his life. And he talked with the Reverend C. J. Ellingham, an unequivocal Christian, to whom Housman's agnostic inclinations mattered little in comparison with the sheer quality of his verse: 'so I saw forever that a poem is not a statement and the poet "affirmeth nothing"' (*Memoirs*, p. 28). A Mr Marsh would lend out editions of verse by Auden and MacNeice; Eliot and Pound were talked about by masters and pupils.

With his peers, Amis discussed sex, radical politics, French verse, Fats Waller, Delius, Charles Morgan and more sex. While 15 per cent of the boys were Jewish, Amis claims never to have encountered anti-Semitism, even in its polite middle-class manifestation.

The City of London School provided a cosmopolitan contrast to Amis's family life. His parents had little time for 'serious' literature. His mother, Peggy, enjoyed the work of middlebrow contemporary novelists which, in Amis's view, were not 'the classics but not "slop" either'. When Kingsley seemed to have little else to do, Peggy would encourage him to 'do a bit of writing', although he was never quite certain what she imagined he would write. William favoured detective novels 'by such as R. Austin Freeman, Francis Grierson and John Rhode from the middle part of the spectrum' (*Memoirs*, p. 15). The only member of his family whose interests corresponded with Kingsley's growing awareness of mainstream literature was his maternal grandfather, George Lucas. Lucas died before Amis was old enough to talk with him about books, but Peggy provided her son with an anecdote that must have seemed consistent with the tragicomic mythology of the rest of his extended family. His grandfather would read out his favourite passages to his wife, who, when his head was lowered to the page, would make faces and gestures at him indicating various expressions of boredom, ridicule and contempt. This, says Amis, 'helped to make me hate her very much' (*Memoirs*, p. 5). And we might recall that this was the woman whose death had caused her mad daughter to regain almost instantaneous sanity.

It would stretch credibility to cite too many direct channels of influence between Amis's early life and his writing, but some parallels are evident enough. Housman became his favourite poet, and he also, at City of London

School, discovered the novels of G. K. Chesterton. Characteristically, Chesterton would use witty and often disturbing paradoxes to startle his readers, to disrupt the comfortable expectation of what a character was really like or what would happen next. Amis's favourites, from his early teens onwards, were *The Napoleon of Notting Hill* (1904) and *The Man Who Was Thursday* (1908). Both novels defy easy categorisation. They mix the genres of fantasy and science fiction with political diagnosis and a style that reflects contemporary habits and locutions. Amis, in such middle-period novels as *The Green Man* (1969) and *The Alteration* (1976), would do something similar, but his attraction to Chesterton ran much deeper than that, because his childhood was in itself not unlike a mixed-genre narrative. His world seemed to comprise not-quite-compatible segments of experience, but he found that he was able to drift between them without much effort or distress.

Larkin usually recalled his childhood with a mixture of feigned forgetfulness and irritation at being obliged, through fame, to speak of it at all. In one poem, however, he says a great deal. 'Best Society' begins:

When I was a child, I thought,
Casually, that solitude
Never needed to be sought.
Something everybody had,
Like nakedness, it lay at hand,
Not specially right or specially wrong.
A plentiful and obvious thing
Not at all hard to understand.

Larkin was twenty-nine when he wrote this, and he goes on to state that the adulthood of 'after twenty' has caused him to realise that solitude now involves effort; other people and the burden of being sociable have to be dealt with. Only then can he properly appreciate their avoidance: 'I lock my door ... Once more / Uncontradicting solitude / Supports me on its giant palm.' In 1951, Larkin was still a relatively obscure poet, but his speaking presence anticipates the figure we would come to know – a man for whom the mundane, the dreary and the mildly depressing were inspirational. The poem is fascinating because it raises questions about the kind of solitude that Larkin claims to have experienced as a child. He was never isolated or maltreated by his parents, and he had a standard retinue of school friends. It was not that he was using childhood, as Wordsworth had done, as a conceit, a vehicle for creative misremembering; not quite. When he wrote the poem his father had been dead for three-and-a-half years, enough time to reflect and take stock of the past as something genuinely irrecoverable. He could now look at his childhood and adolescence with dispassionate sincerity, and what he found was difficult to describe, one might even say bizarre. It was not so much that he remembered solitude, more that the act of remembering caused him to doubt that he could ever really have been a participant in that curious assembly known as the Larkin family.

On the face of things, the Larkins embodied the stereotype of provincial, lower middle-class ordinariness, but Sydney, Larkin's father, was a figure who regularly disrupted expectations. He was descended from four generations of small businessmen – tailors, coach makers, cobblers and finally shopkeepers – based in Lichfield. At Lichfield Grammar School he proved impressive enough to secure a place at the more esteemed King Edward VI High School in Birmingham where he continued to shine as an exemplar of self-discipline, raw intelligence and commitment. He left school, aged eighteen, in 1902, and his first job was as a junior clerk in Birmingham City Treasury. For the next five years he successfully completed a series of part-time courses in accountancy at Birmingham University, sufficient to earn him promotion to Chief Audit Accountant in 1911. In 1913 he moved further up the ladder of local government finance and was appointed Assistant Borough Accountant in Doncaster, and six years after that he moved back to the West Midlands to become deputy treasurer of Coventry City Corporation. In 1922 he applied successfully for the position of treasurer, where he would remain until his death in 1947.

Sydney Larkin is never mentioned in 'Best Society', but for Philip he patrolled the poem's genesis as a spectral presence, felt but not acknowledged. Significantly, the same effect informs the extant accounts and records of Sydney's life. His obituaries, for example, praise his studious efficiency and dedication to the duties of local authority administration, but they read like encyclopaedia entries for some obscure twelfth-century cleric of whose personality virtually nothing is known — except that in Sydney's case the omissions were deliberate. The war had been over for little more than two years, and his family had to be thought of. He had during the 1930s been an ardent and vocal supporter of fascism, particularly its German manifestation.

There are accounts in Sydney's notebooks, preserved by Philip, of how he perceived himself as a necessary and ruthless agent of efficiency in his work in local government. For example, the 'clauses inserted by my suggestion in the Doncaster Corporation Act of 1915' have 'completely reformed the system of short term loans and brought into effect a consolidated system of taxes'. And at Coventry he had created a template of 'financial legislation ... for many years the best in the country' (Hull). The style and temper of these accounts carry echoes of Mr Pooter, but the Grossmiths would have required a much darker sense of humour to have created someone like Sydney Larkin.

On the mantelpiece in the house where Philip grew up stood a 12-inch statue of Hitler which, when a button was pressed, would do a passable imitation of a Nazi salute. Sydney had acquired this on one of his many trips to Germany during the late 1920s and 1930s; he had attended at least two Nuremberg rallies. Sydney's notebooks include no direct references to Nazi Germany as the inspiration for his approach to local authority administration and accounting – or at least those which Philip retained do not – but the parallels were clear enough to everyone who knew him. In the mid-1930s he corresponded regularly with Hjalmar Schacht, the German economics minister. Schacht is credited with rescuing the German economy from the cycle of depression and inflation carried over from the 1929 slump, and Sydney was keen to impose a similar model upon Coventry. He was also by all accounts the only city treasurer in Britain whose office was decorated with Nazi regalia, causing it to resemble the by-then-familiar newsreel of the Führer's headquarters. Even up to the declaration of war in 1939 these remained in place, only to be removed reluctantly and at the insistence of Sydney's superiors in City Hall.

He could not have claimed – as, after the war, did many of the British Union of Fascists, the so-called Blackshirts – that his affiliations were fuelled by a personal experience of poverty. Nor could he have pretended that his preoccupation with Germany was grounded exclusively in the pursuit of economic efficiency: by the mid-1930s Nazi economics had become one strand of an all-encompassing ideology – including, of course, savagely pragmatic anti-Semitism. (At the Nuremberg rally of 1935, two laws were announced: one forbidding any form of sexual contact between non-Jews and Jews, the other depriving Jews of basic civil rights. Sydney was there.) Yet strangely, he possessed a personality which, while less than amiable, was difficult to stereotype. He was an avid reader of contemporary and near-contemporary literature, with a keen taste for Hardy, Bennett, Wilde, Butler and Shaw. By the time Philip was born he had acquired complete collections of their works, alongside an impressive selection of other contemporaneous authors. More significantly, he knew and admired the poetry of Ezra Pound and T. S. Eliot, had read Joyce's *Ulysses* and enjoyed the stories of Katherine Mansfield. Literary modernism was not a particularly widespread interest among local authority figures in the West Midlands, but Sydney's enthusiasm gives some credence to the claim that there was a natural affinity between the fascist notion of disciplined elitism and the view held by some modernists and their followers that accessibility involved populist degradation.

The author who fascinated Sydney most of all was D. H. Lawrence, and the parallels between them are intriguing. Both were self-made men in that they evolved mindsets and ideological viewpoints that unshackled them completely from the formative influences of their respective backgrounds. Above all, they shared a belief in the power and supremacy of the individual. This was not the liberal-humanist notion of the freedom of the individual, but a more exclusive model of individualism as an ability to detach oneself from the weary excesses of collective thinking and consensus – such as a belief in God, attendance to the idealism of democracy, or deference to such abstractions as generosity and compassion. In *Aaron's Rod*, for example, Lilly, one of the principal characters, argues for the reintroduction of 'a proper and healthy and energetic slavery', plus a programme of extermination for the worst of the lower orders and, for the rest, an instilling of respect for a natural aristocracy. The novel was published a few months before Philip's birth in 1922. Whether Sydney purchased his copy at this time is not known, but its subsequent influence upon his son makes one wonder. Sydney had to an extent modelled his life upon what would become Lilly's thesis (which, incidentally, Lawrence treats with respectful objectivity), but Philip's arrival gave him the opportunity to create an embodiment of it from the raw material of a new, male, human being.

Philip was not, of course, the exclusive product of Sydney. Sydney met Eva Day when both of them were on holiday in Rhyl during the summer of 1906. She was twenty, he twenty-two, and their backgrounds were similar. Her father had been a minor civil servant – excise officer and then pensions administrator – in Epping, Essex. She had been to grammar school, and when they met she was a junior-school teacher.

The story of their first encounter, as passed on to Philip, resembles an extract from Arnold Bennett's *Clayhanger* series. They found themselves sheltering from the rain in a hut overlooking the beach, exchanged pleasantries, and Sydney became interested when Eva continued to read her book. Obviously this was a woman for whom literature demanded attention, more so than the potentially unsettling situation of sharing a hut with a male stranger. He introduced himself, persuaded her to meet him again, and within three days they were engaged. It sounds romantic, in a very English, Edwardian kind of way, but in truth it was a moment of misunderstanding that would have miserable consequences. Eva was attracted by Sydney's confidence and impetuosity. She had never met anyone quite so exciting before, yet at the same time his apparent commitment to a respectable secure career reminded her of home. For Sydney she was a manageable version of the new independent woman: educated, moderately cultured but not over-ambitious. These early impressions were sustained by circumstances. Sydney explained that marriage would only be possible when he had a better-paid job, and, because of the distance between Essex and Birmingham, they met for relatively brief periods and exchanged letters. During the five years between their first meeting and their marriage in 1911, Sydney would have no idea that his fiancée was in truth a nervous, jittery individual who craved support, and Eva had no evidence to foresee a life with a monomaniac who would interpret such cravings as evidence of weakness and failure.

Larkin mentions his parents' first meeting only once in his published work. 'To the Sea', written in 1969, is a curious poem. It is a catalogue of images of a seaside town drawn randomly from the past – part-remembered, part-imagined – and the perceived present. It could be anywhere on the English or Welsh coast. Larkin has been there before, as a child: 'happy at being on my own, / I searched the sand for famous cricketers'. The fact that 'my parents ... first became known' in this place is a brief aside, their presence of little apparent significance among the crowded retinue of happy children, bathers, chocolate papers, rusting soup tins and families trekking back to cars as the day concludes. They met there, of that he is certain, but the consequences of the meeting seem to be obscured by matters of questionable significance. What happened after they met is not mentioned; best left unsaid. The poem is Larkin at his most transparent; elegance is mixed with listlessness, not much is said but a great deal is magnificently inferred.

When Philip was born they lived at 2 Poultney Street in a suburb of Coventry. It was a council house but not the type to be mythologised in histories of the Labour movement. Poultney Street had been built by Coventry Corporation as an investment to provide housing for the skilled workforce of the locality. For the Larkins it was a temporary residence until Sydney found something that befitted his status as treasurer. This would be 'Penvorn', Manor Road, closer to the city centre. They moved in when Philip was five, and the house would be the locus for his memories of child-hood and adolescence. It was almost new, and its combination of Tudor and Gothic features gave it an incongruously sinister aspect, fully reflected by life within.

Sydney Larkin had six brothers, of whom at least four lived in the vicinity, but Larkin cannot recall meeting any of them until he was obliged to stay with his Uncle Arthur during the Blitz in 1940. His one maternal uncle, another Arthur, lived in Essex and never visited the family. Apart from there being no relatives to speak of, Philip's parents appeared to have no friends. Penvorn was occasionally visited by people from Sydney's office, but these were not social calls.

When they met, Eva's nervousness presented itself as a tolerable eccen-tricity. Sydney treated her fear of thunderstorms and anxious concern for unforeseen trivialities as superficial elements of her otherwise reliable character. By the time Philip was born, his authoritarian, sometimes short-tempered manner had exacerbated Eva's jittery tendencies, turning her into an involuntary recluse. And one might easily forget that there was a fourth member of the Penvorn household, a daughter, Catherine (Kitty); through no fault of her own she had become in Sydney's view an appendage to Eva. She was born in 1912, and after that Sydney put child production on hold. He wanted a boy, a version of himself, and he was willing to wait until the family had reached an appropriate level of financial security until he tried again.

Sydney ran the household in the same way that he presided over the finances of the City Corporation, and Eva and Kitty became more like possessions than sharers. He was a member of the local chess club – he had always treated chess as an invigorating form of intellectual exercise – he went for long cycle rides, gave papers to the Coventry Literary and Philosophical Society, mostly on contemporary writers, and became a respected after-dinner speaker. This aspect of his life was essentially his own. Eva and Kitty would accompany him to Shakespeare performances in nearby Stratford and to concerts in Coventry, but more for appearance's sake than as a genuine reflection of a family with shared cultural interests. Eva became more and more reluctant to do anything but stay at home, attend to a schedule of duties planned by Sydney and look after the children. This active–passive imbalance was a feature of most lower middle-class marriages of the time, but with Eva and Sydney Larkin, the conventionalism of their relationship intensified their personality traits. The only figure upon whom Eva could rely for advice or encouragement, let alone sympathy, was an autodidact for whom anxiety meant weakness.

Larkin made few public statements about his childhood. The most detailed is probably an article called 'Not the Place's Fault' (1959), an almost nostalgic recollection of his early schooldays and hobbies and of day-to-day life in Coventry in the early 1930s. His parents are hardly mentioned at all. In 1986 he was interviewed by Melvyn Bragg for *The South Bank Show* and the most curious thing about his reflections on childhood is the way in which he appears to want to explain or allude to something in particular without ever saying what this is. He states that children 'don't control their destinies'; they have no choice regarding what they can do and where they live. Then he shifts from the general to the personal. 'This isn't to say I didn't have nice friends I visited and played with and so on, or that my parents weren't perfectly kind to me', but he has also found other people's accounts of their childhoods to be more exciting than his. His 'seemed to have a fairly insulated quality that looking back I can't quite account for'. 'Can't quite' is a suitably ambiguous term, but 'would rather not' is closer to the truth. A more honest account can be found in his notebooks (Hull), written in the early 1950s and never intended for publication. Sydney, according to Larkin, treated Kitty as 'little better than a mental defective', all the more irritating because of her apparent reluctance to find a husband and leave home. Sydney himself had a mind that was 'dominating, active and keen', but he seemed to find difficulties with other human beings. He had no friends, 'he worked all day and shut himself away reading in the evening'.

The notebooks are remarkably candid and at the same time perverse. Rarely, if ever, does he allow his own feelings or his memories of them to intrude upon the catalogue of facts. They read like a physician's report upon the dreadful

circumstances surrounding an untimely death, and in his summing-up he
maintains this mood of cool objectivity. His parents' marriage has left him
with two certainties: 'that human beings should not live together; and that
children should be taken from their parents at an early age'. It is fascinating
to read this alongside the poem celebrating solitude, 'Best Society', written
around the same time. It becomes apparent that the speaker of the poem,
who laments the loss of the unasked-for solitude of childhood and recognises
that he prefers it to the efforts of adult companionability, is in fact a compen-
dium of recollections and recognitions, not least of which is Larkin's growing acceptance that, temperamentally, he has decided to design his life in a
way that abates these affinities. In the third stanza he reaches the conclusion
that the more agreeable aspects of humanity are manifest only when provoked
by the presence of others – lovers, friends, family:

>   ... in short,
>   Our virtues are all social; if
>   Deprived of solitude, you chafe,
>   It's clear you're not the virtuous sort.

So after he has locked his door and retreated from the company of others,
'there cautiously / Unfolds, emerges, what I am'. Or, rather what I prefer.

The short poem 'To My Wife' was written in 1951, the same year as 'Best
Society'. It is a depressing piece uttered by a man who perceives his marriage
and subsequent existence as a kind of living suicide; a single decision has
systematically eliminated all others. It 'shuts up that peacock-fan / The
future was ... for your face I have exchanged all faces'; 'No future now'.
Larkin's biographer, Andrew Motion, suggests that it was prompted by his
feelings for Winifred Arnott, then his occasional girlfriend, but if it was a
grisly projection of the consequences of commitment it was grounded as
much upon second-hand experience as hypothesis. It is a savagely economical account of his parents' marriage and could indeed have been uttered by
his father. In the notebooks, Larkin writes of how Sydney's 'personality had
imposed that taut ungenerous defeated pattern of life on the family, and it
was only to be expected that it would make them miserable and that their
misery would react on him'. Something very similar informs the last three
lines of the poem spoken by the man to his wife:

Now you become my boredom and my failure,
Another way of suffering, a risk,
A heavier-than-air hypostasis.

For the figure in the poem, and Sydney, it is too late, but Larkin still has a choice. In the notebooks he writes of how his parents' marriage has 'remained in my mind as something I mustn't *under any circumstances* risk encountering again'.

Irrespective of our innate dispositions, some aspect of our adult personality will be a consequence of our experiences in childhood. The problem arises, however, when we attempt to estimate exactly how and to what extent we are formed by our past, because memories of childhood are a contradiction in terms. We might recollect events that occurred when we were twelve, but for the adult mind their effects involve as much a process of reconstruction as remembering. For Larkin, this juggling act was further complicated by his having effectively inhabited two separate childhood worlds. One involved the family home and the presence of Sydney, while the other was composed partly of his state of mind and partly of the people and events that he knew outside the home.

Already one becomes aware of parallels between Larkin's and Amis's childhood experiences. Both cultivated strategies of withdrawal and isolation, tendencies that would have a striking effect on them in adulthood and most significantly on their writing. But there are subtle differences too that can be seen as prefigurings of the contrasts between them as grown men. Clearly, Larkin's particular encounter with the way a family works caused him to insulate himself from any inclinations toward marriage and children. This would be the cause of some distress for his long-term partner, Monica Jones, and it would contribute to a broader refusal to affiliate that informs the mood of some of his finest poems: he observes, comments on the beauty, beguiling modernity or sheer ghastliness of the world, but with a hint of relief, as if he is not quite of it. There is no evidence that Larkin disliked his father. But his emotional attachment was equalled by a sense of unease. He admired, even shared, Sydney's commitment to self achievement, and he was certainly impressed by his unorthodox artistic and intellectual tastes, but he also sensed that as a human being, someone obliged to share their world with others, he was, to say the least, clumsy and conflicted. Larkin's own solution was to become prudent and watchful with anything resembling personal or emotional investment.

Amis, on the other hand, chose to set up his father William as a figure against whom he could test his own rebellious ambitions. In two of his novels, *The Riverside Villas Murder* (1973) and *You Can't Do Both* (1994), he incorporated transparently autobiographical accounts of his relationship with his parents and in his recreation of his father there is more than a hint of remorse. There are no reliable or detailed records of what William was really like. We rely on the somewhat partial versions of him related by those who knew him, Amis in particular, and there is evidence, especially in his accounts to Larkin, that Amis carried into early adulthood a tendency to satirise him, deliberately exaggerating aspects of his character that for some might have been amusing, even endearing, but for his son became legitimate excuses for irritation, sometimes vilification. In this respect, his early relationship with his father was a rehearsal for the interdependent relationship between two aspects of Amis the adult: the private individual and the novelist. The latter would use his work as a means of dispersing his cabinet of phobias, hatreds and emotional catastrophes.

In *You Can't Do Both*, Amis acknowledges that in his previous accounts of his relationship with his parents, his mother is always in the background. This, to his regret, is how he tended to recall her, given that the hostilities between father and son would always feature as the most memorable contrast to the otherwise unremarkable routines of life in Norbury. In fact, Peggy Amis, in an albeit unassertive and almost diplomatic manner, played an important part in Amis's early years. Throughout his life Amis had a fear of complete darkness, made worse when he was alone. It began when he was about eight, and Peggy, with a good deal of shrewd and tolerant understanding, would help him through what in modern parlance are called panic attacks. She would also function not exactly as a referee but more as a counterbalancing presence, a friend to both parties, in the disagreements between Amis and his father, a day-to-day activity that would prepare her for the more demanding role of negotiator. Two events, the first involving his affair with a married woman and the second the premarital pregnancy of his eventual wife, would cause William to ostracise his then adult son. Peggy brought them back together, and in *You Can't Do Both* Amis repays the debt.

Amis's first period away from his parents was caused by the Second World

War. Months before it was declared, the City of London School had made arrangements to evacuate its central London premises in expectation of the city becoming the target for German bombers. Marlborough College in Wiltshire agreed to share its buildings and grounds with the City of London School, and, in late August 1939, staff and pupils, the latter allowed one large suitcase each, boarded the train from Blackfriars Station to Paddington and there changed to the Taunton Express.

Amis recalls the experience as both sinister and exciting. War would not be officially declared until 3 September, but most people were aware of its inevitability. The famous 'Walls Have Ears' posters advising everyone to remain discreet about practically everything, given that Hitler's agents might be listening in, would not appear for a year, but the City of London School pre-empted them. Apart from the senior masters, no one knew where they were going. The train made an unscheduled stop at Savernake, a few miles from Marlborough. They had arrived – but until later that day, when officially informed by the masters, Amis and his friends did not know quite where they were.

Amis never made use of the actuality of these events in his fiction, but one suspects that his remembrance of the atmosphere created by them informs the texture of his mid-period novel *The Anti-Death League* (1966). In both, the metropolis and the comfortable Home Counties are visited by a blend of secrecy and subdued anxiety.

Autumn 1939 to early summer 1940 at Marlborough was Amis's final year at school, and it influenced his adulthood in a number of ways.

For the first time in his life he had the opportunity, indeed the obligation, properly to get to know people outside the family home. Leonard Richenberg, then head boy of the City of London School, shared a room with Amis in a decrepit, unheated farm-worker's cottage just outside the school grounds. Richenberg, together with Peter Baldwin, George Blunden, Cyril Metliss and Saul Rose, became Amis's closest friends. He had, of course, known them before, but all were now detached from their families; they spent their days and evenings in each other's company. Marlborough was for Amis a rehearsal for Oxford. He became the figure whose intelligence was respected by his peers but who seemed intent on making everything a lot less serious, more absurd and amusing than it might appear to be. The recollections of his friends are both affectionate and accurately inconsistent.

Blunden remembers him as someone who 'set the standards of cultural and intellectual activity ... the intellectual star', Metliss as 'a great mimic and full of fun' (Eric Jacobs, *Kingsley Amis: A Biography*, p. 60).

When interviewed by Eric Jacobs, all five of Amis's school friends stated that when they read *Lucky Jim*, it was as though they had been returned to the atmosphere of Marlborough, with Amis the at once iconoclastic, hilarious and confidently clever leader of their group. Amis the man would, reinforced by Marlborough, become a puzzling combination of an intellectual and an anti-intellectual farceur, but it was fifteen years before he realised that this blending would be the essence of his early success as a writer.

Marlborough was one of England's senior public schools. Its pupils, then all fee-paying, came from a class above Amis and his City of London School pals; they were the sons of QCs, landowners, rich, socially aspirant business-men and minor aristocrats. The City of London boys were treated by their hosts with a mixture of arrogance and condescending politeness. While Amis and his friends were from comfortably-off homes, he felt that the tension between themselves and the haughtily distant pupils of Marlborough was like something out of Dickens, people who existed in the world mixing uneasily with people who thought they owned it.

It was Amis's first real encounter with the pre-war English class system. His family, Norbury and the City of London School incorporated various strands of lower middle-class London with relatively slight variations in lifestyles, speech patterns and levels of income. His own accent was inherited from his father. It was what used to be referred to as 'BBC English', involving an unflamboyant attention to 'correct' grammar and habits of pronunciation. It was neutrally middle class, suggesting a comfortable enough background but invoking no clear affiliation to a particular region, nor any obvious political allegiance. As such it became the ideal foundation for Amis's talents as a mimic, a bare canvas on to which he could project all manner of caricatures and representations. He began to perfect these at Marlborough.

The evacuation of the City of London School had created something like a bizarre socio-linguistic experiment. The college was not attached to a town of any size, and outside it the quaint verbal mannerisms of the West Country predominated. A regiment of middle-class Londoners had suddenly created an unusual counterbalance to the stark contrast between the upper-class drawl of most of the college boys and the relaxed burr of the surrounding district. Amis thrived on this. It made him more aware than he had previously been of how the way people sound is as much a feature of their perceived personality as the way they look and what they actually say. He started paying closer attention to how vocal habits merged with temperamental and physical attributes, and his unnervingly accurate imitations of the City of London masters had his co-evacuees in stitches. As a means of becoming one of a crowd, his talent would prove very useful in Oxford, but more significantly, he would eventually recognise it as not incompatible with his intellectual astuteness – and out of this, Jim Dixon would be born.

More predictably, the class divisions of Marlborough encouraged Amis's affiliation to Marxism. Despite the fact that both schools now existed in the same place, he could not remember anything resembling a conversation with one of the Marlborough boys – their choice, apparently. He recalls that they behaved as though their privileged part of the world had been invaded by individuals who, simply because of their background, did not deserve to be there. The officer/other ranks structure of the army would, a few years later, further provoke his anger.

This was his last year at school. His masters knew that he would go to Oxbridge and that he was capable of winning an exhibition or scholarship. He had to, given that his parents could not afford to pay his fees. There were far more classics prizes available than for any other single humanities discipline, and Amis was recognised as the best classics scholar at the City of London School. But he chose to read English Literature. There were few English scholarships at either of the old universities, and his choice caused him to spend a year after leaving school at home with his parents. Competition was fierce, and he would not secure an Oxford exhibition until 1941.

Like Amis, at school Larkin found the opportunity to explore and account for aspects of his own personality that were stifled by life at home.

Despite the fact that Sydney was an agnostic, he had Philip christened in Coventry Cathedral: the grandeur of the place offered a suitable starting point for an envisioned successful future. More pragmatically, he made sure that his son was enrolled for King Henry VIII School. KHS, as it was known, was the best grammar school in the region (the fact that it was named after a dictatorial psychopath obsessed with male offspring was purely coincidental). The then-headmaster, A. A. C. Burton, ran the place more like a public school, introducing a streaming system which ensured that bright pupils could be spotted early and introduced to Latin, a basic Oxbridge entrance requirement. Indeed, Burton employed only teachers with first-class degrees from Oxford or Cambridge.

Larkin enrolled at the KHS Junior School aged eight, in 1930. The school was about ten minutes' walk from Manor Road, and most significantly it represented Larkin's first real encounter with life outside Penvorn. Previously he had been educated at home. Eva's experience as a primary-school teacher came in handy here, and Kitty, ten years Philip's senior, was used as a kind of junior assistant, reading to him and encouraging him to write and draw. So when Philip, accompanied by Eva, set out on an August morning in 1930, he was about to experience something unprecedented: never before had he encountered so many people of the same age and size gathered in the same place. Larkin adjusted surprisingly well both to this and to the equally unfamiliar experience of collective schooling. His academic performance was adequate, and although the stammer he had acquired as an infant made him anxious about speaking in class, it seems to have been treated with commendable tolerance by his teachers and peers. No one made fun of him; it was simply part of his physical make-up, like the colour of his hair.

During the three years at junior school he met and became friends with James (Jim) Sutton, a friendship that would endure for the following two decades (and then cease, without apparent cause). After his move to senior school in 1933 he met Colin Gunner and Noel 'Josh' Hughes. As the four of them reached their early teens, Gunner and Sutton in particular would operate as foils, points of correspondence and contrast for Larkin's own attempts to establish an identity beyond the stifling atmosphere of Manor Road. Gunner was the imaginative joker. He would do imitations of teachers and, more significantly, he encouraged Larkin to participate in a kind of surreal, mildly anarchistic version of the Famous Five's adventures. If a particular teacher irritated them they would create around him an unpleasant personal history, such as 'that the repellent-looking dwarf who stumped the town wearing a black cricket cap was in fact his father' (Hull). On one occasion, during the period of the Munich Crisis in 1938, the two sixteen-year-olds imitated newspaper-sellers and ran alongside a stationary train in Coventry station yelling 'War declared!' They had become fantasists in order to contemplate the effects, particularly on the expressions of the passengers, caused by their interferences with fact.

For Gunner, these exercises were an extension of his ebullient personality, but for Larkin they were rehearsals for something more ambitious. By 1936 he had begun to write short stories and make plans for longer pieces of fiction. These veered between pseudo-fictional sketches anchored to the real events and people of Larkin's immediate experience, and self-conscious excursions into the unknown, such as murder mysteries involving famous saxophonists and Chinese detectives. He would recollect that during the late 1930s he 'wrote ceaselessly', and by 1938 he began to supplement his attempts at fiction with verse, his range of styles and subjects being equally eclectic: nature poetry of a descriptive, pre-Romantic temper along with interrogative, subjective considerations of the nature of existence, influenced by a random selection of literary thinkers from Keats to Aldous Huxley.

While Gunner had played a peripheral role in all this, Sutton was more of a stabilising presence. The Suttons lived on the other side of town from the Larkins, and from about twelve onwards Philip became a regular visitor to their house in Beechwood Avenue. Jim's father, Ernest, was a successful building contractor and had built and partly designed the house himself. It contrasted sharply with Penvorn, making concessions to a suburban version of modernism. The rooms admitted generous amounts of natural light, and opened via French windows to a large garden complete with tennis court. Not only did the shape of the building show Larkin that home life could be different; he also found that Sutton's parents were the antithesis of his own. During the summer they would have regular garden parties, and all year round occasional visitors would take a drink, stay on and match the agreeable appearance of the house with the sound of relaxed companionability. Larkin liked his visits, but knew also that the place and the people were made all the more fascinating by his knowledge of their alternative.

By their teens, the temperamental affinities which first drew them together had been supplemented by precocious intellectual and aesthetic partnership. They discovered jazz, graduating from the anglicised mediocrity of Billy Cotton and Teddy Foster to the real thing of the United States – Louis Armstrong, Pee Wee Russell, Bix Beiderbecke, Sidney Bechet. Much later, Larkin would raise the possibility that his early love for jazz had influenced his poetry. Jazz lyrics scanned and rhymed: it was his first private, pleasurable encounter with something that resembled poetry outside the dreary obligations of having to study it at school. By about fifteen, Larkin, prompted by his father, had started reading D. H. Lawrence. Larkin in turn introduced Sutton to him, and the two of them would argue over the qualities and embedded messages of his work. Sutton was more interested in the visual arts and preferred the unemotional detachment of the French post-Impressionists to the loaded turmoil of Lawrence. Sutton would eventually go to art school, but he recognised that his friend's aesthetic inclinations were verbal and encouraged him to write.

Later, Larkin would see the parallels between his teenage friendships with Gunner and Sutton and his relationship with Amis. The latter incorporated aspects of both, providing Larkin with an erudite adult version of Gunner's taste for irreverence and misbehaviour, and a substitute for Sutton's reassuring air of confidence and ambition. But he would also find in Amis a capacity for dissimulation that was by equal degrees guileless and harmful. Larkin would disclose to Monica Jones that what had first attracted him to Amis, the ebullient performer with stimulating ideas on life and letters, he later found to be a facade for something more shiftless and manipulative.

Nothing survives of the prose fiction written during his late teens, but the poems are intriguing. Six appeared in the school magazine, *The Coventrian*, in 1938–9, while others remained unpublished until after Larkin's death. They are, as one would expect of a well-read late adolescent, a patchwork of resonances and borrowings. Snatches of the contemplative-symbolic mood of late T. S. Eliot occasionally interrupt the more pervasive presence of Auden. Just to remind us that this poet is still a schoolboy, we sometimes encounter awe-laden locutions from a Shakespeare-to-Tennyson miscellany – 'footsteps cold ... o'er wood and wold', etc. But despite the chaotic potential of all this learned shoplifting, the young Larkin proves himself to be a skilled technician. It is easy enough to spot the acquisitions, but he fits them together well, if not quite seamlessly. At KHS he would have been taught to recognise and name the devices of poetry, and when we read these early attempts at writing we sense the apprentice trying them out, almost self-consciously. Enjambment, for instance, crops up with studied decorum – rarely more than twice in a poem and executed so as to create a polite *contre-rejet*. For example,

I do not think we shall be
Troubled ...

With thanks to Milton. The most consistent and puzzling feature of these early poems is their anonymity. All manner of themes and inferences are tried out – predominantly isolation, embedded significance, loss – but there is not a recognisably individual presence behind the performance. Certainly most young writers are often difficult to locate among the fabric of debts to their eminent forebears or contemporaries, but with Larkin it seems almost to be a deliberate act of disappearance. This, given his circumstances, was understandable and consistent with many of his other personal traits.

By the age of sixteen he had begun to dress in a self-confidently unconventional manner. Daringly bright waistcoats and bow ties would set themselves off against his expensive, well-polished brogues and country tweed suits. One would assume that he was translating his new-found taste for European *fin de siècle* culture into a fashion statement. As well as offering poems to *The Coventrian*, he would submit letters and diatribes on all manner of subjects (the state of the cricket pitch, the existence of God, etc.) and became an enthusiastic participant in and organiser of sessions of the school debating society. His stammer was as pronounced and unhidden as his bow ties. It would be too easy to classify all of this as merely performance – the standard repertoire of hormone-fuelled late adolescence – because in most instances such rites of passage are involuntary, a necessary state in the process of growing up. It is only in retrospect, having reached maturity, that we are granted an impartial, often embarrassed, perspective upon our activities. There is, however, evidence to suggest that Larkin was engaged in a bizarre process of conscious self-scrutiny; he was watching himself.

Alongside the actual writing of the poems of the late 1930s, he played the roles of publisher and critic. He arranged them into collections, with separate titles. These he would literally sew together as booklets with self-illustrated title pages. In one called 'Poems' he inserted a foreword, offering a disarmingly honest description and evaluation of the contents ('silly, private, careless or just ordinarily bad', for example). If this was a kind of formalised dialogue between the poetic voice and its real-life counterpart, a less restrained version of the latter made its presence felt with longhand comments in the margins adjacent to the poems themselves: 'Bollocks', 'another bucket of shit'.

Between 1937 and 1940 he produced five novels, 250,000–300,000 words of prose fiction, moving between fantasist crime thriller pieces to more conventional, naturalistic accounts of contemporary life; the latter would, however, involve individuals and situations that were purposively distanced from Larkin's own world. Each would be destroyed almost immediately after completion; it was as if the process of writing was an addictive but self-defeating process. Significantly, he also kept a pocket diary (Hull) in which he would record events in Penvorn and at school with brief, dispassionate comments such as 'Mop [mother] in bad form. Pop [father] better', 'awful day', 'pretty awful week'. Although the pocket diary was not a commentary upon the fiction, a parallel can be seen between their relationship and his dialogue with the poems. He was deploying different types of writing in a chameleon-esque manner, the one consistent feature of this being the determined exclusion of anything resembling himself or his circumstances from the literary output. It is a truism that good literature is never exclusively grounded in autobiography, but at the other end of the spectrum ruthless adherence to self-negation is equally damaging. So why was Larkin doing this? Certainly he had literary ambitions, but he was unable to resolve an innate paradox in his early attempts to realise them. In one sense writing literature enabled Larkin to suspend engagement with immediate reality, an escape route from Penvorn, but in his meticulous separation of the world he knew and inhabited from its creative counterpart, he was denying himself access to a more pragmatic long-term prospect, the desired elsewhere of actually becoming a writer. In 1939, aged seventeen, he wrote to Sutton regarding his latest 'very advanced and modern' novel: 'I shall try to have it published by Hogarth Press' (6 November 1939). Within a few weeks he had burnt it.

The cause of Larkin's self-destructive relationship with his early writing is easy enough to locate: Sydney. The image of Sydney as the frightening autocrat, one that he himself did little to dispel, is slightly misleading when it comes to his relationship with Philip. If he had attempted, stereotypically, to create in his only son a more successful version of himself, then at least Philip would have had something to rebel against or retreat from. But instead Sydney behaved more like a Renaissance patron, infinitely flexible and encouraging. Despite having an autodidact's distaste for popular culture, he fully supported Philip's new interest in jazz. He paid for a subscription to the radical jazz magazine *Down Beat*, bought him a drum kit and saxophone and made sure that money was always available for the purchase of the latest American records or for visits, usually with Sutton, to performances by British bands in Coventry. With literature, Sydney choreographed a game of cat-and-mouse. He began by encouraging an interest in respectable nineteenth- and twentieth-century writing, figures who had earned esteem within the conservative purview of English literary culture, but he made sure that his son was always finding fault lines and contrasts. Christina Rossetti's poetry would be promoted alongside that of Housman; the novels of Bennett, Hardy and J. C. and T. F. Powys would show how England could be a different place for different people. And with a magician's sleight of hand, Sydney had also begun to open doors to a different literary world, beginning with Lawrence, leading to James Joyce, T. S. Eliot and Ezra Pound and including the left-leaning, radical and very contemporaneous presences of Auden, Upward, Isherwood and Spender.

Sydney's calculating tutelage ranged far beyond music and literature. In the summer of 1936, he arranged for his fourteen-year-old son to accompany him on one of his frequent visits to Germany. Most of these involved what were euphemistically referred to as his business interests – in truth, his connections with Nazism – but on this occasion he insisted that the trip would be a holiday, an opportunity for father and son to savour the social and cultural delights of a resurgent nation. Wernigerode, in Saxony-Anhalt, seemed the perfect spot: a medieval city of half-timbered houses, overlooked by a Romantic ducal castle and flanked by the Harz mountains. This idyllic reminder of Germany's fascinating history was, of course, like everywhere else, draped with motifs of the present. Apart from the ubiquitous swastika, the Nazi poster campaign was in full flow, involving vivid representations of a muscular, confident ideology along with grotesque caricatures of Jews as the archetypes of greed and deception. Their real-life counterparts had by then been obliged to signal their presence with Star of David armbands.

Sydney had made no secret of his political beliefs, but he had treated Eva and Kitty as his intellectual inferiors and hence unworthy of any attempts at indoctrination. Philip, however, was showing a degree of precocity that seemed adequate enough for this stage in the character-formation process. Germany and its people, irrespective of what they actually represented, were so demonstrably different, so exciting in comparison with the West Midlands that surely this experience would encourage a more involved interest. He repeated the exercise the following year, this time involving Bavaria, home of the German stereotypes of lederhosen, beer halls, oompah bands and fairy-tale castles; it was also the region which most enthusiastically associated itself with Hitler and his beliefs.

The visits are the episodes of Larkin's life over which he drew a calculat-edly impenetrable veil. His school friends were aware of them, of course, but, given Sydney's widely known affiliations, no one was surprised and a diplomatic acceptance was maintained. Much later, when fame had opened up his life to public scrutiny, Larkin chose the wise option of dissimulating candour, claiming that his enduring memory was of confusion and mild embarrassment: he did not share his father's enthusiasm for participating in beer-hall folk singing and he could not speak German. His statement that the trips were probably responsible for his infamous 'hatred of abroad' exploited the largely self-cultivated mythology of the Movement (the 1950s-originated term given to a group of emerging poets that included Larkin and Amis). It is rather like Byron claiming, albeit conversely, that his affection for the sun-drenched vistas of Greece was prompted by the cold, damp misery of his Scottish childhood: the facts hang together but one knows that a fair amount has been left out.

What exactly passed between father and son, and the overall effect of related events upon the latter, are open entirely to speculation; even his closest friend, Amis, knew only of evasive, amusing anecdotes on Larkin's problems with the German language. During the 1950s, particularly after Amis's father was widowed and moved in with Kingsley and his family, Amis included in letters to his friend candid accounts of how he felt about William's continued presence – largely a blend of frustration and barely disguised loathing. By that period Larkin had become more selective with the truth. He cautiously censored memories of his home life and told Amis nothing at all of how his early years might have affected his adulthood. All that can now be observed is that Larkin's childhood and teenage years were touched with a hint of the surreal. The commonplace and predictable features of provincial lower-middle-class existence were present in abundance yet peculiarly configured and informed.

Potted histories of twentieth-century European culture and politics will tell us that in the 1920s and 1930s there was an incursion of radical and unprecedented techniques in music, painting and writing, and that fascism announced itself as the disturbing antithesis to that other recent monolith-in-power, communism. Common sense will interject that while such phenomena existed, their direct impact upon, say, Middle England – at least until 1939 – was minimal. But this was not so in the case of Philip Larkin, and one begins to understand why his early attempts at literary writing, while disclosing precocious assimilative skills, were generically perverse, addressed to putative extremes of the human condition but about nothing in particular. The contrasts and bizarre dichotomies of day-to-day life seemed to amount to something beyond fiction.

There is a cartoon that Larkin drew in 1939, just before his departure for Oxford and for the amusement of Sutton (L to Sutton, 6 September 1939). His father, seated, is reading a newspaper announcing the outbreak of war and he comments that 'the British Government has started this war ... Hitler has done all he can for peace ... well I hope that we get smashed to Hades...', followed by some Lawrentian reflections on the end of a false civilisation as we know it, etc. His mother, 'Mop', is knitting. 'Oh, do you think so,' she answers, and adds, 'I wonder what we ought to have for lunch tomorrow ... well, I hope Hitler falls on a banana skin ... by the way I only washed four shirts today.' Kitty, standing, is more concerned with her account of her visit to Munich (she replaced Philip on Sydney's final journey) and how George the 'Storm Trooper' was asking after her despite her being too tired to attend the dance. Philip himself is seated, his face a dark shade of something, probably a mixture of rage and confusion. He seems apparently unable to speak or, with a pen prominently detached from paper, write (L to Sutton, 6 September 1939).

The cartoon is an impressive piece of work. Apart from disclosing a talent for visual caricature, it shows us that the seventeen-year-old Larkin had a fine ear for the inadvertent comedy of dialogue, of the ways in which, with a small amount of adjustment and some tactically astute juxtapositions, people and their relationships with each other can be made both vivid and hilarious via speech. It also prompts the question of why Larkin did not see potential interfaces between his undoubted literary ambitions and this inherent talent. The easiest answer would probably be that for a seventeen-year-old, alive to the adolescent attractions of modernism, writing like a provincial version of Evelyn Waugh (whose work he had read) was an unattractively conservative, downmarket option. Just as significant, and more obstructive, was the fact that, as yet, the material from which such realist black comedy could be drawn was exclusively his own, immediate experience. Sydney, who took trips to Munich with as much joyous insouciance as his colleagues savoured the annual delights of Yarmouth and Llandudno, was, literally, beyond parody: he was also very much – too much – part of Larkin's existence.

Within a week or two of the cartoon, he wrote in his notebook 'half my days are spent in a black, surging, twitching, boiling HATE!!!' (Hull). He does not specify the cause or direction of this feeling, but it is possible to read between the lines. Larkin was subject to a strange panorama of conditions and their attendant emotional registers. He did not hate his father or any other member of his family, and his feeling was not self-directed in any conventional manner; rather, the upper-case monosyllable was his way of killing a sentence that would otherwise have continued as a sequence of adverbs indicating frustration and confusion.

Sydney was by even the most generous measure a bizarre and unsettling individual. He was immensely learned, and he followed enthusiastically, and indeed judgementally, the twists and turns of contemporaneous cultural radicalism in a way that would put Bloomsburyites to shame. Yet he was a self-educated West Midlands local authority official – T. S. Eliot at his best could not have invented him. He loved England – its landscape, its architecture, its, as he saw it, esteemed past – yet he saw the hideous spectre of Nazi Germany as something even more venerable, a lesson for an empire in decline. Larkin's maintenance of a degree of composure during those years is commendable.

In the summer of 1938, the year after his two visits to Germany, he sat for a standard retinue of subjects in the School Certificate – the equivalent of what would become O levels and GCSEs – and gained only one A grade, in English, with Ds and Es distributed liberally through his other six subjects. In normal circumstances this would have prompted the school to offer polite discouragement regarding entry to the sixth form – his D in Latin presaged a poor chance for Oxbridge consideration. However, Burton, the headmaster, was aware that the results were, for whatever reason, incongruous with Larkin's inherent intelligence and potential and allowed him to proceed. L. W. Kingsland, head of English, recognised that this would be the most promising subject for university entry. In March 1940 Larkin took the train to Oxford to sit the entrance examinations to read English at St John's

College, the only Oxbridge college with which his school had connections. He passed, and in June won distinctions in English and History for the Higher School Certificate. In October he would for the first time begin to spend lengthy periods away from his family.

2

Early Years

Much of Larkin's life involved either making do with the routine and mundane or anticipating disappointment. A precedent for this had already been set with his bizarre family existence, and Oxford established a sense of continuity. Larkin arrived on 9 October 1940, little more than a decade after Waugh's *Decline and Fall* had presented the place as an agreeable combination of decadence and absurdity. Now it appeared as though doleful farce had taken a hand.

The traditional academic calendar had been replaced by a random, capricious timetable, with undergraduates beginning, graduating or deferring the completion of their degrees according to the demands of military service. The undergraduate population of St John's College now rarely rose above seventy, and all had to take rooms in the Front Quad. The New Quad was occupied by civil servants whose 'secret' work involved the administration of the white fish and potato ration, earning St John's, one of the richest and most prestigious colleges, the nickname of Fish and Chips.

The Blitz had not yet begun – it would a few months later and, terrifyingly for Larkin, would soon involve Coventry – but it was generally assumed that the *Luftwaffe* would at some point shift their bombers to urban centres, including morale-sapping raids on the glittering prizes of Oxford and Cambridge. Consequently St John's, like the rest of the colleges, had taken on the uniform of expectation. Fire buckets, extinguishers and sandbags decorated the staircases and quads, and the mullioned windows had tape on the glass and blackout curtains on the frames. Each undergraduate had to do an all-night 'fire-watching' stint every ten days or so. Most teaching was done by dons ranked too old, infirm or inappropriate for civil or military service. The glamour and elitist self-confidence of the city appeared to have been absorbed by a fabric of ominous dreariness. But some things did not change, such as the place's distillation of the British class system into the undergraduate population. The majority of Larkin's new peers were from public schools, and for them Oxford was a continuation of the customs and routines of a life spent mostly away from the family home. Larkin, although reasonably secure regarding his intellectual abilities, was visited by various registers of anxiety. 'Public schoolboys terrified me. The dons terrified me. So did the scouts' (*Required Writing*, p. 40). He dealt with this in a number of ways, initially by spending his first few months almost exclusively in the company of friends from Coventry. He shared rooms at St John's with Noel Hughes with whom he had co-authored in September 1940 'Last Will and Testament', a parody goodbye-note poem to the masters at KHS. Ernest Roe and Frank Smith, also from KHS, were respectively at Exeter and Hertford Colleges. His close friend Jim Sutton had gone to the Slade School of Art in London, but just before Larkin's arrival all Slade students had, for the duration of the war, been moved to Oxford. This sense of extended provincialism would eventually be embodied in John Kemp, the hero of *Jill*, except that Kemp had no friends at all and was made to feel even more isolated by being dropped a class from middle to working. And unlike Kemp, Larkin in his early months made an attempt to create a bohemian self-image. Before leaving Coventry he had acquired, with Sydney's approval, an unusual and dazzling variety of clothes: cord trousers ranging in colour through green, purple and red, waistcoats of slightly contrasting brightness, most notably yellow, and a selection of flamboyantly patterned bow ties. Sometimes he wore a slouch brimmed hat, and his cerise trousers soon earned fame as allegedly the only pair in Oxford. Larkin did his best to supplement his blink-inducing appearance by cultivating the verbal mannerisms of a wit, rehearsing clever and sardonic observations on the dons and the curriculum; both, he noted, favouring the ancient and the obscure. His stammer presented problems here, of course, and he took up pipe-smoking as a nonverbal means of diverting attention from his frequent mid-sentence truncations. Who or what he imagined he was creating is given some indication in the dozen or so poems, most unpublished in his lifetime, that he wrote in his first eighteen months in Oxford. Many of these are promising, precocious pieces. Or they would be if they did not also give the impression of being manuscript drafts written by someone else, most obviously Auden.

'Ultimatum' (June 1940) was Larkin's first published poem and reads like a thesaurus of Auden's phrasings and metrical orchestrations. The 'Auden Generation' (a.k.a. the 'Pylon Poets') had yet to attain the status of an enduring cliché, but the fact that *The Listener*'s sagacious literary editor, J. R. Ackerley, had accepted Larkin's poem indicates that their radical edge had within a decade become a fashionable idiom. The one significant difference between Auden's contemporaneous verse and Larkin's rehearsals of it is that while the former offers a stark impression of civilised Europe moving towards a fascist-inspired apocalypse, Larkin maintains a studied avoidance of any particular frame of reference. They are like poems written by an Auden afflicted with aphasia, and it is likely that Ackerley's decision to publish 'Ultimatum' was influenced as much by external events as by the piece itself. It resonates with suggestions of collective anxiety and uncertainty leavened with an image stolen shamelessly from Auden's 'Look Stranger': 'For on our island is no railway station, / There are no tickets for the Vale of Peace ...'

Read as a text in its own right it is an exercise in modernist-licensed discontinuity, intimating much but saying nothing, but before it arrived at *The Listener*'s office the battle for France was entering its disastrous final phase, and by the time Ackerley came to look at it, Dunkirk had turned Britain into an island from which there were indeed 'no tickets for the Vale of Peace'. 'Ultimatum' was a lucky break, its shambolic obscurity given apparent coherence by Hitler's military successes. In Oxford it lent credibility to Larkin's cultivated self-image; he looked like a poet, albeit of *fin de siècle* vintage, and now he had been published.

Tutorials were done in twos, and Larkin's partner was a man called Norman Iles. Iles was the Oxford variation on Gunner, a cross between a *Brideshead* throwback and a self-promoting vandal. Larkin frequently found himself alone in tutorials; Iles attended when he felt like it. He hardly ever went to lectures and he earned an unenviable reputation as a burglar: he stole coal, jam, beer and other rationed consumables from everywhere in college, including the rooms of his fellow undergraduates. Despite all of this Larkin got on well enough with Iles. It was not a close friendship, but one incident would make it a very memorable one.

Amis arrived in Oxford just before his nineteenth birthday in April 1941. No other City of London boys had gone to St John's, but the dozen or so in the rest of the university welcomed Amis in his first week with a sherry party, held next door in Balliol. This, he recalled, was his first experience of extreme drunkenness. He tells in his *Memoirs* of how, after staggering back to his St John's rooms, he had his vomiting session interrupted by canvassers for the Oxford University Conservative Association. Taking account of the chamber pot on his lap, their spokesman politely acknowledged that 'perhaps we had better return at a more convenient time' (Amis, *Memoirs*, p. 36). Amis began telling this unconfirmed story in the 1980s when the Conservatives had certainly returned, for himself and everyone else. But perhaps this is merely a coincidence.

Within a week of his arrival Amis recognised in St John's one of his Cambridge co-failures from the previous year, Norman Iles, and forty years later remembered him with a fair degree of loathing. But Iles was responsible for introducing Amis to the man with whom he shared a tutor, a meeting that would affect both of them for the rest of their lives and change the history of twentieth-century English writing. It is the stuff of myth and legend.

According to Larkin, Iles said he knew a recently arrived freshman who 'was a hell of a good man ... who could shoot guns'. Later that same afternoon, 5 May, Larkin found out what he meant. Iles pointed his right hand, pistol style, at 'a fair haired young man' emerging from the corner staircase of the Front Quad and did a passable imitation of a shot. The stranger clutched his chest and half collapsed against the piled-up laundry bags. After introductions, Kingsley Amis offered them his own recently practised pistol-shot performance, supplemented with ricochet and echoes. Larkin's account of this ends with the comment: 'I stood silent. For the first time in my life I felt myself in the presence of a talent greater than my own' (Larkin, *Required Writing*, p. 20). There is, of course, more than a hint of sarcasm in this. Larkin wrote it twenty years after the event, reflecting perhaps on how the time he had spent with Amis in Oxford was rather like a living parody of serious young writers honing their skills and exploring their ideas. Their friendship would be important; each would significantly affect the development of the other's work, and as individuals they would be two of the most influential figures in the history of post-war British literature. But Wordsworth and Coleridge they were not.

Amis's 'talent' for sound-effects and imitations is part of the mythology of those years. What is rarely mentioned is that in Oxford at the time practically everyone else was doing this. Another St John's freshman of 1941,

Edward du Cann, later to become one of Mrs Thatcher's Cabinet ministers, was celebrated for his 'set piece' reproduction of a Soviet propaganda film 'full of small arms fire and shell noises' (*Memoirs*, p. 39). Larkin and Amis traded imitations of senior English faculty dons. Amis would offer a version of Lord David Cecil's effeminate, upper-middle-class drawl, celebrating the delights of 'Chauthah ... Dvyden ... Theckthypyum', in return for Larkin's rendition of J. R. R. Tolkien's semi-audible mumble which added an extra layer of impenetrability to his special subject, Anglo-Saxon. Impersonation enabled Larkin to suspend completely his stammer and played a small part in his gradual removal of the affliction from normal speech.

Larkin and Amis helped to found a group called 'The Seven', the other five being Jimmy Willcox, Philip Brown, Nick Russel, David Williams and Norman Iles, all St John's undergraduates. Ostensibly the model for this circle was the early eighteenth-century Scriblerus Club, comprising among others Pope, Swift, Gay and Arbuthnot, and whose object was to 'ridicule all false tastes in learning' and by implication uphold their meritable counterparts. Such lofty antecedents soon gave way to a less purposive opportunity to meet at least once a week, tell jokes, share cigarettes, get drunk and maybe discuss contemporary literature. Sometimes they would pass round a poem that one of them had written and talk honestly about its various qualities and shortcomings, at least until the drink began to take hold.

This combination of high culture and disorganised indulgence accurately reflects the nature of Amis's and Larkin's early friendship. The two of them would spend long periods, usually in Amis's rooms, listening to jazz records, often prancing around in an attempt to embody the rhythms and improvisational nuances of the piece. In the Victoria Arms in Walton Street Larkin could sometimes be persuaded to do a twelve-bar blues number on the battered piano, and 'if there were no outsiders present' (*Memoirs*, p. 53) Amis would join in with lyrics borrowed from their records. Larkin's recollections of his time with Amis in Oxford often carry a slight but tangible note of envy and resentment, and there was sufficient cause for this. It was as though they were two versions of the same character created by a novelist who was uncertain about which would make it to the final draft.

Their backgrounds were remarkably similar. The City of London School was the metropolitan equivalent of King Henry VIII School, Coventry, and for each of them school was a treasured alternative to their relationships with their respective fathers. William Amis could have been Sydney Larkin rewritten as a more tractable, easy-going presence. Both were hard-working, self-made office men, and both were agnostics. When Amis and Larkin talked with each other of their lives before Oxford and their families, it must have seemed to the latter as if his new friend had drawn the longer, more generous straw. At every turn it appeared as though some omnipotent word-smith was having fun with two parallel scripts, choosing to reframe Amis's as suburban comedy and Larkin's as provincial Gothic. Amis, when he arrived in Oxford, was an enthusiastic communist, proudly exhibiting a polemicist's knowledge of the works of Marx and Lenin, but even then he admitted that his commitment was acquired partly as a way of irritating his father, a means of asserting his independence. He had become a radical among lower middle-class Tories. How, wondered Larkin, would he too have acquired a similar, albeit immature sense of a separate identity? By declaring his loyalty to Stalin? Sydney would probably have relished the challenge – the polarities of European fanaticism embodied in father and son.

And then there was jazz. 'Our heroes', wrote Amis in his *Memoirs*, 'were the white Chicagoans, Count Basie's band, Bix Beiderbecke, Sidney Bechet, Henry Allen, Fats Waller, early Armstrong, and early Ellington ... and our heroines were Bessie Smith, Billie Holliday, Rosetta Howard ... and Cleo Brown' (*Memoirs*, p. 52). These enthusiasms were not unique to Larkin and Amis – every undergraduate not prematurely middle-aged was a jazz fan – but what was striking for the two new friends was the weird contrast between how they had acquired their tastes. Amis told of how his father regarded Duke Ellington records as evocative of dark-skinned savages danc-ing round a pot of human remains and much classical music, without the human voice, as a form of grandiose self-indulgence. Amis senior preferred Gilbert and Sullivan. So again Amis made sure that his early encounters with Mozart, Haydn, Schubert and, particularly, American jazz were accom-panied by a learned polemic. His love for music, jazz and classical, became transparent and unflagging, but it was inspired by his early instinct to rebel against anything his father espoused. Sydney encouraged and promoted all the activities that in the Amis household functioned as symbols of youth-ful dissent. Classical concerts in Coventry were standard fare, and, as we have seen, Larkin was encouraged in his love of jazz. Amis's parents enjoyed middle-market contemporary fiction; women novelists such as Ursula

Bloom, Norah C. James and Ann Bridge being his mother's favourites, William preferring the detective writing of Austin Freeman, Francis Grierson and John Rhode. At Amis's school the likes of Auden, MacNeice and Eliot were coat-trailed by masters and pupils as examples of something almost dangerous. How different from Penvorn where modernism was perfunctory, *de rigueur*. The literary, political and cultural affiliations that Amis used as a means of projecting himself into an impertinent adulthood appeared for Larkin to have been anticipated and pre-empted by his father. Certainly his taste for caricature and practical jokes amused Larkin, but more and more each found in the other dimensions of their own personality either more fully developed or comfortably contained.

They talked a lot about literature, and Amis later claimed that Larkin 'was always the senior partner ... the stronger personality, always much better read'. This was true in that Larkin knew a lot more about contemporary writing than his friend. He encouraged Amis's slight interest in Auden and introduced him to the idiosyncratic fiction of Flann O'Brien and Henry Green. He also recommended to him Julian Hall's *The Senior Commoner*, a humourless exploration of class difference, isolation and repressed sexuality. This would influence Amis's first novel, 'The Legacy', completed after the war and unpublished. 'The Legacy' was like none of the works that would sustain his career as a novelist. It was introspective, lacked narrative energy, contained nothing resembling wit and in a paradoxical way it reflected the nature of Amis's early friendship with Larkin. Amis's presence encouraged, even licensed Larkin's taste for visiting upon respectable culture a blend of the satirical and the obscene as a valve for his frustrations and uncertainties regarding his serious literary ambitions. At the same time Larkin's learning and sophistication offered Amis a stabilising counterbalance for his own addiction to irresponsible humour.

According to Amis, Larkin would write obscene clerihews about the college dons, and they collaborated on a record cover involving 'Bill Wordsworth and his Hot Six': 'Wordsworth (tmb) with "Lord" Byron (tpt), Percy Shelley (sop), Johnny Keats (alto and clt), Sam "Tea" Coleridge (pno), Jimmy Hogg (bs), Bob Southey (ds)'. During their discussion of other people's poems, including those of friends from 'The Seven', they considered having two rubber stamps made, reading 'What does this mean?' and 'What makes you think I care?' Larkin later commented that there would be 'one for each of us', and we will never know which question best reflects the attitude of either himself or his friend. They even evolved a private, ritualistic habit of speech in which, to save time, any idea or person they regarded as pompous, boring or pretentious would be attached without connectives to an obscenity: 'Spenser bum, piss William Empson, Robert Graves shag'. This mildly juvenile practice survived in their letters until Larkin's death. Despite being much shyer than Amis and less inclined to turn his taste for mockery and caricature into a public performance, Larkin could be far more cynical. He wrote a parody of Keats's 'La Belle Dame Sans Merci', which included the sensitive Romantic's confession that:

And this is why I shag alone
Ere half my creeping days are done
The wind coughs sharply in the stone ...
There is no sun.

Amis's copy of Keats's *Poems* contained a comment by Larkin on that famous moment of ethereal unification and transcendence in *The Eve of St Agnes*: 'YOU MEAN HE FUCKED HER.' It was as though both were in private able to enjoy breaking down the institutionalised borders between comic irreverence and high culture, while in their attempts to produce proper literature they deferred to the humourless conventions of the latter.

Around the same time as this Amis had taken on, for a term in 1942, the editorship of the University Labour Club *Bulletin*, and in the spring issue he included two of Larkin's poems called 'Observation' and 'Disintegration', the titles of which bespeak their intense, self-focused moods.

In early 1942 they collaborated in what Amis later called a series of 'obscene and soft-porn fairy stories'. One was entitled 'The Jolly Prince and the Distempered Ghost' and was a parody of the sometimes dreary medieval narratives that were a compulsory element of the Oxford curriculum. It involved a ghostly presence whose insubstantiality is belied by his constant habit of farting. Another, called 'I Would Do Anything for You', was about two beautiful lesbians who discover in their Oxford flat a collection of jazz records left there by the previous, male, occupant. Scrupulously these records are listed, and they are ones that both Amis and Larkin had read about but never heard. This is a fascinating evocation of circumstantial and psychological pessimism. If the man had returned to the flat to reclaim his property he would have found women to whom he was attracted but who would never feel anything similar for him. The records, similarly observed but not experienced by the authors, testify to their own anticipation of failure – although for Larkin, much less attractive and confident than his co-author, the symbolism would have been more cutting. The story, combining in one figure characteristics of each of them, would remain a token of their early friendship: Amis refers to 'IWDAFY' on at least six occasions in his letters to Larkin during the 1940s and 1950s.

The sense of stoical gloom that underpins the story would re-emerge in Larkin's first published novel, *Jill*, four years later. It is a work that is addressed to his own ever-present sense of vulnerability. The element of mildly pornographic irresponsibility and the sheer fun that had attended his collaboration with Amis had disappeared. It was only when he began to write his early-1950s poems that the assertive, sardonic spark of the unpublished novel began to show itself.

Although Amis described Larkin as the 'senior partner' in their friendship, this is more a tribute to the latter's learning than an accurate reflection of their conventions of exchange. For Larkin their co-authored stories involved a degree of self-mockery. He had become a devotee of the psychologist John Layard, whose theories of sexuality, identity and socio-cultural enclosure found parallels in the fiction of D. H. Lawrence, whose work Larkin also admired. Amis summed up his own view of Layard and Larkin's preoccupation with his ideas as 'all that piss about liar's quinsy', and he loathed D. H. Lawrence. Lawrence, in Amis's opinion, was a psychosexual evangelist masquerading as a literary writer. Amis always believed that whatever else literature might be it should not become the vehicle for an explanation of the human condition. Amis and Larkin did not argue about this, because Amis simply forbade from their exchanges anything that in his view was spurious, intellectually pretentious and consequently boring, and Lawrence was top of the list.

So while their stories might appear to be the products of similarly disposed farceurs, they grew out of the unevenness of their relationship. For Larkin they provided some relief from the harsh and unsettling world of self-examination that constituted his early writing. Amis, as Larkin has stated, did not really have another world; he 'lived in a zone of the most perfectly refined pure humour' (Motion, 1993, p. 54).

The relationship formed between Larkin and Amis in the year before the latter left Oxford for military service is fascinating principally because we fail to appreciate its immense significance. It would be a decade before each of them had served their apprenticeships as writers and begun to produce prestigious work, and this process was informed, instigated, by their friendship. The reason why we do not recognise the influence of one upon the other is because it was involuntary. Few if any writers would be willing to concede that the essential character of their work, its success, was due to an accident for which they were only partially responsible.

The most widely quoted and returned to account of Larkin's Oxford years, particularly 1941–2, is his introduction to the reprint of *Jill* written more than twenty years later. For some reason, which Larkin does not bother to explain, Amis holds centre stage. The other characters – Noel Hughes, Iles, his tutor Gavin Bone, his other close friend Bruce Montgomery – feature as a graciously acknowledged cast of extras. Amis takes precedence, but Larkin makes sure that we do not get the wrong impression. After telling of his friend's abilities to render everyone incapable with laughter he adds: 'This is not to say that Kingsley dominated us. Indeed to some extent he suffered the familiar humorist's fate of being unable to get anyone to take him seriously at all' (Philip Larkin, 'Introduction', *Jill*, p. 16). This must come close to a record for breadth of implication generated by economy of words. Virtually everyone who read it, in 1964, would see not the undergraduate farceur but the bestselling novelist. Moreover, those who had followed Amis's work would see a writer whose claims to be taken seriously had been regularly undermined by a solid core of reviewers who treated his apparent addiction to comedy as his Achilles heel, the characteristic that denied him admission to the rank of proper novelists. Certainly Amis was a far more talented joker and imitator than virtually anyone else in Oxford, but to imply, as Larkin does, that this was an accurate anticipation of his literary presence is a calculated distortion of fact. Larkin does this as much as a private means of repackaging the past as a snide gesture towards the public reputation of his friend. As we shall see, by 1964 Larkin had virtually ostracised his friend, and an ugly combination of envy and bitterness played some part in this.

Among his friends, Amis, at the time, seemed to Larkin the least likely to succeed as a literary artist. Before he met Amis, Larkin had, albeit tentatively, begun to cultivate a friendship with Bruce Montgomery. Montgomery was already a legendary figure in Oxford: composer, painter and author of two novels and a monolithic tome entitled *Romanticism and the World Crisis* (all at the time unpublished). His background, looks and behaviour were those of a lazy, idiosyncratic sybarite – a talented version of Sebastian Flyte. Also, he presented himself in his dress and manner as potentially bisexual. Larkin was fascinated and influenced. In 1942, for example, he began to make hesitant sexual advances towards Philip Brown, a medical student with whom he had shared rooms in 1941 and a co-member of 'The Seven'. Brown later confessed to being more puzzled than offended by this, given that Larkin himself appeared to be trying to recreate himself as a version of Montgomery. He was attempting to build a world around himself where any form of unorthodoxy and radicalism – sexuality included – indicated artistic promise. Amis, the boozy, talented jester, seemed to belong in a completely different sort of drama.

Larkin and Amis had known one another for little more than a year when the war interrupted their friendship – Amis was conscripted into the army but Larkin's poor eyesight exempted him from military service. This period of prolonged separation, particularly the eighteen months when Amis was serving in Continental Europe, was immensely important because they began to exchange letters regularly. It was the beginning of a correspondence that would last, with a notable interruption in the 1960s, until Larkin's death and which is unique in the history of literature. Never before or since has there been an extended record of two writers disclosing aspects of their private worlds to each other, sharing dimensions of their personalities in such a way as Amis and Larkin did. Their correspondence provides an index not only to the progress of their relationship but also to each of them as individual writers.

In July 1942 Amis arrived at Catterick Camp in Yorkshire for basic army training. He had completed only a year of his degree when he was called up. After two months as a private he was posted to the neighbouring Royal Corps of Signals depot as an officer cadet; and six months after that was awarded a commission as a second lieutenant.

Amis was well prepared for the shift from university to military service. At City of London School, aged fourteen, he had joined the Officer Training Corps and he transferred to its adult version, the Senior Training Corps, at Oxford. In the Officer Training Corps he had become an excellent rifle shot, and at City of London and Oxford he proved to be a talented practitioner of drill and marching. New, physically fit soldiers could choose their regiments and specialisation, although practically all able and mentally competent men were obliged to join active service units. Amis, following the advice of his Oxford acquaintance Norman Manning, went for what seemed the safest. The Signals, as its name suggests, was the communication department of the army. They set up and maintained radio links between fighting troops and their support and they worked largely behind the front line. Amis during his period in Europe in 1944–5 witnessed the consequences of war but never quite its practice. He landed in Normandy three weeks after D-Day, and he followed the advance through France, Belgium and Germany always at a relatively safe distance from the exchange of fire.

'Who Else Is Rank?', a novel, was co-authored during his time in Europe with his fellow Signals officer E. Frank Coles. It was never published, and the typescript is deposited in the Huntington Library, California. The parts of 'Who Else Is Rank?' written by Amis involve Frank Archer, a young, sensitive lieutenant in the Signals, whose story is based almost exclusively upon Amis's experiences in 1943–5. Archer undergoes basic training in Catterick, and one evening he meets a young woman in the King's Arms, Richmond, a market town a few miles from Catterick Camp. The woman is attractive, has 'dark brown hair and rather peculiar eyes a long way apart and rather long from corner to corner'. Her name is Betty Russell, and she is an exact reproduction of Elisabeth Simpson whom Amis did meet in Richmond, in the King's Arms. Her fictional name reflects Amis's continued attachment to Larkin. In their letters in 1943–4 he always refers to her as Betty, and the other name that occurs most frequently in these letters is Pee Wee Russell, one of Amis's favourite jazz players.

Coles and Amis wrote the novel over several months in the winter of 1944–5 when their signals company was stalled a few miles from Brussels. As Amis put it in his *Memoirs*, 'Ennui had time to set in' (*Memoirs*, p. 86). Their temporary officers' mess was a well-furnished bourgeois house, and after dinner they would compose and read to each other their respective chapters. Amis's Archer and Coles's Stephen Lewis were first-person narrators whose experiences and observations would often intersect. Significantly, however, Coles/Lewis tells us a great deal about Amis/Archer, while the latter is more preoccupied with his own activities.

Amis's chapters are, as one would expect of first attempts at fiction, uncertain exercises in how to blend the message with the resources of the medium. The two chapters entitled 'Rhapsody' and 'Ecstasy' concentrate on his relationship with Elisabeth Simpson and are as much a means of exploring his own feelings and recollections as an attempt at publishable fiction. In one episode in 'Rhapsody' he describes in about 160 words several days in the lives of Betty and Archer, but the phrase 'A few days later in the waiting room at Catterick Bridge Station' is the only specific reference to place and time. The rest of the passage is concerned with 'kissing' (three references), Betty's 'breasts' and Archer's contact with them (twice), her 'legs' and 'thighs' and, predominantly, her response to his attentions: 'her heart ... beating as fast as mine', 'she seemed very tense and quivering', 'still didn't say anything', 'she writhed in my arms', 'she was breathing very deeply'.

'Ecstasy' tells us of a weekend they spend in York in a hotel, of how Archer feels something more than desire for Betty and eventually of Betty's declaration that their relationship must end. Her husband is on active service in the Middle East. She does not love him, but she feels she must return to him for the sake of her daughter. When Amis wrote this in 1944–5 it was an accurate account of the state of his relationship with Elisabeth Simpson. He concludes the chapter with Archer saying, 'I'm seeing you again', as Betty boards her train. After the war they kept in occasional contact by letter, but their relationship was effectively over before Amis left for Europe. Amis even includes in 'Ecstasy' a version of his father's discovery of his affair with Elisabeth. Archer tells Betty that his father is 'a bit suspicious' and that he thinks of her as 'a designing woman', which, in the light of William Amis's actual reaction, is a trifle generous. In truth, William ostracised Kingsley who was home on leave. Only Peggy's shrewd, diplomatic policy of persuasion caused him to resume communication with his son.

In the letters exchanged between Amis and Larkin in 1942–3, when Amis was in Catterick, we can recognise parts of the narrative of 'Who Else is Rank?' In practically every letter Amis mentions Elisabeth or 'Betty'. On 20 August 1943 Larkin replies to a letter of the week before in which Amis had told him of how Elisabeth effectively dominated their relationship, referring to him as a 'funny, silly creature'. Larkin writes that a woman who had said this to him 'would find herself on her back before she knew where she was' and he was not referring to sex. He adds that Elisabeth 'sounds delightful, honest she does. I know she isn't really.' It is clear that Amis has presented Elisabeth to Larkin as someone who both excites and, to an extent, intimidates him, and in his letters he includes examples of fictional dialogue based upon his own exchanges with her. In a reply to him on 16 September 1943 Larkin writes that 'these "pattern conversations" are the last word'. Amis provided Anthony Thwaite, Larkin's letters editor, with an explanation: 'a pattern conversation was a typical conversation between young man and young woman showing how she could twist y.m. round her little finger – "What's wrong?" [asks y.m.] – "Nothing" – "If there's something wrong I wish you'd tell me" – "If you like me as you say you do you wouldn't need telling", etc.' (Anthony Thwaite (ed.), *Selected Letters of Philip Larkin, 1940–1985*, p. 70).

Amis supplied Anthony Thwaite with these details in the late 1980s when the latter was preparing his edition of Larkin's *Letters*, but what he did not recall was the function of pattern conversations both as a private joke between himself and Larkin and as a testing ground for his first attempts at writing fiction. Writing to Larkin from Catterick (26 October–6 November 1943) Amis suspends the gossipy flow of the letter and offers his friend an example of pattern conversation.

'It was awfully nice of you to come and see me tonight, darling, when you've got all that work to do.'
'Don't say that. I wanted to.' (Liar.)
'It's been awful this week. I've missed you so much.'
'It hasn't been nice for me either. I've missed you too.' (Liar.)
'You know, Bill ... it's just like having ... pins and needles ...'
'You'll have to get used to being without me, you know.' (Bastard.)
'Yes, I know.'
'Never mind, May. I shall never forget you.' Yes, I really did say that.

The 'May' to whom he referred was a soldier in the Auxiliary Territorial Service (the women's branch of the army) based at Catterick with whom Amis (Bill) was having an affair alongside his one with Elisabeth, and one assumes that this is a transcribed recollection of an actual exchange. A very similar conversation appears in 'Who Else Is Rank?' following the 160-word description of Archer fondling Betty.

'Are you all right?' I said.

'Yes, I'm all right,' she said. 'You mustn't do that,' she said. 'I felt like crying.'

'But I like you very much,' I said.

'You wouldn't have done that if you really liked me.'

One wonders if Amis adapted a transcription of his exchange with May for the one between Archer (himself) and Betty (Elisabeth). The only significant difference is that the former includes, for Larkin's benefit, disclosures of Amis's blatant insincerity ('Bastard', etc.). 'Who Else Is Rank?' bears practically no resemblance to the fiction that Amis would eventually publish, with the exception of the pattern conversations. These resurface in a more accomplished, merciless form in the exchanges in *Lucky Jim* between Dixon and his horrible girlfriend, Margaret Peel. And again we encounter a connection between the closed, confessional exchanges between Amis and Larkin and the former's writing, first in 'Who Else Is Rank?' and more significantly in *Lucky Jim* where Margaret Peel, the pushy woman attempting to 'twist the y.m. round her finger', is based upon Larkin's girlfriend, Monica Jones, whom Amis openly disliked. It is also worth noting a close resemblance between Amis's pattern conversations and the dialogues between the nervous, hesitant John Kemp and practically everyone else, particularly the women, in Larkin's first novel *Jill*, which he first mentions to Amis in a letter written three weeks before he congratulates his friend on this misogynistic contribution to the novelist's task.

At one point Archer obtains an evening pass for a few drinks with some of his Oxford friends – he, like Amis, has had to interrupt his degree for war service. One of his friends is wearing purple corduroys, very thick glasses and an orange bow tie, and his manner drifts between the anxious and the affected. His name is Bruno Coleman. One of the mildly surreal and unpublished short stories that Larkin wrote, without Amis's cooperation, although he read it, was about a dominant lesbian figure called Brunette Coleman.

Aside from the pseudo-erotic pieces co-written with Amis, most of Larkin's own literary output during his undergraduate years can best be described as outlandish. It comprises principally two pieces of fiction, 'Trouble at Willow Gables' and 'Michaelmas Term at St Bride's', and a verse sequence called 'Sugar and Spice: A Sheaf of Poems'. The work is fascinating in its own right but even more so because all of it is written by a figure invented by

Larkin, the aforementioned Brunette Coleman. It would be tempting to treat the two novels – the first set in a girls' boarding school, the second involving some of the same characters a few years later in Oxford at a version of Somerville College – as a blend of mild pornography and self-parody: women's sexuality, specifically lesbianism, appears to be the predominant theme, and it would, of course, have been both satisfying and a compensation for his own sexual immaturity for Larkin to have set his own most lurid fantasies against his imaginative and technical skills as a writer. However, on closer scrutiny it becomes evident that he had involved himself in something far more strategic and complex than an exercise in vicarious gratification.

In 'Trouble at Willow Gables' the style shifts between three registers: cautious indifference, archly overwritten symbolism with a hint of Lawrence and prose that appears to disclose its writer's involuntary feelings of sexual excitement.

He pretended to his friends that Brunette was a joke, but in truth she was a rehearsal for what he knew he would give proper time to after graduation. She enabled him to invent a writer, to stand outside this presence, sometimes allying her with his own inclinations – sexual and familial – and sometimes watching her operate as a figure attempting to reconcile what she was with what she put on the page. Within a year of completing the strange fabric of texts that created Brunette he would begin his first serious attempt at fiction. There would be parallels, in that the principal figure would be a fantasist, not unlike the creator of Brunette, for whom life and fiction involve fragile, nebulous borders. Brunette was the preamble for *Jill*.

Considering the amount of time and effort given over to the creation of Brunette and her literary constellation it is extraordinary that he had any in reserve for other activities, such as his final examinations in June 1943. Throughout the spring and early summer he complained regularly to his friends that he was, variously, unprepared for finals, unsuited to academic study per se and indifferent to the nature of his degree. To Norman Iles he wrote that 'There's so much to be learnt – and of course the best thing to have is a "genuine love of literature". I haven't got one ...' (7 April 1943). To Iles he predicted 'a Second if I'm lucky', for Sutton 'a Third, at most a Second' (12 April) and for his parents 'a Third or lower' (4 April). His pessimism was genuine in that he was aware that he had spent too long doing other things to make the best of his innate talents as a literary scrutineer

– perversely Brunette's 'What Are We Writing For?' discloses the analytical talents of its, and her, creator. When, in mid-July, he ascended the steps of the Sheldonian Theatre to look for his name on the degree lists he was well prepared to be ranked as mediocre or worse, and the combination of surprise and elation was all the more priceless when he found that he had a First. For once the Larkin family shared an unalloyed feeling of happiness. Eva and Sydney attended his graduation ceremony in late July, and afterwards the three of them went to lunch with Diana Gollancz and Bruce Montgomery.

He spent the rest of the summer in Coventry with occasional visits to friends still in Oxford, and it is during this period that he exchanged experiments with Brunette for plans for a piece of fiction that might be taken seriously by publishers. At the end of 'Michaelmas Term at St Bride's' there is a curious passage in which one of the two principal characters, Pat, informs the other, Marie, that the 'story' in which they had both been involved is 'over now' and that reality beckons. The specifics of this non-fictional world involve a bar-room full of young men, some of whom she has met before and others not. Members of 'The Seven' would probably have recognised versions of themselves. 'Teddy' is, no doubt, Edward du Cann, and one man, Bruce Montgomery, is even referred to as author of *The Case of the Gilded Fly*, as indeed he was. Not only had Larkin introduced his fictional character to some of his actual acquaintances, he further guaranteed the authenticity of this world by basing it upon a real event. On 5 June 1943 he wrote to Iles:

> We went drinking last night with Bruce Montgomery, Philip and two fresh-men and Lt Colin Strang and Kingsley did The Man in the Pub and The Man in the Train etc. etc. ...

As Marie pushes ajar the Smoke Room door she witnesses them, including 'a fair haired second-lieutenant talking about a man in a train': 'Marie shut the door hastily. If this was reality, she decided, she would rather keep in the story.' So also concludes Larkin's period in a world inhabited and created by someone else. He had allowed Marie to return to it, but he was moving elsewhere. He wrote to Sutton a couple of months later, 'I am writing a story called (provisionally) "Jill"' (20 August 1943).

John Kemp, the main character, fails to engage the interest or sympathy of anyone inside or outside the novel, so perhaps his real function is that of an embodied device, the means by which the fictional text folds into itself and contemplates its own status as fiction. He invents a separate life for himself involving the creation of a younger sister, Jill, a process which begins with him writing letters to and from her in which he presents himself as the witty, confident figure he aspires to be but for some unexplained reason finds himself unable to become in real life. This spirals into a private fantasy, with Jill becoming the subject of an extended short story and then the author of her own diary. Soon after that he encounters a real Jill (or rather Gillian) who spoils the fantasy by proving to be not quite what he expects and certainly not, as he hopes, interested in him.

Larkin's attempts to distance himself from John Kemp read like an alibi offered by the accused. Kemp's working-class background, his childhood in Huddlesford, a Lancashire industrial town, and, worst of all, his parents, are assembled from second-hand stereotypes. He tells in the Introduction of how he and Norman Iles had invented a 'Yorkshire Scholar' when amusing each other on trips to and from tutorials by conversing in music-hall versions of northern working-class speech. However, a more revealing example occurs in a letter to Amis (14 July 1942) in which he places himself, with his own classless accent unaltered, in an imaginary exchange with two Leeds University undergraduates.

> Me: Of course, the fundamental quality of Russell. [Pee Wee Russell, the jazz musician]
> 1st Scholar: E-e-ehhh! Dust mean Professor Russell of Awld English Philologee?

He prefaces this with the comment that he and Amis were lucky not to have ended up in the University of Leeds, but within a year this joke had rebounded. Kemp's parents' speech habits are not quite as excessively provincial as those of the scholars, but they nevertheless come close to sounding like a parody of Elizabeth Gaskell's *North and South*. Joe Kemp: 'You ain't talkin to a man with backward ideas ... I want to do t'best by the lad as I can.' Clearly John Kemp had to lose his accent.

It would have been apparent to Larkin that his dressing up of Kemp as a working-class northerner was unconvincing, but he kept at it because it was his only hedge against his increasing and uneasy awareness that he was indeed writing about himself. He wrote to Amis that 'John Kemp is getting rather clever, but that's because he is growing like me, a tendency I shall sternly redress in the third draft' (12 October 1943). He was referring here to Kemp's imaginative cunning, evidenced in his preparation of the false letters to and from Jill. But he did not redress the tendency and a month later he reported to Amis that 'the diary and the short story he writes ... may have to be cut out. A little twerp like John Kemp couldn't think of anything so perverse' (8 November 1943). He could not because nowhere else in the novel does he indicate anything resembling literary talent or ambition; again the problem originates in Larkin's attempt to separate himself from his character. In the end, however, Kemp's inventions become a key element of the novel, and he becomes even more like his creator than Larkin had envisaged. The diaries and the short story are a cannibalised version of 'Trouble at Willow Gables'. Jill's boarding school is called Willow Gables, many of the characters from the original manuscript are there too and only the mildly pornographic material is left out. More significantly, he disclosed to Amis that, with regard to this transference, 'Brunette Coleman, who wrote "Trouble at Willow Gables", is helping me' (20 August 1943), and throughout his account to Amis on the progress of the novel Brunette is indeed always there helping him. This might seem to be a joke, but in truth it is an acknowledgement by Larkin that he had effectively lost control of the balance between invention and autobiography.

Brunette was based partly on Diana Gollancz, at the time Larkin's closest woman friend. They had met during his final undergraduate year, and he had kept in touch with her during 1943–4 when writing *Jill*. She was an art student at the Slade, daughter of the publisher Victor Gollancz and given to the mixture of moneyed flirtatiousness and bohemianism with which Waugh's novels had drenched the image of Oxford between the wars. There could hardly have been a better model for the author manquée of Larkin's erotic fantasies, and when he refers to Brunette in the Amis letters as his helpmate in the planning of *Jill*, fantasy was yet again bleeding into fact: Diana read and commentated on Kemp's letter and diaries. Brunette could not, of course, feature as herself in Larkin's first attempt at publishable fiction, but her real counterpart could, and Diana becomes Elisabeth Dowling. She, like Diana, is self-consciously and proudly attractive to men and dresses in a way that enhances both her erotic and artistic self-image.

Apart from Kemp's eventual obsession with the real Jill, Elisabeth provides the novel's one moment of almost unbridled sexuality. She is advising Kemp on how to wear his newly acquired bow tie (blue silk with white spots, one taste he shared with his author), and as they move closer together and make physical contact Kemp begins to feel a 'flaring theoretical lust'. Elisabeth's expression indicates that she wants him to touch her: 'He saw in a second that she expected him to do this, that she was waiting for it.' This is an economical version of a more extended dance of mutual attraction between Larkin and Diana. He reported to Amis that he had heard that 'Diana Gollancz thinks very highly of me and would like to get into the same bed that I do ... she waits for me to make the advances' (19 October 1943). In the letter he cannot quite make up his mind about whether he will respond to Diana's apparent attraction to him (actually his account is touched by vain optimism and in the end nothing happened between them), while in the novel he expands on this by having Kemp's narrator helpfully explain the curious notion of 'flaring theoretical lust': 'A horrible embarrassment tingled and shuddered inside him, that what he had imagined to be his most secret feeling was almost cynically common.'

Larkin's anxiety about separating himself from Kemp might appear to be driven by the standard elevation of imaginative and intellectual sophistication over a dependence upon given facts. In fact, his fears were far more rudimentary. Kemp was a version of him – he had come to accept that – but now he had to decide the extent to which his creation would improve upon or embody those aspects of himself that caused him most discomfort.

After informing Amis of the sexual potential in his friendship with Diana he adds in the same letter that he only mentions this 'as a vague answer to your weekly Rabelaisianism'. What he means is that Amis had over the previous eighteen months kept him regularly informed of his prodigious sex life. Larkin was fascinated and amused by Amis's accounts of his exploits and, when comparing them with his own attempts to initiate something resembling a relationship, he was envious and disappointed. He had made tentative and ultimately unsuccessful advances to Margaret Flannery and Hilary Allen of the University English Club, both involving a mixture of uncertainty and, on his part, nerves. He had arrived for a date with another undergraduate, having prepared his strategies carefully, including the presentation of a bunch of flowers. She had disrupted his calculated sequence of charm and chat by opening the door too early, causing him to present her with the bouquet and, fearing an attack of the stammers, depart hastily down the road. On one occasion he had attempted to kiss a woman when both were savouring the romantic ambience of a shared punt on the Cherwell. 'I'd sooner not, thanks,' she had said, as if he'd offered her another drink. He reported to Sutton that 'Women (university) repel me inconceivably ... they are shits' (20 November 1941). In truth, they did not, and on the whole the ones he knew were not. It was just that while he felt sexually attracted to them he did not have Amis's enviable combination of charm, wit and looks. As compensation, of sorts, he theorised about sex with the assistance of Lawrence and Layard. Kemp was born out of this cheerless meshing of sexual vacuity and unspecified ambition. When he informed Amis that he was thinking of cutting out Kemp's creation of the diaries and the short story, Larkin was actually addressing his own confused and intermingled notions of fantasy and creativity.

From 1940 onwards he had kept Sutton regularly informed of his thoughts about Lawrence, whose entire works in print he was reading again and again and in which he was finding a web of speculations that might explain, if not compensate for, his own feelings about sexuality. For example: 'We drew strength and life from Lawrence's works, and I don't think one can do any more from any book' (21 December 1942). 'WHY conventional critics don't admit DHL into the holy of holies as a prose writer alone never ceases to baffle me' (16 March 1943). 'When Lawrence says "only the mind tries to drive my soul and body into uncleanness" by creating rules in the soul's judgments, he means surely that beauty is untangible and unreliable' (4 April 1943). What attracted Larkin most to Lawrence was his ability to break down the established borders between speculative, theoretical discourse and literary writing. His novels did not simply record and enact elements of the human condition; they informed representation with ideas, even solutions. Larkin: 'Imitation is absurd. Perhaps plots are the thing – someone [Lawrence] with a lively penis kicking a hole in society ...' (6 July 1942). If Larkin could similarly integrate his literary ambitions and sexual uncertainties in a novel then he might at least realise the former while offering himself a more secure perception of the latter. It was no accident that Sutton was the first to hear of plans for Gillian:

he [Kemp] begins to construct a complicated sexless daydream about an imaginary sister who serves as a nucleus for a dream-life. Then he meets a girl who is exactly like this imaginary sister (the sister-aspect having by now changed into a rather more emotional relationship) and the rest of the story in action and in a long dream, serves to disillusion him completely. (10 August 1943)

The contrast between the Sutton letters and those to Amis during the same period is hilarious. Often the subjects are the same – sex and literature particularly – but the Lawrentian high-mindedness of the Sutton correspondence is, for Amis, exchanged with something closer to Rochester. 'My flogging chart [daily record of masturbation] reads 2.3. My writing, when it happens, is the only happy thing ... I don't fuckin' drink, I don't fuckin' smoke ... I don't fuckin' fuck women – I might as well be fuckin' dead' (14 July 1942); perhaps not quite what Lawrence meant when he reflected on the mind's role in driving soul and body into uncleanness. Larkin is honest enough about his own failures to attract women and concentrates on his friend's reports of doing little else. Sometimes Amis would amuse Larkin by reporting conversations with his lovers, with pseudo stage directions, partly as a rehearsal for the use of dialogue in fiction, and all the time their exchanges shifted the emphasis from the pragmatic theorising of the Sutton letters to celebrations of ribaldry. When he informed Amis, a week after Sutton, of his plans for *Jill* his synopsis was far more tough and succinct – 'a young man who invents a younger sister and falls in love with her' (20 August 1943) – and in case Amis suspects some intellectual complexity he adds the tone-lowering reference to Brunette. Amis's subsequent enquiries on the progress of the book, particularly the invention of Gillian, were obviously consistent with this mood because Larkin answers on 19 October 1943 that 'No, he [Kemp] doesn't "slap a length on her, ole boy".'

In *Jill*, Kemp's rejection of Elizabeth Dowling was a sign of Larkin's commitment to a Lawrentian prototype for the novel, and earlier in the book there is another passage that reinforces this and which is laden with enough clues to make its private resonance very clear. Kemp has just arrived in Oxford and is meeting the group of people who will variously intimidate, attract and irritate him during the remainder of the story. Kemp feels excluded from the conversation, which at one point turns to an absent Julian who has recently volunteered for the Royal Corps of Signals.

'That's right. In the Signals.'

'Oh I see. I thought there was something in it.'

'You bet.'

'Aren't the Signals dangerous then?' Elizabeth asked ...

'Is that what you mean?'

'Can't be if Julian –' (p. 29)

Apart from reinforcing Kemp's feeling of exclusion the exchange seems oddly redundant, but one reader at least would have recognised its significance. Amis's and Larkin's acquaintances in Oxford frequently made amused but by no means pejorative references to shrewd young Kingsley finding the best option in choosing the Signals as the safest of all active service regiments. The exchange is followed by an even more enigmatic one involving Elisabeth and a recollection of having met Julian 'in Town' when they went to see a show. Patrick adds that 'what Lizzie means ... is that he [Julian] ...' '*Shut* up!' says Elizabeth. It is interesting that on 26 October 1943 Amis had written to Larkin of his trip to London also involving a show, and sex, with his married lover. And the lover's name? Elisabeth Simpson. In their correspondence Amis always refers to her as Betty, but Larkin for no obvious reason insists on calling her Lizzie, and the passage involving Julian (Amis) is the only moment in the novel when Elizabeth Dowling is given the same abbreviated version of her Christian name.

Julian is never again mentioned, and for the ordinary reader the episode appears as a gratuitous, peripheral moment in the text, which further strengthens its significance as a token, private register. In a crude sense he is signalling to Amis that he will not feature in the novel, but more significantly he is attempting to make a choice between those dimensions of his personality that would inform the book and those that would be excluded.

As stated, Dowling is based partly on Diana Gollancz, who remained, sexually, a hypothesis, and partly upon Amis's story of his relationship with Elisabeth Simpson, another woman to whom Larkin has been introduced, vicariously, but didn't actually know. His linking of her with Amis/Julian anticipates the moment when Kemp spurns her gaudy attractions. He is desperately attempting to detach Kemp from the world of bad behaviour, bravado and decadence proffered to him by Amis in their letters, and in which he could only participate as a correspondent. He could share Amis's manner, indeed his world, verbally but in reality he could only treat it with a mixture of unease and envy. Through 1943–4 Amis kept his friend regularly informed of his juggling act of shameless infidelity. Before D-Day he managed to sustain his affair with Elisabeth alongside equally energetic sexual liaisons with May. Before he was called up he had begun an affair with an Oxford undergraduate, June, to whom he continued to write from Catterick, professing his ongoing commitment, and before his regiment decamped for the south coast prior to the invasion he began a relationship with a young lady called Gail. Typically 'I did not meet Betty on the Saturday before we left, and she came to see me off at Darlington. I like this because I want to take her trousers down, but I didn't like it because I couldn't then' (A to L, *c.* 26 October–6 November 1943). 'My posting with Betty was heartbreaking, because we love each other, or so we say ... We certainly want to make the beast with two backs, eh? Yesh ... this is funny. I didn't say goodbye to May' (A to L, 6 November 1943). Amis takes particular pleasure in transcribing for his friend passages from letters written to him by Gail, in which a commendable attendance upon moral principle is swept away within a few sentences by an abundance of anatomical self-scrutiny.

> I have thought it over quite a lot and have decided that I cannot come away with you ... I have been brought up very strictly and have been taught to look on it as rather despicable ... Don't think I don't want you because my God I do, so much so that at times it torments me ... Maybe if you tried to persuade me I would change my mind ... My cunt is small owing to the fact that I am a virgin and my hymen is not intact. The hair extends about an inch behind my cunt and several inches in front. My clitoris is warm and soft ... In spite of all I have said I still want ... to stroke your cock and feel your hands on my cunt and feel our bodies pressed together.

Amis comments wryly: 'I quite agree; I don't believe it either. But it's true all right' (A to L, 25 November 1944). Later in the letter he speculates on life after the war 'knowing so much more about sex ... I should be able to ... see how two halves of my life fit together ... Can you imagine showing Elisabeth to Castin [Fellow in History, St John's]? Or introducing Gail to Freddy Hurdis-Jones [undergraduate at Magdalen]? ... The thought of it makes me scream.' At the time the hypothesis might have seemed faintly absurd, but the act of fitting together 'two' apparently incongruous 'halves of my life' would become the working principle of his fiction, beginning with *Lucky Jim*. In his debut novel he brilliantly redistributed the man he wanted to be and the man that circumstances obliged him to become between his narrator and Jim Dixon, and the fact that this first hint at what would be the key to his success emerges in a letter to Larkin is prescient. Larkin would play the straight man and to an extent the failure in their ongoing double act. They would share confidences on everything from the dullness of their homes, friends and relatives to their true feelings about the women they pursued, but even in these early letters aspects of their roles were already prescribed: Larkin the erudite failure, the man for whom the world, particularly when it involved women, was a gallery of crisply observed disappointments, and Amis the reckless Cavalier, always seemingly caught between the 'two halves' of his life, respectively the accountable, public one and the other involving excess, irresponsibility and the sheer joy of disclosing it to his friend.

It is significant that while Sutton serves as his sounding board for Lawrentian theorising – part of his planning procedure for *Jill* – Larkin never once mentions Lawrence in his letters to Amis. It was not that Larkin was intimidated by his friend or afraid to argue his case. He, too, had doubts regarding the validity of Lawrence's spiritual-aesthetic philosophy, but for the time being he needed for pragmatic purposes to decide upon what kind of method and thesis would underpin his first serious attempt at fiction. He did not, however, recognise that while we can and do alter our persona according to circumstance this activity has self-determined limitations, and that to systematically exclude from his writing the element of his person-ality that had a natural affinity with Amis was suicidal. He was pretending, at least as an author, that part of him did not exist. He treated Lawrence as his guide, substitute and mentor in a process of self-immolation.

The writing and rewriting of *Jill* had taken up most of Larkin's time during the summer and autumn of 1943. Occasionally he visited Oxford to meet old friends and, reluctantly, apply for jobs. His interview for the Civil Service, in August, was unsuccessful, and Larkin told Sutton that this was partly his intention. He claimed to have informed the panel that he would be happy to offer them his services if they provided him with a decent livelihood to pursue his true vocation as a writer. Something must have impressed them, however, because his name and details were passed on to the department of the War Office which ran the counter-intelligence and code-breaking establishment at Bletchley Park. Since recent disclosures of what actually went on there – particularly the breaking of the German Enigma Code – Bletchley has achieved legendary status, and, while little if any of this was made known to Larkin at his interview on 14 September, he offered Amis a parodic account of how the Admiralty official had intimated that the work was vital to the war effort. 'Of course, yah're workin' against the clock all the tahm ... one day orf everah seven ... one week everah three months ... Christmas, Eastah, Bank Holiday – they don't exist ...' (L to A, 16 September 1943). Again he was deemed unsuitable for the job.

In October he applied for the post of librarian in the public library at Wellington, Shropshire, was interviewed on 13 November and given the job. Reporting this to Sutton he states that he is 'not very proud of the fact ... [I] spend most of my time handing out tripey novels to morons' (13 December 1943). In fact, he was remembered by people who used the library during his two years there as courteous, helpful and willing to make use of the inter-library loan service for anyone whose interests extended beyond the somewhat limited stock. 'The books in the library are mostly very poor, but there is a copy of *Aaron's Rod, Bliss, The Garden Party* and *Crome Yellow*, all of which make me feel at home. I can't imagine how they got there. There's no poetry later than Housman' (L to Sutton, 13 December 1943). Wellington was one of the more disappointing towns of Housman's favourite county. Redbrick Victorian and Edwardian buildings cast a dismal shadow over what remained of its more engaging pre-nineteenth-century architecture. Larkin found a bedsit in an ill-heated Victorian house about five minutes' walk from the library. He shared a small kitchen and bathroom with two other residents, and his landlady, Miss Jones, would not allow him to play his jazz records. Social life, at least for strangers, was generally non-existent and Larkin compensated by making regular train journeys to visit Bruce Montgomery in nearby Shrewsbury.

Montgomery had been teaching at Shrewsbury School for more than a year, and his presence there was one of the reasons Larkin had applied for the job. Montgomery had always enjoyed alcohol as a stimulant to easy acquaintance, but during their encounters Larkin took the lead, probably as an antidote to the general sense of dullness that seemed to him to embrace the locality. Accounts of their wild nights in Shrewsbury include

Larkin interrupting their conversation on the way back from the pub by falling sideways over a garden wall, passing out on the train and missing his stop at Wellington and one night, after eight pints of local bitter, attempting to break into a shop. The most famous outing involved an evening when the two of them attended the school's literary society, after several hours on the town. Larkin found that his bladder was demanding more of his attention than the debate and, given that he did not, characteristically, wish to draw attention to himself by leaving the room and estimating that his heavy overcoat and several layers of winter clothing were sufficiently absorbent, he decided to urinate *in situ*.

When sober the two friends discussed and advised each other on their respective writings. Montgomery was particularly helpful with the final draft of *Jill*, which Larkin completed in spring 1944. To an extent their partnership resembled that of Amis and Larkin in Oxford before the former departed for wartime service, with one significant difference. Amis had willingly played foil to Larkin's creative fantasies and caricatures, even co-authoring one of them, but Montgomery was already a published and respected novelist – albeit in the sub-genre of crime fiction – and had a network of useful contacts. Montgomery was sufficiently impressed by *Jill* to recommend it to Charles Williams of Oxford University Press who, if he shared Montgomery's opinion, would forward it to T. S. Eliot at Faber. He didn't and returned it to Montgomery who next tried Gollancz. They, too, rejected it. J. A. Caton's Fortune Press was Larkin's last hope, and eventually in late summer 1944 Caton replied with contractual impositions – including no royalties to the author – which confirmed Larkin's suspicion that Caton made his money from pornography while acting as little more than a vanity publisher for 'serious' writers. This suspicion was challenged, however, when in October Caton wrote to Larkin to ask if he would care to submit a volume of poems for consideration. He did, and the collection, *The North Ship*, appeared three months before the novel in 1945.

Apart from himself and his writing Larkin's frame of reference was severely limited. He found the world cheerless and often depressing and, as a self-proclaimed instrument for literary transparency, he did not attempt to improve on this by making the poems themselves more engaging, let alone agreeable, than their emotive underpinnings. There is, of course, a long tradition of beautifully executed poems about melancholia that succeed because the poet generally has a clear perception of its cause. This might remain undisclosed, but its pervasive presence will prompt the reader to reach for clues. With *The North Ship*, however, the promptings require close and diligent scrutiny and remain in the end indiscernible. They coalesce around the presence of a figure other than the speaker who stalks from poem to poem and is certainly female. For example:

'Your lips that lift at mine' ('Is it for now or for always')

'And if she were to admit / The world weaved by her feet' ('The Dancer')

'Within the dream you said: / Let us kiss then, / In this room, in this bed' ('Within the dream you said')

'Love, we must part now: do not let it be / Calamitous and bitter' ('Love, we must part now')

'Last night you came / Unbidden, in a dream?' ('Morning has spread again')

Beyond her existence as a pronoun little more is disclosed of this figure, which, on Larkin's part, is involuntarily candid. His experience of 'love' (mentioned nine times in separate poems) and its attendant, embodied causes was that of the sophisticated but endlessly frustrated adolescent, and the dreary atmospherics of the whole collection suddenly seem more appropriate.

During early spring 1944, Larkin found himself forming a friendship with one of the library borrowers; five years later he would propose marriage to her. Ruth Bowman was intelligent, interested in high- and low-brow literature and impressed by the cautious, learned Oxford graduate who ran the library, and she was sixteen years old. Larkin never commented on what first attracted him to Ruth. She was short, although not petite, wore spectacles and while not distractingly pretty was not unattractive either. Motion contends that she reminded him of himself. 'Her apprehensive, short-sighted face mirrored his own self doubt and potential self disgust' (Andrew Motion, *Philip Larkin: A Writer's Life*, p. 118). It might be true that Larkin's sense of an alliance between his physical shortcomings and temperamental inhibitions caused him to feel unthreatened by Ruth, but there was more to it than that. He was, when they met, a man whose existence was comprised as much of invented hypotheses as of endured experience, and she became a channel between the two states. It was not that he saw her as a living model for further writing, at least not at the beginning. She embodied a pervasive element of work complete and in progress. She did not intimidate him, as Diana Gollancz and her fictional counterpart Elizabeth Dowling had done with their erotic sophistication. She carried the same attractions that Jill had done for Kemp, but Larkin did not have to contend with Kemp's experience of an unwelcoming competitive context; this was dull provincial England and Ruth was not part of the high-living set, up from London. Most significantly she was innocent, inexperienced and very real, a perfect replacement for the ill-defined presence who in *The North Ship* seems as threatening as she is attractive and for whom 'fear' might easily be substituted for 'love'. Ruth lived in the town, in modest circumstances. Her father had died when she was eleven and, encouraged by her grandfather, who had been assistant editor of the local newspaper, she had ambitions to read English at university – she eventually went to the University of London. Larkin at first acted as a kind of informal tutor, advising her on what to read and locating books not otherwise available. Their courtship developed out of this. They were observed walking in the town, reciting poetry to each other, and Ruth was advised by her teachers to be less arrogant and rebellious, tendencies which, as gossip suggested, Larkin had inculcated. When Larkin was first invited to her home for a meal his diffidence had registered for Ruth's mother as something more unsettling and sinister: he was 'arty', an intellectual, a type known to cause heartbreak and personal catastrophe, at least in the opinion of the English lower middle classes of the 1940s. Ruth's mother was attuned to local unease about this man who had encouraged the reading of Lawrence, Huxley, Joyce and other unsuitable authors.

Much later, after Larkin had achieved literary fame, Ruth Bowman reflected on their relationship as something that at the time had confused her. He could be unpatronisingly erudite, share her taste for literature and bring to it his own tendentious breadth of reading. And he could make her laugh. He adapted his Oxford-practised talents to caricatures of local dignitaries. His stammer, always present in the library, fell away when they were alone and together. But she was never certain of when this exclusively caring and entertaining presence would be exchanged for a mood of withdrawn introspection, a sadness he never explained. She knew of his ongoing publications and was, as she put it, 'star struck', but what he did not tell her was that she had become part of the weirdly fatalistic interweaving of his life and his writing.

In June 1946 Larkin applied for and got the post of sub-librarian at University College, Leicester. He was at the time halfway through a correspondence course that would eventually qualify him as a member of the Library Association, and he persuaded the Leicester selection board that his commitment to the profession was genuine; he claimed that the war had delayed his full-time training and his job at Wellington operated as a practical introduction. His reasons for the move were various. Obviously a city and an academic environment were more attractive than a rural backwater, and there was a degree of truth in his presentation to the interview board. He was finding more and more that the way in which libraries worked suited his temperament and to an extent operated as a fitting compensation for many aspects of his non-working life. The relationship between writing and everything else might have seemed capriciously unreliable, but in libraries books were obliged to know their place and librarians maintained order.

Ruth Bowman knew that the job and his life in Wellington had been temporary contingencies, but in a letter she wrote to him the day after he left she seems uncertain of what exactly the move would mean for each of them. Alongside customary lamentations on how she would miss their day-to-day companionship she indicates a fear that something more significant has changed: 'how can I battle my way through life ... without you?' She concludes that they 'mustn't let the mere fact that we do not live in the same town come between us irrevocably' (4 September 1946). The letter gives the impression that it was written in response to one from Larkin, suddenly announcing a momentous change of circumstances; this is puzzling since one assumes that they had talked of the move over the four months since his interview in June. A year earlier Ruth had been accepted by King's College, London, to read English, and her elevation from schoolgirl to independent woman was reflected in their relationship. They had started having sex and, particularly during Larkin's visits to London, had behaved like a mature couple, attending the theatre and cinema, visiting the National Gallery and the Tate and going out for meals. Over the period between 1946 and 1948, Ruth accompanied Larkin on what seemed to be a tour of his enthusiasms. In summer 1947 they had spent a week in Oxford, and shortly afterwards Larkin had taken her to Eastwood, where he had shown her the

D. H. Lawrence family home and they had wandered through the locality looking for the likeliest original settings for their fictional counterparts. A year after that they had gone to Hardy country. Larkin had exchanged Yeats for Hardy as his poetic mentor, read the novels along with the poems, and during their visit they had repeated the Nottinghamshire exercise, trudging avidly between the landmarks around Dorchester.

Given these continuities and apparent signs of commitment, her anxieties about his move to Leicester appear unfounded, but it is possible that the longer she knew him the more she began to detect a chameleon-esque dimension to his personality. It was not that he was misleading her, at least not in the conventional sense, rather that he was dividing up his life into components, some of which he shared with her but often only obliquely. This is indicated in his renewed friendship with Amis. Larkin introduced Ruth to Amis in January 1946, and they met on several occasions after that, up to and following Amis's marriage to Hilary Bardwell. Much later Ruth informed Motion that she found Amis to be a divisive presence, often displaying a tendency to draw Larkin away from her and towards his own self-image of boozy debauchee. She didn't know the half of it.

3

The Return of Amis

From 1945, when Larkin first informed Amis of her presence, Larkin referred to Ruth either as the 'schoolcaptain' or 'Misruth'. In effect she became a real version of the fantasies he had shared with Amis and used in the Brunette writings and *Jill*. He was watching her grow up, and he shared with his friend some of the questionable pleasures derived from this blend of involvement and voyeurism. He does not change facts for Amis, but he adapts them to a mood and a setting that had since 1945 become their exclusive terrain. His anecdotes include an account of a step-cousin 'who used to watch misruth undressing' (L to A, 24 September 1946). This turns out to be Ruth's cousin Isobel who, Larkin implies, causes Ruth to fear that when she is away at university 'Miss Isobel and I would instantly get into the same bed' (L to A, 12 July 1946). Jane Exall, a friend of Ruth, would later be presented as the 'bosomy English Rose' of his 1962 poem 'Wild Oats'. At the time, he wrote of her to his friend as inspiring men 'to want to FUCK HER UP TO THE NECK' (30 September 1946). Larkin's presentation of himself to Amis as a lecherous bon viveur was one feature of a letter-writing style that had evolved between them since the war, a pun-laden discourse in which their opinions on literature, details of their private lives and ambitions, resentments and invectives on life in general became an exclusive and usually hilarious dialogue, sometimes accompanied by photographs or sketches.

One letter in particular is fascinating. On 26 February 1947 he informs Amis of how his relationship with 'misruth' was going through one of its occasional bouts of uncertainty. He wonders about the benefits or otherwise of sex with Jane Exall and reflects that in the end 'a pock is a pock'. Would the effort of getting Jane into bed be worth it when this 'wouldn't be nearly so nice in reality as it is in my imagination WHEN I'M TOSSING

MYSELF?' So, he asks, why doesn't he just put up with 'what is to hand', in this case figuratively, and 'resign myself to misruth'? There is no evidence that Larkin kept copies of all of his letters, but it is almost certain that he did with this one, given that it reads as a prose version of 'Wild Oats', the poem he would write thirteen years later. For instance, in the poem Ruth is referred to as 'her friend in specs I could talk to', the one he 'took out', despite the attraction of Jane, the bosomy rose. In the letter Ruth and he 'got on ... because we are really quite alike', she being less attractive, less a reminder of his own inadequacies and in whose company he could 'start thinking about something else' – something other than sex.

He had ceased any kind of contact with Ruth when he wrote the poem, and while one might be tempted to treat it as insensitive, confessional would be more apt. The poem tells us much: principally that the figure he felt himself becoming in the late 1940s would soon be the abiding influence for its public, literary counterpart. In his most celebrated poems he uses the artefact in much the same way that he used his letters. There is a confidential openness interweaved with mundane, sometimes embarrassing, personal detail, and then the focus shifts abruptly to a reflection on general significance or, just as likely, prevailing insignificance.

Amis returned to Oxford in October 1945 and was given comfortable rooms in the New Quad, the part of college previously occupied by the Ministry of Food and Fisheries. He felt relieved that his army experience had introduced him more to institutionalised boredom than warfare, yet resentful that he had lost two-and-a-half years of his normal life. Most of his friends and acquaintances from 1941–2 had avoided military service, finished their degrees and gone on to other things. Larkin had got his First in English, published more poems and *Jill*. His second novel, *A Girl in Winter*, was finished and would be accepted by Faber & Faber a year later. Amis had almost two years of his degree course left. He would work hard at this, but he decided also to give much of his available time to writing. In Catterick, before D-Day, he had begun to plan a novel involving half-formed ideas on marriage, sexuality and the influence of the family upon the individual. A number of these found their way into 'Who Else Is Rank?', but the original project had been sidelined by Amis's years of active service in Europe. Back in Oxford he decided that these early drafts and sketches would form the basis for his first serious attempt at prose fiction. He would finish 'The

Legacy' in 1948, and it would never be published. (The typescript is in the Amis Collection, Huntington Library, California.)

Larkin and Amis had returned to regular correspondence. They met in Oxford in November 1945, and Amis confessed to feeling uneasy about his lack of material in print. Over the previous two years Amis had written about forty poems and published none. Larkin advised him to send this collection to Reginald Caton, the proprietor of the Fortune Press and the publisher of *Jill*. Two weeks later Amis forwarded thirty-one of these pieces to Caton and they were accepted for publication in May 1946. Larkin later wrote to his parents that 'If one can't get out of a mess oneself, the best thing is to drag someone else into it' (5 May 1946). The mess referred to was Caton's unreliable, careless treatment of Larkin's first novel.

Caton was an enigma. The Fortune Press made him money principally through its steady output of pornography, including novels entitled *Boys in Ruin* and *A Brute of a Boy* and monographs such as *Chastisement Across the Ages*, a detailed study of corporal punishment in German women's prisons. Caton's interest in proper literature was a means of providing his pornography list with a shroud of respectability and, given that it made him little money, as a tax dodge for his other role as landlord of a large number of low-rent, barely habitable properties in Brighton. Alun Lewis, one of his serious authors, accused him of publishing poetry without having read it, and Amis suspected that his own volume spent the six months between submission and acceptance gathering dust in Caton's office. But Caton's apparent status as a low-life charlatan is belied by the impressive list of authors that he did choose to publish, including Larkin, Amis, Alun Lewis, Julian Symons, Dylan Thomas, Roy Fuller and C. Day-Lewis. During the war years the Fortune Press provided a valuable outlet for new writers who experienced more difficulties than usual with the established presses, cash-strapped and paper-rationed as they were. In 1944 it published *Poetry from Oxford in Wartime*, including verse by Larkin and John Heath-Stubbs, and a similar collection from Cambridge.

Caton certainly left an impression on Amis. He met him once at his dingy basement office in central London, and he reproduces the episode in 'The Legacy'. Caton's fictional counterpart, L. S. [Lazy Sod] Caton, appears, albeit briefly, in each of Amis's published novels from *Lucky Jim* to *The Anti-Death League* (1966). In *Lucky Jim* he features as a suspect academic who promises and fails to publish Jim's article on medieval shipbuilding in his new journal, and in the rest he resurfaces as a similar figure whom we never actually meet. He communicates with the characters only by post, telephone or rumour, a shadowy, distant presence who makes promises that he never keeps and disappears when his fraudulent activities become known.

Caton features in Amis's novels far more frequently than any other life-based character, apart from the author himself, and there are several reasons for this curious obsession. For the episode in 'The Legacy' in which the narrator, called Kingsley Amis, meets the potential publisher of his volume of poems, Amis did not have to change many details. The real Caton was almost beyond parody, dressed in a greasy suit and collarless shirt and equipped with a strategy of substituting digressive diatribes for answers to questions. Most of his statements would conclude with the phatic verbal question mark of 'what?' The office itself carried an air of dissolute imperma-nence. On the door Fortune Press announced itself with a cardboard notice in red ink; the phone was disconnected, and most of its flat surfaces were covered in dust-laden typescripts that Caton seemed either to have forgotten about or abandoned.

In the novel Caton demands £20 to cover initial publicity costs, and in life Caton required Amis to buy, wholesale, and resell the first fifty copies of *Bright November*. Many of these would be purchased in Berkhamsted by friends and acquaintances of Amis's proud mother.

Amis first saw Hilary Bardwell in a café in High Street, Oxford, one morn-ing in January 1946. She was pretty and blonde, and he arranged for a girl he knew to pass on his name to her, along with a polite enquiry as to whether she might like to go for a drink some time. A few days later he found a note in the porter's lodge with her name and telephone number.

Hilly was a popular date with undergraduates, and Amis's request was one of many. She did not, initially, find him particularly attractive or charm-ing, but the more they discovered of each other's personalities the more they began to find unlikely points of attraction. Hilly, despite looking and behaving like a woman in her twenties, was seventeen, and for a female teenager in the 1940s she displayed an unusual, almost rebellious, tendency towards eccentricity. She had left her decent middle-class boarding school, Bedales in Hampshire, aged fifteen, having run away from the institution on several previous occasions. After that she had become a trainee kennel maid in a dogs' home in Surrey run by two lesbians, enrolled as an art student at Ruskin College in Oxford, abandoned her course and, when Amis met her, was earning a small amount of money as a model at Ruskin. Superficially, Amis and Hilly were ill-matched. She was clever but she had no real interest in literature or politics. She was articulate and certainly not shy, but she regarded lengthy conversations as a waste of time and effort.

In August 1946 Amis, Hilly and Amis's friend Christopher Tosswill spent a three-week holiday in the Vosges, close to the France–Germany border. Amis had first persuaded Hilly to have sex in May, an event he triumphantly announced in a letter to Larkin, but the holiday was their first attempt at living together, and it did not go well. He wrote to Larkin complaining that, while he enjoyed her company, she was too quiet, and he compared his time with her, unfavourably, with the dynamic exchanges that took place between himself and Larkin. But by the end of the trip they had made things up. Something kept them together, something more than the sexual attraction that each could easily have found elsewhere. Almost half a century later, in his *Memoirs*, Amis tells us what it was. He states that apart from a few facts and dates he will say very little about Hilly, 'after just one mention of the word love' (*Memoirs*, p. 47). This word tends to mean what we want it to mean, and I would venture that for Amis and Hilly it meant finding that you felt something exceptional for someone with whom you had practically nothing in common.

Socially they became a double act. Amis would play his by then established role as raconteur, mimic and polemicist, while Hilly would appear interested in something else and complement his verbal energy with distracted behavioural gestures. She would drink beer and swear – most unladylike habits – and sit on the floor. Anne Cleary, the wife of Amis's Swansea colleague, Esmond Cleary, had first met Amis and Hilly in the late 1940s. Her family lived in Berkhamsted, near Amis's parents, and she recalls that even before *Lucky Jim* Amis had developed an almost charismatic reputation. He and Hilly were, in Oxford, the couple to know. They were unusual, slightly anarchic in a manner that would not become fashionable until the 1950s, and in a peculiar, indefinable way they seemed to belong together.

At the end of 1947 Hilly discovered that she was pregnant. Amis announced Hilly's pregnancy to Larkin in a letter on 6 December 1947 and one can assume that the couple had known of her condition for some time already since he adds that on the informal advice of a GP friend they had 'assembled a lot of chemicals which are inimical to the continued retention of the fertilised ovum': that is, a DIY abortion. It did not work and by mid-January 1948 they were arranging for a surgical procedure, then illegal. They consulted a number of doctors in London, and one of them was honest about the dangers to Hilly of the operation. Amis wrote to Larkin that for both of them marriage and a baby seemed a far better prospect 'than such a disaster as might happen' (12 January 1948). (Amis would recollect these events almost fifty years later in his penultimate novel, *You Can't Do Both*.) The wedding took place on 21 January 1948 in the Oxford registry office, then conveniently situated next door to St John's and above the Lamb and Flag public house. Neither family was happy with the arrangement, but both eventually conceded that there was no alternative. In February they found a cramped, expensive flat in north Oxford, which by June they had exchanged for a more spacious farm-worker's cottage – 'Marriners Cottage', in the village of Eynsham, twenty minutes by bus from Oxford. Hilly gave birth to Philip (named after Larkin) Nicol on 15 August 1948.

Soon after Hilly became pregnant, Amis gained a First in English, and shortly before their marriage he enrolled as a B.Litt postgraduate student. He won a small grant, and the remainder of the costs of supporting a wife and child was provided by his and Hilly's parents. In 1947 decent although modestly paid jobs for graduate ex-servicemen were easy enough to find, and his decision to spend the next few years in relative poverty was inspired partly by advice from John Wain, with whom he had become friendly in 1945. Wain was three years younger than Amis but had avoided military service and secured for himself academic posts in English both at Oxford and the nearby University of Reading. Wain assured Amis that with his First and a postgraduate degree he would find a lectureship in one of the expanding provincial universities, rather than 'the suburban schoolmaster's job I had vaguely envisaged' (*Memoirs*, p. 42). Hilly, to her credit, did not complain about having to spend the first year of her married life largely on her own in a dull Oxfordshire village with little to spend or do, while her husband travelled every day to the Bodleian and St John's to research his thesis, finish his novel and draft a few poems.

These are the principal events in Amis's life between his return from army service and the beginning of his experience as husband and father. More interesting is how these developments affected his relationship with Larkin and his own ambitions as a writer. We should note first of all that while Larkin corresponded with virtually every one of his acquaintances, from Sutton and Gunner through his Oxford friends to his mother and father, Amis wrote almost exclusively to Larkin. The fact that, aside from formal letters to his seniors in Oxford, no correspondence at all survives in the possession of his peers and acquaintances is not due to their carelessness in retaining it. All surviving figures were consulted by Zachary Leader when he prepared his edition of the Amis letters and their replies were uniform: no letters from him were received. This is curious but not because it discloses Larkin as a more prodigious letter-writer than his friend. He was, but he wrote not merely out of politeness or a companionable sense of duty. As is already evident from the contrast between the manner of his correspondence to Sutton and his pieces to Amis, for Larkin letters were already a means by which he could isolate often incompatible or discordant aspects of his character from each other, a tendency which would play an important part in his abandonment of aspirations as a novelist and his commitment exclusively to verse. For Amis they played a similarly important role in his progress as a novelist. Even before he saw active service in Europe there is evidence that Amis was beginning to use Larkin as a release for his various frustrations and anxieties. On 6 November 1943 he virtually begs his friend to join him at his parents' house where he is soon due to spend leave.

> How I hate Berkhampstead. What a place to spend leave ... you can surely come over here for *two* or *three* days. Please try. It is very nasty here on one's own. My parents would be very glad to have you, if you see what I mean. I think they regard you as a 'stabilising influence' on me. ('Does Philip care for girls much?' 'Well, not an awful lot; he likes them, though.' Silent registration of approval.)
> If you come, bring all your obscene stories and things, especially Willow Gables.

The deft choreographing of bitterness and irony bears no relation to his attempts at fiction writing during the subsequent six years but it is a remarkably accurate pointer to the style he discovered in 1949 when he began 'Dixon and Christine', later to become *Lucky Jim*.

After Amis's return to Oxford Larkin introduced him to Ruth Bowman ('I'm glad Ruth likes me ... "unnatural vice" what had you said to her ...

"much better looking than you had led me to suppose" ... WHAT HAD
YOU LED HER TO SUPPOSE???', A to L, 18 January 1946) and despite
her later, uneasy, reflections on Amis's influence on Larkin they seemed
to get on well, as did Larkin and Hilly when a few months later Amis
introduced him to her. Indeed, she and Larkin immediately formed a
friendship of their own quite separate from the latter's attachment to Amis
and which endured well beyond the break-up of Amis and Hilly's marriage.
Yet even after Larkin and Hilly had met, Amis assumed that he could bypass
her with his confidences and observations, that whatever he said to Larkin
would, because of the special nature of their friendship, remain private
and confidential.

Amis's reports to Larkin on the first year of his relationship with Hilly
are faintly bizarre. 'Hilary is coming on nicely. She does really like jazz. Her
breasts are concave on top. And she likes me' (A to L, 7 March 1946, Bod).
One might assume that the opening sentence refers to Amis's strategy of
seduction but Larkin would understand things rather differently. They had
begun their co-authored story, 'I Would Do Anything for You', around two
months before this letter and while there was no initial connection between
the project and Amis's courtship of Hilly, Amis gradually began to discover
overlaps between his girlfriend and his, and Larkin's, fantasies. The two
lesbians of the story share their authors' tastes in jazz and, to Amis's evident
incredulity, so did Hilly. Instead of simply offering accounts of what they
had talked about Amis causes Hilly to participate in 'pattern conversations'
so that the border between invention and authenticity becomes all the more
uncertain. When she told him of her experiences with the two lesbian owners
of the dogs' home he could hardly believe that the overlap with IWDAFY
was a coincidence. He offers an account of their exchange, with third-person
comments for Larkin's delectation.

> 'I can't stand Ellington after about 1930'
> 'After that I worked at some kennels with some dreadful women, two of them.
> They were lesbians.' (Me; 'Did they lezz with each other or with other people?'
> – Geuss Who I maent eh you old Bugar I know my sort) 'With each other and
> with the dogs too. It was rather sordid.'
> 'Sex, sex, sex, nothing but sex all day long.'
> She is seventeen. I like that. (A to L, 25 February 1946)

Marsha, one of the lesbians of IWDAFY, is an art student, as was Hilly briefly before she gave up her course and became a model for the Ruskin. Amis, further astonished by this pre-empting of the actual by invention, decides that it is appropriate to cooperate further. By March 1946 Marsha has a specified age, seventeen, plus physical characteristics including physiognomy and hair colour that make her an exact replica of Hilly. She never learned of this because despite the fact that it all occurred before she and Amis became a proper couple it bore an unnerving resemblance to later, similar exercises in fantasy and, crucially, duplicity involving Amis, Hilly and Larkin.

It is interesting to compare the chain of events regarding Hilly's pregnancy with another that occurred almost simultaneously. Whether they entwined in Amis's thoughts will remain a matter of speculation, and fascination. Throughout 1947 Amis had corresponded with his erstwhile lover Elisabeth Simpson, informing Larkin in June that her most recent letter was 'a kind of reward from destiny' (A to L, 5 June 1947), meaning that she had promised they would meet. He also reported to his friend on his fascination with at least two schoolgirls, one of whom he had seen in a Lyons tea shop and considered asking her out and another he encountered at a dance, to which he went to 'see if there were any young ladies worth getting on top of. There was one. Her name was Susan Cox.' He spoke to her but despite 'her noticeable breasts' and her alluring gesture of 'look[ing] back disinterestedly, half closing her eyes', nothing further occurred that evening: 'She was TWELVE YEARS OLD TWELVE YEARS OLD TWELVE' (A to L, 13 January 1947, Bod). A few weeks later matters had progressed. 'There's only one fresh thing to report about my schoolgirl; whatever I did she would not respond beyond blushing and giggling and wriggling a little as if tickled, smiling affectionately at me and rubbing her warm cheek against mine, saying softly "You *are* funny, Kingsley"' (February, no specific date, 1947, Bod). In late summer he tells of several dates with a young woman called Helen, and with Norma, yet another schoolgirl: 'I removed a lot of her clothing in Xt ch [Christ Church] meadows, but I didn't shag her because it would spoil things with Hilly' (5 June 1947, Bod). One might be forgiven for assuming that Amis's reference to 'things with Hilly' being spoilt had he taken things further reflects a degree of caution, even contrition, on his part. What actually concerned him was the possibility of spoiling the prospect of something more exciting involving the three of them. Six months earlier he had reported on how he and Hilly discussed a threesome with 'the Norma schoolgirl'. The plan was that Hilly, who knew her, 'will speak to her next term [i.e. next year when the Christ Church meadows encounter occurred] and "see what comes of it". We are going to pretend to be much younger than we really are, to make things easier (WHAT THINGS DO YOU MEAN?)' (23 December 1946, Bod).

There is no record of how Larkin felt about Amis's reports but a great deal may be construed. Their co-authored pieces such as 'Trouble at Willow Gables' are more than pastiche and self-caricature; they are erotic fantasies despatched to fiction, fantasies that generally involve schoolgirls. After his return to Oxford, Amis was enjoying what they had both craved. Larkin might have been envious, incredulous, but what is much more certain is that during the next fifteen years he would see these episodes as prescient. Amis would prove himself an alchemist, able to turn the tantalising into the gratifyingly real. Even worse, for Larkin, would be the recollection of how Amis employed his comic talent in these accounts. Shortly before his encounter with Norma:

> Kingsley Amies, 24, stated to be a former member of Oxford university, was sentenced to six months' hard labour here today for a serious offence against a thirteen year old girl. Amys pleaded guilty and asked for forty-five other offences to be taken into consideration. When sentenced and asked for anything to say, he said: 'I am really sorry for all the trouble I have caused, and when I come out of gaol I hope to make a fresh start. On someone else.' Aimis was taken to the cells in a collapsed condition. (A to L, 21 November 1946, Bod)

The humour – barbed, provocative and for many unacceptable – anticipates *Lucky Jim* and Larkin, much later, would come to realise that Amis's talents as a seducer and a literary comedian had granted him a status that he, Larkin, would only be able to contemplate. Amis would live the lives that sold his books to readers and this eventually would cause Larkin to sever links with him.

During the later months of Hilly's pregnancy and in the period following the birth of Philip, it was almost as though the fact of Amis's new status as married man and father, while intractable, panicked him into the creation of brief replicas of the life he had enjoyed less than a year earlier. On 2 March

1948 he reports to Larkin on how he 'met *Joan* [one of his previous girl-friends], riding on her bicycle, this morning ... She gave me her telephone number, though I don't think I really want her coming round here' (A to L, 2 March 1948, Bod). Three months after Philip was born he observes, 'I get pretty lonely sometimes, you know, shuttling back and forth from the sweet city.' But a few days earlier:

> I was rather bucked ... when I got talking to a girl on the top deck ... only a schoolgirl actually, of fourteen and a half. Better than nothing though; I must says she's damn pretty, with blonde hair and a tiptilted nose, and quite bright too ... the other evening she called out to me as I was leaving the bus. 'I nearly came up and sat with you but I couldn't pluck up courage.' Pity ... (A to L, 18 November 1948, Bod)

Within a month he had telephoned Joan and restarted their relationship, now clandestine. The night he and Hilly welcomed their first guests for drinks at Marriners Cottage, Amis had other things on his mind. 'I didn't enjoy myself much, partly because the girl I particularly wanted to come, because she is beautiful ... didn't come, and another who did come was shagged by 2 men during the evening but I wasn't either of them' (A to L, 5 December 1948, Bod).

More important than one's opinions on Amis's moral compass is the part he allocated to Larkin in his world of disclosures and concealments. Since they had begun to correspond, such was the amount of draft material for novels-in-progress that accompanied their letters that very often the borders between invention and reportage became porous: characters such as Brunette and others from Larkin's fantasy fiction and Amis's 'Kingsley' of 'The Legacy' regularly appear alongside real events and people. By 1946–7 this had mutated for Amis into something more perplexing and, it must be said, faintly sinister. It is unlikely that at the time he was fully conscious of the parallel but Amis had begun to treat his friend as the personification of the generally rather nebulous figure to whom the novelist addresses his work. The letters are far more improvised and discursive than fiction but in one crucial sense they capture a unique feature of novel-writing. The people who feature in his accounts are rather like invented characters, at least in the sense that he enjoys a greater knowledge of their world than they do themselves. His reports on the firm-breasted Lolita at the dance and her equally alluring counterpart in the teashop are disconcerting not only because of their age. In each case Hilly is with him and he appears to find extra satisfaction in disclosing to Larkin his feelings of excitement and guilt that at the time he masked from his wife. The only other opportunity to play these games is in fiction-writing. He offers Larkin portraits of his life in a way that combines the perspective of the first-person narrator with the omniscience of his third-person counterpart, moving among these figures and affecting their lives directly. For Larkin, he takes a step back and broadens the perspective to allow himself the opportunity to speculate on what they think and how they feel, to blend this with reflections on life in general and mix in some black comedy; the resulting confection emerges as a means of distancing himself from an unprotected encounter with reality.

In 1946 he replied to a letter from Larkin, now lost, in which the latter appeared to express dissatisfaction with having to choose between his affection for Ruth Bowman, which was genuine but which involved fidelity, and his equally strong desire for unconfined debauchery. Amis replies in the manner of a wise epicurean and sets out his personal manifesto for promiscuity. The letter provides a valuable insight into the lifestyle that this handsome, witty young man foresaw for himself, and puts into context what he felt when it was derailed by Hilly's pregnancy and their eventual marriage barely eighteen months later. Even more interesting is the effect of the passage when the pronouns are changed from 'I' to 'he' and 'you' to 'his friend' and 'Philip', etc.

> He knew exactly what Philip meant about getting bored with Ruth, when you cannot ... etc. When these things have reached a certain stage they must be completed. Why didn't he have it out with her, he wondered? Kingsley really thought it might be a good idea. He certainly didn't think there was anything even a little wrong with him in feeling bored. He knew well what Philip meant because he'd had a similar experience with June, though he went even farther without than he hoped, for his self-respect, Philip had gone without. And however fond Kingsley is of a young lady he liked to do things away from her occasionally, which is only the same sort of thing as playing other records than Spider Crawl when Sp. C. is still one's favourite record. (Adapted version of A to L, 1 April 1946)

In *Take a Girl Like You* (1960) Patrick Standish spends much of the novel in pursuit of Jenny Bunn, whom he professes to love but who is reluctant to have sex with him. Following a night out in London he sleeps with another women, Joan, and later:

> During the next half hour, the background of Patrick's consciousness went on with its propaganda ministry job on the events of the last eighteen hours ... His eventual capability [to have sex] belonged elsewhere, far away from Jenny or anything into which she entered or could enter – belonged to the image of himself – a rakehell with a heart, but a rakehell – that he had been trying so long and so staunchly to manhandle across the threshold of reality. With that settled, he was free to start being in love with Jenny again ... (*Take a Girl Like You*, p. 236)

Ostensibly the subject of Amis's letter was Larkin's problem of getting bored with Ruth, or more specifically dealing with her reluctance to have sex, but this segues into his almost identical feelings about Hilly. It would be almost two months before she agreed to sleep with him ('Hilly has yielded', A to L, 22 May 1946), and in the meantime he satisfied himself with Joan. The parallels between the two passages do not require explication and there is convincing evidence that the novel spliced remorse with self-exculpation, a faux apology for his previous fourteen years with Hilly (and one cannot treat the re-emergence of 'Joan' in fiction as a coincidence). But rather than view the letter, albeit abridged, through the lens of the novel consider instead how the correspondence prefigures key elements of the fiction.

Amis's candour is extraordinary; had he committed a murder it is more than likely that he would have explained to Larkin, with a suitable degree of remorse and puzzlement, why exactly he'd killed someone, but without fear that this might disclosed to anyone else. In part, Amis was using Larkin as his confessor but there was no sense in which he expected moral disapproval or even some reward for contrition; they were, he assumed, far too similar in temperament and outlook for that. This allowed him leeway to use his disclosures as a means of steadying his own potential feelings of unease about the sort of person he was and the life he lived. The only other way in which one can reconcile confession with discretion and thus become slyly accountable to oneself is in the novel. Frequently Amis acknowledges

Larkin's unique role in his world, even thanks him, and on 19 June 1946 we come across a passage in which he positions him as by equal degrees closest friend and exact replica; Larkin is gradually becoming that figure who for any aspiring novelist must be their imagined correspondent and without whom their ambitions will remain unrealised.

> I enjoy talking to you more than to anybody else because I never feel I am giving myself away and so can admit to shady, dishonest, crawling, cowardly, brutal, unjust, arrogant, snobbish, lecherous, perverted and generally shameful feelings that I don't want anyone else to know about; but most of all because I am always on the verge of violent laughter when talking to you and because you are savagely uninterested in all the things I am uninterested in. (A to L, 19 June 1946)

There was certainly some truth in Amis's presentation of the two of them as temperamental twins, but the image was also selfish and partial. He chose to ignore anomalies such as Larkin's respect for Homer Lane, Lawrence, Auden, Yeats, even Freud, assuming that his own criticisms had set right his friend's delusions. At the same time Larkin became alert to Amis's tendency to mock and then reshape the absurdities of the world according to this model of how they ought to be. For example, as early as 1946 Larkin decided that he would say nothing at all to Amis of Sutton, his closest friend since adolescence. Until the publication of Larkin's letters, seven years after his death, Amis knew absolutely nothing of Sutton's existence. Sutton was, during Larkin's teens and early twenties, the antidote to those aspects of his personality that Amis mirrored. He wrote to Sutton about literary and artistic figures that Amis would have dismissed as unworthy of comment but he also confided in him on his difficulties with Ruth Bowman. Consider this:

> What mainly worries me, if you'll excuse my speaking on my own affairs for the moment, is a strengthening suspicion that in my character there is an antipathy between 'art' and 'life'. I find that once I 'give in' to another person, as I have given in not altogether voluntarily, but almost completely, to Ruth, there is a slackening and dulling of the peculiar artistic fibres that makes it impossible to achieve that mental 'clenching' that crystallises a pattern and keeps it still while you draw it. It's very easy to float along in a semi-submerged

way, dissipating one's talent for pleasing by amusing and being affectionate to the other — easy because the returns are instant and delightful — but I find, myself, that this letting-in of a second person spells death to perception and the desire to express, as well as the ability. Time & time again I feel that before I write anything else at all I must drag myself out of the water, shake myself dry and sit down on a lonely rock to contemplate glittering loneliness. Marriage, of course (since you mentioned marriage), is impossible if one wants to do this. (L to Sutton, 7 April 1946)

He tells Sutton of his relationship with Ruth but mainly as a pretext for exploring grand abstracts, notably 'love', 'art' and 'death'. His accounts to Amis mostly involve his record of 'pocking'. He would never have written anything to him even faintly resembling the above. Typically he interrupts a report on his library duties to note that 'Already I have wasted hours, and Jane [Exall] came in and I wanted to lay her and SHAGG her, Yes I did, she looked that way and I felt that way but no ...' (L to A, 8 January 1946, Hull). Later that year, after telling of a disappointing day out with Ruth, he reflects: 'Don't you think it is ABOLUTELY SHAMEFUL that men have to pay for women without BEING ALOUD TO SHAG the women afterwards AS A MATTER OF COURSE? I do: Simply DISGUSTING. It makes me ANGRY' (L to A, 18 August 1946, Hull).

His reports to Amis on Ruth were mostly concerned with sex and the various frustrations of having to deal with a regular girlfriend. Never did he allow anything like emotion to break through the bravado performance — a replica of Amis's candid portrayal of himself as a shameless lecher — but with Sutton one could easily mistake him for a completely different person. He informed each of his closest friends of his engagement to Ruth on the same day, 18 May. In the letter to Sutton he presents himself as a figure who might have walked out of a novel by Lawrence.

To tell the truth I have done something rather odd myself – got engaged to Ruth on Monday ... It has been putting me backwards and forwards through the hoops for a long time now ... No one would imagine me to be madly in love and indeed I'm more 'madly out of love' ... The engagement, to me ongoing, is to give myself a sincere chance of 'opening out' towards someone I do love in a rather strangled way. (L to Sutton, 18 May 1948)

No record of his letter to Amis exists but the latter's reply was brisk and one might say brutal. 'Do you wish that I should congratulate you on its account?' (A to L, 28 May 1948), rather as if his declared commitment to someone else was self-evidently an affront to the special arrangement between them. Sutton's reply seems to have been far more thoughtful, considering Larkin's response in which he gratefully attends to his enquiries.

> My relation with her is curious, not at all as I imagined one's relation to one's *fiancée* (why isn't there an English word?) – we are sort of committed to each other by our characters, at least I think we are. I can't imagine, judging from the women I meet casually, that any other girl would come within a mile of my inner feelings. (L to Sutton, 18 June 1948)

One might be forgiven for assuming that 'any other girl' is intended as a mere hypothesis, the kind of philosophical conceit that litters his addresses to Sutton. Perhaps, for Sutton; but in his other world, with Amis, such figures were anything but abstractions, as is evident from a letter from Amis of a year earlier, a response to Larkin's eager enquiries about 'Marie' to whom Amis had introduced him during a visit to Oxford.

> You ask ab8 Marie. As far as can be ascertained with any degree of reliability, old boy, not much in the physical line has occurred between Xtopher and her YOU'RE GLAD ABOUT THAT AREN'T YOU but she did tell him, *in some detail,* that although she enjoys *being pocked,* she has *lesbian leanings,* and not long ago while she was having an affair with a man she was having one with *a young lady* too. The other girl was *very nervous,* but M *went to bed* with her ... and although her friend was still *shy,* had an *orgasm* all right ... Chris isn't going to go any further with her; I expect he feels, understandably, that a girl who would engage in that kind of perversity isn't worth 2 pins to a decent man BUT WE'RE NOT OF MEN WHO ARE BEING DECENT ARE WE? WE DON'T MIND THAT DO WE? (A to L, 4 February 1947, Bod)

It's tempting to regard Amis as a bawdy Mephistopheles conducting a private exchange with his hapless apprentice, but another fascinating element of their early years should be taken into account: Hilly. Amis deceived her, certainly, and would continue to do so but his confessions to Larkin involved a great deal more than louche confidences. On 12 January 1948 he composed a long letter to Larkin that is quite unlike anything he would ever write to his friend or anyone else. It was in this letter that he told of how their plans for an abortion had been abandoned, of how they had decided to have the child and marry. That he should offer him such a detailed record of what happened is not surprising; they'd known each other for seven years and Larkin had got on well with Hilly since they met two years earlier. The most stunning aspect of the letter is its manner. It reads like something put together by a ten-year-old with a precocious command of correct syntax but no proper sense of style. It is difficult to decide on whether he is determined to leave nothing out or if his accumulation of details is a way of obviating feelings of distress that prey upon the account. Typically:

> I have had a lot on my mind; more on it than I have ever had on it in the whole of my life before. Hilly and I went up to London on Tuesday to see the nasty man, and stayed in London until Saturday, seeing other nasty men: at least I did. What happened was that on Tuesday we went to see a doctor, and he said that he couldn't do anything, but a friend of his could, only it would cost 100 gns. He would give us the address of his friend on Thursday. Tuesday night we spent at the house of my friend Frank Coles, who offered to accommodate Hilly after the operation. On Wednesday we went down to Mitcham to see Chris and borrow 100 gns (before you read any further you would probably like to be assured that I'm not trying to borrow 100 gns or any other sum from you). Chris said he would help if he could, but his money was in the Post Office and he couldn't get it for at least a week. So then Hilly and I went to Kingston (a long bus journey) and stayed that night with her granny, who is 92 and beat her at Halma. When the granny had gone to bed I 'phoned Nick to borrow 100 gns. Nick said he would help if he could, but his money was in the Post Office and he couldn't get it for at least a week. So then I rang up my father and got the address of Lightfoot, whom I think I've mentioned and who is rich and on military duty in the city of Paris. Then we went to the doctor's ... (A to L, 12 January 1948)

The letter continues in this manner for a further eight pages, and Larkin is spared none of the details. What is lacking, notably, is comment or any hint of the wry humour that was a keynote of their exchanges for forty years. It is, of course, impossible to second-guess Amis's exact state of mind as he wrote this extraordinary piece but it is not inconceivable that he had decided, for once only, to dispense with language as entertainment, gesture or protection and opt for pure transparency. He had experienced a traumatic series of events with the woman he loved and wanted to report it to his closest friend, stripped completely of ostentation.

Even before Hilly became pregnant she treated Larkin as the only one of Amis's friends in whom she could confide. They got on well from the moment they first met. Amis's other female acquaintances seemed to Larkin to be figures from a story; convincing enough, but evanescent, insubstantial. Hilly was different.

In November 1947 Amis wrote to Larkin on his imminent visit to Oxford, stating that he had found him a room in Hilly's digs. In the same envelope he enclosed a letter he'd received from Hilly, with her approval.

> Billy darling [Hilly sometimes called Amis by the familiar version of his middle name, used in the army and thereafter only among those closest to him]
>
> I must just tell you; this bed of mine just aches for you, it's one of those beds which can't simply bare bedding just one person. It absolutely gets upon its hind legs and eats me up, and it's all down on one side.
>
> (Postmark Oxford, 10 April 1947, Hull)

The passage is followed by a sketch of the bed, occupied only by Hilly. His reason for enclosing the letter becomes evident from the very much tongue-in-cheek admonition in his own.

> Now, Phil old man, we've been pals for long enough now for me to speak frankly. To put it bluntly, Hilly's an attractive girl, and you're rather a susceptible type. So – forgive me old boy – don't let there be any nonsense, will you? I trust you, of course, but I just thought I'd get the subject out of the way before we meet. (A to L, 14 November 1947, Bod)

Amis's implication that this first meeting required moral rectitude was part of the joke. The three of them had already spent weekends together:

Hilary liked you very much which is nice, isn't it? '…attractive…' '…charming stammer…' '…amuses me a lot…' '…the nicest of all your friends including Chris…' '…I love him going all small when he's saying something he doesn't like…' (A to L, 24 June 1946)

At the time the banter of the 1947 letter probably seemed harmless and good-natured to all three of them, yet there is something faintly ominous in Amis's implication that Larkin's chance of seducing his girlfriend is farcical. In 'Letter To A Friend About Girls', the poem which signalled Larkin's loss of patience with his friend, he would remark with bitter resignation that 'we play in different leagues'.

Hilly's letters to Larkin from when they met in 1946 disclose a feeling of unforced mutual affection.

Now listen Mister, did you know that Albert Ammons plays the piano *just* like you, on Early Mornin' Blues?; it quite breaks my heart to hear it, also Billy Kyle on 'Down House Blues' plays like you do. I'm looking forward very much to your coming down to Oxford. (Hilly to L, 29 October 1947, Hull)

Only two days after Amis sent Larkin his emotionally bare stream-of-consciousness description of their decision to have the child, Hilly tells of

all the amazing things that have happened. I still feel very dazed, I'm very happy and flattered and I can't help feeling pleased about the troublesome baby – if a little alarmed. I'm going to have some very nasty minutes soon when I tell my mother's Father that I'll have to get married soon *because* a baby's turning up in July, but not half so bad as it would have been having it cut out by a Slimy Pole only *partly asleep*. (Hilly to L, 14 January 1948, Hull)

The contrast between their manner of address – Amis stunned, fixated; Hilly anxious but quietly ecstatic – testifies to their shared perception of Larkin as the one figure in whom they can confide feelings and anxieties that they might keep from others.

Three days after the birth of Philip, Hilly found time to write her first

letter from the Radcliffe Infirmary, to Larkin. He had sent her his drawing
of a rabbit, the kind used to decorate infants' rooms:

> it's the nicest picture you could have possibly done ... some time when you
> have the time you might do one for Philip's room... [I'm] really glad that we
> are calling him Philip after you, I only hope he'll live up to the name ... I'm so
> looking forward to your visit ... Next year we must all go on holiday together
> ... (Hilly to L, 21 August 1948, Hull)

Over the next few years Hilly's and Larkin's friendship strengthened and,
as Amis became a more adventurous and successful adulterer, Larkin found
himself drawn even further into a discomforting situation he could neither
control nor escape from.

During the summer holiday of 1949, Kingsley, who was now facing
the prospect of supporting a second child, scoured the *Times Education
Supplement* for any university jobs in English, anywhere. Prague and Buenos
Aires turned him down, as did Bristol, London, Manchester and Durham.
Then, on 23 September, he was invited for interview at University College,
Swansea and subsequently offered an assistant lectureship with the derisory
salary of £300 per year. He left Oxford within a week, alone, to begin work
and search for accommodation while Hilly, Philip and the new-born Martin
stayed with his parents. Impatient and anxious, Hilly joined him, with
Martin, in mid-November and found a flat within two days of her arrival.
On 16 December she set off in a rented van with all of their possessions and
two noisy infants to rejoin her husband in the cramped second-floor flat of
82 Vivian Road, Swansea.

It is significant to note that Kingsley played hardly any part in the move,
having spent two months searching unsuccessfully for a suitable residence. He
commented to Larkin that 'I need all the time I can get for *house hunting*, and
thinking about house hunting.' The placing of this activity in italics, and the
droll coda in which he admits to giving as much time to contemplating
the task as executing it are revealing. Hilly stated to Zachary Leader that
he was 'totally impractical'; a somewhat generous abridgement to what in
truth was a predilection for selfishness. It was not that he did not love his
wife and children, simply that for the time being he took every opportunity
to postpone the tiresome responsibilities that came with them. Kingsley's

salary was pitiable and Hilly, as well as looking after the children, worked part-time five days a week in the local cinema, and later at a fish and chip shop in the Mumbles, whose leftovers were frequently brought home for family suppers. Nonetheless, Hilly later recalled the period as probably the most blissful of their marriage. 'We were perfectly happy. We saw the funny side of it' (interview with Leader, 2006).

The death of Hilly's mother followed by an endowment in her will enabled the Amises to move from the cramped flat in Vivian Road – where the two baby boys were bathed in the kitchen sink, recorded in the first-ever photograph of Martin – to a house, 24 The Grove, for which they paid £2,400. Hilly, not Amis, reported these events to Larkin: 'I have been meaning to write to you for ages, we've got this lovely house, with 3 floors, it's the sort with a sitting room and kitchen, and all on quite a big scale, we've got some very nice and comfortable furniture from London and some very nice curtains'. (Hilly to L, 30 April 1951, Hull)

Amis got on well with his colleagues, most of whom were also new recruits, part of the post-war expansion of provincial universities. Willie Smith, a Dubliner and new lecturer in Classics, shared Amis's digs in St Helen's Place, before the arrival of Hilly and the boys, and his taste for drink. James 'Jo' Bartley had previously held a Chair in English in New Delhi. He had departed shortly after independence and rarely spoke of his experiences there, except during his frequent bouts of drunkenness when his most remembered line was 'Mountbatten shot my bearer'. Esmond Cleary, of the Economics department, and Sam Dawson, lecturer in English, were close to Amis's age, both recently married and quite soon regular guests at the raucous house parties held at 24 The Grove. Even before *Lucky Jim* plucked him to fame Kingsley was treated at Swansea as a minor celebrity: still in his twenties, a First from Oxford, handsome and, as a lecturer, like no one that his students, his colleagues or, to their unease, his seniors had previously encountered. He taught the canon but encouraged his students to question the apparently inviolable qualities of great authors. One of his first students, Mavis Nicholson, remembers his disparaging remarks on Keats – 'self-indulgent and impenetrable' – along with his dashing appearance at his first lecture, when he strolled on stage with his 'chic' overcoat hung over his shoulders and a lock of hair falling distractedly across his forehead. 'There's talent', she commented to a friend.

In 1949 University College, Swansea was informed by the Chapel-based morality that was still influential in South Wales. During the first year of Amis's appointment alcohol was forbidden on campus and until 1951 the recently opened Senior Common Room offered only tea and ersatz coffee. Amis rejoiced in the fact that the board of local dignitaries who appointed the first chief barmaid were apparently the only people in town unaware of her previous profession as a prostitute. Sam Dawson had been in post a year before Amis's arrival and comments that:

> he and Hilly were like the parting of clouds ... they brought sunshine to a drab monochrome place. On every Saturday after pay day Kingsley and Hilly, a few staff, *and* some students would begin with drinks at the Grand Hotel, go on to the Metropole for a cold table lunch, and more drink, and then back via several pubs to The Grove. Generous refreshments would be available there, and things would go on into the early hours, some dancing, and jazz records of course.

Swansea was a small town and the spectacle of academics carousing with their students caused whispers of imminent social decay. The College Council included a number of non-conformist ministers and businessmen who saw themselves as guardians of local morality. W. D. Thomas, Amis's first head of department, was an indulgent sort who advised Amis to practise at least a little discretion while still in his probationary years. Amis, though grateful, ignored him. He enjoyed his reputation as a rebel and it was to Larkin that he announced his intentions for his first lecture. 'At 11 a.m. I deliver my first lecture. It's about the aesthetic movement (don't grin like that) ... "Wilde united the qualities of silliness and high intelligence in a degree unparalleled since Keats" – yes, I'm going to say that' (A to L, 9 January 1950).

All seemed well and as Hilly had written to Larkin, 'I think we shall like it here' (31 December 1949, Hull), but there is a revealing coda to her letter to him of 30 April 1951 (Hull). She comments that 'Billy seemed to enjoy his stay with you very much, I want to come and see you too, but there seems to be a hell of a lot on just lately.'

The 'stay' to which she referred was Amis's visit to Larkin at his new base in Belfast where he had recently been appointed as librarian at Queen's University. The trip would also involve a drunken excursion to Dublin and, though neither of them recognised it at the time, the episode marked the beginning of a shift in their relationship. After her statement that she too wanted to come to Ireland, Hilly adds, 'The thought of Billy getting a job in Ireland is good and bad, bad because of all the filthy moving, selling, and endless arranging, but good because of being in your sweet company darling.' A post in English had come up at Queen's and it was clear that Amis and Hilly were prepared to undergo the horrors of another move and give up their agreeable lifestyle just to be close to the man each of them saw almost as a member of the family. There is no record of whether Amis's application was turned down – he was not called for interview – or if he withdrew it. In Larkin's notebook from this period there is a brief undated observation in verse. 'I am in Ireland, you in Wales / Let us, among these Celts and Gaels, / Grow more Saxon' (Hull). Amis would visit Larkin once more in Belfast in July 1952 and never again would he travel to his friend's place of residence. Thereafter Larkin would always be the visitor, the guest, a status he did not particularly resent. However, he knew that it involved more than practicalities, that after 1952 power relations between them had begun to shift. Amis was by then at work on the novel that would make him famous.

4

Lucky Jim

Although he was not fully conscious of the parallels, Amis was during this period becoming an almost exact simulacrum of the man who in 1954 would cause a minor earthquake in the otherwise torpid zone of English domestic fiction, Jim Dixon. The feature of Jim – and indeed his quiet accomplice, the narrator – that made him so popular, particularly for those looking for something both unorthodox and selfishly optimistic in the still-gloomy aftermath of 1945, was the fact that he was a magnificent fraud. He was an academic who loathed the pretensions of academia and most of all he was much cleverer, and indeed more cunning, than he pretended to be. The subtle alliance between Jim's sardonic, cutting private ruminations and the merciless orchestrations of the narrator was a kind of revenge against fate. He detested the provincial world in which the need to earn a living had placed him, treated those similarly grounded with a mixture of pity and scorn, and dreaded the prospect of ending up in a long-term relationship, marriage, with the leech-like Margaret. The novel's conclusion was for some of its more scrupulous admirers its only weakness; even John Betjeman, hardly an advocate of harsh realism, found it slightly implausible. Suddenly, Jim's dismal existence is exchanged for the realisation of his fantasies. He is offered a job in London by a wealthy entrepreneur – well paid but with no onerous duties – and the girl of his dreams, the magnificently busty Christine, leaves with him arm in arm on the train for the capital.

Christine was a compromise. In part she was Hilly, the innocent but outstandingly sexy girl he had come across in Oxford and married. She was also a fantasy endemic to maleness, the kind of woman that men long for but with whom they don't necessarily wish to have children and spend the rest of their lives.

Amis's relationship with Hilly – particularly when it became permanent – altered his life in ways that were not at the time self-evident. Before that he and Larkin had confided in each other if not exactly as equals – they recognised their respective differences – then at least as friends whose world neither required nor abetted other occupants. Hilly changed this, subtly but irrevocably. She was, as we have seen, closer to Larkin than to any other of Amis's friends but the idyll of an affectionate trio is belied by Amis's implicit imposition of rules of exchange. Hilly knew how close they were, how much they enjoyed each other's company, and for this reason Amis was aware that she would be less inclined to suspect that within this extended family of the three of them she would remain entirely excluded from a dialogue that resembled subterfuge. Men, and women, have routinely concealed from their partners matters that they obsessively confess to their closest friends. There is no doubt some psychological formula that accounts for this but rarely has it become a model for fiction writing. Third-person narrators alienate or engage the reader in a variety of ways but the most divisive aspect of their activities involves a combination of dissembling and mockery. When they form an alliance with a particular character everyone else in the novel is excluded. We, the readers, watch and listen as they seem to be whispering behind the backs of all others involved in the story. Sometimes, depending on our sympathies and levels of credulity, we might want to walk into the book and tell the deceived what is actually going on, but then we remind ourselves: it's only fiction. What then would Larkin have felt when he realised that the role he had played for Amis in life was becoming a piece of fiction, one moreover that had acquired a magnetism because of his involvement?

Amis wrote to Larkin only six months after his arrival in Swansea to report on the weekend he had spent in London with his friend James Michie, 'where I drank a lot, and talked to sweet ladies, and smoked a lot of cigarettes, and spent some money on myself' (7 March 1950). Already, it seems, the exercise in wish fulfilment so brilliantly realised in the novel four years hence was being played out in Amis's sullen, frustrated disclosures to Larkin.

He goes on:

As I came back on the train on Sunday evening, sinking as I did so into a curious trance-like state of depression, some ideas began clarifying in my mind:

(a) The proportion of attractive women in London and Swansea is 100:1 or more – this is a sober estimate;

(b) Nobody in Swansea really amuses me;

(c) Children are not worth the trouble;

(d) I would rather live in London, than I would live in Swansea;

(e) Consequently the best thing I can do in Swansea is to keep on shutting myself up on my own and writing poems and a novel.

A more exact moment of gestation for his first novel is hard to locate. Jim's constant sense of inhibition and infuriation, his irritation at having to spend his time in a place and with people he dislikes, and the prevailing mood of having failed to secure the lifestyle and career he genuinely wished for; all are present in Kingsley's list. Just as significantly he betrays, no doubt unwittingly, a key aspect of himself post-*Lucky Jim*. There is no evidence that he disliked his children nor even resented their intrusion upon his battles against thwarted ambition, quite the contrary, yet at the same time he rationed the time he felt it necessary to spend with them. His university job was moderately demanding, though by today's standards it seems as much a salaried hobby as a profession, and the rest of his days involved the realisation of his 1950 objective to '[shut] myself up on my own ... writing poems and a novel'.

Through their parties, Kingsley and Hilly seemed intent on reclaiming the opportunities for youthful irresponsibility that pregnancy had denied them at Oxford almost a decade earlier. Hilly's endowment also enabled them to take on regular domestic help in the form of Eva Garcia, a woman of mixed Celtic/Iberian stock married to the similarly provenanced Joe, a solidly built, hard-drinking steel-rigger. Eva's principal duties involved repairing the post-party damage – according to Philip the house smelt for most of the time 'like a pub' – but she also took over tasks routinely undertaken by the woman of the house. She looked after the children when Kingsley and Hilly were exploring deferred opportunities for hedonism.

On the surface, the Amises seemed to making a promising if slightly intemperate start to married life and despite their separation geographically from Larkin the friendship between him and Amis, and indeed with Hilly, appeared strong and enduring. But in both instances there were flickers of doubt and disenchantment, apparent to all but Amis himself. In Oxford

Hilly had developed an affection for Larkin that carried an air of flirtatious first cousins about it but soon after the move to Swansea she came to detect beneath his ribaldry a genuine capacity for kindness and sensitivity, something she was beginning to feel was lacking in her husband. She wrote to him shortly after becoming pregnant with Martin in 1948, 'I do hope that my husband has expressed to you enough how you must come to our party and get drunk and be *my* boy at it'. (Hilly to L, 9 November 1948, Hull)

The plea appears light-hearted, slightly coquettish, but there is evidence to suggest that Hilly was coming to rely on Larkin as a counterbalance to her husband's unfeeling carelessness regarding his infidelities. She later told Leader that in Marriners Cottage Amis would 'leave it [his notebook/journal] around with private written on it'. It would include references to his plans for liaisons with other women and reflections on successful encounters. But despite her distress she was not confident enough to confront him with what she knew. 'I went very quiet and that was the only sort of way I could deal with it' (Zachary Leader, *The Life of Kingsley Amis*, p. 228). She might have been too anxious to disclose to her husband her knowledge of his activities but she confided in Larkin. Shortly after they moved to Swansea she wrote to him. 'I think we shall like it here ... Poor Kingsley will miss his Oxford mistresses, but alas I had no masters to miss, but I shall see what I can do among the Welsh – Welsh persons may be rather nice' (Hilly to L, 30 December 1949, Hull).

Clive Gammon, one of Amis's students in his first year at Swansea, described his arrival: 'as if a brilliantly-hued tropical bird had come winging into our still blitz-battered town' (Leader, 2006, p. 238). He was not referring only to his manner and dress sense. Within a year of his arrival he had begun clandestine relationships with an undergraduate and the girlfriend of a colleague. Mavis Nicholson: 'He was more promiscuous than anybody we'd ever met.' She too would have an affair with him, but her portrait of the early years in Swansea is touched more with amiability than debauchery.

We [she and her boyfriend, later her husband, Geoffrey Nicholson] babysat for Kings and Hilly, then got to know them well, became friends. It was a lovely house. When Bruce [Montgomery] was over he'd play the piano and Hilly and I would sing, with our legs crossed drinking Martinis, as if their front room was a nightclub. He was sweet, like a teddy bear. When

Philip came there was clearly something special between him and Kingsley. Sometimes they'd whisper to each other and they'd never stop laughing. They thought each other very funny but there was a feeling of deep mutual affection too. In their letters you feel that you're intruding on something particular to them. It was the same in real life. Philip was shy and lovely. He was stuffy but kind. He would go on about how mean he was, how he'd sharpen his pencils until they were too short to pick up. I was never quite sure if he was deliberately making fun of himself but everyone found him hilarious. Kings would join in and tease him, usually about his meanness. No offence was taken. They were a natural double act, but there was something between Philip and Hilly too. She clearly loved him, as a close friend, someone she could trust.

During the Amises' first five years in Swansea Larkin found himself sole recipient of his friend's boasts and confessions, while Hilly, for whom he cared sincerely, was coming to rely on him as someone with whom she could share her own feelings and uncertainties. She knew what her husband was doing but, at least during this period, she was prepared to persevere as mute victim rather than confront him directly and risk disrupting the precarious stability of their family life. The two boys were between infancy and primary school and their daughter, Sally, would be born within a few months of the publication of *Lucky Jim*. Four months after the 1949 letter in which she commented with weary resignation on Amis's 'Oxford mistresses', Hilly updated Larkin on her husband's more recent acquisitions at Swansea: 'I'm sick to death of all the men I love and admire going off with other women, usually much better looking than me. There's Kingsley with Barbara and Terry [Swansea undergraduates], James Michie with a Jamaican girl, and now you with this schoolgirl or whoever she is [Jane Exall]' (Hilly to L, 3 March 1950, Hull). She reports that 'Kingsley has just gone off for the weekend', which he would spend with Michie in London and about which he wrote to Larkin in his letter of 7 March. He was not accompanied by either of his Swansea girlfriends but Hilly was confident that other conquests would be available: 'They are having a party on Sat. night and I'm sure K will "do" all the pretty women there.' Again she permits herself a degree of permissive irony: 'here I am at Skatty, Swansea, where *all* the men are dull, stupid and too short'. She assumes that Larkin will not take seriously her hint that, if only circumstances allowed, she would revenge herself by replicating Kingsley's ill-concealed profligacies. But what, one wonders, would he make of her closing suggestion. 'I've got a weekend off in April, when I shall be going to London, I dream that I'm meeting you there, and that we'll have loads to drink and then go to bed together ... Lots of love Sweet Meat – and remember, no more women unless it's me.'

It reads as flirtatiousness flecked with despair and it is likely that Larkin treated it as such. However, his indulgence would have been tested later that year when Amis himself began to disclose more details of Barbara. He was 'a trifle implicated with a lady student' (A to L, 28 October 1950, Bod), adding, two weeks later, 'I am a little more involved with that lady student' (A to L, 12 November 1950, Bod). Larkin could have replied that, yes, he was fully aware of this involvement, given that his wife had confided to him details of it months earlier. He did not. Amis's assumption that he had covered his tracks, sustaining for Hilly a contented ignorance, would have seemed to Larkin by parts farcical and odious. In the letter of 12 November in which he referred to his lady student, Amis also reports without comment on how Hilly, seemingly deliberately, had broken an Eddie Condon record, his favourite. This has, he comments, 'made me more fed up with being married than anything that has ever happened to me ... why did she have to *choose* that record to break ...?' Later that same week, during a night out with friends, Hilly 'spewed 5 pints of cider over the pub floor ... a bad time was had by all'. Amis was clearly unaware that *he* was the cause of his wife's seemingly arbitrary acts of obtuseness. Aside from the infidelities themselves, his arrogant assumption that she knew nothing of them had driven her to behave as she did. Larkin observed from a distance as two of the people closest to him kept secrets from each other. As if in response he was keeping one of his own from them.

He met Monica Jones, lecturer in English at Leicester, soon after his arrival there in 1946. They became lovers two years later, shortly before he would move to Belfast and while he was still, nominally, engaged to Ruth Bowman. Amis only learned of her existence by accident when he visited Larkin in Leicester and Monica called on him at his mother's house, 12 Dixon Drive. He almost immediately took against her, not because of her personality but because he sensed she would pose a threat to the, as he saw it, unique and

confidential partnership between him and Larkin. As we shall see, his bitterness and wish to alienate her would become a key element of *Lucky Jim*, but
from the beginning Larkin was fully aware of his friend's antagonism towards
Monica, and even before he decided to recreate her in fiction, Amis's letters
during the late 1940s are peppered with disparaging comments. Invariably
he sounds like an embittered adolescent so determined on ridiculing an
enemy that his own immaturity becomes apparent. 'As soon as I saw the
picture and shape of the Jones dame, and that she was speaking something
out with her mouth, I knew everything was all right [that in his view his
notion of her as pretentious had been confirmed]' (A to L, 29 September
1948, Bod); 'that postcard of Jones' was turdy. It carries to me the stamp
of pride in unconventionality (or rather such peoples' conception of it)'.
He proffers an image of her that blends precise observation with malice, an
effect that would become more deftly executed, and effective, in his portraits
of Margaret Peel in *Lucky Jim*. 'I think of her rimless geometrician's glasses
and her voice contentedly forging ahead in shit, like a little flag-decked
pinnace bravely steaming with the dung it carries below its polished deal
decks' (A to L, 27 October 1948, Bod). After Larkin had informed him that
he was thinking of Monica as a serious alternative to Ruth, Amis refused to
treat their potential relationship as anything other than a distasteful farce. 'I
laffed like bogray over the Monicker bizness; if you aren't very careful you'll
find you-self back in the renning. The relationship wd dateless go well into
my Leicester novel, with a piss of fisticuffs' (A to L, 2 November 1948, Bod).
Once again, there is an unnervingly accurate foreshadowing of *Lucky Jim*,
and even Hilly was persuaded by her husband to join the tirade. 'I do hope
things will cheer up a bit for you soon, and that you will take the piss out
of Monica Jones' (Hilly to L, 21 August 1948, Hull). Given that Hilly had
not yet encountered Monica in person and only heard of her via Amis one
must assume that this curious sub-clause was inserted at his bidding. Mavis
Nicholson confirms this.

> It was very hard for Hilly to dislike anyone, and on the few occasions that
> Monica came to Swansea with Philip she [Hilly] always welcomed her. They
> seemed to me to get on. I thought Monica a nice, jolly woman, eccentric,
> attractive. Very different from Philip, but in some ways perhaps not. Maybe
> they belonged together. I knew Kings didn't like her, but I don't know why.

At one point Amis turns her literary tastes – which Larkin shares but rarely mentions to Amis – into a crude attempt to convince Larkin that her affection for him is equally suspect: 'if she can see beauty in a derelict shit-house, she must have more said see, Billy T than you' (A to L, 8 September 1948).

> If Money-cur tries to tell you that E. Sitwell on Wyld Bille [Shakespeare] is any good, you might quote this. E. says that Bill was keen on Plato and the simple life, Diogenessh, and quotes from Leer in support as follows:
>
> > Allow not nature more than nature needs:
> > Men's life is poor as beast's
> > Two assertions you see. Bill *wrote*:
> > Allow not nature more than nature needs,
> > Man's life is poor as beast's
> > That's quite different ...' (A to L, 9 November 1948)

Irrespective of whether Amis is correct there is something rather desperate in his use of close critical scrutiny to sabotage Sitwell's and more particularly Monica's ideas. And just as he employs sleight of hand to make Larkin look again at Shakespeare's proper meaning, so his concluding comment is malevolently double-edged: 'She's a dishonest old bag, isn't she?' So many words have passed since his last specific reference to Sitwell and Monica that these might well apply to either of them. There did not seem to be a particular aspect of Monica's character that caused Amis's explosions of contempt and derision. Rather, he seemed to be searching desperately for a pretext for his antagonism, something that might serve as a substitute for what he really felt, or feared. Ruth, whom he indulged, was harmless in that her youth and consequent lack of temerity always meant that she would remain on the margin of the threesome of Amis, Larkin and Hilly. Monica was, he sensed, capable of drawing Larkin into territories that he and Hilly might not share. The parallels between Amis's early attempts to persuade Larkin to get rid of her and the means by which Jim Dixon and his narrator expose her fictional counterpart Margaret Peel as a vindictive fraud are unnerving. Again we find that Amis was scrupulously harvesting key aspects of his friendship with Larkin for the novel. Throughout this period Larkin neither connived in Amis's disparaging comments and nor did he reprimand him. Instead, he became secretive, never denying that he remained in contact with Monica but allowing Amis to assume that their acquaintanceship was, as Amis hoped, casual and distant. In truth he was, as early as 1947, discovering that her characteristics and temperamental affinities – particularly regarding their tastes for music, film and literature – were very similar to his own. Gradually she began to provide him with refuge from his role as intimate and foil for the Amises. It would not be until his departure for Belfast that their relationship began properly and by the mid-1950s Monica had, involuntarily, usurped Amis as the person to whom Larkin would disclose the more deeply buried aspects of his temperament and state of mind. She also replaced Amis as his most trusted adviser on his poems-in-progress.

It should be stressed that throughout the 1940s both men were primarily set upon succeeding as novelists. Each wrote and published poetry but more as a testament to the enduring legacy of verse as the paramount genre than an all-consuming ambition. Even then the notion of the professional poet was an oxymoron. The history of Larkin's career as a writer of fiction, his initial promise that ended in a weary acceptance of failure, is absorbing, all the more so because of the part played in it by Amis.

He is best known for the two pieces that appeared during his lifetime, *Jill* and *A Girl in Winter*, but these and other unpublished works reflect only one strand of his prodigious output during 1945–50, the one which took its cue primarily from his exchanges with Sutton. But there is another that progressed simultaneously and lasted a little longer. This one was very differ-ent, involving prose fiction similar to that we would come to associate with Amis, who would also be the cause of its sudden abandonment.

When *A Girl in Winter* was almost complete Larkin wrote to Sutton of how the book 'picks up where John [Kemp of *Jill*] left off', by which he means Kemp's feeling of isolation.

He concedes that *The North Ship* and *A Girl in Winter* were both part of the same almost involuntary process of withdrawal and isolation. In the former he had mixed a prevailing mood of discontent and melancholia with stylistic borrowings from Yeats, and in the latter he had written a novel about a communicative impasse. Their unifying theme, which they share with *Jill*, is their author's compulsive, addictive relationship with language. Kemp uses it to invent both the person he wants and wants to be, Katherine is estranged by it and the poems submit themselves to its distortive capacities.

By early 1947 he had begun work on a third novel about a visual artist. Sutton was his point of inspiration, a man who was as committed to painting as a profession as Larkin was to becoming a writer. In September 1947 he wrote to Sutton that the novel comprised '44 pages now of almost complete bunk' (14 September 1947) and asked his friend for advice. Can a man teach himself to paint? When you start a picture do you know in advance what effects you want to achieve? The novel came to nothing because his objective to move 'back to life' was effectively a further process of distancing. The visual arts theme was an extension of Katherine's brief moments of consolation when she communes non-linguistically with the natural landscape. Between 1946 and 1948 Larkin includes in almost all his letters to Sutton verbal pictures, perhaps as rehearsals for what he hoped would make up the texture of the novel.

What he did not tell Sutton, or anyone else for that matter, was that he had simultaneously begun to try out what was, for him, a completely unprecedented type of writing: naturalistic prose fiction that offered an unadorned account of the lives of ordinary people without making any claims upon significance.

'No for an Answer' is comprised of five draft chapters, which would have formed about a third of the novel if he had made anything of the plans in the succeeding workbooks and finished it. He did not, and although there is no obvious reason for his failure to complete the book, circumstances invite speculation. Since late 1946 Amis had kept him informed of the progress of 'The Legacy' and it became the principal stylistic influence for 'No for an Answer'. Its substance involved yet another attempt by Larkin to reshape his experience as fiction.

What exists of the novel centres upon the relationship between Sam Wagstaff and his girlfriend Sheila Piggott and between Sam and his father Samuel. The Wagstaffs own an agricultural machinery firm on the outskirts of Birmingham – an idea probably inspired by Ferguson tractors (which became Massey Ferguson and had a factory near Coventry). The most striking feature of the text is the way in which Larkin creates an atmosphere scrupulously devoid of intellectual or literary issues without implying that the characters are in any way lacking in intelligence or significance. Had the novel been completed and found a publisher – likely, since *A Girl in Winter* had recently received promising reviews – it might have subtly altered the course of post-war literary history. Braine, Barstow, Sillitoe, Storey and to a lesser degree Amis and Wain dismantled the stereotypes of class determination by showing that good writing could coexist with states of mind that had little time for high culture, but this new wave of writing did not make its presence felt until the late 1950s. Larkin with 'No for an Answer' would have set the precedent ten years earlier.

By far the most impressive aspect of the existing text is the dialogue. Larkin had always been a talented impressionist, and in *Jill* we detect only a slight inclination to adapt this ability to the verbal idiosyncrasies of his fictional characters. In 'No for an Answer' the text becomes energised by exchanges between characters, and the inspiration for this was the so-called 'pattern conversations', a technique which Larkin and Amis had discussed since 1943.

Larkin did not inform Ruth even of his application to become sub-librarian in the Queen's University of Belfast, and when on 17 June 1950 they met in Lincoln, where she was then working as a teacher, the evening was a disaster. Over the previous two years their engagement had dwindled to the status of a token gesture, never fully revoked by him and regarded with seasoned scepticism by her. Now he went so far as to wonder if she might be willing to accompany him to Northern Ireland. She was happy enough to consider this, but as the evening wore on and drink took effect it became apparent to both of them that his application and acceptance had been a kind of undeclared act of uncoupling. But that was not quite the end of things. During the three months between his interview and his move to Belfast in September 1950 they exchanged letters regularly and met on at least four occasions. It was as though Larkin was waiting for a sign, even an order, regarding the future of their relationship; or more likely he was, by vacillating, trying to provoke one. He was successful. Ruth wrote to him in September stating that there should be no final meeting. It was over for good. Shrewdly and, given his behaviour, generously, she hoped that he 'will find yourself able to write, for I know you will never rest until you do' (22 September 1950).

The novel, along with Larkin's relationship with Ruth, suddenly came to a halt, but there was one other reason for its eventual cessation: Amis. By the end of 1949 Amis's 'The Legacy' had been rejected by Longman and

Gollancz. Doreen Marston, a reader for Collins, sent Amis a report on why she regarded the book as unpublishable. It suffered from 'redundancy and lack of conflict', it lacked anything resembling a narrative that might interest the reader, and 'there is no suspense; there is, in its place, a good deal of boredom' (Marston to A, 1 January 1951). While Marston's estimation of the book is dismissive, she had accurately detected the effect that Amis had strenuously attempted to achieve. He was intent upon producing a book in which unalloyed mimesis overturned both experiment and the lazy vulgarity of escapism. Amis informed his friend of this and soon afterwards Larkin replied that he too had given up. 'Sam Wagstaff has finally gone for a Burton has he?' (A to L, 7 March 1950). In truth, Larkin would not completely abandon his own attempt at unostentatious social realism until 1951, when he found himself reading drafts of a work that incorporated something that each practised quite brilliantly but which neither had previously considered as a vehicle for fiction: comedy.

Within months of Marston's letter Amis announced to Larkin a new strategy, prompted specifically by what she had said about 'The Legacy'. This time he would make the reader interested in the outcome – it would involve a relationship and a professional dilemma – and it would be funny. The working title, at least in the letters, was 'Dixon and Christine' and the result would eventually be *Lucky Jim*. The novel succeeded because it dismantled and ridiculed virtually all of academia's claims upon significance, and according to Amis the idea for this first occurred to him, about a year before 'The Legacy' was abandoned, on a visit to Larkin in Leicester.

> On the Saturday morning he had to go into college and took me ('hope you won't mind they're all right really') to the common room for a quick coffee. I looked round a couple of times and said to myself, 'Christ somebody ought to do something with this'. Not that it was awful – well, only a bit; it was strange and sort of developed, a whole mode of existence no one had got on to from the outside, like the SS in 1940, say. I would do something with it. (*Memoirs*, p. 56)

Amis wrote this in 1982 and while it remains a matter for dispute as to whether he had forgotten or carefully sidelined the truth, clear evidence shows that the real inspiration for the novel lay elsewhere.

In 1950, shortly before Larkin was to depart for Belfast, Amis had written him a curious letter of thanks; curious because the cause of Amis's gratitude is not immediately evident. The letter is crammed with nostalgic recollections of stages in their friendship – odd for 28-year-olds who had known each other for less than a decade. 'Do you remember, old trencherman! reading my sheaf of poems in Johns (that room I had in the North Quad) sometime in late '45 or early '46 and sang you liked them on the whole and thought they were quite good?' (27 August 1950).

Amis goes on in this manner for a few hundred words, recalling events more or less at random but returning continually to moments when Larkin had helped him out with his writerly ambitions – most of which he omits to add, diplomatically, have been failures – and one wonders, as indeed would Larkin, where all this is leading. Weirdly, Amis does not say, but he provides a clue. 'During the week I turned out all my drawers, and re-read some of your letters ... they are much *funnier* than mine ever were ... Today you are my "inner audience", my watcher in Spanish, the reader over my shoulder, my often mentioned Jack and a good deal more!'

Larkin would have understood most of these private code words, but the full implications of the letter would only become clear to him later. Amis was announcing, albeit obliquely, that he had found the formula that would eventually become *Lucky Jim*.

There were effectively two Jims: one inside the narrative, struggling with his various feelings of impatience, frustration and rage; and the other controlling and orchestrating the story, ensuring that the reader will share Jim's private thoughts on the idiocies and pretensions of his colleagues and acquaintances. This arrangement, as indicated in Amis's letter, was inspired by his correspondence with Larkin. They would discuss and disclose to each other things that no one else would ever hear. For example, in July 1946 Larkin included in a letter a shameless imitation of Ruth Bowman's self-consciously upper-class habits of pronunciation, such as 'the same (sam) time' (L to A, 17 July 1946). Ruth was never aware of this but she would, via Larkin, become ultimately responsible for one of the most widely quoted comic episodes of Amis's novel. Amis transplants the same vocal idiosyncrasy to Bertrand, the pretentious 'artist' son of the Welches, and it eventually leads to the fight with Jim in Chapter 20. '"If you think I'm going to sit back and take this from you, you're mistaken; I don't happen to be that type, you sam." "I'm not Sam, you fool," Dixon shrieked; this was the worst taunt of all ...' (*Lucky Jim*, p. 209).

The most blatant borrowing from their language game occurs when Jim, signing himself as Joe Higgins, sends a letter to the nasty, obsequious Johns accusing him of the attempted seduction of a university secretary. It begins, 'this is just to let you no that I no what you are up to with yuong Marleen Richards, young Marleen is a desent girl and has got no tim for your sort, I no your sort ...' (ibid., p. 153). It closely resembles Amis to Larkin on the latter's sexual relationship with Ruth: 'All right. I know why you don't. All the sam, I bet you wish you could, eh (ha ha)! you old bugar, I no yor sort', and bears some similarity to a piece from Larkin to Amis where he thanks him 'for Yuor letar, yuo can certainly Spinn a yarn, I was fare peng myself at the Finnish: rekun you ave the nack of writing' (17 July 1946). Amis's borrowing from Ruth's verbal idiosyncrasies was not simply a matter of convenience. It was more personal than that. While far less tolerant of Monica, he resented Ruth for coming between him and Larkin and there was a history of malevolence in the caricature. The letters themselves provided Amis with inspiration for a large number of the comic set pieces for the novel – as early as 1946 he had recognised the uniqueness of their private, shared discourse by starting to keep copies of his own to Larkin – and also they were a token of something unique in their friendship. Amis believed that they knew each other better than anyone else knew either of them – hence the untidy metaphor of the 'watcher in Spanish' indicating that their exchanges were, at least for others, a mixture of the silent and the inaccessible. In naming Larkin as his 'inner audience' Amis borrows a phrase he had invented in his Oxford BLitt thesis to describe a private interior dialogue that occurs during the writing of poetry. For him Larkin was a real, embodied version of one half of this exchange, and as well as drawing upon moments from their friendship and sewing them into the early drafts of the novel he began to send these pieces to Larkin for comment. There is no evidence at that point that Larkin regarded the project as potentially successful. Amis had already had a completed novel turned down by three publishers. His new excursions into what appeared to be working-class Wodehouse-in-academe were not the kind of thing which, in Larkin's experience, mainstream fiction publishers were likely to welcome. Nevertheless he worked as Amis's adviser and copy-editor.

Between 1950 and 1953 he received something like 150,000 words of sprawling, uncertain, sometimes directionless drafts from Amis. He worked hard,
particularly on cutting out characters that seemed superfluous to the most
interesting parts of the story, the latter principally involving Jim's tenuous
status as an academic and his relationships with the irritating Margaret
and the alluring Christine. In the letter of 8 September 1952, for example,
Amis responds to a list of his detailed suggestions on various stages of the
narrative including what would turn out to be the most famous passage
of the novel: '*The lecture:* I see what you mean about this, though it would
be awfully difficult to do. I could have a shot at it, anyway, and you could
decide whether it could go in ...'

We will never know exactly the extent to which Larkin was responsible
for the brilliant timing of this scene, but later in the letter we encounter
something that suggests that, at this stage at least, the novel was operating as
the site for private jokes:

> I think the best thing about Veronica's name would be to change it to Margaret
> Jones; then I could enjoy cutting at Margaret Ashbury as well as at Monica.
> You tell Monica I'm cutting at some frightful Welch girl, and I'll tell Margaret
> that I'm cutting at some frightful Leicester girl. How would that do? It's a
> common enough sort of name, God knows. (8 September 1952)

It is beyond dispute that Monica Jones was the model for the odious Margaret
Peel of *Lucky Jim*, but the story that attends this particular borrowing by
Amis shows her to be a pivotal figure in post-war literary history; that she
played this role unwittingly adds a note of drollery to the tale.

Despite Amis's argument that Larkin could claim that Margaret was based
on a woman social worker friend of the Amises in Swansea, the rhyming
association of Monica's full name of Margaret Monica Beal Jones with
Margaret Peel's would have been clear enough. Also the effect of Margaret
upon the texture of the novel is both striking to the general reader and, for
Amis, Larkin and Monica, privately reverberant.

Every time Jim meets her, or even thinks about her, the passage involves
a precise description of what she is wearing, often supplemented by a
comment on her posture or physiognomy. She wore 'a sort of arty get-up of
multicoloured shirt, skirt with fringed hem and pocket, low-heeled shoes,

and wooden beads' (p. 76), and in the next chapter 'She was wearing her arty get-up, but had discarded the wooden beads in favour of a brooch consisting of the letter "M".'

> As if searching for a text he examined her face, noting the tufts of brown hair that overhung the earpieces of her glasses, the crease running up the near cheek and approaching closer than before to this eye socket (or was he imagining that?) and the faint but at this angle unmistakably downward curve of the mouth (ibid., p. 20).

Jim's apparent obsession with her appearance might be his way of emphasising his dissatisfaction at being attached to a woman he finds unattractive. But at the same time one suspects that Amis is suggesting a causal relationship between women who look and dress like Margaret and a propensity for pretentiousness and faked psychological intensity.

Margaret's face, hair, spectacles, her taste in clothes and jewellery, would have shown anyone who knew Monica, and knew of Larkin's friendship with Amis, that Margaret was based on her. And there were parallels, too, between their cultural predispositions and their verbal habits, so much so that Larkin was later prompted to ask Amis if 'you weren't actually there taking notes [of our conversations] were you?' (Jacobs, *Kingsley Amis*, p. 146).

And how did Monica feel about this? She knew that Larkin was helping Amis with the book, but she did not find out about her part in it until after publication. There is no record of her immediate response, but if she had read *The Times* review we can assume that it was less than ecstatic. *The Times* praises Amis's representations of the most affected, pretentious characters, particularly 'the neurotic woman lecturer' with whom Jim has 'brilliant' exchanges. When asked years later about Amis by Larkin's biographer, Andrew Motion, Monica recalled that Amis would try to take charge of any exchanges that the three of them had, and would attempt to exclude others from the Amis–Larkin double act. 'Kingsley wasn't just making faces all the time, he was actually trying them on. He didn't know who he was' (Motion, *Philip Larkin*, p. 169). When asked by Motion about Monica, Amis said that 'There was a sort of adhesive thing about her ... Not quite predatory, but still ...' It was not so much that Amis disliked Monica herself, more that he disliked her apparently close attachment to Larkin, a Larkin who was willing to talk to her about things that were forbidden from their own exchanges. This sense of Amis as resentful of women who interfered with their association is borne out by Ruth Bowman. She felt that Amis 'was possessive of Philip and tried to keep me separate from him', and she tells of how she was offended by Amis's clear attempts to turn Larkin into a version of himself, particularly in his attitude to women (ibid., pp. 123, 138). In a strangely similar way, Margaret interferes with the relationship between Jim's inner and outer worlds, causing him to make continued concessions to her personality that privately he finds almost unbearable. This might explain why both women appear in the novel not only as caricatures but as irritants to the laddish alliance that is its essential feature.

Over three years Larkin not only witnessed the fictional recreation of Monica, he assisted in it and in the construction of the world she would inhabit. Indeed, Larkin read the novel as a better-organised version of their private chronicle of complaints, confidences and daydreams. Amis informed Larkin that 'I have jotted down a few notes for my next book about Daddy B; I don't see how I can avoid doing him in fiction if I am to refrain from stabbing him under the fifth rib in fact' (A to L, 16 January 1949). Daddy B was Amis's father-in-law, Leonard Bardwell, who would eventually become the model for Professor Neddy Welch, Jim's boss. The notes, which Amis continued to make during 1949, took their cue from the letters to Larkin. Throughout the year, with the move from Eynsham imminent and job prospects uncertain, Amis became more and more aware of the dreadful notion of actually having to live with the Bardwells. Since meeting and marrying Hilly he had been variously bored, enraged and frustrated by her father's obsessive interests in cultural arcana: Bardwell was keen on English 'folk culture', particularly morris dancing, and was fluent in three languages – Welsh, Swedish and Romanish – whose common feature was that they were spoken by practically no one he was likely to meet.

Amis in 1949 reports incidents to Larkin that would also go into his notes, be reformulated a couple of years later and fitted into the plotlines of the novel. In the January 1949 letter he writes of how, following an evening of being bored by Bardwell's accounts of Sweden, folk dancing and folk cultures, and the language of the Romaneschi, he is next morning lying in a half-filled bath with him [Bardwell] in the room underneath accompanying on the piano, his foot regularly tapping, folk tunes which he was playing on the gramophone ... As one vapid, uniformly predictable tune ended and another began I found that the hot tap was now dispensing cold water, and, getting out of the bath, began drying myself.

The notes-inspired memory of this weekend at the Bardwells' would become the foundation for Jim's enforced weekend at the Welch house with an evening of compulsory participation in madrigal singing. Jim escapes to the pub and wakes up next morning, hung over. This time Welch is in the bath, singing a piece 'recognisable to Dixon as some skein of untiring facetiousness by filthy Mozart'. The tune might have become upmarket and classical, but Jim, like Amis, is still obliged to 'marvel at its matchless predictability, its austere, unswerving devotion to tedium' (*Lucky Jim*, p. 64).

In the same letter Amis writes that 'I have been thinking of a kind of me-and-the-Bardwells theme for it all, ending with me poking Hilly's brother's wife as a revenge on them all'. (He didn't.) This instinct was surely still present when he used the horrible weekend-with-the-Welches as the occasion for Jim and Christine's tentative indications of mutual attraction. Christine is almost engaged to Bertrand and she is, for the Welches, a socio-cultural trophy, upper class and well connected with the London-based arts establishment. Her preference for Jim certainly registers as an 'act of revenge'.

The 'me-and-the-Bardwells theme' emerges again in Amis's report to Larkin on his Whitsun weekend at the in-laws' house (9 June 1949). Bardwell is, as usual, 'a proper scream' with his accounts of 'folk dancing'. This is supplemented by music from Hilly's composer brother William ('conchertoes and sympathies', 'a talentless flavourless sonata played me gratuitously'), which might explain the eventual upgrading of Bardwell's folk playing to an equally unpleasant rendition of a classical piece by Welch in the novel: the Bardwells' badness transcends musical boundaries. William Bardwell, 'Bill B', causes Amis more irritation with his arty obsession with French cuisine, culture and lifestyle, 'his I'm-more-at-home-in-France-than-England balls'. The Welches are similarly obeisant to Frenchness, giving all of their children French Christian names (Bertrand is Bertrond, with the second syllable predominant and pronounced 'ornd'). 'He [Bardwell] said to me, "They've just reprinted that, you know." I said, "What Roger?", pronouncing the proper noun with a short "o" ... "Yes, Roget," he said, prouncing it "Roh-zhey" ... *Correcting* me you see' (A to L, 25 August 1948). In the 1949 letter Amis writes that 'Two things only pleased me. Bill B has *given himself the shits* by his own *filthy French cooking*' (transposed perhaps to 'filthy Mozart' in the novel). The other agreeable incident involves Marion, the three-year-old child of the Bardwells' daughter Marion. As Bill picked her up, 'She instantly shat over his trousers'; 'amn't I telling you we had the big laugh there the two of us, me and myself.' There are no defecating children in the novel, but one wonders if the incident was in Amis's mind when, in a confidential moment, he has Jim ask the Welches' cat to 'pee on the carpet'.

Amis kept carbons of his letters to Larkin and these, with his notes, would have been with him as he wrote *Lucky Jim*. A few particular incidents were recycled as set pieces for the book, but equally fascinating are the more oblique, peripheral connections. On 9 May 1949, for example, Amis reports that the 'best news from here for a long time is that old Bardwell was taking part in some lunatic folk-fandango [morris dancing] in which the men swung the Staves about and ducked and jumped over them'.

> Well, old B's opposite number swung his stick at the wrong time, or old B mistimed it or something: anyways, the upshot is that old B takes *one hell of a crack on the brain box,* and is laid out for some time, and *suffers a lot of pain,* and has to be treated for shock. NOW THAT'S FUCKING GOOD EH?

Throughout *Lucky Jim* Dixon wants something like this to happen to Welch. He wants to hit him, dump him in a lavatory basin or whirl him around the swing doors of the library. Jim cannot tell Welch that he really thinks him an idiot almost beyond parody because his job is at stake, just as Amis is prevented by decency and convention from saying the same to Bardwell. But, for both, moderate violence, actual, accidental or imagined, is a fair compensation.

Two months later (12 July 1949) Amis writes to Larkin of how an otherwise agreeable weekend in Eynsham was spoilt by the arrival of Bardwell. A village carnival was taking place, and Hilly, Amis and some friends from Oxford were enjoying themselves 'until old ape-man turned up – he had "come to see the country dancing"'. Bardwell as 'ape man' is the keynote of the letter: 'WITHOUT THE APE we should have been a merry party, but

THE APE WENT ON SITTING ABOUT AND GRINNING and *spoiling* everything by his presence and *not realising it* ...' The joke, with Larkin, is that Bardwell's obsessive concern with folk culture, his view of medieval England as an artistic reviver, is about as useful and relevant as the case for a return to the instinctive prelinguistic communities of our simian ancestors: apes. Again Amis states that he wants to take revenge by putting Bardwell in a novel: 'I shall swing for the old cockchafer unless I put him in a book *recognisably* so that he will feel *hurt* and *bewildered* at being so *hated.*'

The letter is echoed in *Lucky Jim* on several occasions. Jim, via the narrator, offers the reader a private account of what he really wants to say to Welch, much as Amis had in his letter about Bardwell: 'Look here, you old cockchafer, what makes you think you can run a history department, even at a place like this, eh, you old cockchafer. I know what you'd be good at, you old cockchafer' (p. 85). Jim has been coerced by Welch into researching and delivering a public lecture on 'Merrie England', and Chapter 20 opens with what appears to be Jim's performance, an endorsement of 'the instinctive culture of the integrated village-type community ... our common heritage ... what we once had and may, some day, have again – Merrie England'. He is not in fact delivering the lecture but writing it, transcribing Welch's thesis on the lost idyll of medieval life and culture. His own opinions on this are disclosed by the narrator. He stops writing and

> With a long jabbering belch, Dixon got up from the chair where he'd been writing and did his ape imitation all around the room. With one arm bent at the elbow so that the fingers brushed the armpit ... he wove with bent knees and hunched rocking shoulders across to the bed, upon which he jumped up and down a few times, jibbering to himself (p. 205).

The ape-man joke with Larkin on his father-in-law's revivalist medievalism becomes in the novel a craftily orchestrated set piece. Welch's, and Bardwell's, ideas are too absurd to merit verbal criticism; the ape-man performance is enough.

Wales and Welshness would feature in Amis's second novel, *That Uncertain Feeling*, and in the letters to Larkin during his first two years in Swansea Amis has a great deal of politically incorrect fun with the locality, particularly the accent and mannerisms of its people. The place is mentioned once in *Lucky Jim*, seemingly as a harmless, peripheral gesture but in fact as a private joke. Academia had provided Amis with the perfect setting for his fictionalised Bardwell – his absurd interests could become a professional commitment – and the fact that Amis's own introduction to the profession took place in Wales involved an irony he just could not ignore. When Bardwell heard that his son-in-law might be moving to Wales, his enthusiasm for the country and its culture went into overdrive. 'Won't it be *marvellous* if Kingsley gets the job!!! Professor Dai ap Faeces is there, who wrote the first really Scholarly-Welch grammar, I'll get it and show you ... So handy for the National Scheissbedsodd, too' (A to L, 6 October 1949). The carbon of this letter would have been on Amis's desk as he had Neddy Welch offer a piece of characteristically irrelevant advice to Jim about his article on medieval shipbuilding: 'I was having a chat the other day with an old friend of mine from South Wales. The Professor at the University College of Abertawe, he is now. Athro Haines; I expect you know his book on medieval Cwmrhydy ceirw' (*Lucky Jim*, p. 82). Abertawe is Swansea in Welsh and Athro Haines is Welsh for Department of History. Would Bardwell have recognised the link?

Amis would certainly have revelled in the almost fatalistic ironies that underpinned it. When summoned for interview, Amis was still suffering the after-effects of a debilitating bout of flu, and Bardwell had offered to go with him. 'He would enjoy the trip so! To his beloved Wales!!' (6 October 1949). Amis politely declined the offer but, of course, Bardwell would go with him, in his notes, and become part of his novel. But what would he call him? In all of the letters Amis wrote to Larkin during 1949–50 telling him about his new home in Wales 'Welsh' becomes 'Welch'.

The private exchanges between Amis and Larkin provide the former with a kind of scurrilous rehearsal for the cautiously framed exercises of the novel. Larkin participated willingly in his role as foil to Amis's angry projections. Indeed, he sometimes unwittingly provided Amis with ideas. In a letter to Amis in July 1946 Larkin responds to Amis's early reports on Hilly's relatives: 'an awful price to pay for Hilary', writes Larkin, and he goes on to declare that:

I HATE anybody who does anything UNUSUAL at ALL, whether it's make a lot of MONEY or dress in silly CLOTHES or read books of foreign WORDS or know a lot about anything or play any musical INSTRUMENT (menstruin) or pretend that they believe anything out of the ordinary that requires a lot of courage, or a lot of generosity, or a lot of self-cunt-roll, to believe it – BECAUSE THEY ARE USUALLY SUCH SODDING NASTY PEOPLE THAT I KNOW IT IS 1000–1 THAT THEY ARE SHOWING OFF – *and they don't know it* but I *know it* (L to A, 17 July 1946).

This is Larkin's general response to Amis's opinions on the sham hypocrisies of the Bardwell family, and it closely resembles Jim's first public disclosure of his inner world. In Chapter 20, when Bertrand bursts into his room to warn him against flirting with Christine, Jim tells him what he thinks of him. 'You think that just because you're tall and can put paint on canvas you're a sort of demigod. It wouldn't be so bad if you really were. But you're not: your sensitivity works for things that people do to you. Touchy and vain, yes, but not sensitive' (p. 208). Again, Larkin found himself at one corner of Amis's triangle of confidentiality, deceit and invention. Not since he had first been introduced to members of Hilly's family had Amis fully disclosed to her how he felt about them. To his credit he did not wish to cause her distress. She did not share their various enthusiasms and idiosyncracies but what she found endearing her husband treated as preposterous and unendurable. He reserved these outpourings for Larkin and once more his game of hide-from-one and disclose-to-another resurfaced in the relationship between Jim and his narrator. Hilly did not realise that key figures in the novel were based on members of her family until several of the letters disclosing Kingsley's opinions on them were included in Jacobs's biography forty years later. She was upset and one wonders how Larkin dealt with the knowledge that he and Hilly were reading what amounted to two versions of the same novel.

In the 1949 letter where Amis thanks Larkin for encouraging him to be funny, for being his 'inner audience', he comments on how their friendship only really began after they had stopped seeing each other in 1942, and he states that he has 'just laughed like necrophily' at a spoof address that Larkin had used in a letter to Amis at Catterick army camp: '6477599 Fuc. P. A. Larkin, Excrement Boy, 1st BUM, Mond's Lines, Shatterick Ramp, Forks'. This letter, which was making Amis laugh in 1949, had been written to him in July 1942.

Soon after they became friends in Oxford it became clear to Larkin that exchanges on such topics as literature, culture and politics were permissible only if woven into a fabric of farce, ridicule and pun-laden invective. This peculiar blend of learning and anti-cultural mannerisms would eventually become Jim Dixon, or at least the dimension of Jim that drew the attention of the book's more hostile critics. Jim is an articulate, clever graduate, but practically all of his encounters with learning are accompanied by a disclaimer indicating boredom or indifference. When Jim sees Christine at the College Ball he comments to himself on her attractiveness and adds that 'he'd read somewhere or been told that somebody like Aristotle or I. A. Richards had said that the sight of beauty makes us want to move towards it' (*Lucky Jim*, p. 107). He can't remember which of them said this, and he does not care. At the same event he reflects on how Bertrand continually uses his status as a potential artist as though it were a guarantee of his complex and intriguing personality. 'Dixon himself had sometimes wished he wrote poetry or something as a claim to developed character', and he makes it clear that he never will (ibid., p. 107). Alfred Beesley is an English lecturer with whom Jim shares digs and who has, on occasion, lent him books. One is about love by 'somebody like Plato or Rilke' and another is a modern novel involving a character who feels 'pity moving in him like a sickness ... or some such jargon' (ibid., p. 72).

At the end of the novel Dixon and Christine are about to board the train to London, and they encounter the Welch family on the platform.

> He saw that not only were Welch and Bertrand both present, but Welch's fishing-hat and Bertrand's beret were there too. The beret, however, was on Welch's head, the fishing hat on Bertrand's. In these guises, and standing rigid with popping eyes, as both were, they had a look of being Gide and Lytton Strachey, represented in waxwork form by a prentice hand (ibid., p. 256).

The narrator tells us that Jim 'drew in breath to denounce them both', but instead he collapses with laughter. '"You're ..." he said. "He's ..."' He does not complete these sentences and we will never know if the narrator's learned allusions to Gide and Strachey are shared by Jim, which is appropriate since he is about to make his triumphant departure from the world in which high-cultural coat-trailing is a measure of importance. It is impossible to overstate the importance of the moment at the dance when Jim, for the reader, completely renounces his claims upon any interest in culture and discloses instead his far more gratifying contemplation of the spectacle of Christine. We do not really believe that he is ignorant of the aesthetic ideas of I. A. Richards, Plato, Aristotle or Rilke; more that he has relegated each as distractions. One is reminded of his letter to Larkin of 13 January 1947 (Bod) in which he tells of meeting the impressively built schoolgirl at a dance. The disclosure to Larkin is deliciously confidential. He takes pleasure not only in confessing to his friend something that Hilly would never know but especially in exchanging his and Larkin's intellectual and cultural interests for something far more important; sex.

Jim's ostentatious philistinism would become the most controversial aspect of the novel. If he had been presented as an ill-educated, working-class type, a 1950s version of Hardy's Jude, or even as an English counterpart to the anti-intellectual intellectuals who had flourished in Tsarist Russia and more recently in France, that would have been fine. But Jim does not even pay culture the backhanded compliment of bothering to dislike it, let alone wanting to know more about it as a step to self-improvement. When *Lucky Jim* was published, few people had ever heard of Amis, but through 1954 and 1955, as the book became a bestseller, it was attended by interviews with and profiles of its author, and the parallels between Jim and the junior don at a provincial university who had created him raised questions, which on 17 February 1956 were addressed by J. G. Weightman in the *Times Literary Supplement*.

> Kingsley Amis's *Lucky Jim* has spread the impression that Redbrick is peopled by beer-drinking scholarship louts, who wouldn't know a napkin from a chimney-piece and whose one ideal is to end their sex starvation in the arms of a big breasted blonde ... If the book were directly autobiographical, as many people assume it to be, Amis would presumably have long since lost his job, and rightly so.

While Weightman had never met Amis and perceived the novel as a symptom of moral degeneration, his suspicion that Jim grew out of his author's anti-cultural inclinations is obliquely accurate.

The letters Amis wrote to Larkin between 1945 and 1953 show how the unsettled, often contradictory features of Amis the private person were eventually recognised by Amis the novelist and reconstituted as Jim.

Most of the major English writers are mentioned in the letters, and most appear to cause various moods of boredom, disappointment and irritation. He regards Chaucer as comparable with 'the big pipe, that takes away, the waste matter, from a public lavatory' (15 May 1946; the intrusive commas being a parody of the locutionary habits of his tutor J. B. Leishman). 'Dryden is A SECOND RATE FUCKING JOURNALIST' (8 October 1946). He agrees entirely with the *Edinburgh Magazine* reviewer who 'saw through our young romantic parvenu [Keats] from the start', and in the same letter he states that Pope and Wordsworth, while differently inclined, are equally overrated (20 March 1947). The Renaissance sonnet, bedrock of formal discipline and stylistic exuberance, is a horrible, ridiculous exercise. 'I always thought that Eng. Lit. *ought to be good*; I still think it, but it *isn't* ... Do not refrain from scorning the sonnet at *every available* opportunity' (2 December 1947). Milton, Cowper, Crabbe, Blake, Hardy, Dickens and Hopkins receive similar treatment. Shakespeare is spared, by omission.

More recent writers, many of whom had been introduced to him by Larkin, do not fare too well either. The verse of the Imagists and Symbolists is incomprehensible, formless; 'like what I used to write when I came in pissed in 1943. It kept PRETENDING to mean something and NOT MEANING ANYTHING' (30 January 1947). Dorothy Parker is 'TOO OBVIOUS AND ELEMENTARY' (29 March 1946). The characters of Flann O'Brien's *At Swim Two Birds* are '[not] at all funny' (8 August 1946). Joyce's *Ulysses* is unreadable (16 January 1949). D. H. Lawrence is an ideologue masquerading as a novelist (6 August 1948). Dylan Thomas writes self-indulgent nonsense (24 March 1947) and Waugh's *Brideshead Revisited* is pseudo-elitist fantasy (8 October 1948). Graham Greene, on whom Amis had in 1948 been commissioned to write a monograph, is found to be humourless and tedious (9 November 1948). Even Auden, whom he once admired and whose imprint on Amis's early verse is very evident, now irritates him (9 March 1949).

Before concluding that Amis in his twenties appreciated nothing, we should recognise that he was reading not as a critic, an evaluative scrutineer, but more like someone obliged to watch a game while all the time wanting to be a player. His abusive diatribes were symptomatic of his frustrations, and it is noticeable that after 1950 these splenetic, irritable attacks on other writers almost ceased. He had begun *Lucky Jim*.

Further parallels between the novel and the letters to Larkin are remarkable.

The 1952–3 letters are different from their predecessors in a number of very slight but tangible ways, evident only if we read them alongside the novel. He gives Larkin reports on the rapid progress of the final draft, and it is as though there is a dynamic relationship between the letters dispatched to Belfast and the other text, in progress and destined eventually for Gollancz.

On 9 December 1952 he lists the 'vital books' on his shelf, presumably the shelf in his study in 24 The Grove. These include all of the authors vilified in his letters of the previous seven years. He does not explain why they are 'vital' (the inverted commas are his), but unless he had undergone a personality transplant we can assume that he means necessary to own and have read – he is, after all, a lecturer in English. There is a confident irony in the remark, because he does not bother to comment on their relative qualities; he's done that. Now he's more interested in something else: 'tally-ho for Dixon. I am about to start the pin-Welch-down sequence. There has been a lot of stuff about the burnt table which you might laugh at.' He might also have noted that he had decided that his 'vital books' are those that Dixon cannot be bothered to read. Obviously he has, for his fictional counterpart, transformed his literary irritations and obligations into a state of happy ignorance.

Larkin would remain embittered for the rest of his life by what he saw as Amis's act of plagiarism. Sometimes he disclosed his feelings to others but never to Amis, even much later when their friendship appeared to be mutating into quiet antagonism. The most touching memorial to the novel is a letter to Larkin from Hilly. She begins by thanking him for his card and drawing – 'one of the nicest things about having a baby [Sally] is the letter or card and creature I get from you'. The poem. 'Born Yesterday', dedicated to Sally, is 'the most beautiful poem I've ever read, and I've put it in my special box of letters and things to keep for her ... I was quite overcome when Kingsley read it to me'. She continued: 'it's such a lovely relief to me to think that in spite of having married and got kids Kingsley has managed to write *Lucky Jim* – I always had a fear that I might have buggered it up for him one way and another' (Hilly to L, 26 January 1954, Hull). As Larkin was aware, Hilly's feelings of guilt were completely misplaced. The novel had been *driven* by Amis's frustration regarding his marriage, his in-laws and his job. Hilly asks Larkin to 'come and stay this easter ... stay a nice long time'. Politely he declined the invitation.

5

Belfast

Larkin's first impressions of Belfast are recorded in a postcard to his mother sent on the day of his interview in June 1950: 'Belfast is an unattractive city. Oh dear, oh dear.' The words seem unambiguous enough, but with knowledge of Larkin's maturing temperament one detects a hint of masochistic glee.

After boarding the Liverpool–Belfast ferry in September he sat on deck and composed a poem called 'Single to Belfast', a title which refers, of course, both to the nature of his ticket and his love life. The poem was never completed, but what remains is a series of rather pompous reflections on this moment of departure, such as 'The present is really stiffening to past / Right under my eyes'. And so on, with an echo of the workbook of 'No for an Answer', which has Sam Wagstaff departing for a transformative new existence. But the *Ulster Duke* ferry was not quite the *Queen Mary* and Belfast was certainly not New York.

Larkin's first rooms, a bedsit in a Victorian hall of residence, overlooked the old quadrangle of Queen's, which unlike many of its Oxford counterparts did not attempt to disguise its medievalism as anything other than nineteenth century. As an institution, however, Queen's dutifully imitated Oxbridge traditions and not simply as an aspiration to status. Northern Ireland was part of the UK but was also a uniquely devolved pseudo-state, with its own Parliament, legislative structure, education system and unusual police force. Also it was obsessively concerned – or at least 60 per cent of its population was concerned – that its neighbour the Republic was continually plotting to swallow it up. Queen's was its only university and quite accurately saw itself as serving a vital role as a production line for the local Establishment. A fair number of the doctors, lawyers, politicians, senior civil servants and policemen of Ulster were the products of Queen's. So quite soon Larkin found that he was living within what appeared to be aspects of his student life in miniature, with touches of the surreal thrown in for good measure. Queen's was a middle-class version of Oxford, while Belfast and the rest of the province resembled a kind of neurotic, torpid parody of Britain at war.

Appropriately he began to revert to the kind of lifestyle he had enjoyed as an undergraduate. The bright shirts, bow ties and patterned sports jackets replaced the relatively sober attire of his Leicester years, and Larkin soon began to realise that he could operate much as he had in Oxford, comfortably displaying his mildly exotic artistic persona among a group of tolerant peers – now made up of junior academics rather than undergraduates. Within weeks he had met Alan Grahame (history), Arthur Terry (Spanish), Evan John (music) and James Bradley (classics), all lodging in the same hall of residence. Soon he bumped into Colin Strang, a near-contemporary of his at St John's who had recently been appointed to the philosophy department at Queen's. In the intervening years Strang had met and married Patsy Avis, another Oxford graduate. The Strangs had a house in Kincotter Avenue, South Belfast, and Larkin became a regular guest.

More and more Larkin began to find that Belfast was not simply a rerun but a considerable improvement on Oxford. Now he had independence. He no longer dwelt in the intimidating, expectant shadow of his late father; he had his own money, and the responsibilities for his widowed mother were devolved to his sister and her family. Despite the dour influence of Presbyterianism, Belfast could be a lively town. The city-centre pubs were busy meeting places, particularly the famous Crown; there were regular jazz concerts in the University Union and the city hospitals; and the Queen's Senior Common Room parties would often be riotously drink-fuelled. Larkin entertained his new network of friends with well-matured versions of his Oxford retinue of anecdotes and imitations and gradually acquired the reputation in Queen's-based society as an agreeable, multi-faceted personality – a comic extrovert and boozer but also learned and cultured; after all, he had published two novels and a volume of poems and was busily producing more of both.

The Strangs's marriage was not quite deserving of the term 'open' – this was still Britain in the early 1950s – but 'ajar' would not be an overstatement. Patsy came from an immensely wealthy South African family – owners of diamond mines – and had spent a relaxed, culturally rich childhood in London. After Roedean she had, at Oxford, made the best of her natural brilliance, temperamental flirtatiousness and taste for the idiosyncratic. Colin Strang, lecturer in philosophy and son of a distinguished diplomat, was her alter ego, her stabilising presence, an arrangement which is often successful but which by 1951 was becoming strained.

Larkin's improved reinvention of his Oxford style certainly worked with Patsy. She found him entertaining, enigmatic and, in Belfast, agreeably incongruous. For Larkin she was a version of Diana Gollancz, but because she was married and he had become a friend of the family – he also got on well with Colin – the prospect of sex was far more realistic. She could, as it were, be borrowed and, like the glossy magazines, she required no long-term attention.

Most of the private diaries that Larkin himself had not destroyed were shredded by Monica and his secretary Betty Mackereth after his death, and the only surviving account of what they might have mentioned came from Patsy via her second husband, the poet Richard Murphy. One day she had arrived early at Larkin's rooms and while waiting for him read his recent entries. When later in the day she disclosed this to him she generated a once-only encounter with Larkin in a state of anger verging upon rage. The most prominent entries involved detailed accounts of his masturbatory activities. Patsy, being a broad-minded, indulgent sort, was mildly amused and not at all unsettled by the disclosure that Larkin was indeed like most other people, but for him it was worse than being caught, literally, in the act. He was not infuriated so much by the nature of what Patsy had found out as by the fact that she had caught him writing about it. She had known him for little more than eighteen months, and despite the fact that they had become lovers he was still cautious about showing her what really went on behind the presence with whom she shared secret liaisons. It was already evident to her that he was capable of disingenuousness – how else could he maintain an unflustered social life with her and Colin while conducting their affair? The diary had shown her briefly, and to his distress, another level of secrecy where the different segments of his public and private worlds would become part of the same experience – writing. For Larkin, aged thirty, his notebooks and diaries had become the point at which the sometimes divergent, irreconcilable dimensions of his life intersected. The writing of them did not provide a solution to his problems but it offered an adequate compensation – confidential omniscience. He could contemplate the entirety of what he had, for others, distributed only as perspectives.

The dynamic between secrecy and quiet disclosure that fed his addiction to the diaries and notebooks – and in an adjusted way his exchanges with Amis – would become an equally important feature of his finest verse. In 'Best Society', completed shortly after Patsy's discovery of his notebooks, he contemplates the pleasure of being alone: 'I lock my door' and 'Uncontradicting solitude / Supports me on its giant palm'. (And one cannot but wonder if the nature of what Patsy found might have played some part in the formation of the final image: he had once remarked to Amis that 'I don't … want to take a girl out and spend circa £5 on her when I can toss myself off in five minutes, free, and have the rest of the evening to myself' (*Memoirs*, p. 61)). He did not crave detachment from other people; rather, he was becoming aware that solitude meant something more than being alone. It was the point at which the various strata of his life were available only to him and from which he could cautiously select, perhaps edit, and reassemble material for writing poems. The anger provoked by Patsy's inquisitiveness would eventually be transposed into something cautiously planned. We, like Patsy, would be fascinated, amused, even shocked, but in the poems Larkin would maintain control. Almost thirty years later he might well have recalled the incident with Patsy when planning the opening line of what would be his last significant poem, 'Love again: wanking at ten past three'. It reads like a diary entry; and by 1979 he was beginning to lose interest in what his poems said of him, and running out of things to say.

Along with his affair with Patsy Strang, Larkin became closely attached to two other women while at Queen's. Judy and Ansell Egerton's marriage was, relative to that of the Strangs, stable and would endure until 1974. Ansell lectured in economics and after leaving Queen's employed his expertise more profitably first by becoming city editor of *The Times*, later as a merchant banker and eventually as a director of Rothmans International. Judy was born in Australia, did a degree in history and, in London in the 1970s, made use of her interest in art, working first on Paul Mellon's collections and then as curator at the Tate Gallery. Larkin found in Judy reflections of the more agreeable aspects of his own character. She often gave the impression of being shy and unsettled by the presence of loquacious and intelligent companions, but in truth she was keeping in check a shrewd, thoughtful perspective upon matters in which she and genuine friends shared interests. She and Larkin found that they had similar tastes in twentieth-century fiction and poetry – predominantly English and conservative – and he enjoyed encouraging her interest in jazz with his encyclopaedic knowledge of it. After Belfast he, sometimes with Monica, would stay with the Egertons in London, usually at the time of the Lord's Test Match – Ansell, seconded by Harold Pinter, would in 1973 successfully propose Larkin for membership of the Marylebone Cricket Club.

Larkin's relationship with Judy was not exactly asexual – she was pretty and he was certainly attracted to her – but it came more and more to resemble that of brother and sister. Their letters read like the correspondence of two people intimately acquainted in an agreeable but diplomatically restrained way.

Winifred Arnott was born in London in 1929 but during the Blitz joined her father's family in Belfast and stayed on to read English at Queen's. In 1950 when Larkin arrived she had recently graduated and had taken a part-time job in the library. Quite soon she would become Ruth Bowman the Second. She was seven years younger than Larkin and, although intelligent and well read, in awe both of his presence – a mixture of the esoteric and the early middle-aged – and his reputation as a writer. They attended parties together, went to concerts and the cinema, and on Sundays would cycle along the Lagan and into the countryside south of Belfast. She already had a boyfriend, C. G. Bradshaw, in London and although they were not formally engaged theirs seemed to be the kind of conventional relationship that would eventually result in marriage. This was an attractive prospect for Larkin. He could play the role of learned suitor, comfortable in the knowledge that things would never reach the stage that they had with Ruth where he would continually equivocate between commitment and fear of the same.

In 1952, she returned from a visit to London and announced that she and Bradshaw were formally engaged and would be married within eighteen months. Things had not gone quite as Larkin had expected. It was not that he was stricken with her choice of Bradshaw before him – he had seen this as inevitable, on his part as a kind of goods-returned-with-thanks – but he was mildly irritated by the timing. They had not had sex and he had hoped that her continued presence in Belfast would enable him to consummate the relationship before the unavoidable closure of operations. She now insisted that the suggestive, flirtatious element of their earlier attachment would not continue.

'Lines on a Young Lady's Photograph Album' was begun soon after Winifred's announcement of her engagement and completed in September 1953. The poem strikes a brilliant balance between a mood of intimate informality, as if addressed to the young lady of the album, and a series of more introspective reflections on emotions prompted by the photographs themselves. The quality of the piece is without doubt, and critical accounts of it abound, but what is never mentioned is the curious image of the speaker, which stays in the mind long after one's appreciation of its artistry. It invites comparison with Browning's 'My Last Duchess', except that Browning's speaker is deranged and self-evidently an invention of the poet. With 'Lines' Larkin is evasively present, and he gives away just enough to suggest that the deeply moving nostalgia of the apparent theme – the past recorded beautifully and timelessly – is intercut with something else, a kind of lewd masochism. There is a subdued sensuality in the opening stanza, in which she 'yields up' the photographs 'matt and glossy on the thick black pages': 'too rich: / I choke on such nutritious images'. And later: 'the theft / Of this one of you bathing ...' Read by a sensitive and incorrupt person these images could remain just on the decent side of ambiguous, but the more inquisitive might be prompted to speculate on what lies behind them.

'Maiden Name', again inspired by Winifred and written shortly after her wedding in 1954, would be one of the poems that made *The Less Deceived* so popular and successful, and its closest formal relative would probably be the early-seventeenth-century lyric practised by the likes of Donne and Herbert. The syntax and diction sit somewhere between the elegant and the languid, and both carry their stanzaic framework like a well-made suit of clothes. The title introduces the conceit with which Larkin plays games, turning it this way and that and opening it out into figurative excursions. Mostly he switches between reflective tenderness and tongue-in-cheek stoicism:

> ... you cannot be
> Semantically the same as that young beauty:
> It was of her that these two words were used.

Occasionally, however, there is a hint of something less agreeable. Her marriage is described as her being 'so thankfully confused / By law with someone else', with the phrase 'thankfully confused' carrying a smirking ambiguity. Is Larkin thankful for her departure or does the term involve its older usage of fortuitousness and to her benefit? Similarly, 'confused' could involve both its archaic meaning of combined (including physically combined) and its more familiar usage. Appended to the manuscript draft of the original poem is the phrase 'you are not she', which raises the question of whether Larkin was wondering about incorporating it into a rewritten text or leaving it simply as a private comment. Either way it opens a new perspective upon the furtive verbal gymnastics of the piece: 'you are not she' = 'you Arnott she'. The girl has gone from the almost intimate familiarity of 'you' to the absence of 'she', the transformative phrase involving the aurally identical and equally effective 'Arnott' (maiden name) and 'are not'. Rarely can one claim to have access to the conditions and thought processes that brought a poem to completion, but it must be the case that the above piece of verbal quiddity was in his mind as he put together 'you cannot be / Semantically the same as that young beauty'.

During his period in Belfast, Larkin's relationship with Monica acquired a degree of continuity, or so it appeared to her. On his visits to Britain he would divide his time between periods with his mother and sister, trips to the Amises in Swansea, occasional meetings with Bruce Montgomery and regular encounters with Monica. They might stay at her flat in Leicester or after 1951, particularly during the Easter and summer vacations, take holidays in various parts of southern England, North Wales or Scotland. She first visited Belfast in March 1951, and after a few days in the city they took the train to Portrush and then on to the Glens of Antrim, staying in the pretty, well-preserved village of Glenarm. In later summers they would explore Donegal, and on one occasion they briefly visited Dublin; generally they preferred the countryside.

The remarkable thing about their relationship during these years was the way in which Larkin organised and oversaw it. Monica met Patsy on several occasions but at the time did not suspect that anything other than close friendship existed between them – indeed, she knew little of the affair until after Larkin's death. Similarly, she knew of Winifred but trusted Larkin's account of her as a junior colleague with whom he shared interests and often socialised. Again, until the 1960s she assumed that the subjects of 'Lines on a Young Lady's Photograph Album' and 'Maiden Name' were inventions, conceits.

Patsy was the living realisation of the fantasies for which pornography provided Larkin with more reliable deliverance. Several times she suggested that since they enjoyed each other so much, sexually and temperamentally, they should go public and have a proper relationship. She once offered to leave Colin, marry Larkin and work full-time so that he could concentrate on his writing. Larkin was honest enough in his responses. Theirs was an affair in the deliciously improper sense, and he enjoyed particularly its furtive aspect. They would leave letters for one another in post offices under the false names of Mr and Mrs Crane and book into hotels in Larne or other Belfast satellite towns, again as the Cranes. Belfast with its dour Victorian countenance and abiding distaste for anything indulgent or exciting – bar the marching season and 12 July bonfires – provided the ideal counterpoint for their secret adventures. The choice of Crane was their amusing commentary upon all of this, given that the most omnipresent public couple in Belfast were the two giant Harland and Wolff cranes. On 13 March 1953 he wrote to her with a further explanation of how they were unsuited to a long-term relationship. She was, he contended, far more exuberant and impassioned than him. 'Please don't think of me as frightfully sophisticated ... I'm not. You're only my second young lady, and look like being my last.' The first, as far as Patsy knew, was Monica. He said nothing of Ruth. Moreover, he managed also to maintain for Monica a convincing performance as her monogamous partner even when on several occasions during her visits to Belfast she joined the hectic, partying milieu of the Strang household. When he wrote to Monica, reporting on events in Belfast, it would of course have seemed curious, perhaps suspicious, if he had deliberately omitted mention of two of his closest friends, the Strangs. Here he writes of a conversation on the Amises that he, Patsy and Monica had had during the latter's recent visit: 'What I *remember* saying was that Hilly must regret marrying Kingsley so early when she sees her sister married to a respectable husband who will (very likely) go far', implying that despite encouraging his friend's attempts at his next novel he did not, in truth, see it as securing him success: how ironic this would prove to be. He adds, 'Patsy's reaction to this was "What's the use of a respectable husband going far if you don't like him?" which is true enough, I suppose ... I did say that Hilly regretted "missing fun" [and] I expect every married woman does ...' (L to Monica, 1 November 1951). One might, too easily I think, feel awed at the various levels of dissembling that went into this: he clarifies for his supposed girlfriend (Monica) an exchange they shared with a mutual acquaintance, with whom he had recently begun an affair (Patsy) on the state of his supposed best friend's marriage and his sense, as Hilly's confidant, of it as a grave disappointment for her. This might seem like mendacity but it is not. He is disarmingly candid and honest and he makes no pretence to feelings he does not have. There are no lies, only tactical omissions.

Even more extraordinary is a letter he wrote to Monica two months later:

> your letter today seemed especially pleasing. Thank you for it. Possibly at the bottom of this impression was your long acclamatory passage of me as a food & wine man – & woman man – wch it never occurred to me not to take seriously until you said not. Of course it bears little or no relation to the facts of life, but then nor do my visions of myself. I was trying to think of the number of women who had been in my rooms alone, & apart from Miss Leach the Welfare Officer, Mrs Farrell the caretaker, & Patsy I can't think of any. (L to Monica, 11 January 1952)

It is almost as though he is admitting to being the only person present at the commission of the crime while not quite admitting to guilt.

Strictly speaking it was true that the only three women 'who had been in his rooms' were the ones named but whether or not he felt any private thrill from splicing a statement of fact with his private knowledge that it involved sex will forever remain open to speculation. However, his careful cultivation of a confession that involved only part of the truth suggests that he did.

In midsummer 1953 Larkin spent a week in Mallaig in the Highlands of Scotland with Monica, and following that they went south for ten days in Weymouth. Larkin never disclosed a particular taste for the epistolary novel, but during this period it might occasionally have occurred to him that he was in one. On 20 July he wrote to Winifred from Mallaig, informing her of the view from his hotel window of a church 'with a cross on top (and a gull on the cross)', a cottage and 'beyond, the grey sea and the dim shape of Skye. I can hear gulls calling and hotel guests padding about.' Later he shifts to the anecdotal – an account of a notoriously drunken fisherman of the village – and finally to the intimate, recalling their cycle rides around the Ulster countryside, particularly the one just before his departure 'ending

with your soft *shy* goodbye (lock this up) on Thursday in the darkness'
(20 July 1953). Before he left he had set her a task. In his absence she was to
read a number of seventeenth-century amatory poems, chosen by him. (The
exercise would in due course inspire his own borrowing from the metaphysical sub-genre in his poem on and to Winifred, 'Maiden Name'.) All involved
the commanding yet gentle and learned presence of the seducer addressing
his generally innocent and always subdued addressee. 'How are you getting
on with *your* holiday task? When you know it thoroughly, you might go on
to Herrick's *To virgins, to make the most of time.*' This must have seemed,
at least to him, mordantly appropriate. He had clearly not given up in his
pursuit of her despite the presence of her London-based fiancé, and he was
writing her provocatively amusing letters. He ends, 'I rage, I pant, I burn
for a letter from you ...', knowing of course that, like Herrick's virgins, she
would remain the secret recipient of his beguiling sophistry.

And where was Monica when he was writing this? 'The only time I can
write to you [Winifred] is before getting up, which is what I'm doing now
...' Larkin and Monica were sexual partners, but this was 1953 and offering
false names to hotel receptionists and other guests was simply too much
trouble, given that their relationship had already taken on aspects of the
reliably mundane. They took separate bedrooms.

Two days later, on 22 July, he begins, 'Hotel paper, hotel pen, but I can
still write you the beginnings of a letter before breakfast, as M hasn't finished
dressing yet.' On this occasion the letter is to Patsy, and one cannot help
finding parallels with Fielding's *Clarissa* or Smollett's *Humphry Clinker* as
Mr Larkin, hidden in his study, hurries a message across the paper before
the return of 'M'. A few days later he is in Weymouth, snatching a few
spare moments while Monica is elsewhere, this time 'sitting in the sun
lounge looking across the front' and informing Winifred of how, when no
one was looking, he had 'plucked your letter from the rack like a cormorant
snapping up a bit of bread'. He commends her for reading the next on his
list of lyrics, this time Marvell's 'To His Coy Mistress', adding that 'I'm not
really playing my *own* game in all this. By the time I've convinced you that
virginity is just an underdeveloped talent you'll be setting yourself off alone and
defenceless, with young Sparks [Graham Bradshaw, her fiancé]' (26 July 1953).

His ability to switch personae for three different women, let alone overcome the practical difficulties of secretly writing to two while holidaying

with the third, is formidable, and on 28 July he delivered an urbane finale in a letter from Weymouth to Colin and Patsy, simply as if writing to two close friends, on what he and his girlfriend Monica had got up to in the Highlands and on the English south coast.

It is impossible to ignore the parallels between the situation orchestrated by Larkin and the numerous confessions of adulterous mishap related to him by Amis. In fact there is a letter from 1947 in which Amis is hardly able to conceal the sense of exhilaration which undermines his claims to anxiety. He was seeing Joan while at the same time managing a threesome comprising her, 'Helen' and Hilly.

> My time with Helen passed without mishap – 1 ½ hrs – but I was hard pressed by her twin enquiries. I why had I got to 'get back' so soon? And when was I coming up to see her *and spend money again*? By a sodain turne of the whele of the goddes [of] Fortune, as I was conducting an unplanned with drawl at the entrance to her office [a term routinely associated by both with 'orifice']. [Mervyn] Brown came up and starting speaking out of his mouth I never imagined I should be *glad* to see him under any circumstance, but that just shows the defects of my imagination: *I was then VERY* glad. Helen later helped matters by ringing me up ... while Hilly was ... plang records in my bedroom. That is the sort of situation I used to laugh at when I saw it presented over the footlights or on the silver screen, but I didn't then. (A to L, 29 September 1947, Bod)

Amis was revelling in the thrill of being caught. He feared he could not quite manage this precarious balance between deceit and gratification and as a consequence he enjoyed the experience all the more. The Amises knew the Strangs from Colin's time in Oxford but Larkin certainly did not make use of his affair as an act of oneupmanship against his friend's well-established record of infidelity. In fact, Amis did not know of the affair until after it was over. It was Hilly in whom Larkin confided. Hilly wrote to him in 1954, shortly after their relationship had ended, reporting on her recent conversation with Patsy in London, 'A lot of talk and hints – but nothing one doesn't know already' (Hilly to L, 2 August 1954, Hull). He would remain on close affectionate terms with Hilly until the early 1960s but, as indicated here, his apparently candid exchanges with Amis were becoming on his part gradually more selective.

Larkin's attempt at duplicitous promiscuity carried with it the atmosphere of an Ealing comedy, that characteristically English sense of something naughty going on beneath the calm surface of nothing terribly untoward. He could share a bed with his clandestine, adulterous partner while he and her unconcealed long-term counterpart were obliged to have separate rooms. And then there was Winifred, the Coy Lady he would like to share with Marvell, if only she were not so determined to begin a proper relationship with someone a little more conventional. Larkin, like Amis, was enjoying himself, and he knew that before too long matters would reach a conclusion, all the more painlessly because he would not be a participant. The comparison is an accurate reflection of the writers they were becoming. Amis's novels of the 1950s involve the dynamic of subterfuge and disclosure while Larkin during the same period recorded lyrics of weary resignation.

Soon after his return to Belfast in August Patsy wrote informing him that Colin had applied successfully for a lectureship in Newcastle and that, apart from clearing their house, they would not be returning to Ulster. Their relationship was not over, not quite, but the move would cause practical difficulties. It was at this point that she suggested that she leave Colin for him, and he with disingenuous concern for her advised against such a precipitous act. She left Colin anyway, went to Paris to study at the Sorbonne and there met the poet Richard Murphy. At the end of November 1954 she informed Larkin that she and Murphy were to be married. He answered tactfully that 'I think I'd better retire into the background of your life for a bit' (7 December 1954), and both of them knew that he meant for good. Later in the letter he informs her, offhandedly, that 'I got this blasted Hull post, and am going there in March'. He had first mentioned the Hull post to Patsy in October. It was one among many that his boss Jack Graneek had advised him to apply for, 'but', he informs Patsy, 'it is true that I shall not' (9 October 1954). He adds enigmatically that he does not 'think that's the answer'. Three weeks later, however, he had almost changed his mind, telling Patsy that, yes, he wants the job but only 'in a way; knowing that it will mean harder work and more responsibility' (28 October 1954). For his mother he shows the same display of ambivalence shot through with indecision, writing to her when called for interview that 'it's a bit chilly here – and smells of fish' (23 October 1954).

Larkin had at some point made a final decision to leave Belfast. He had been happy there, but the move was an acknowledgement that he had become, more than ever before, unflinchingly, almost dispassionately aware of who he was and to what his life amounted. The five years in Belfast had contributed to this, not by virtue of the place itself, but the place would, if he remained there, provide memories of mutation when what he required was a sense of completion. For those who knew him, the move was simply that: a change of place to a new, more senior post. It neither indicated nor reflected a significant change in him, at least not in terms of the personae he shared with friends and colleagues. It was, however, connected with something that had begun to happen at a more private level in his poems.

The poems he composed during his last two years in Belfast contain the quintessence of what would become Larkin the acclaimed poet. They would form the core of *The Less Deceived*, the collection that effectively altered his status from obscure, occasional novelist and versifier to one of the outstanding voices in the motley chorus of post-war English writing.

'Success Story' is an uncomplicated reflection upon failure, inferring that his – and the speaker is certainly Larkin – lack of success involves an unrealised literary ambition. The closing two stanzas are fascinating:

> The explanation goes like this, in daylight:
> To be ambitious is to fall in love
> With a particular life you haven't got
> And (since love picks your opposite) won't achieve.
> That's clear as day. But come back late at night,
>
> You'll hear a curious counter-whispering:
> Success, it says, you've scored a great success.
> Your wish has flowered, you've dodged the dirty feeding,
> Clean past it now at hardly any price –
> Just some pretence about the other thing.

What, he prompts us to ask, has he failed at in 'daylight', yet compensated for with the private counter-whisper of the night? It seems that he has become aware that his governing, overarching ambition was a falsehood, weirdly described as 'dirty feeding' or, more mundanely, the 'pretence about the other thing'.

The poem was written on 11 March 1954. A week earlier he had written to Patsy, caught between admiration for a novel that he had helped to construct and pure envy that it had piloted Amis to a position he had so long craved: 'Success, Success', he had written of Amis in the letter, with teeth clenched in indignation, but in the poem this becomes endurable irony. The alternative to what has been denied to him is not specified, but it does not need to be: the speaking presence of the poem is perversely aroused by failure because of his self-evident mastery of something else, the poem that he is writing.

The letters to Patsy during this period are like a sketchbook of his literary progressions and an index to their promptings. On 6 March 1954 he writes that having 'hurled himself at the novel again' he has now, finally, 'packed it up ... and I am still suffering from injury to self esteem'. Six weeks after that he tells her of his Easter break in Britain, including a weekend in Swansea with the Amises 'which rather put me out of humour ... I was rather jealous of his success' – that word again – and the newly acclaimed novelist and old friend who has attained it. Ten months later he remains unable, perhaps unwilling, to rid himself of the envious feelings that had become stubbornly attached to a single word. 'I came up from London this morning, feeling pretty tired and fed up after another glimpse of the rich life of the Amis household', he wrote to Monica in January 1955, and added, 'It's not his success I mind so much as immunity from worry and hard work, though I mind his success as well.'

He finally gave up all ambitions to become a novelist just prior to leaving Belfast and shortly after *Lucky Jim* was published. His reason was in part a sense of having his life plagiarised by his friend. Imagine how you would feel if your heroic attempts to build a novel from a blend of imagination and personal experience resulted in persistent failures and alongside this you witnessed your friend, and, in a still-amicable sense, closest rival, borrowing material from that same source for something that seemed to gather an implacable energy week-by-week, after which it took the literary world by storm. Weariness bordering on desperation would be an understandable response, but there was something else too that ensured that Amis's book would finally close the door upon Larkin's hopes of succeeding as a novelist.

In the workbook outlines for 'No for an Answer' we encounter the mysterious figure of Margerie.

She is a gay young Oxfordian, regarding herself etc. And wanting to be regarded by others as a real misfit in the funny little town she has chosen by a pin in the *TES* [*Times Educational Supplement*] but slowly by an emergence of personal dullness and Conservatism fitting into her job more and more ... (Philip Larkin, *Trouble at Willow Gables and Other Fictions*, ed. James Booth, p. 312)

The portrait is less than flattering, but the subject is undoubtedly Monica Jones, and she became the centrepiece for what would turn out to be his final attempt at fiction. 'A New World Symphony' was begun almost immediately following his abandonment of Sam Wagstaff's story, at the same time that Amis was reporting to him on the progress of the Dixon and Christine project. Although Larkin was happy to act as an adviser on Amis's rough drafts – tidying up the style, expelling redundant characters, etc. – there is no evidence that he expected it to be successful. It seemed to him to be Amis's version of the 'Willow Gables' exercises – writing as an escape valve for personal discontent – with rebarbative satire and farce substituted for sexual fantasy. What it did do, however, was to provide Larkin with a new idea for a novel about Britain *circa* 1950. It would be set in a university, certainly, but a provincial university where the contrast between high-minded bohemianism and post-war ordinariness was almost absurdly conspicuous.

As soon as Larkin met Monica Jones he was beguiled by her, for the simple reason that she was more than an attractive woman. Her background and her intellectual presence made her the equal both of Larkin and Amis. Both had met but neither had pursued a woman like this before and although there is evidence that Amis was particularly annoyed by this – hence his vindictive targeting of Monica/Margaret in *Lucky Jim* – Larkin was inspired. Amis's 1992 account of his experience of the Leicester Senior Common Room as the inspiration for *Lucky Jim* bears a close and unnerving resemblance to a letter that Larkin wrote to Monica on 13 April 1949. He is in the common room and takes particular delight in picking out the dreariness and unwitting absurdity of a gathering of provincial academics.

I have eaten the last lunch of the term now & opposite me Zandy, C. G. Wilson & Taylor are reading: Taylor in particular is reading *Punch* – he read this all yesterday, & has not finished it yet. I mention these things because I always believe in telling my correspondent what is around me in case it seeps into my text...

A small *Apparatus* has appeared in ye Common-Room, marked 'H2S test – Do not move. L. Hunter'; and dyd occasion a Witticism from me about the no. of bad Eggs on the staff. Mr Martin has donn'd a Fair Isle pullover and a curious jacket, cut for riding but made of gents' suiting, that doth in no wise enhance hys amiability. The College Visitor ... When his vacuous alert face came round the door on Saturday I felt I wanted to shriek at him what Llywelyn & John Cowper Powys shrieked at Baron Corvo in Venice: 'We're engaged! All the time! Right up to the bloody hilt!'

This, we should remind ourselves, was written before Amis had disclosed to him that 'Dixon and Christine' would be set in a university. Later in the letter he tells Monica that recently his friend Kingsley had visited Leicester and of how he'd introduced him to this patchwork of eccentrics and curiosities, ending with the observation that it would provide excellent raw material for his friend's skills as an impersonator. 'By god he'd do it well, wouldn't he?' Indeed he would, but not quite as Larkin imagined.

A redbrick university as the setting for his novel had indeed come from his visits to Larkin in the late 1940s, but Amis would only be able properly to build on this idea when he moved to Swansea. By then Larkin had already begun a novel that would, had it been completed and published before 1954, have eclipsed *Lucky Jim*.

Augusta Bax, the heroine of 'A New World Symphony', was Larkin's Jim Dixon. As characters they had absolutely nothing in common, nor did their real-life counterparts Monica Jones and Kingsley Amis, but in Larkin's view Augusta would prove far more effective than Jim as the focus for a groundbreaking tale of provincial academia.

Monica was an attractive woman, a natural blonde with piercing blue eyes. There is a photograph of her by Larkin from 1947 in which she appears about to either seduce or wreck the camera or possibly both. She wore the kind of handmade, brightly coloured clothes that might feature in contemporaneous films about Americans in the Mediterranean. Her taste in jewellery was self-consciously eccentric, ranging from ropes of imitation pearls to bejewelled rings that looked as though they put severe strain on her arm muscles. There was certainly a fair degree of sexual chemistry between them during their early, tentative meetings, owing partly to the fact that they were continually discovering similarities between their respective temperaments, backgrounds and behavioural peculiarities. She had grown up in Worcestershire, the child of a lower middle-class family – her father was an engineer – and went to high school in Kidderminster. There, in her mid- to late teens, she won the approval of her teachers for her abilities in English literature. She went up to Oxford, St Hugh's, on a scholarship to study English in October 1940 and graduated with a starred First in 1943 – an identical profile to that of Larkin, although they never met at university. She taught briefly at a private school near her home, but she had been advised that her future lay in academia. She narrowly missed getting a job in King's College London, but in early 1946 was appointed lecturer in English at Leicester. Her glowing Oxford references – one from the esteemed Helen Gardner – opened doors.

Soon Larkin began to find that their resemblances masked as many differences. Both projected a colourful unorthodox image to shield various states of inadequacy and uncertainty, but while Larkin combined his with an almost manic creative output Monica's inner character was of the inescapably defensive, watchful type. She knew that she had intellectual strength – Oxford had assured her of that – but she did not know what to do with it.

A number of temperamental features shared by Amis and Larkin were very similar to those that attracted Larkin to Monica. She, too, was irritated by the tendency for provincial universities to concern themselves obsessively with bureaucratic ritual. English literature as a university discipline was in Britain attaining a reasonable level of acknowledgement and respect; in the interwar years it had been widely mocked as an upstart, amateurish affair, a second-rate alternative to Classics. After the war, English gradually, systematically, set about creating a scholarly and disciplinary framework for itself that would rival established arts subjects. Monica, while showing an impressive ability to engage critically with literary texts, found herself at Leicester becoming more and more irritated by the systemisation of criticism. She was a curious combination of a Johnsonian and an anarchist. Like the good doctor she was opinionated and judgemental – some writers were good, others were not – but she balked at grounding evaluation in consensual or abstract formulae. Instead, she favoured such quixotic measures as instinct and inclination and as a consequence developed a reputation in

Leicester as an eccentric rebel. She never published a word of criticism in her life, but in lectures and tutorials and in the marking of student papers she was the model of idiosyncratic arbitrariness. This, along with wearing tartan to lecture on *Macbeth* and a waist-length rope of pearls for *Antony and Cleopatra*, made her a small legend in her equally compact provincial domain. Leaving aside her reluctance to publish anything, and differences conferred by gender, Monica was a near-exact replica of the young rebel of University College Swansea.

Larkin in 'A New World Symphony' offers a complex and unnervingly honest picture of Monica. When the unfinished draft was eventually published after Larkin's death Monica read it for the first time and drew the editor James Booth's attention to a passage describing Augusta Bax's youthful, creative enthusiasm for clothes both fashionable and unusual. She conceded that this was based on the way she dressed, but she did not, however, comment upon how this unremarkable trait was only a slight element of Larkin's depiction of a more puzzling, almost baroque persona: the printing of a hundred cards 'reading Miss *Augusta Bax*' and kept in 'an ivory and silver case with concertina pockets inside'; the attendance at Evensong on Sundays (despite her indifferent agnosticism); the placing of a three-branched candle on her writing desk; her singing of nineteenth-century love songs in French while being punted on the Cherwell. During the early years of their relationship, before Larkin finally broke up with Ruth, each of them had cultivated an image of affected, perverse bohemianism. His stationery, for example, included pink, searing lemon and, most strikingly, the black-bordered mourning paper left over from his father's funeral and he sent Monica elaborately designed cards like those that Augusta has printed for herself. Larkin, sensing Monica's taste for arch formality, advised her to use them 'for cancelling tutorials, refusing dinner parties, postponing lectures and declining invitations to rambles, discussion groups, coffee circles …' In the novel:

> By setting up as an eccentric – vague, wispy, slightly distracted but exquisitely-bred – she gained a reputation in College many envied …
>
> What prompted this attitude? … Partly it was a daydream of the kind of person she most admired. Partly it was a reaction against the kind of person she most disliked … But partly – perhaps mostly – it was a guard, a mask, hiding an enormous vacancy. (Larkin, *Trouble at Willow Gables*, p. 399)

By 'vacancy' Larkin most certainly does not mean shallowness. As the novel and its central figure evolve it becomes evident that he is creating what would have been his most intricate fictional presence, based principally upon Monica and, more obliquely, himself – a character for whom vacancy was synonymous with absence of realisation, anticipation of failure. Augusta/ Monica compensated for this by becoming the person Larkin had met, and to a degree recognised, during his first year in Leicester.

> Augusta admired the amateur tradition, the dislike of plodding, the careless production of masterpieces. She saw herself reading widely, pointlessly, fantastically, trailing through eighteenth-century libraries, lounging in embrasures with folios, one hand turning a globe. Then a subject would spring up in her mind: a single strand electrifying several centuries ... one followed one's nose, perhaps now and again a book might result (ibid., p. 399).

It is fascinating to compare Larkin's version of Monica with that of Amis. Provided that one accepts that perception is partly a function of the predispositions of the perceiver, then both are accurate and realistic.

As already mentioned, Amis was introduced to Monica by Larkin during a 1947 visit to Leicester, and although she was willing to tolerate some of the more strident social habits of Larkin's closest friend, Amis decided almost immediately that she was not the right kind of partner for Larkin. Monica and Amis would meet five or six times thereafter up to 1950, but following his move to Belfast, Larkin made sure that their encounters were as infrequent as possible. She rarely accompanied Larkin on his regular visits to the Amis house in Swansea. It was not that Larkin felt unable to deal with the simmering antagonism that soon became a standard feature of their meetings; more that he found their incompatibility reflected a division within his own personality, which he was content to maintain. 'It doesn't surprise me in the *least* that Monica is studding Crab; he's *exactly* the sort of *priggish, boring, featureless* (especially that; there isn't *anything* about him, is there?) *long-winded, inessential* man she'd go for' (A to L, 8 September 1948). This could be Jim Dixon speaking at the end of the novel when he, and indeed the reader, have become fully aware of the nasty manipulative tendencies of Margaret Peel. Crabbe, one should note, is described not as the poet but the 'man' Monica would 'go for'. The implied message is that while Larkin is the complete antithesis of this, Monica would try to mould him suitably to meet her expectations – exactly the way that Margaret had behaved with Jim.

In truth, Monica provided Larkin with a counterbalancing alternative to Amis. The latter had from their Oxford days onwards virtually forbidden from their exchanges anything that resembled the – as Amis saw it – false earnestness of tutorials. Literature could be discussed, certainly, but in a manner that had more in common with Byron than F. R. Leavis. Larkin and Monica shared a genuine, thoughtful enthusiasm for the profundities of Hardy, Yeats and Lawrence, and would exchange ideas and reflections on them without a hint of self-consciousness.

The other main character of 'A New World Symphony' is Dr Butterfield, Augusta's head of department. Butterfield, thirty years her senior, embodies the amateur tradition of scholarship to which she aspires, and the plot focuses upon the conflict between Butterfield's ethos and the commerce-based pragmatism of post-war England. The university wishes to expand and its administrators are attempting to supplement government funding with local business sponsorship. Chairs for all departments are being advertised and the successful candidates will be expected to show as much entrepreneurial flair as scholarly dedication to their subjects. Clearly Butterfield will not get the job.

In Amis's version Jim exposes academia as a nest of neurotic bohemians, egotists and audacious timewasters; he gets the pretty, unpretentious girl and after dumping Margaret/Monica exchanges scholarship for a well-paid job in the real world of industry and high finance. Larkin would have been entertained by this. It was an amusing, fantastic rewrite of the retinue of complaints about colleagues and working life with which Amis's letters from Swansea had been strewn for the previous five or six years. It was not, however, a presentation that he imagined would be taken seriously by a publisher. 'A New World Symphony' would; it involved themes and narrative foci that Larkin had cautiously selected from Amis's material and inverted, so that civilised, almost languid intellectualism became a bulwark against the invasions of corporate anti-culture.

He never discussed 'A New World Symphony' with anyone. There are vague references in letters to Amis and Sutton between 1950 and 1954 to his having restarted a novel, but nothing more. He was convinced that Amis's work would not get into print, and while he was preparing his own he understandably did not want to admit that he was using his friend's writing as inspirational counterpoint. Proof that he was can be found in the draft itself.

The likeliest candidate for the Chair is an egotistical bully and his name is Welch. Amis had bombarded Larkin with material in letters on his loathing for his father-in-law Bardwell and in drafts on his vengeful caricature of him as Professor Neddy Welch. Throughout 'A New World Symphony' there are randomly distributed references to matters 'Welsh', involving the nationality of minor characters, places sometimes visited, locutionary habits and so on. These seem to be completely arbitrary, at least regarding the novel itself, but they gather significance with the knowledge that Amis was continually sewing into his letters and drafts jokes about Welch the character, and the Welsh, in whose country Amis lived and with whose culture Bardwell was obsessed. It was often Larkin's habit in early drafts of fiction to name characters in a talismanic, idiosyncratic manner, with the intention of changing these to something more unpremeditated when the text was offered to the public. We can assume that had 'A New World Symphony' been completed and published he would have done so here, too. (And we should here recall 'Sam' Wagstaff, boyfriend of a fictionalised version of Ruth, whose pronunciation of 'same' as 'sam' became a running joke with Larkin and Amis.)

Amis stalks the pages at this early draft stage like the ghost of Larkin's conscience. There is even a reference to a minor character called 'Mumbles the Librarian'. Mumbles was the suburb in which the Amises had lived during their first three years in Swansea and which, of course, appeared atop Kingsley's regular letters – letters to a librarian with a slight speech defect.

The exact date at which Larkin finally abandoned 'A New World Symphony' is uncertain, but the cause is clear enough. He became aware, during 1953, that *Lucky Jim* was turning into something more than a shared joke. John Wain had known Larkin and Amis from their Oxford days and had thereafter done well as a writer and academic. He had spent the war years as a junior fellow at St John's and then acquired a lectureship at Reading University where he established himself as a kind of amateur patron of the arts. He launched a series of short poetry volumes, sponsored by the university, which can be seen as the first recognition of a new wave of contra-modernism, and in 1953 he secured a contract with the BBC to edit a radio series called 'First Readings', which would introduce Third Programme listeners to the work of new writers. Larkin's poem 'If, My Darling' would appear on this in July, but the opening broadcast on 26 April featured an extract that had far more significant reverberations. It was a short piece from Amis's as yet unpublished novel. The typescript was with Gollancz and, following the broadcast, Amis's eventual editor Hilary Rubinstein found most of his office colleagues discussing it and in states of uncontrollable laughter: he immediately telegrammed Amis with the offer of a contract. Amis informed Larkin of this on 5 May, adding 'It will be dedicated to you.' He concludes that he is 'Glad about your novel ...' but confesses that he can't remember 'what "The Leicester one" was going to be'. The 'Leicester' novel was up to that point a private reference to Larkin's admiration for William Cooper's *Scenes from Provincial Life* (1950), which he had christened, with well-meant irony, 'the great Leicester novel'. It appears that Larkin had recently informed Amis that his own contribution to this sub-genre was under way. He did not tell him that it was to be an alternative to *Lucky Jim*, and Amis would also never learn that his letter of 5 May would effectively put an end to it.

Later that summer Larkin wrote to Patsy Strang, who had since moved to England: 'You know, I can't write this book: if it is to be written at all it should largely be an attack on Monica and I *can't* do that, not while we are still on friendly terms, and I'm not even sure it interests me sufficiently to go on' (5 July 1953). This is fascinating in its disclosure that Patsy was the only person with whom he had discussed anything regarding the nature of the book, and also because he seems to be addressing the problem as much to himself as he is explaining it to her. The emphatic, repeated '*can't*' relates not to his inability to write the book but to his realisation that he needs comprehensively to alter it, shift the perspective so that Monica's/Augusta's flaws and idiosyncrasies are no longer treated sympathetically. As he states, this would be difficult while he and Monica are still on 'friendly terms', but he does not explain why such a major change has to be made in the first place. A week later he offers, involuntarily, a clue, writing to Patsy that 'I still feel a good deal worried by art (writing) and life (MMBJ) [Margaret Monica Beale Jones] ... Now I've begun writing I find I've nearly nothing to say' (12 July 1953). The rest of the letter is mostly a chronicle of general complaints regarding the replacement of gloom and depression with a 'restless and bored' condition, and, for no apparent reason, the observation that 'I expect getting his novel accepted has made Kingsley a bit cocky'.

The workbook for the new draft, all done during 1953, reads like the jottings of someone lost in a maze, constantly choosing another potential route while knowing that he will never reach the exit. Larkin plays with alternatives: Perhaps he could give more attention to Butterfield (now called Praed) as the central figure? How can Augusta be changed? Focus upon her background – her parents' marital problems – as the cause of her serrated temperament; make her more forceful, even irreverent? Transform the story itself, with Augusta leaving the English provinces for the USA? All the time the options are driven by an unstated imperative: Try not to prompt comparisons with *Lucky Jim*. Larkin knew this was impossible, and at the end of November 1953 he gave up for good, little more than a month before review copies of Amis's novel went out.

In February 1954 it was again to Patsy that he offered his genuine feelings about the attention being generated by its publication: 'the reviews it has been getting are the kind of thing I *don't like to see* – Anthony Powell for instance in today's *Punch*. Well, well. Success, success.' He concedes that 'The Kingsley humour I think quite unrivalled, quite wonderful'. But, of course, he always had; Amis had been one half of a private double act. Now, however, their world was public property and Larkin's unease is evident. 'Apart from being funny I think it is somewhat over simple'; 'It's in the general thinness of the imagination that he falls down'; and he compares *Lucky Jim* with a story from Angus Wilson's *The Wrong Set*, which 'to my mind makes the Welch family hardly satire at all' (3 February 1954). He did not add that the reason none of this occurred to him while he was spending so much time helping Kingsley rewrite the first drafts was that he had misjudged the literary world that would in a month turn his friend from a nonentity into a star.

In a letter to Monica in February 1955, Larkin offers an account of his friendship with Amis which is partly an apology for the latter's creation of Margaret Peel and, more strikingly, a moment of recognition that Amis had exploited their friendship. He states, with regard to *Lucky Jim*, that 'I refuse to believe he can write a book on his own – or at least a good book', a clear disclosure that for Larkin his role as unwitting collaborator in Amis's ascent to first-novel fame had now become part of his menu of dejection.

Lucky Jim has been held responsible for many things – progenitor of an unprofound, witty, rational, sardonic mood in post-war fiction and so on

– but it should also be recognised as a pivotal moment in the creation of a poetic repertoire that few would dispute is one of the finest of the twentieth century. The novel and its author played this role unwittingly but nonetheless effectively; Larkin gave up fiction.

Amis and *Lucky Jim* are acknowledged in the typescript of 'A New World Symphony' as the presences that brought about its stagnation. No direct reference is made to them in the 1953–4 verse, but if we bring them with us into a reading it becomes evident that they were present when Larkin wrote the poems. 'Poetry of Departures' and 'Toads' are meditations upon the same condition felt, it is inferred, by everyone at one time or another: ennui, *Weltschmerz*, the irksomeness of having to work and live in a way that is a dispiriting obligation. It is a familiar theme, but in both poems there is something opalescent in Larkin's treatment of it. In 'Poetry of Departures' he first harnesses his frustration to familiar escapist clichés:

> So to hear it said

> *He walked out on the whole crowd*
> Leaves me flushed and stirred,
> Like *Then she undid her dress*
> Or *Take that you bastard*;
> Surely I can, if he did?

One is prompted to ask; if you can, then why don't you? He goes on to add that

> I'd go today,

> Yes, swagger the nut-strewn roads,
> Crouch in the fo'c'sle
> Stubbly with goodness, if
> It weren't so artificial,
> Such a deliberate step backwards
> To create an object:
> Books; china; a life
> Reprehensibly perfect.

The first set of images seem drawn from the world of B-movie fantasy, but the second, the ones potentially open to him, are equally unreal, although this time with a tinge of adolescent adventurism: 'swagger the nut-strewn roads', 'crouch in the fo'c'sle', 'stubbly with goodness'. Humphrey Bogart has been replaced by the Famous Five. He posits two types of release from an apparent sense of dissatisfaction, one self-evidently unattainable, the other perversely irrelevant; so why bother with either? The answer involves tracing a thread of meaning only half-disclosed in the fabric of the poem itself. Both types of release, while apparently incompatible, share certain characteristics: they are disagreeably 'artificial' and involve 'a deliberate step backwards / To create an object: / Books ... a life / Reprehensibly perfect'.

The one person to have made them compatible and to have revelled in the outcome was Amis. *Lucky Jim* was a fairy-tale that had, overnight, earned its author immense literary esteem. It was, and only Larkin knew this, fantasy made real and vice versa; a blending of Amis's actual life with that of Jim Dixon, who 'walks out on the whole crowd', taking with him the kind of girl who will, we know, undo her dress for him, after of course he had belted her unworthy boyfriend. Jim had not said, 'Take that, you bastard', but '"You bloody old towser-faced boot-faced totem-pole on a crap reservation," he said', just before thumping Bertrand, would do.

The imperatives of the first part derive in truth from Amis's letters, which read like the promptings of an amiable demon. He responds, for instance, to Larkin's convoluted account of his pursuit of Winifred with 'I fucking give you up as far as sex is concerned. Don't you e pe *want* a poke? More impressive too, to stop believing in sex *after* pocking AWA rather than before' (16 April 1953).

Barely a month before *Lucky Jim* was published and little more than two before Larkin composed the poem, Amis wrote to him that 'I wish that something would happen to me, like having a fuck or selling the film rights to *Jim*. That'd be funny wouldn't it? Dixon, Alex Guinness; Christine, Gina Lollobrigida; Margaret, Dulcie Grey; Bertrand, Orson Welles; Welch, Boris Karloff ... Directed by Alfred Hitchcock. Just pipe dreaming dear' (26 November 1953). By the end of January 1954 the pipe dream was becoming real. John Betjeman wrote Amis a private letter, at the same time as his fulsome review in the *Daily Telegraph*, complimenting him on a beguiling mixture of fairy-tale and realism. Amis had informed his friend of this, adding that 'they can't stop me now!' (14 March 1954). Larkin had witnessed and been kept regularly informed of this unlikely incidence of adolescent escapism made real from its very adult initiator. Five days after he completed 'Poetry of Departures' he included in a letter to Patsy an aside on his writing. 'I sometimes read a poem over with a tiny Kingsley crying *How d'you mean* at every unclear image, and it's a wonderful aid to improvement' (3 February 1954).

One suspects that alongside this imagined helpmate is the recollection of how he, Larkin, had played a similar role in the making of Kingsley's fantasy. In 'Toads' he returns to the same field of complaint. He asks,

> Why should I let the toad *work*
>   Squat on my life?
> Can't I use my wit as a pitchfork
>   And drive the brute off?

As rhetorical questions go it is one of the best, sullenly pre-empting its answer, but the alternative seems to involve unfocused absurdism.

> Lots of folk live on their wits:
>   Lecturers, lispers,
> Losels, loblolly-men, louts –
>   They don't end as paupers;

'Lecturers' probably found their way into this alliterative cascade by an accident of 't's and 's's – probably. Later he concedes that he is not 'courageous enough / To shout *Stuff your pension!* because not only does 'the toad *work*' squat on his life,

> ... something sufficiently toad-like
>   Squats in me, too;
> [...]
> And will never allow me to blarney
>   My way to getting
> The fame and the girl and the money
>   All at one sitting.

It is not that he cannot do this; rather, that his innate toad-like characteristics cause him not to. All of a sudden the digressive whimsy has become precise in the fame, the girl and the money. The lecturer who is now anything but a pauper has indeed got them all: Amis again.

The final stanza,

> I don't say, one bodies the other
> > One's spiritual truth;
> But I do say it's hard to lose either,
> > When you have both

seems at first puzzling, but the first 'one' is the toad that sits on him, the second the 'toad-like' condition that configures his temperament. The subtext for 'Toads' becomes bitterly evident in a letter that Larkin wrote to Monica ten months after completing the poem.

> I sought his [Amis's] company because it gave me a wonderful sense of relief – I've always needed this 'fourth form friend', with whom I can pretend things are not as I know they are – and pretended I was like him. Now I don't feel like pretending any longer ... He doesn't like books. He doesn't like reading. And I wouldn't take his opinion on anything, books, people, places... (L to Monica 15 February 1955)

The most striking, puzzling feature of the letter is Larkin's apparent sense of surprise. He writes as though he has only just discovered that this friend's intellectual hooliganism was not a pretence, while he, Larkin, had treated their 'fourth form' antics as a release, an escape from 'things ... as I know they are'. The shock was due to the fact that Amis had turned their private, adolescent fantasy world into a recipe for literary success. The letter was written six weeks after W. Somerset Maugham had, in the *Sunday Times* 'Books of the Year' supplement (25 December 1954), cited *Lucky Jim* as presaging the decline of Western civilisation. Its author, a provincial academic with an Oxford degree no less, had written a distressingly autobiographical novel which recommended and justified a blend of hedonism and philistinism. 'They [that is, Amis *and* Dixon] do not go to university to acquire culture,' wrote Maugham, 'but to get a job, and when they have got one scamp it.

They have no manners, and are woefully unable to deal with any social predicament.' Larkin had read the piece, and Maugham's litany of negatives is echoed in his letter to Monica. He knew that their private fantasy had become Amis's route to fame and also that what faced him was the 'toad', work, a career as a librarian. How else would he earn a living, at least enough to allow himself the time and opportunity to abandon 'pretending' and turn his attention to the unprofitable realm of 'things ... as I know they are' in his poems?

'Toads' leaves us with an impression of curmudgeonly contentment, signals of the misanthropic presence of his later work, but there is something else. Three years earlier Larkin, in response to Sutton's praise for the self-published pamphlet *XX Poems*, had offered perhaps his most coherent account of how and why he writes verse. 'For me, a poem is the crossroads of my thoughts, my feelings, my imaginings, my wishes and my verbal sense: normally these run parallel.' He then stops typing and provides a diagrammatic representation of these five elements following parallel lines adding in longhand that 'Often two or more cross ... but only when all cross at one point do you get a poem' (10 July 1951). All this is leavened with a hint of self-mockery – he also provides a diagram of the lines conjoining, adding, 'Poem!! Yippee!!', and a sketch of a glass of bubbling champagne – but such was his habit with Sutton when he was saying something about himself where significance was not quite matched by confidence.

Larkin does not claim that such interweavings come about by accidental promptings or unsolicited moments of inspiration. They are, on the contrary, the result of planning, calculation, stylistic design and, most significantly, selective appropriation. He sews together the elements so that each is variously reshaped, obscured, transformed or delineated by its convergence with the others. In 'Poetry of Departures' and 'Toads' the predominant mood is that of stoic resignation, an acceptance that some aspects of his world cannot be altered but are by their intransigence recognisable to him as appropriate, albeit distorting, mirrors of his temperament. In a letter to Judy Egerton he comes close to disclosing that this was his new source of inspiration and he is honest about its cause. In 1958 Hilly had done a newspaper article on her now famous husband and the piece struck Larkin as a reminder that celebrity had once more improved upon the friend he thought he knew. 'Kingsley's "very good degree"', he complained to Egerton, 'was a "shortened" one, designed to rush ex-Servicemen through in 1948. First Class, admittedly, but *only in five papers.*' Beneath what appears to be a rather pedantic strand of bitterness runs a subtext which surfaces in the next sentence. 'Sometimes I think I'm preparing for a huge splenetic autobiography, denigrating everyone I've ever known: it would have to be left to the nation in large brass-bound boxes, to be printed when all of us are dead' (7 March 1958). Not all of his poems would be splenetically autobiographical, but most contain a nuance of a particular now-soured friendship. When we examine the circumstances of their composition, best evidenced in his letters, we can almost watch how the diagram he had offered to Sutton is brought into operation. The abandonment of 'A New World Symphony', the success of *Lucky Jim*, the recollected and still present voice of Amis as at once his alter ego and enviable opposite, are never in the poems explicitly referred to, of course, but they become hidden talismans and provide the 'crossroads of my thoughts, my feelings, my imaginings, my wishes and my verbal sense'. Evidence of Larkin's developing expertise in negotiating such interchanges emerges when we compare these poems with those inspired by and addressed to Winifred, in which the mysterious subject engages our attention almost as determinedly as the poem itself. Now Larkin leads us into the texture of the poem, and the question of why he is doing so becomes a dimension of the experience, not its pretext.

It would, of course, be preposterous to assert that the death of Larkin the novelist was the exclusive cause of the emergence of a poet of extraordinary significance, yet certain facts should be noted. Within months of abandoning his final attempt at fiction he would begin work on arguably his finest poem of the mid-1950s, 'Church Going'. As we shall see in the next chapter the woman on whom the principal character of 'A New World Symphony' was based, and whose status in Larkin's emotional life was precarious, would during the same period replace Amis as his literary sounding board, even his adviser.

In his letter of 6 March 1954 to Patsy he reports on his week in the Midlands spent mainly with his mother. On Easter Tuesday they had paid their annual visit to the 'family graves' in Lichfield, and the Easter weekend had involved 'a queer mixture of hell and a rest cure, with a bit of gardening and church-going along with the big meals'. The term 'church-going' rests among his weary report on family obligations like a diamond in the mud. We will never know if Larkin recollected his use of it in that passage, but three weeks later (10 May) he wrote to Patsy that 'I have been writing a long poem about churches recently that I hope will be finished tonight.' It would be his most celebrated early piece.

'Church Going', like all other poems, is not perfect, yet it shares with a select few the condition of being unimprovable. One is aware of that token of excellence, the contrast between the easy, elegant passage of the words and the immense difficulty of making this effect possible. The register with which Larkin informs the poem involves a mixture of incongruity, discordancy and acceptance. He feels comfortable in this vast, ancient building and persuades us that his presence, alone, as a dry commentator upon its span of false mythologies and centuries of unremembered ritual is somehow fitting. The church both as a physical setting and an accumulation of significances is treated neither dismissively nor with customary respect, but with sympathy; which, via the words of the poem, it seems to return.

The idiomatic coupling of the title is reinterpreted by the poem. This is a particular, personal encounter – not the kind that one would share with members of a congregation. Nowhere, however, does Larkin treat those who might still be churchgoers as pitiable or credulous. The final stanza is a masterpiece of consolidated meditation. There appears to be a covenant formed between his own scepticism and a building resonant with faith, yet he does not force the issue. And one here recollects the sentence in the letter to Patsy containing the phrase 'church-going' where he describes his period with his mother as 'a queer mixture of hell and a rest cure'. It was not quite that he resented having to accompany his mother to church services, nothing so unambiguous as that. His relationship with her was always at once a wearying necessity and a gathering of intimate, emotional registers. It seems appropriate, then, that this same sense of states incongruous but not dispersible should re-emerge three weeks later in a poem where again he is 'Church Going', except this time he is alone, better able to choreograph the conflicting states of mind that attend his presence in the church. He is able to do this because he can rebuild them as something else, a poem which, like the church building, contains and prompts but does not coerce him. At the same time that he wrote the poem, he began to discover that he and Monica shared a respectful secular appreciation for church buildings, particularly when they seemed, unlike so many man-made structures, to belong within the contours of the natural landscape. She would accompany him to Arundel and the two of them talked of the tomb that inspired the poem, and she would, at his request, comment on early drafts of 'Church Going'.

It was not the case that before the Belfast years Larkin had lacked the mental conditioning or stylistic competence to produce excellent poems. Both were certainly present, but with a few exceptions they failed to cooperate. Yet gradually he perfected a technique that fed upon his temperament. He was a man who selected and redistributed aspects of himself for different people and different circumstances; he had become a poet who had found a means of controlling and harvesting moments of contact between these otherwise separate dimensions.

Evidence of this is provided by Larkin himself in his unpublished and unfinished piece 'At thirty-one, when some are rich'. The provisional title is its first line, and the topics of the poem involve a fascinating, introspectively candid account of who and what he was.

> At thirty-one, when some are rich
> And others dead,
> I, being neither, have a job instead ...

When he wrote this, *Lucky Jim* was four months short of going into print, but Larkin knew it would succeed. And what does he do with the time not given over to his 'job'?

> ... instead of planning how
> I can best thrive,
> How best win fame and money while alive,
> I sit down, supper over, and begin
> One of the letters of a kind I now
> Feel most of my spare time is going in ...

He was aware, of course, that their private correspondence was the foundation for his friend's forthcoming novel. With this recognition came another: that his destiny lay not with the genre that might 'win fame and money while alive'. He does not refer to poetry specifically; more revealing is his focus upon the kind of letters that he now feels have become at once an addiction and a reflection of his personality: 'letters to women ... Love letters only in a sense: they owe / Too much elsewhere to come under that head'. The poem was begun and left unfinished during the three weeks following his return to Belfast in late summer 1953 after the period spent variously in the company of two women – Monica and his mother – while two others – Patsy and Winifred – received accounts by letter; his curious epistolary odyssey from Mallaig to Weymouth. Now he comes, 'each evening back to a high room', and writes letters to all four. They are, as he states, love letters 'only in a sense'. He is not telling lies exactly ('I'm kind, but not kinetic'), but rather

> Just compromise,
> Amiable residue when each denies
> The other's want?

He is selecting appropriate dimensions of himself for each correspondent, and the question posed is whether this technique of splicing and redistributing Philip Larkin will amount to anything more than an emotionally bankrupt, private world of letter writing. The answer is at once implied but blindingly obvious. The poem he is writing is about the poet he recognises himself becoming.

6

The 1950s

When *Lucky Jim* was published, Amis had reached page 40 of his next novel, *That Uncertain Feeling*. This was finished by the end of the year and came out in July 1955.

The plot is relatively simple. It is a first-person account of a couple of months in the life of South Wales librarian John Lewis. Lewis spends the greater part of the novel considering the attractions and consequences of adultery with Elizabeth Gruffyd-Williams and the likelihood of promotion to a modestly senior post in Aberdarcy library. Both prospects are complicated by the fact that Elizabeth's husband, Vernon, is a local industrialist and council executive who will have a decisive influence on the placing of the library job. Lewis treats his wife, Jean, with exceptionally foul expediency, and there is enough circumstantial evidence to place Elizabeth in the category of a tragically unstable victim. We know this, and Lewis seems disarmingly honest about his own moral and emotional shortcomings, but at the same time his clever, dry, sardonic presence always short-circuits our inclination to judge him properly.

John Lewis is showing us the John Lewis that none of the cohabitants of his story properly appreciate or understand. This is a man who knows true feeling and affection, while being able to intersperse his transparent sincerity with recklessly dark humour. Moreover, he can draw together these apparently incompatible states into an impressively seamless discourse. It is as though Lewis's condition of being different people at different times is what enables him to tell his story with such confident verbal dexterity. He seems to feel uneasy about his inclination to fabricate and deceive, but it is evident that it is the task of sewing together these conflicting elements of his life and character that drives the narrative forward and makes him such a good storyteller. And in this respect John Lewis *is* Kingsley Amis. It is not simply that Lewis's story mirrors Amis's life in the mid-1950s – and there are many very close parallels – more that Amis the man, like his fictional creation, seemed to thrive on an existence that involved functioning as very different personae.

Amis, too, was an adulterer who loved his wife and family, but in his former role he was far more prodigious and calculating than Lewis. Amis had met Robert Conquest in 1952 at a party in Chelsea held to launch a new PEN anthology of poems in which they both featured. Conquest went on to edit the *New Lines* collection of 1956, which is credited as a yardstick for the Movement style of poetic writing, but their friendship had as much to do with a shared taste for boozing, irreverent humour and laddish self-indulgence as it did with an interest in the state of English verse. Throughout the 1950s Conquest would put up similarly inclined writers and their families in his house in Hampstead: 'Amis and his wife, Enright and his wife and daughter, Davie, Wain and Larkin stayed with me for the odd night or nights for one time or another – the Amises quite frequently' (Blake Morrison, *The Movement: English Poetry and Fiction of the 1950s*, pp. 47–8). Just as frequently, particularly after *Lucky Jim*, Amis would visit London on his own, ostensibly to see his publisher, to promote his own writing or in connection with his regular work for *The Spectator* and *The Observer*. By the time he wrote *That Uncertain Feeling* Amis was also writing to Conquest with requests to borrow his other residence, a flat, for sex. He often used Conquest as his fellow conspirator. Conquest was on close terms with Hilly; she trusted him and Amis exploited this as a means of providing plausible alibis for his adulterous liaisons. In 1957 Amis sent Conquest a letter that resembles the plan for a chapter of a novel. It specifies, in five sections, the narrative for the afternoon of Friday 13 September – including the invention of 'a vague cousin or brother-in-law of yours – a nice circumstantial touch, I thought' (Jacobs, *Kingsley Amis*, p. 172). Lewis plans his liaisons with Elizabeth with far less tactical precision, but the parallels were evident for all who knew Amis well and it is no accident that the novel marked a significant change in Larkin's sense of who his friend was and how much of his life-improved-by-fiction he was prepared to indulge.

Larkin never ended his friendship with Amis, at least not in the customary manner of telling him that he had grown to dislike him, which makes the fact that he nurtured a persistent (if infrequent) loathing for him from at least the end of the 1940s all the more extraordinary. Larkin kept this from Amis until his death but confided his misgivings to Monica, and in this regard we must treat his relationship with her as being as significant as his friendship with Amis.

In 1948 Larkin produced something that can only be described as a hybrid, somewhere between a letter and a poem.

Then, when I visit my friends in Oxford,
Their lives seem happier and more successful than mine:
Kingsley in particular seems to live at the centre of gratified desire.
But when my desire is for the past, or for immortality,
Who can gratify that? (Hull)

Two years later:

And I thought: Well I hate him at least, put that down for a start,
And the piss-culting stench of success – that goes witout saying,
Though everyone says it.

Each echoes passages in his letters to Amis where Larkin concedes his lack of success with women and his general sense of failure – but the letters always deflected the self-pity of such concessions via their farcical, self-parodic manner.

The passages anticipates 'Letter to a Friend about Girls' which he would begin during the mid-1950s, but, just as significantly, it carries an air of desperate insularity that in his best pieces he deflected with artistic genius. Here the sense of failure is uncrafted, unalloyed. The voice seems to be searching for a listener, and with Monica he found one – a person who, temperamentally, had much more in common with him than Amis, and with whom he would share his increasing sense of unease about their friendship. As early as 1951 he was offering her accounts of his meetings with Amis in which the latter appears as boorish and intemperate, a figure whose company he endures rather than enjoys.

Kingsley has gone, leaving me just able to support the horizontal weight of my salaried employment, but only just. He certainly dropped plenty of plates around, though only 10 of my 15 pounds. On Saturday we went to Dublin, drinking all the way there, all the way back, and back: I am only just about recovered. He left me as usual feeling slightly critical of him: despite his organised self defence, I detect elements of artlessness? – no, what I mean to say is that despite his limpet-grip on life, terre-à-terrish & opportunist, there are times when I fancy I can see further than him in his own way. More of that, if needed, when we meet. However, he also intensified my predominant sensation of being a non-contiguous triangle in a circle [diagram of triangle within circle] – the inner life making no contact with the outer. Buried alive! (L to Monica, 18 April 1951)

The atmosphere of the Amis household in Swansea, described by many, including their son Martin, as relaxed, hospitably hedonistic, is shown in a very different light by Larkin. Despite his fulsome thanks to Amis and insistence on how much he enjoyed his visits, Monica is offered what seems a more candid account. Even the italicised notes of anxiety regarding his flight to Belfast are cruel jibes against Amis's fear of flying.

Swansea was a big contrast to what came before it or after it as could well be. (Oh dear! *suppose* we hit something?) The contrast to our 2 days of planned exploration was profound. Sluttishness, late hours, drink, squalling children & (*Here is the flight bulletin. Over Liverpool going about 160 m.p.h., 10 mins. behind schedule.*) poor, insufficient food. Nor did the compensations for these seem as sufficient as in days of yore. I was read nearly ALL Dixon & Christine, & suggested it should be called The man of feeling, an idea wch Kingsley quite took to, but will probably not entertain finally…

I met Kingsley's ex-'mistress', a curious dark crooked-mouthed prognathic girl whose scarlet cheeks & burnt-cork eyebrows reminded me of Tod Slaughter made up for some villainy or other. Truly one man's meat is another man's buttered parsnips. (L to Monica, 11 August 1951)

Esmond Cleary, one of Kingsley's colleagues and recently married to Jean, sometimes looked after the children at their house or visited the Amises for parties. Cleary:

Everyone seemed to look on The Grove with a mixture of envy and bafflement. The children were happy, bright, quite well behaved but the place was wonderfully disorganised, an endless cocktail party. A strange combination. You have to remember that this was provincial Britain in the '50s, everything seemed hopelessly dreary, but Kingsley, Hilly and the children were determined to enjoy themselves. Don't misunderstand me, they weren't irresponsible hedonists. The children were loved and cared for ... yet there was an energy and optimism about the house that was at odds with the time and the area.

Cleary's indulgent image is treated by Larkin with succinct disapproval: 'Sluttishness, late hours, drink, squalling children ... and the ex-"mistress".' The inverted commas surrounding 'mistress' should also have accommodated 'ex', given that the lady in question was the wife of a local rugby player whose Saturday afternoon commitments would continue to enable her to pursue her own sporting interests with Amis. She would be vividly represented in Larkin's 'Letter to a Friend about Girls'. A year later he observed: 'Patsy [Strang] says their house [that of a friend] is filthy. I pressed her: "As filthy as Kingsley's?"' (L to Monica, 16 October 1952).

It was not merely that Larkin treated Monica as a convenient sounding board for his complaints about Amis and his family. The letters between them involve levels of honesty, mutual concern, indeed commitment, that always wrestle with obfuscation and self-caricature in his exchanges with his close friends. Despite the fact that during the 1950s in Belfast, and later in Hull, he cheated on her with other women, there was a touching uniqueness about their relationship. Regarding monogamy one might judge him no better than Amis, but while Amis was unfaithful both physically and in ways that were even more hurtful – such as showing disdain for Hilly and others by complaining about them and boastfully announcing his extramarital successes to others – there was at the core of Larkin's relationship with Monica an implacable seam of tenderness and sincerity. Their letters on relationships, sex and marriage reveal in Larkin an extraordinary willingness to speak candidly about his desires and uncertainties. In his letters to Sutton, whom he treated as his closest temperamental intimate, and to Amis, what he actually felt is always clouded by swathes of bitterness, self-recrimination and farce. To Monica, typically:

... someone might do a little research on the inherent qualities of sex – its cruelty, its bullyingness, for instance.

It seems to me that bending someone else to your will is the very stuff of sex, by force or neglect if you are male, by spitefulness or nagging scenes if you are female. And what's more, both sides would sooner have it that way than not at all. I wouldn't. (L to Monica, 1 November 1951)

This goes some way to dispose of the image of Larkin, cultivated by left-leaning commentators, as a purblind misogynist. For a male writing in 1951 it is remarkable, prefiguring the supposedly groundbreaking feminist notions of sex as an inherently brutal male-dominated activity. And one should remember that it was written to a woman with whom he was having a sexual relationship. More than anyone else Monica caused him to explore his true feelings about gender and sexuality. 'It seems more to me that what we have is a kind of homosexual relation, disguised... I mean, I seem entirely lacking in that *desire to impose oneself*, that is such a feature of masculine behaviour' (L to Monica, 29 January 1958). He would never have betrayed such confidences to Amis. It is surely not a coincidence that in the previous paragraph he commented that 'I see "W" John Morgan [a journalist whose wife had been Amis's mistress when a student at Swansea] is interviewing Kingsley next Saturday – *Get Kingsley Amis to sleep with your wife, You'll find it will give you a bunk up in life.*' He seems to be inviting Monica to compare their emotionally grounded intimacies with Amis's regime of unconsidered self-gratification.

When he arrived in Hull, Larkin went through a well-rehearsed ritual of finding the most convenient and consequently disagreeable place to live and then repeating the act. In March 1955 he moved into Holtby House, a student residence, in Cottingham – once a village but now part of the northern suburbs of Hull. After a month he moved out of Cottingham to a private boarding house through an arrangement with the university. This, too, turned out to be 'a nightmare' with the constant irritation of a 'blasted RADIO which seems to feature in everyone's life these days' (L to D. J. Enright, 26 April 1955). Similarly, his move to an apparently superior set of rooms in Belfast brought with it only a variation in grievances: 'so many flies ... smelly and untidy ... dirty marks on my living room walls. Who's going to get them off?' (L to Patsy Strang, 25 August 1952).

In June 1955 he moved once more to another boarding house a few streets away in Hallgate, owned this time by an elderly lady, Mrs Squire, with quieter

habits – but again the rooms were cramped, poorly heated and uncomfortably furnished. Within a week Mrs Squire fell ill and announced that her
lodgers would all have to find alternative accommodation, which Larkin did
with the Drinkwaters in the same street. This time the top-floor rooms were
a little more spacious, but one reason for the Drinkwaters' acceptance of a
lodger was to provide extra cash for their new and reliably noisy child.

'Mr Bleaney' was, of course, the result of all this. It was his first full
excursion into mordantly dark comedy, and it also began to indicate, while
maintaining a cautious film of indifference, his sense of distaste for many
people with whom he was obliged to share time and space.

The landlady's dreary account of the previous occupant of the room is
supplemented by its appearance:

> Flowered curtains, thin and frayed,
> Fall to within five inches of the sill,
>
> Whose window shows a strip of building land,
> Tussocky, littered.

The bed inspires no comment, the 'upright' chair is, one assumes, uncomfortable, the 'sixty-watt bulb' – not forty or one hundred, you understand –
seems unshaded, the door has no hook and there is no room for 'books'. He
adds a dash at the completion of this itinerary, indicating the brief moment
between impression and decision. 'I'll take it,' he states. Thereafter he settles
down to enjoy the ambient misery and reflect upon his occupation of what is
not just Mr Bleaney's room but the summation of his drab existence. 'I knew
his habits,' he relates, particularly regarding the choice between sauce and
gravy, summer holidays in Frinton and Christmas with his sister in Stoke,

> But if he stood and watched the frigid wind
> Tousling the clouds, lay on the fusty bed
> Telling himself that this was home, and grinned,
> And shivered, without shaking off the dread
>
> That how we live measures our own nature,
> And at his age having no more to show

Than one hired box should make him pretty sure
He warranted no better, I don't know.

In a letter dated 18 August 1955, Monica wrote after listening to a broadcast of his work on the BBC *Third Programme*:

> Mr Bleaney sounded so very like you – yr catalogue of the room's shortcomings! Like you & like me – I smiled at the radio as if I were smiling at you as it was read. And I like your poetry better than any that I ever see – oh, I am sure that you are the one of this generation! I am sure you will make yr name! yr mark, do I mean – really be a real poet, I feel more sure of it than ever before, it is you who are the one, I do think so. Oh, Philip – I don't know what to say! You will believe me because you know it doesn't make any difference to me whether you are or not, I shouldn't think any less of your value if yr poems seemed to me bad & if everybody said so; and because I've never said to you this is magnificent, this is greatness triumphant, in yr hands the thing becomes a trumpet …

She catches perfectly his ability to make a poem so seemingly transparent – 'Mr Bleaney sounded so very like you' – while weaving his sense of guileless authenticity into a beautifully crafted composition. He had not bothered to send a draft of the poem to Amis and there is no account of his friend's impressions of it even when it appeared in *The Whitsun Weddings*. His only recorded remark on it came in a letter to Robert Conquest after Larkin's death: 'Makes you think of Mr Bleaney … Christ what a life' (7 June 1986). By the mid-1950s Amis was still sending his friend sprawling pieces of fiction for comment, and Larkin was responding with some early drafts of his poems, but he was becoming wary about discussing his work with Amis. Amis would often read what he was sent, but his responses betrayed a reluctance to look beyond what he expected Larkin to produce, and were often patronising. 'Church Going' marked a turning point in Larkin's trust in Amis as an attentive reader.

On 11 August 1954 Amis commented on the early draft sent to him by Larkin:

> As regards the poem, my general werdick is definitely favourable, and, though I don't feel at all as you do about consecrated edifices, I sympathise with you

having a shot at saying what you feel, even at such length ... Hayever, as expected no doubt, I have a few particular objections. I don't myself much care for the historic present: it makes me think of George Eliot and of school boys chorusing 'Makes it more vivid, sir' when asked why it's used. I realise, however, that changing it would be a chore and shag up the metre if not the rhymes. Also, I think the last stanza isn't right yet; not because of the punctuation – couldn't see anything wrong with that – but because of one or two highly poetical words and constructions: the inversion in the first line, for instance, which makes me think of 'A casement high and triple arched there was' and such bits of flannel. I'd say you've got to be extra careful, at the point when you ease your foot gently down on the accelerator, to avoid reminding the reader that 'this is poetry'. See what I mean? 'Blent', too, seems a bit 18th-c. to me. Friend, look to 't. But as I say, it seems okay on the whole, and certainly meet to be published ...

As Larkin reported several days later to Monica: 'Church Going didn't interest him ... he wants the inversion removed from the 1st line of the last verse ... and objects to the "historic present" ... Not a word about the poem as a whole, except he "doesn't feel as I do"' (L to Monica, 16 August 1954). On only one more occasion would he send unpublished versions of his pieces to Amis for scrutiny. It was not that he resented his opinions. He expected constructive criticism, but what he received were dismissive, heedless projections of Amis's prejudices. His comments were about his own sense of how things ought to be rather than attempts to think about what Larkin was trying to achieve. The latter were now provided by Monica. She had been sent a copy of 'Church Going' at the same time Amis received his.

Thanks for all the nice things you said abt my poetry, but I think you put your paw on the flaw in Churchgoing, a lack of strong continuity – it is dangerously like chat, 4th leader stuff. The most important emotion – the church as a place where people came to be serious, were always serious, & all their different forms of seriousness came to be intermingled, so that a christening reminded of a funeral & a funeral of a wedding: nowadays these things happen in different buildings & the marvellous 'blent air' of a church is growing rarer – this emotion I feel does not come out nearly strongly enough. (L to Monica, 10 August 1954)

He incorporated Monica's suggestions in his final draft.

Jean Hartley states that while Larkin's friendship with Amis remained 'strong and intimate', it was just as consistently 'tinged with a perhaps inevitable rivalry' (Jean Hartley, *Philip Larkin: The Marvell Press and Me*). Larkin would call regularly at the Hartleys' House in Hull Road during the eighteen months following the publication of *The Less Deceived* and, with Jean and George, pore delightedly over that week's accumulation of reviews and related articles, and note with equal satisfaction the increasing number of subscription slips. With a mixture of admiration and stoical despondency, Larkin would also give accounts of how *That Uncertain Feeling*, published within two months of *The Less Deceived*, was astounding the reading public: most were amazed by how rapidly the author of *Lucky Jim* could produce yet another book, which, while impressively different, could so brilliantly paint a picture of contemporary life and mores. 'Philip told us, good humouredly,' says Jean, 'how after reading ... *That Uncertain Feeling* he complained that Kingsley had cannibalised his letters for some of the material. "Life transmuted into art," Kingsley had retorted. Philip replied, "But God damn it, Kingsley, my letters ARE art."' In truth, Larkin's good-humoured complaint provided only a selective account of the complex web created by the two men and used by one of them with such ruthless versatility.

The dynamic of Amis's second novel also evolved out of his friendship with Larkin. While Conquest played a straightforward role in the provision of accommodation in London and plausible alibis, Larkin was Amis's emotional release mechanism. Amis's letters to him would mix anxious reports on how he was concealing his latest liaison from the increasingly suspicious Hilly with reflective passages on life as a successful seducer and a family man, and its inherent paradoxes. In this respect the letters were a rehearsal for the fabric of effects spun by John Lewis. Throughout the novel the reader's potentially empathetic relationship with him is tested by the growing suspicion that if he were not such a brilliant raconteur we could easily come to despise him. We wonder what we would have felt, indeed what we would have done, had we known real versions of John and Jean, rather than listened to an exclusive account of events by the former. Larkin had to deal with the fictional and non-fictional experiences simultaneously. Amis provided him with a private commentary on his extramarital activities plus a philanderer's disquisition on life in general, while on visits to the Amises' house Larkin was obliged to behave with Hilly, whom he considered as much a friend as the wife of one, as though nothing was happening. When he read the novel he would have undergone the disquieting experience of having to share all of this with tens of thousands of amused readers, knowing privately that it was based on fact and that he had played the role of reader-surrogate in its construction.

It was *Lucky Jim* revisited, except on this occasion it was the adulterous subterfuge and reflective contrition played out in Amis's letters that had been transformed into the successful novel. For Larkin it would have seemed as though his friend had discovered the key to fashioning all aspects of life, however licentious and paradoxical, into a profitable vehicle for literary fame. A subdued, even tolerant level of envy might have attended this were it not for the fact that Amis seemed intent on continually reminding Larkin of his role as contributor and spectator.

As early as 1953, Amis had written to Larkin confessing that he could not think of a setting for his next piece, specifically a profession for his main character. He had done 'carledge life' in *Lucky Jim*, and his only other significant personal experience had been in the army, which offered too limited a menu of plots. But he did have access, albeit secondary, to a lifestyle that was so mundane that it yearned to be made more interesting. John Lewis becomes a provincial librarian, and the contrast between the grinding monotony of his working life and his droll, expertly timed account of it is one of the best features of the book. Larkin would, when reading it, have recognised his letters to Amis, particularly those offering caustic accounts of his time in Wellington Public Library. Jean Hartley had either misunderstood Larkin or he had offered her a diplomatic account of things. Amis had not cannibalised the letters verbatim. He had, from Larkin's perspective, done much worse than that by stealing part of his friend's life and reconstructing it in a way that could cause Larkin to feel a combination of bitterness and amazement. John Lewis is a hybrid of Larkin and Amis in the sense that he draws all of his disgracefully hedonistic and undeniably attractive features from the latter and presses the former into service for everything else. Larkin was watching his friendship with Amis re-enacted in a single fictional presence, an embodied double act in which he was an involuntary participant.

Amis had kept Larkin up to date with the progress of *That Uncertain Feeling* throughout 1954, and when they met in Cheltenham in late November he showed him the substance of the final draft. Larkin laughed, dutifully, but saved his actual feelings for Monica to whom he wrote in February 1955, shortly after Amis had informed him of having sent the finished text to Gollancz.

I have 3 regular correspondents – you, Mother & Kingsley, & Kingsley never writes. I shouldn't be surprised if he were fed up with me, in a shoulder-shrugging sort of way: I am of him, except as you say 'the dog is so very comical'. I was interested to hear the book had gone to Gollancz – oh please God, make them return it, with a suggestion he 'rewrites certain passages'! Nothing would delight me more. And I refuse to believe he can write a book on his own – at least a good one. Still, we'll see. In a sense he has behaved more consistently than I have: I sought his company because it gave me such a wonderful sense of relief – I've always needed this 'fourth form friend', with whom I can pretend that things are *not* as I know they are – and pretended I was like him. Now I don't feel like pretending any longer, *&* I suppose it looks like 'turning against him.' (L to Monica, 15 February 1955)

He was particularly aggrieved by Amis's presentation of Lewis the librarian. At no point in the novel does he confess to literary ambitions, which is puzzling given his dextrous command of so many stylistic registers. To this extent he is an unnerving and pitilessly accurate version of Larkin as he presented himself in his letters to Amis: a man with no enthusiasm for his job but at the same time not blind to the irony of having to spend his working life with the material of literature and cater for the ridiculous range of obscure and philistine tastes of his daily customers. The subtext in both instances – self-evident in the novel and a continuous feature of their correspondence – is that we find a writer with enormous potential and ambition in circumstances that resemble a living parody of each.

Larkin's commitment to librarianship was born out of immutable realities. By the middle of what would be his last year in Belfast he had come to accept that even if he could find a publisher for one of his ongoing attempts at fiction this would be no more profitable than his two previous novels. He knew he could never support himself as a writer, and his decision to apply for such a senior post at Hull was prompted by this recognition. Within months he was obliged to undergo a transformation of his professional life. On arrival he found himself in charge of eleven members of staff, a library stock of approximately 125,000 volumes and library premises that involved a random collection of buildings, including Nissen huts, adapted from other functions.

Alongside his new role as linchpin in this process of post-war university expansion, Larkin found himself for the first time as a boss. His post at Belfast had involved some degree of seniority, but now he ran everything and everyone. He became within a year an image of the kind of benevolent dictator that bitter irony would have caused to form in his private hall of recollections. He had always known that some aspects of his father's temperament and disposition were evident in his own. Now he was faced with a very similar set of professional challenges and responsibilities, and he responded almost identically. When he moved into his large, generously appointed new office during the completion of the first stage of the library's redevelopment in 1959, the parallels with Coventry City Hall struck him immediately; ever the dark ironist, he gave the place occupied on his father's desk by the operational statue of the Führer over to a photographic portrait of Guy the Gorilla, more a comment perhaps on the absurdity of Sydney's enthusiasm than historical revisionism. His office became his space for retreat, reflection and control. Access would only be granted via his secretary, which meant that Larkin could plan his day according to, as he saw it, the most efficient division of his time between unavoidable encounters with bodies such as the Senate Library Committee and periods during which the long-term future of his library and its staff could be planned and reconsidered without unnecessary disturbance. In 1957 he took on a new private secretary, Betty Mackereth, a woman he recognised as formidable of character and unwilling to suffer fools or insignificant visitors gladly. Their alliance would develop effectively and amicably and last until his death.

The gloomy presence of Larkin who trails behind his reinvention in Lewis freezes him in time as the frustrated denizen of a provincial backwater. It was the Larkin of Wellington who had amused Amis with his masochistic self-caricatures of life, but what fuelled Larkin's bitterness in 1955–6 was the fact that his friend seemed to assume that nothing had changed. Certainly, he was still a librarian, but he had long since ceased to report to Amis on what his job now actually involved. He either ignored such accounts or came back with reminders that while he still worked in a library, Amis was now a novelist who had seized the attention of the press and news media.

That Uncertain Feeling fed Larkin's surmise that he was playing the passive, indeed anonymous, half of the double act that was impelling Amis's considerable and growing literary fame, and in September 1956 he received a letter from his friend that provided confirmation. As was their mutual habit it drifted between trivialities and matters more profound – as if their shared discourse transcended such distinctions – but one issue rose continually to the surface: their letters. Amis had been reading those from Larkin, most of which he had kept. It was, he states, like reading an unpublished novel by, say, Isherwood or Hoff, an experience that 'made me feel happy and contented as if I was doing something significant in a significant mode of existence, just like I felt, I remember describing to you, while I was reading *Scenes From Provincial Life*'. He goes on to praise Larkin for his at once engaging and amusing accounts of his encounters with Monica, Winifred Arnott and Ruth Bowman. 'But apart from lots of causes for yelling laughter what came over was [how] you seem to observe women much more closely and sensitively and well lovingly ah ha well perhaps not that than I do' (24 September 1956). Larkin, who had only two years previously given up his ambition to become a major novelist, is informed by his closest friend that his letters are as good as fiction. The novel he could not write is according to Amis already existent in this sad chronicle of provincial lust and farcically distended pessimism. 'Anyway,' continues Amis,

> ... it all made me feel what a feast is awaiting chaps when we're both dead and our complete letters come out ... Made me think we ought to try to get back into ... our old tempo of screedswapping ... there is a novel there, about you in Wellington-Leicester-Belfast-Hull and I shall ... probably write it one day, if you don't.

Larkin did not respond directly to this but we can offer a confident account of what he felt. The novel suggested by Amis would involve a picking of the bones, given that the body of their friendship had already been successfully plundered by him in his fiction so far. What would, however, have struck Larkin as pertinent to their respective standing, as writers, although perhaps not entirely intended as such by his friend, was Amis's fascination with their letters. Amis had used them in various ways as dialogic rehearsals for his fiction and his comment that they would constitute a 'feast' for critics when 'we're both dead' would have prompted Larkin to consider how his own work might be re-examined in terms of their 'tempo of screedswapping'. He would have recognised that the evolution of the quintessential poetic voice of Philip Larkin through the 1950s had come about not just through his acquisition of a new and better stylistic register but also because he had begun to feel more comfortable with regard to his putative readers.

He had given up on fiction and although his new sense of confidence as a poet was, in part, a means of establishing for himself a literary territory that owed nothing to his – as he now saw it – cloying friendship with Amis, he still felt that the latter had kidnapped him as part of his reckless rise to fame, and exploited him as an editor, a character and an unacknowledged ghost writer.

> What the NS & N [*New Statesman and Nation*] terms a brilliantly funny opening scene in a public library is, I am prepared to swear, taken from one of my Wellington letters. I remember writing it: 'a sample encounter with a borrower.' Really, I do find it irritating – of course, I'm not in possession of the text, or of my own letter of ten years ago, but I do dislike being used to open the show, to put everyone in good humour, to make them think 'ah, this is going to be just as funny as the other one' – see what I mean? It irritates me powerfully to see this stuff, small though it may be, used for his credit & advantage, when I wrote it just for my & his amusement. Well, I seem to be getting rather 'psychotic' about one little scene – but I'm not sure that will be all, and I think I do well to be irritated. Don't you? I mean, though it stands to reason that K. couldn't write a scene like that without help, nobody will think of it that way – it'll just be 'a brilliant opening scene'. (L to Monica, 19 August 1955)

Larkin was an addictive, almost fanatical letter-writer. When he was not producing literature, working, socialising or sleeping, much of his time was given over to composing letters for friends, literary acquaintances, family or lovers. For most he selected personae to accommodate their expectations, but with a small number – Monica, Judy Egerton and Robert Conquest to some degree, and Amis extensively – he provided a more abundant, comprehensive account of himself, embarrassments, trivialities and self-contrarieties included. While the poems that built his reputation did not, of course, carry to their readers the same agenda of private knowledge, they offered a comparable level of arch confidentiality, at once intimate, informal and cautiously entertaining.

As his letter to Monica indicated, the opening passage of *That Uncertain Feeling* was a small instance of a much deeper sense of grievance: Amis, he now realised, was obviously pillaging the correspondence in his own pursuit of literary fame.

Amis's musings on the letters, albeit self-focused, caused Larkin to begin work on the most significant poem to remain unpublished in his lifetime. The ostensible topic of 'Letter to a Friend about Girls' was sex, but its more engrossing subtext was Amis's treatment of their friendship as at once special, secretive and something that might be worth writing about. Accordingly he made sure that the poem would register differently for Amis and the general reader.

> After comparing lives with you for years
> I see how I've been losing: all the while
> I've met a different gauge of girl from yours.
> Grant that, and all the rest makes sense as well:
> My mortification at your pushovers,
> Your mystification at my fecklessness –
> Everything proves we play in different leagues.
> Before, I couldn't credit your intrigues
> Because I thought all girls the same ...

The mood of sanguine resignation carries with it the inference that his sense of recognition, almost revelation, is recent, confirmed by the first word of stanza two:

> Now I believe your staggering skirmishes
> In train, tutorial and telephone booth,
> The wife whose husband watched away matches
> While she behaved so badly in a bath,

And all the rest who beckon from that world
Described on Sundays only, where to want
Is straightway to be wanted, seek to find,
And no one gets upset or seems to mind
At what you say to them, or what you don't:
A world where all the nonsense is annulled,

And beauty is accepted slang for yes.

Why 'now', one might wonder? A particular reader would know the answer, given that the stanza is assembled from Amis's anecdotes of the previous decade, and one of these is particularly significant: the wife 'who behaved so badly in a bath' while her husband was watching away matches. In the letter that prompted the poem Amis had told of how he was 'getting tied up with a young woman here, not to say really tied up, just started fucking her what', an arrangement scheduled by her provision of the fixture list of the Swansea Rugby Football Club and marked with matches to be attended by her husband, 'Her meaning being, then YOU CAN SLIP IN AND SLIP IT IN BACH.'

He goes on to describe the lady rather in the manner of a farmer who has just acquired an average-quality beast for a knock-down price. 'Good breasts, yes, but a bad face, narrow eyes, long nose, cheese-like skin. Her hair smells slightly of watercress. Started fucking her out of charity really,' adding, as a condescending thought for Larkin's possible feeling of exclusion, 'no need for envy on anyone's part here'.

Larkin's statement that 'now I believe' all the reports of sexual conquest on which Amis had kept him regularly updated does not imply that he ever doubted their veracity. It indicates his recognition that Amis had almost magically caused fantasy and fact to become compatible. He had witnessed first Amis's use of their friendship as the dynamic for *Lucky Jim*; next he had read *That Uncertain Feeling*, where the private correspondence between the narrator and the reader is a replica – confessions, reflections and celebrations included – of Amis's with him. Finally, he had seen a curious spiralling of the fact–fiction alliance, with Amis's success as a novelist and public personality causing his real-life career as a lady-killer to improve upon its made-up counterpart.

The third and fourth stanzas invite a comparison between their sex lives,

at least ostensibly. When he asks, 'But equally, haven't you noticed mine?'
one should remember that by now he expects Amis to pay attention to the
established subtext, writing, with girls

> ... you mine away
> For months, both of you, till the collapse comes
> Into remorse, tears, and wondering why
> You ever start such boring barren games ...

This is a direct response to the section of Amis's letters where he thanks Larkin
for his amusingly despondent accounts of his relationships with women,
such as when 'AWA [Winifred Arnott] slipped-off-from-the-expensive-
dinner-I-was-giving-her-to-go-to-a-Bach-concert ...' This raises the question
of why he asks Amis, 'haven't you noticed mine?', when it is evident that
he has. What Larkin would like Amis to notice, or at least consider, is the
ways in which their respective literary careers have interfaced with their lives.
Just as Amis had made his life and his fiction enviably interchangeable and
interdependent, so Larkin's poetry had become a kind of testament to his
dismal retinue of disappointments with women. The melancholic, almost
masochistic presence that had come to inhabit his verse had also made it
successful. It was an honest reflection of the man behind the poems, the
same man who had since Oxford played his role as mordant hanger-on to
Amis's witty seducer in their mutually accepted double act.

> I'm happier now I've got things clear, although
> It's strange we never meet each other's sort:
> There should be equal chances, I'd've thought.
> Must finish now. One day perhaps I'll know
> What makes you be so lucky in your ratio
> – One of those 'more things', could it be? *Horatio*

The speculative circling is arch and rhetorical. Of course, he knows why they
never 'meet each other's sort' or what makes him so 'lucky' in his 'ratio'. That
knowledge is a condition of his having 'got things clear', but he is content
to play his role of dismal failure in this rich and varied pageant of male
philandering.

'Horatio' is, of course, a figure in *Hamlet*, the old university friend of the Prince left alive to tell the story, which seems appropriate. Amis, too, had lived beyond his fictions. His principal male characters seemed always to get away with so much that credibility was threatened. But it and they survived, just like their author in his reckless pursuit of excitement beyond the ordinary. Alternatively, Larkin is the failed novelist, the poet who has found his natural accomplishment in fashioning the elegant text from irredeemably depressing material.

There is an almost cruelly appropriate and risible appendix to Larkin's reflections. In October 1957 he sent Amis a rough first draft of the piece, and the latter replied that it 'sounds like an absolutely fucking marvellous idea ... But don't get me wrong (though I suppose it needn't be "me" in the poem); what I mean is I am no Don J. at all, really, I merely work a pennyworth of fucking in with an intolerable deal of wire pulling' (9 November 1957). There is no record of Larkin's response, but one might safely assume that at this point he was slightly puzzled by Amis's inference that the 'absolutely fucking marvellous' idea was Larkin's own. Amis continues that 'it [the poem] might easily stir me to a reply, not a polemical one of course, but a further discussion of the points you raise'. It might all, he states, be 'bumper fun' and concludes, without a hint of irony, 'Or isn't that in tune with your original conception?' Well, no, Larkin would have mused, given that the poem was a thoughtful response to their exchanges of the previous ten years. After dismissing the off-chance that Amis might have been visited by a bout of clinical amnesia, it is possible that Larkin's taste for self-lacerating dark comedy would have prompted him to see the 'friend' of the poem as an even more accurate picture of Amis than he had first imagined. The preening false modesty of 'I am no Don J. at all' was apt. Amis had variously overlooked and forgotten screeds of past reports on his Don Juanish conquests, his cannibalisation of their friendship for his own literary purposes and, apparently, his original suggestion – that they write about all this in a co-authored novel (24 September 1956) – which had prompted Larkin to compose the poem. The image of the 'friend' in the poem as so magically successful that such irritating encumbrances as memory can be sidelined is superbly accurate. It should be noted that while the version shown to Amis in the mid-1950s closely resembled the one that appeared in the posthumous collections, another, much longer, set of revisions exists. It dates from late 1959 and records the point at which

Larkin completely lost patience with his friend. Larkin did not send Amis any further drafts of the poem and the latter forgot about it, which is consistent with the impression Amis had left upon him during one of their meetings in London a couple of months earlier. To Judy Egerton, Larkin wrote, 'Three old friends – myself, B and K [Bruce Montgomery and Kingsley] – met in London ... last week ... Kingsley has less and less conception of talking *to* you: you are simply an audience, and the more intelligent the better, since the better you can appreciate him' (4 August 1957).

The ever-extending gallery of Amis's reports on his excesses are the inspiration for 'Letter to a Friend about Girls', but one also wonders if it was intended as a specific reply to some poems, autobiographical and unapologetic, that Amis had shown him in draft form.

Amis's *Case of Samples* (1956) is a selection of the poems published over the previous nine years in magazines and journals, and these are radically different from the verse of *Bright November* (1947).

The title is taken from the closing line of a poem called 'A Song of Experience'. The poet and his friends are in a pub where they meet a travelling salesman who tells them of the women he has known and seduced. The tone is informal, familiar; the conversational diction is slipped into the quatrains as easily as the traveller slips in, and out, of the lives, emotions and bodies of his women.

> He tried all colours, white and black and coffee;
> Though quite a few were chary, more were bold;
> Some took it like the Host, some like a toffee;
> The two or three who wept were soon consoled.

The traveller is a projection of Amis himself. True, 'A Song of Experience' is not simply a means by which Amis can displace his life of lechery on to the figure of the traveller. He also projects the traveller into an exploration of the relationship between literature and sex.

> The inaccessible he laid a hand on,
> The heated he refreshed, the cold he warmed
> What Blake presaged, what Lawrence took a stand on,
> What Yeats locked up in fable he performed.

The named writers are part of a literary tradition that turns the pure pleasure of sex into apocalyptic metaphors, in contrast with the traveller who, without apology or explanation, simply appreciates it. And we should note that two of them, Yeats and Lawrence, were favourites of Larkin. Eventually he stopped mentioning them in their correspondence, having become weary of Amis's ridicule. Instead, he talked and wrote to Monica about them. Aside from his sideswipe at Larkin's enthusiasm, Amis seems to be exploring complementary versions of himself. On the one hand, he shares a genre with his eminent predecessors – as he shows in his self-confident reproduction of William Blake's method – on the other, he is a writer who has detached himself from their brand of moral and aesthetic elitism. They, he implies, would have treated the traveller as an intriguing specimen. For Amis, he is part of experience, his own included; something that poetry should involve and not patronise. Amis concludes:

> I saw him brisk in May, in Juliet's weather,
> Hitch up the trousers of his long-tailed suit,
> Polish the windscreen with his chamois leather,
> And stow his case of samples in the boot.

We know that the traveller would probably neither recognise nor care about Amis's Shakespearian allusion – he is more interested in real-life Juliets – but this is not Amis invoking his cultural superiority; quite the opposite. The traveller's case of samples enables him to enjoy a life of promiscuity, and it is significant that Amis chooses this phrase for the title of his collection. Amis's case of samples is his writing, which involves a combination of his literary talents and his less sophisticated traveller-like persona. Here, too, there is an element of confession with apology; Amis's literary reputation, his own case of samples, played an important part in his successful career as a seducer.

The most famous of this sequence was begun soon after the publication of *A Case Of Samples*. 'Nothing to Fear' is an account of the thoughts that run through the mind of a man in a flat 'lent by a friend, whose note says *Lucky Sod*'. He is waiting for a woman:

> ... the cover story pat
> And quite uncheckable; her husband off
> Somewhere with the kids till six o'clock.

He reflects with covetous glee on her impressive face, legs, hips and breasts, and at the end of the first stanza he dismisses feelings of guilt, compunction and 'all that cock; / It'll wear off, as usual'. But it does not, and in the second stanza the pace of the language quickens as he asks himself why he feels so uneasy:

> This slight trembling
> Dry mouth, quick pulse rate, sweaty hands
> As though she were the first?

The sense of anxiety that he had earlier dismissed becomes tangibly present in the closing lines.

> Sitting here, a bag of glands
> Tuned up to concert pitch, I seem to sense
> A different style of caller at my back,
> As cold as ice, but just as set on me.

Conventional guilt can be coped with in the manner of the traveller in the pub, and Amis in his letters, but this is different: a fear of something that can only be himself, a figure who lives two lives and is rightly terrified at the thought of their intersection. The 'different style of caller' disturbs the self-contained pleasure of the illicit liaison which the rest of the poem tries so desperately to celebrate.

The poem is Amis's most blatantly autobiographical. The 'friend' whose flat he borrowed was Robert Conquest, who had access to a number of West London flats owned by friends and colleagues, and he personally leased a basement in Eaton Square, Chelsea. As mentioned, he would lend one of these to Amis whenever he needed a site for sex, which he frequently did. Amis in his *Memoirs* tells of how on one occasion, after 'Nothing to Fear' had been published, Conquest set up a tape recorder that was triggered by the main door and caused a disembodied voice, Conquest's, to recite the first few lines of the poem.

Amis no doubt includes this anecdote to indicate that his prodigious sex life and clandestine dealings with Conquest were more the basis for laddish humour than anything resembling guilt or uncertainty. If it is also intended to disperse the very convincing mood of discomfort generated in the poem itself it fails, because 'Nothing to Fear' is the most explicit of a series of poems in which Amis explores various states of anxiety, depression, even self-loathing, which surround the sexual act. If these were not rooted in actual feelings then Amis is the most hollow and talented liar ever to have written a poem. While preparing 'Nothing to Fear' he wrote to Larkin: 'Still haven't finished my adultery poems, but shall have a bash today' (15 December 1959). Next, he shifts from his writings on adultery to its real counterpart: 'Tackling of adultery, my activities in this direction ...' involved the discovery by Hilly of more letters from one of his girlfriends.

'Nocturne' seems to be a Movement poem par excellence, a very short story in verse where Amis describes the view from an upstairs window on to a dark, damp street after the pubs have closed. It is probably Swansea. Two people, apparently with nowhere else to go, fondle each other in a shop doorway, watched by a drunken sailor with an empty beer flagon 'looking for something good to smash it on'. Amis wonders what the local guardians of decency, the Watch Committee, would make of this. They would probably describe them as 'mere animals', and Amis agrees. They are animals, but of the human variety whose bestial instincts are altered by their ability, need, to keep in their mind 'the image of another creature'. It is a poem about sex, loneliness, even envy – Amis implies that the drunken sailor's anger is partly the result of the couple's reminder that he is alone. And it is also about Amis. He knows nothing of what these people feel, but their image of drab desperation causes him to speculate on its emotional underpinnings; it is as much a moment of introspection as observation.

In 'A Point of Logic' two verse stanzas describe the same act. In the first, a couple climb a staircase 'of marble / Or decently; scrubbed boards', the uncertainty perhaps an indication of the many different staircases that Amis had used on his way to Conquest's flats. In the second he advises them to 'put out the light':

Lurch to the bare attic
Over buckets of waste
And labouring bodies;
Leave the door open
And fall on each other ...

Throughout the poem Amis causes us to wonder if the couple is involved in a random, illicit liaison in an unfamiliar building or whether the location is their new home. Do the 'labouring bodies' and 'buckets of waste' indicate builders at work on the house, or are they part of some degenerate fantasy? At the end he advises them to:

> Stay only a minute
> Depart separately,
> And use no names.

This could be an echo of Amis's brief, almost anonymous encounters, or it could be a description of the impersonality of all sexual acts, even those with a regular partner, in which satisfaction is selfish, physical. The bizarre, almost surreal uncertainties of the account are a distillation of Amis's experiences in the 1950s. He enjoyed his life with Hilly and feared its loss, but it was not enough. In his 1957 letter to Conquest on how he had made peace with Hilly and resumed his other encounters he concludes, 'Oh, why isn't there *more* of that kind of thing?'

'Alternatives' is even more disturbing. The first three stanzas offer a brief cinematic narrative. A woman is alone in a dark house, playing the piano. A man moves from the pavement and up the stairs. He enters her room and strangles her. In the fourth stanza, Amis stops the film and asks if the reader would like to alter its conclusion. Perhaps the house should be empty; or maybe the woman knows and is expecting the man, whose hands will move not to her throat but to her 'eager breasts'. Amis is not suggesting that sex is the equivalent of murder, but the fine distinction between killer and lover recalls the 'different style of caller' that he senses in 'Nothing to Fear'. This time a woman is waiting for a man. At the beginning of the last stanza Amis considers the choice between the two stories, 'Neither or both for you', and against this is an echo of his own life.

Amis had no clear plans for his next novel, but at the end of March 1955, fate helped him out. He received a telegram in Swansea from Hilary Rubinstein of Gollancz informing him that *Lucky Jim* had won the Somerset Maugham award for fiction. Amis was gratified and amused. It was only three months earlier that the esteemed benefactor of the prize had written of *Lucky Jim* as a symptom of widespread moral and cultural degeneration:

evidently Maugham was not on the panel of judges. The award of £400 was generous, more than Amis's academic salary, but it was attached to a condition: that the author 'agree to spend [it] on three months' travel or residence abroad'. Amis would be able to fit the three months into the Swansea summer vacation, but he had no particular interest in foreign travel and no contacts abroad. Apart from periods with family, local excursions to the Gower and a few weeks in a caravan near the Thames, the Amises had never been on a proper holiday since their marriage, and Hilly was more enthusiastic about the prospect than Amis. They thought about returning to France, which they had visited briefly in 1947, but eventually they sought advice from their wealthy friends the Aaron-Thomases. John Aaron-Thomas said he would contact Signor Pintos Bassos, a businessman with whom he and his wife had stayed in Portugal. Dates and addresses were forwarded, and the Amises with their three children boarded the Southampton–Lisbon ferry on 23 June.

They would not stay with Pintos Bassos but with one of his employees, a senior clerk called Billy Barley. Barley was proud equally of his Portuguese nationality and his English father, which for him recreated the sixteenth-century alliance between Portugal and England. He was honoured to play host to a writer from his paternal homeland and from whom he would ask £3 7s. a day for board and lodging, an exorbitant amount in Portugal in 1955. Barley had spent the previous month building extra interior walls into his modest single-storey house in Estoril, half an hour from Lisbon. When the Amises arrived they found a bizarre assembly of rooms the size of large cupboards which would accommodate Barley, his wife and two children, and the Amises and their three. Amis did not dislike Barley – he described him to Larkin as 'very amiable in a childish way' – but he felt that the cramped quarters, the heat, the mingled smells from the kitchen and the adjacent lavatory and their attendant insects were a kind of Maughamian revenge. By the end of July the Amises had decided to move to a boarding house in the Algarve.

In *I Like It Here*, Billy Barley becomes C. J. P. Oates. Barley's wife and children, his Anglo-Portuguese background, his accent, the cramped house with its smells and discomforts, even his transport – a dangerously decrepit moped upon which Amis is offered a lift, which he politely declines – resurface with little embellishment or alteration. In the Algarve the Amises met an

Ulster couple, the Tyrrells, who were renting a mountain chalet. When the Tyrrells moved on, they offered the chalet to the Amises, who gratefully accepted it. Again, all of this is reproduced in the novel with autobiographical verity. Mr Tyrrell becomes Bannion, and Bannion, like Tyrrell, is prone to embarrassing imitations of foreign persons, including a Frenchwoman who seems to have acquired her native language in an Ulster grammar school, plus recitations of 'The Charge of the Light Brigade' by four individuals from different parts of Europe.

The Barleys, the Bannions and the Amises' farcical trek through Portugal had great comic potential in themselves, but this was the only occasion in his literary career when Amis borrowed so blatantly from real life. He did so as an act of convenience. The figures and events that almost wrote themselves provided Amis with a subplot for the book that is one of his least satisfying.

Garnet Bowen's trip to Portugal is sponsored by his publisher, Hyman, and in return for a free holiday Bowen is asked to unravel a literary detective mystery. Hyman has recently received a manuscript from a person claiming to be the Wulfstan Strether who had published five acclaimed modernist novels in the 1930s and 1940s, who has not been heard from for a decade and has since acquired cult status. Strether is an assembly of all the traits and affectations that Amis associates with the mythology of the British writer abroad, and Bowen has to find out if this is the real Strether or a talented pretender.

On 10 July 1955 he wrote to Larkin of how the worst aspect of being 'abroad' is:

> You haven't got any of your friends with you, you see, and you can't make friends with the locals because they're foreign and don't understand what you're saying and you're not here long enough ... Now I'm funny. I like talking to chaps I like talking to and wd. rather not ... talk to chaps I'd rather not talk to ...

Bowen's struggle with the relationship between linguistic exchange and its context is an encoded statement by Amis about what, in his view, were the necessary conditions for writing literature that is not detached from the inclinations, preconditions and, crucially, the linguistic habits of its readers, and Amis created Strether as the precise opposite of this creative manifesto.

Another part of the narrative involves an oblique commentary on Amis's private life. He began the novel as soon as he returned to Swansea in late 1955, but by the following summer had barely completed the first two chapters. His marriage was in a seemingly irretrievable state of decline. He and Hilly had become friendly with the journalist Henry Fairlie during their occasional visits to Robert Conquest's house in London for weekend parties. Fairlie had been invited back to Swansea and by early 1956 had begun an affair with Hilly. In September 1956 Hilly told Amis that her relationship with Fairlie had progressed beyond its original, tacitly agreed, status as a compensation for his own frequent and incompetently disguised bouts of infidelity. She was thinking of divorce; she would take the children and move in with Fairlie in London. Nothing was certain, but she had decided that for the next few months she and Fairlie would 'decide whether they are victims of an "infatuation" or of "something more important"' (A to L, 22 October 1956), and during this period marital relations with Amis would cease. They would live in the same house but separately. Amis informed Larkin in October that 'my marriage has a one in four chance of surviving till next summer', but by December the odds had improved: 'much increased cordiality between the partners to the matrimonial arrangement in question' (A to L, 6 December 1956). (This state of things had been helped, from Amis's point of view, by Fairlie's arraignment in November for fraud and his brief imprisonment for contempt of court.) By January 1957 Hilly had decided that her affair with Fairlie was over and had engineered a post-hostilities agreement, with Amis promising restraint and, when this was unsteady, candour. (Amis's observance of it can be judged by his letter to Larkin of 27 January on their forthcoming weekend in London: 'We can both stay with my girl...')

During all of this the Portugal novel had been shelved. 'Can't seem to work much these days, somehow. My novel had rattled along merrily to p. 49 when the blow fell; now remains there' (A to L, 4 November 1956). By spring 1957 he had returned to it. The notes from Portugal provided plenty of incident and contextual detail but nothing resembling a story. Once the Strether mystery was solved, all that was left was the Bowens' departure, so at the twelfth of the sixteen brief chapters Amis has Barbara Bowen summoned home by telegram to look after her seriously ill mother; and she takes the children. The parallels between the Amises' near break-up and the Bowens' benign separation might seem slight, and at the time no one outside a very confined circle of friends knew anything of the former – Amis in his 22 October letter to Larkin had asked him to keep it all in the strictest confidence. However, Amis uses the closing chapters as a channel for, perhaps a purgation of, the feelings of uncertainty that attended the months after October 1956. In the letter to Larkin, Amis admits that the 'light and bantering tone' of their correspondence is for once beyond him and would in any case be 'a poor index of how I feel this evening'. Despite having behaved in a way that justified Hilly's inclination to leave, he is still disturbed by the suddenly very real possibility of being on his own.

> [I]t means presumably that the children, about whom I feel strongly, will accompany their mother to her new home. I shall be able to see them 'often' of course. But that isn't the same as having them in your home all the time, you see ... Having one's wife fucked is one thing; having her taken away from you, plus your children, is another, I find ... Dividing the records, selling the house, storing the furniture and all that, it seems inconceivable. Reckon I shall resign here and go to London or somewhere when the time comes. It'll be odd to be a bachelor again. (22 October 1956)

Through Chapters 13 and 14, Bowen's Portugal experience appears suddenly to have become more engrossing, now incorporating a variety of enigmatic and sinister figures, but he seems to find it difficult to maintain any interest. Every thousand words or so a more persistent feature of his mindset interrupts his perception of actual events: 'He was thinking about Barbara, whom he had seen off on the plane to London, together with the kids, ten days earlier ...'; 'Why hadn't he gone back with Barbara?'; 'sitting on Buckmaster's veranda with a glass of Madeira before him, and thinking about Barbara'; 'Since his marriage he had never spent more than a few days away from Barbara'; 'too sleepy to think about Buckmaster. He thought about Barbara instead' (*I Like It Here*, pp. 139–71). Why, one is prompted to ask, is Bowen so unsettled by a mutually agreed few weeks away from his wife and children?

At one point he is about to have alfresco sex with a young friend of Strether, Emilie, but is prevented from doing so by a wasp bite on his leg. As a piece of fiction the moment is both arbitrary and unconvincing: Emilie features nowhere else and Amis's male characters generally require a more significant cause for restraint. But, like the rest of the closing chapters, it indicates that Amis has more on his mind than the scrutiny of the suspicious reader.

Amis weaves into his account the very personal hypothesis of his letter to Larkin: what would it be like if he were on his own again, a freewheeling bachelor? And he also addresses this to a particular reader. He was not attempting to convince Hilly, via Bowen and the Emilie incident, that he had become a natural monogamist by inclination – hence the wasp bite as an unconvincing act of fate. He knows and implicitly confesses that he will go on being attracted to attractive women, but he also makes it clear, through Bowen's persistent and intrusive thoughts about Barbara, that such instincts can be overruled by his attachment to his wife. In effect, he writes into the novel a version of the agreement he had reached with Hilly in January 1956; an uneven but circumspect blend of candour and restraint. The more unsettled, non-fictional counterpart of this can be gauged from a comparison between the letters he wrote to Larkin during this period and the one he sent to Fairlie (1 November 1956). In the latter (*c.* 1856) he adopts the style of a distraught victim, a decent husband and father who faces the loss of all that is dearest to him.

> This [separation of Amis from his wife and children, who would live with Fairlie] will be agonising for them, but not as agonising as it is for those who are suffering instead of merely inflicting cruelty, and if they are already selfish and ruthless by nature, as I think you are, they will be less agonised still.

Three weeks earlier he had reported to Larkin on which of his new first-year students would 'be best for a bit of ah ha ha'; the 'dreamy freckled lascivious Heather Harding' or maybe the 'high-breasted squirming Wendy Roberts' (8 October 1956). (And one wonders why Amis did not try out the epistolary novel; he could certainly reinvent himself in letters.)

When Bowen returns to London and is waiting for Barbara on the station platform, he reflects on how the likes of Emilie mean nothing to him compared with the woman he is about to meet. Barbara leaves the children with the luggage and sprints towards him. 'They kissed. Bowen had never felt so relieved in his life' (*I Like It Here*, p. 224). Why 'relieved'? There was absolutely no suggestion that their separation was anything more than a practical inconvenience, at least not in the novel. But in one word Amis had allowed his own feelings to undermine the pretence of fiction. There are no reasons for Bowen to feel 'relieved' at his sudden reunion with his wife, but for Amis there were many. As he wrote to Larkin (6 December 1956), 'I am less of a misery now, because I have more or less got my wife back (no Henry for 6 months; resumption of marital relations; much increased cordiality between the partners ...) and that is sodding good-oh, believe me, sport.' However, one should not treat Bowen's feeling of relief at being united with his beloved wife as an exact version of that of Amis. Later in the same letter to Larkin, he reports that 'I have got my girlfriend back too. And that, as well, is very nice (indeed to fook) ... yes my love-life is quite near an even keel at the moment.'

Mavis Nicholson offers a more poignant recollection of the episode.

Hilly had a particular fondness for Philip. She admired him as a poet but more than that she felt at ease with him. There were times when she very much needed his support, because of Kingsley, and he gave it. The worst was during the near-break-up, involving Henry Fairlie. It wasn't that she chose to have an affair, she'd no choice. It was her only way of altering Kingsley's regime. Apart from arguing with him [Kingsley] the only person she really felt able to talk to, the only person who knew Kingsley and who'd listen, was Philip.

Again, Larkin found himself obliged to listen to Amis and sympathise with Hilly but limited in what he could say to either of them.

I Like It Here became a novel that Amis wanted to forget. He talks of it in a self-critical 1973 essay, but more significantly neither it nor the summer in Portugal are mentioned in his *Memoirs*. Here he states that he intends to leave out 'as much as possible of potentially hurtful topics' (p. 47), particularly those relating to Hilly. This is a creditable decision and, given that the events of 1955–7 were a prelude to their actual separation five years later, it is understandable that the novel that refers, albeit obliquely, to these events is proscribed.

During Amis's period of anxiety and recklessness Larkin played his standard part of droll respondent, but throughout 1955 he kept his true feelings about his friend largely to himself, with the exception of Monica. On 15 February 1955 he wrote to her:

And as you say he's not like us. The idea of Kingsley loving a book – or a book 'feeding' him as K. M. wd say – is quite absurd. He doesn't like books. He doesn't like reading. And I wouldn't take his opinion on anything, books, people, places, anything. Probably he has been mistaken, to himself, about me.

Ever since their time as members of 'The Seven' they had treated the high-mindedness of literary criticism with a degree of caution, sometimes allowing this to slide into caricature and apparent philistinism. For Larkin, this was a protection against his low self-esteem as a writer, but as he matured he began to appreciate that literary evaluation was a necessary concomitant to genuine appreciation, or, as he puts it to Monica, 'loving a book'. Amis, however, went in the opposite direction. Undermining the reputations of major authors was one of his trademarks as an academic during his early years at Swansea. It earned him a reputation of being more unorthodox and consequently more interesting than his colleagues, and bought him the admiration of his students, particularly the women. Once *Lucky Jim* had been accepted for publication he began to treat other writers, particularly his contemporaries, not as fellow artists but as competitors. He had never been particularly patient or indulgent with work that he had decided was in some way irrecoverably flawed (hence Larkin's decision to talk of his continued interest in D. H. Lawrence only to Monica, knowing that any mention of him to Amis would summon rants and abuse), but once his profile as a novelist had become more secure he saw others as threats and legitimate targets to be ruthlessly disposed of. Typically, regarding John Wain: 'Saw old Johnny boy [Wain], who seemed pretty well, considering ... His book [*Hurry on Down*] did less well than mine – miaouuuu!!!!!' (A to L, 20 December 1954). 'Wasn't John's first poem frightful? I wanted to take out my pencil and scrawl COULD HAVE TOLD YOU THAT SHITFACE across it' (A to L, 19 April 1956). Later in the same letter: 'What's all this about you having written a review? [Gordon Wherton] said you praised "Katie". Kate RAINE? you must be lso pso losing your mind.' Larkin was not a dedicated fan of Kathleen Raine but he did not believe that the quality of a writer's work should be based on an implacable foregone conclusion. More significantly, he resented Amis's sense of acting as censor for any aberration from their (as Amis saw it) shared literary tastes and prejudices.

Amis's reports to Larkin on his misfortunes in Portugal read like a rehearsal for weary, sardonic mood that surrounds Bowen during his equally ghastly trip. He tells him that the 'Tyrrells are well worthy of fictional transcription' (28 July 1955), and his deadpan account of their religiosity could quite easily be transposed with the portrait of Harry and Isabelle Bannion from the novel. Amis's trademark mimicry finds an easy target in Mrs Tyrrell, who is Goanese: 'Meezda Emmess's glarz is ampty. Order another of thawz mwontles (bottles) off vine. The rad.' Larkin tells Monica: 'This makes me laugh' (L to Monica, 3 August 1955). No doubt it did but it stirred other feelings too. Although he does not proffer a full explanation, Monica would undoubtedly recognise a connection between his amusement at Amis's mercilessly funny treatment of Mrs Tyrrell and a similar performance some five years earlier in the letters that would gestate into *Lucky Jim*. Larkin adds, without comment:

> One letter I 'sorted' at home was from Kingsley, thanking me for the schedule of chapters 1–7 and containing 2 pages of detailed questions for 8–15 ('I see what you mean about the lecture, though I don't know if I can do it'). I told him how to do it. He did it. Oh well.

He muses, 'it seems LJ is going to be filmed and broadcast (18/– a minute) so he can afford it [more expensive accommodation in Portugal]'.

We have to ask, which is the real Larkin? Is it one who replies to his old friend, maintaining his well-established role, or is it the one who casts off this persona to confide in Monica? The answer, indisputably, is the second. For one thing, he has by the mid-1950s subtly adjusted his manner with Amis. He certainly does not betray to him any of the unease regarding their friendship that emerges in the letters to Monica, but he omits both the disclosures of insecurity that marked his early exchanges with his friend and, just as crucially, he no longer speaks to him of his writing. The fact that these mutations are imperceptible to Amis – that the latter never finds cause to mention them is testament to that – goes some way to reinforce Larkin's notion of him as now almost completely self-absorbed, so preoccupied with his own success that he fails to notice how his friends are feeling.

We have seen already how with 'Church Going' Larkin preferred Monica's advice to his friend's flippant comments, but in his letter to her of 3 August 1955, we encounter an equally significant shift of allegiance. The collection that projected him from the status of a respected, slightly parochial writer to the poet that the nation took to its heart was *The Whitsun Weddings*, and its title poem germinated in this letter: 'I went home on Saturday, 1.30 to Grantham – a lovely run, the scorched land misty with heat, like a kind of bloom of heat – and at every station, Goole, Doncaster, Retford, Newark, importunate wedding parties, gawky and vociferous, seeing off couples to London.' By this time the poem was at draft stage, and between 1955 and 1958 he would make the Whitsun journey three times, a silent witness to this curious social ritual. In the finished poem he would, as in 1955, accompany the new couples the full distance to London.

The figures he observes in the poem, the 'girls' 'grinning and pomaded' 'in parodies of fashion', the fathers 'with broad belts under their suits / And seamy foreheads', the mothers 'loud and fat' and the uncle 'shouting smut' all seemed possessed of a beguiling transparency. They are not exactly dignified, but their honest vulgarity is something that Larkin uncritically accepts.

The closing lines of the poem are a masterpiece of evasion.

> ... and what it held
> Stood ready to be loosed with all the power
> That being changed can give. We slowed again,
> And as the tightened brakes took hold, there swelled
> A sense of falling, like an arrow-shower
> Sent out of sight, somewhere becoming rain.

The poem ends, but its concluding juggling act between inference and bold imagery will go on forever. The 'arrow-shower' might well, as he disclosed to Jean Hartley, have been inspired by Olivier's *Henry V*, but this does not account for it 'becoming rain', unless one simply accepts that both images involved things quintessentially English – outdated patriotism, dismal weather and a sense of resignation. Whatever all of this signifies, Larkin gathers himself into it with the collective 'We'.

The letter to Monica, in which he gives an almost exact listing of the stations in the journey, might be treated as coincidental to the poem were it not also for his continued, almost obsessive references to his recent travels as offering a prism to the strange amorphous notion of Englishness. A friend at Hull had told him a story of soldiers rescued from Dunkirk 'sleeping it off on the grass verges of the streets in Dorchester: 'He saw it as "This England" ... Talking about England, did you see Henry V is to be shown at the Academy, Oxford St? I want to go' (L to Monica, 3 August 1955). He did, later that year, and it is difficult not to treat the stunning cinematic moment of the bowmen and the arrow as part of a chain reaction which also involved the particulars of a train journey through the length of England and the elusive question of what England actually is. It all began in his fascinated account for Monica, and while it would be facile to present her as his muse, she had most certainly replaced Amis as the person to whom he confided details of work-in-progress, and sometimes even asked for advice. Amis did not see 'The Whitsun Weddings' until it appeared in print.

Along with his growing respect for Monica as scrutineer of his poems-in-progress, Larkin had since the early 1950s disclosed to her aspects of his temperament that few close to him knew anything of. From Belfast he wrote to her:

> It is a fine mild autumn Sunday and I've ridden up into the hills, aided by a kind south wind ... the weather was soft and fine like the end of Wuthering Heights: I grubbed about for blackberries. In all I must have done nearly 20 miles and I feel tired and virtuous. I like the country up there, barren and featureless ... (L to Monica, 30 September 1951, Bod)

On those relatively few occasions that Larkin betrays some form of enthusiasm, admiration or affection, the disclosure seems qualified by doubt; enjoyment for him seemed to cultivate a corresponding level of torture. But not here. Soon after his arrival in Hull he reported on a dreadful party held by people in his lodging house, and then suddenly the mood lifts.

> I went for a walk this afternoon. People had told me to 'walk the wolds' or the Dales ... It was a sunny afternoon but there were cloudy intervals. Near home I stopped and watched about half a dozen Jersey cows. How lovely they are! Like Siamese cats, almost: the patches of white round their eyes and the soft way the coffee colour melts into their soft white underbelly. They were licking

each other affectionately in pairs, on the chest and along the neck. When
one stopped the other would begin licking back. The peaceable kingdom! ...
Never a rabbit did I see, alas. (L to Monica, 6 August 1955, Bod)

There is no hint of affectation here. For once, he allows someone – Monica –
access to his unguarded sense of empathy with the landscape and his love for
animals. He was sometimes honest with Amis, but it was a prudent sincerity,
calculated to show his friend something of the man he thought he understood
better than anyone while stifling features of his temperament he preferred to
keep to himself. He would never have disclosed anything like the above
to him. Yet it was not that he reserved a different type of performance for
Monica; for her he was not performing. She, uniquely, was provisioned with
the complete spectrum of his sometimes contradictory traits.

Larkin wrote an extraordinary letter to her on 3 May 1955 in which he
presents himself as facing a crossroads. He feels that he must exchange those
people he sees as inhibiting his creative temper for one whose constitution
mirrors his own: Monica.

I think one thing I can say about the progress of our relation is that I've grown
tired of all my friends except you – all my close friends, that is: not many
really. This is worth mentioning because you have often felt that you were
in a different camp from all sorts of points of view, haven't you? 'Socially,
politically, morally' as one might say. I kept you apart because I know, myself,
that I acted a different part with them from my behaviour with you, and since
I couldn't do both at once it was well not to try. And in any case I couldn't
see you mixing into, nasty phrase, life as it was led at Kingsley's house or the
Strangs'. Therefore I kept them away from you, and as I did myself still enjoy
their company I suppose I was keeping part of my life hidden from you in a
suspicious way. But when I met Kingsley in Cheltenham, & the Strangs on
Boar Hill, & Bruce in Abingdon, I thought on each occasion: I'm through
with this. Basically. You have shown me better things!

This was sent shortly before Amis's departure for Portugal, and though they
exchanged letters during that summer one suspects that the notion of Amis
being elsewhere prompted Larkin's musing on a complete break from him.
The letter is immensely revealing in another way too; specifically his admission

that he 'acted a different part with them from my behaviour with you'. Since Oxford Larkin had become more and more a chameleon, selecting and often exaggerating those aspects of his character he thought most suited the expectations and habits of his different friends. At the beginning of their friendship he was transparent in his dealings with Amis; his role as the more sardonic, embittered and to an extent pitiable half of their partnership was based largely on fact. It reflected his state of mind. But over the subsequent decade he became if not more content then at least reconciled with the man he was. With the new responsibilities at Hull he came to treat librarianship less as an obligation or sign of failure and almost a vocation; secondary, of course, to his writing. With Monica he cultivated a love of the countryside, old buildings – particularly churches, though neither of them held religious beliefs – and walking. He said absolutely nothing of this to Amis, aware that it would draw mockery. Indeed, after seeing 'An Arundel Tomb', and with no knowledge that it was inspired by Larkin's visit to the cathedral with Monica, Amis's only comment was 'don't you ever go anywhere except into bleeding churches? Hope you aren't getting this chic faith thing' (A to L, 19 April 1956).

Aside from the Portugal visit there is no obvious reason for Larkin's contemplation of a precipitate decision at that moment. But during the previous five years, following the Amises' move to Swansea, Amis gradually eroded those boundaries beyond which lay matters best kept to oneself. This could be seen as a blend of secular confession and self-administered psychiatric care, the use of a confidant to purge one's system of its more distasteful elements. But there is something in Amis's letters that goes beyond this, a slight but detectable implication that they share seedy characteristics and by exchanging them guilt is supplemented by unalloyed gratification. On 3 August 1953 (Bod), Amis wrote him a long letter giving a detailed account of a family outing to the beach in Swansea Bay. Amis always professed a certain amount of distaste for Nabokov, and while never condemning him morally as a writer one can't but help wonder if, when *Lolita* was published two years later, he felt a twinge of disdain for himself. Even the style – shamelessly epicurean – carries an air of Humbert Humbert about it. He begins triumphantly. 'On Saturday on the beach I saw the most beautiful person I have ever seen in my whole life.' Note the asexual 'person'. He is releasing parts of the picture to his friend with delectation as if this is something he knows Larkin will appreciate. The next sentence opens with 'she': 'blond and fair skinned, with a face of great sweetness and placidity ...; she was tall, she had long childish legs ... she had a light refined voice; she had a friend called Wendy; she walked with a slow pliant step; she had enormous breasts.' Such is the care taken in assembling this gallery of her physical characteristics, one might be forgiven for overlooking an observation that Amis slips in to the list midway: 'she was about fourteen'. He continues. 'I had my eye on her for about 15 seconds at a range of 4 or 5 yards; at the end of that time I had a considerable horn, no mean achievement when sitting on a crowded beach surrounded by family and friends and wearing wet bathing trunks'. The obsessive attention to detail then gives way to an account of his state of mind, beginning with a description of 'feeling great fear' and then a 'feeling of great happiness and release from tension which took some hours to disperse'. He concludes with a reflection on how 'youth and physical beauty' are at once 'exciting' and 'important', causing both happiness and sadness. There is no record of a specific response to this by Larkin but when seen as part of an accumulation of effects one can see how it played some part in the seemingly precipitate mood of his letter to Monica, his contemplation of a complete break with Amis.

As we have seen, the near breakdown of Amis's marriage did not deter him from further extramarital excursions but during that same year something else happened too. Not only did he continue to deceive Hilly, he sometimes did not bother to conceal his activities. The rugby player's wife, herself the participant in other covert liaisons, told of one dinner at the Amises' when several of the female guests were invited by Kingsley to join him outside in the greenhouse. Several did, and despite the fact that no one present actually witnessed sex taking place, everyone knew exactly what was happening. In a memoir, Al Alvarez gives an account of a similar party at which he was present when Amis, seemingly without much use of persuasion, was accompanied to the garden by a number of women. Alvarez comments on how over breakfast, by way of apology, he 'launch[ed] into a long rigmarole about his fear of death' (Al Alvarez, *Where Did It All Go Right?*, p. 210). This is almost an exact replica of what happens in his description of the day at the beach: both involved a shameless celebration of gratification and impropriety (albeit hypothetical paedophilia as opposed to near-public adultery), followed by the sort of self-analysis that might in some way excuse or account for his failings.

Amis kept Larkin updated on his Bacchanalian revels, and while there was a slight alteration in Larkin's routine duty as sharer of secrets – given that Amis was now cautious and discreet only when this seemed a tactical obligation, both with Hilly and the husbands of his lovers – he continued nonetheless as his 'inner audience'. He remained the one person to whom Amis felt comfortable not only in divulging his misdemeanours but also who he could rely upon as the patient listener. It was not just that Amis found lurid pleasure in the telling of his stories, more that he seemed obsessed with putting into words events that in real life appeared variously fantastic, inexplicable, even unbearable. There is, for example, a letter to Larkin sent on 20 October 1954 in which he reports in detail as precise as his account of the day on the beach a drunken evening with friends, including his colleague James Bartley. Hilly, apparently keen to rescue the flagging mood of debauchery, had removed Bartley's trousers and persuaded him to hold out his penis for inspection. Amis concludes, 'He held it for half a minute or so, gazing around. The party broke up soon after. I got to bed 3.45.' The clipped mode of the piece, bringing to mind a policeman's notebook, is not I think a means of laying out the scene for a similarly inclined voyeur; rather, he needs to be meticulous because precision is his only means of keeping at bay such questions as: 'can this really be happening?'

In a period of less than two years Amis's life seemed to have been trans-formed from weary endurance to an outrageous realisation of the fantasies he had entertained, for the benefit of Larkin, before *Lucky Jim*. Yet even though this cornucopia of sexual excess expanded virtually by the week, he continued to treat Larkin as a buffer against complete anarchy. Alvarez, albeit with the benefit of almost five decades of hindsight, diagnosed Amis's tendency to explain away his sexual appetites as baulk against 'neurotic preoccupations' – fear of death included – as typical of the 1950s generation of writers as a whole, who 'pretend that all's well with the world provided they keep their backs turned on what they really feel' (Alvarez, *Where Did It All Go Right?*, p. 210). In my view he was wrong, both in terms of his general observations on 1950s writers and with regard to Amis in particular. Amis was genuinely neurotic. His catalogue of fears was seemingly preposterous in its range – involving everything from a refusal to drive cars, travel in aeroplanes, sleep on his own with the lights out and venture down dark streets to a frequent inability to distinguish between nightmares and reality, which would leave him screaming in the middle of the night – but all were underpinned by a single, ever-present fear: that his death, despite all evidence to the contrary, was lurking and imminent. There is not, as far as I am aware, any particular psychoanalytic case study in which hyperactive sexual activity with as many different women as possible is seen as an attempt to compensate for this state. But the lack of such a model is probably due to the fact that few if any men suffering from this particular anxiety found themselves with the same escape route as Amis did. There can be few more reassuring testaments to life as an apparently limitless opportunity for sex.

All of this goes some way to explain why he felt it necessary to tell everything to Larkin. In his report on the beach episode he describes how, after a period of sexual arousal, 'a feeling of great fear took its place, the old narrowly-escaped-being-run-over-in-the-street one, with trembling and disturbed breathing'. By 'the old' he does not mean a commonly experienced sensation of anxiety; no, it was one of the numerous private phobias that plagued him and which he knew Larkin would recognise from earlier reports. Only Larkin and Hilly knew him well enough to accept that there might be a causal relationship between his disturbed state of mind and his behaviour and she, being his wife and mother of his three children, was a little less inclined to indulge it as a self-exculpatory compensation for bad behaviour. As Alvarez put it, describing the effect on those present (Hilly in particular) of Amis's breakfast-table confessions, 'everyone was miserable ... but nobody said a word' (p. 210). Larkin, Amis assumed, would listen, sympathetically, but as the letter to Monica revealed, he overestimated how much of it his friend could continue to accept.

At this point we must raise a further question. Why did he go no further with his claim to Monica that he'd 'grown tired of all my friends except you ... I'm through with this.' It would, of course, be near-impossible for someone so averse to change to completely detach himself from the man who, whether he liked it or not, was part of his existence. Larkin did not even indicate to Amis in letters or in person any sense of mortification or disillusionment. On the surface he remained for his friend the figure he had always been, but more and more he had begun to reserve his candour, indeed his true personality, for others – Monica in particular. He would never grow to despise Amis – there was always something implacable in the relationship that endured – yet from the mid-1950s onwards the figure that Amis thought he knew was becoming more a performance, a performance that he hoped would satisfy Amis's expectations of their unique attachment, yet one that served as a cover for his genuine feelings. That he continued this act for a further three decades – even during the peculiar breakdown of communications in the 1960s – showed not that he was too lazy or weak to gradually allow their ties to unravel. Rather, it was a curious act of kindness, partly a testament to something unique they had once shared and also a reluctance to hurt a man whom he still respected and sometimes found amusing, despite his growing reservations.

Larkin's private and emotional life changed considerably in the period between 1953 and 1955, and the fact that he mentioned none of this to Amis shows again that he was gradually building a wall between the figure Amis perceived him to be and who he actually was. That Amis did not detect even a nuance of this change is a further confirmation of his self-absorbed inclination to see things as he wanted them to be.

On 2 October 1955 he wrote Monica a more significant letter than the one in which he had considered cutting his ties with Amis. In this he confesses to behaving 'rather shabbily' during the 'low ebb of our relations and '51 and '52', adding 'I *was* rather dazzled by Patsy in those days.' His disclosure that Patsy had 'dazzled' him was an apology, of sorts. He had convinced Monica that his dazzlement never became an affair.

Since then I *have* changed, but I think my great worry has remained fairly constant – that our relation did not seem to contain the force that would turn it into something else – marriage for instance, or affair-and-parting – and worrying whether it was my fault or your fault or just nobody's fault, whether it did and I was trying to pretend it didn't, or *vice versa*, or whether it was just my fault for being so self centred – and in any case what I ought to do about it. That is the sort of worry that leads me to make these occasional outbursts. If they have any 'spurious' quality it's that they *are* emotional outlets to some extent, as well as being attempts at apology for prolonging a state you must find rather wounding, no matter how nice about it you are and anxious not to seem possessive. I hate leaving you at the end of a holiday, as if all that was over now and the toys were being put back in the box, yet the impulse to make it real and permanent doesn't seem strong enough to shift me off

the sandbanks – or if it is then I'm too feeble to obey it – And all this absurd
havering revolts me too.

Love and contrition are discharged with reticence, but this was not because
Larkin was protecting the truth. It was the closest he could come to transparency. He was responding to a letter from Monica where she states that she now
perceives him differently. 'I think you have changed more than I have in the
progress of our "relationship".' On his closeness to Patsy, 'I don't think that it
entered my head to think there was "anything between" you and P, I can truly
say that never occurred to me so don't think I mean that; no ...'. She explains
that 'more depressing' than their actually having an affair was Larkin's seemingly
selfish management of his time, making space for Monica only when his busy
social commitments in Belfast allowed. Her point is that being able to talk to
him about this now shows that they are much closer than ever before. 'Dearest,
dearest, I feel very close to you to be able say this – please be pleased and feel
close to me too, you ought to be, and not troubled at all' (Monica to L, 28
September 1955). Despite the fact that Larkin had not corrected her impression
that his infatuation with Patsy was no more than that (and one might charitably
assume that he was simply sparing her the knowledge of an affair that was over),
there are indications that their relationship had undergone an extraordinary
change, and this is evident as much in his own work as their correspondence.

The mood of sardonic melancholia that informs 'Mr Bleaney' would soon
find more to fuel it in the real world. As usual he arranged to spend Christmas
1955 and New Year with his mother in Loughborough. On arrival he found
friends and neighbours in a state of concern regarding a curious affliction
besetting Eva and of which he had not been forewarned. No specific record of
what this amounted to survives, but enough can be inferred from the fact that
her GP found he could do little, and referred her to the nearby Carlton Hayes
Hospital. Carlton Hayes dealt with various forms of mental illness and instabil-
ity, and for Larkin this prospect of a living purgatory was made no less dreadful
by the fact that he had for at least a month been suffering from a persistent
stomach disorder and was booked to undergo a barium meal and X-ray in Hull
in late January, these being the tests generally employed to identify cancers.

Between his mother's return from Carlton Hayes and his own return to
Hull he met up with Monica, and they decided upon an impromptu visit
to somewhere that might relieve the preponderant sense of gloom. They

went south to the Sussex coast and stayed in Chichester: pretty, quintessentially English and at that time of the year almost empty. It was here in the cathedral that they encountered the tomb of the Fitzalans, Earl and Countess of Arundel. Larkin scribbled some notes, including details provided by the cathedral authorities on the history of the monument, but he was not sure at present what he would do with them. The resulting poem, 'An Arundel Tomb', would become one of his best known and most frequently cited and reprinted. He wrote it during the two weeks following his tests in mid-February 1956, before he knew the results.

Below the finished poem on the manuscript draft he wrote that 'Love isn't stronger than death just because statues hold hands for 600 years', which is generally taken to reflect the poem's mood of cynical detachment, but something more than this emerges in 'An Arundel Tomb'.

Among its diction and syntax is found a light distribution of registers that are, if not quite anachronistic, self-consciously unusual. 'Their proper habits vaguely shown' carries a hint of the naughty ambiguity of the Renaissance lyricist, and the words 'lie in stone' would, if found in a poem three centuries older than this, prompt a suspicion that the verb 'lie' is playing beyond its apparent reference to a recumbent final posture. This suspicion is further encouraged in the final stanza, in which we learn that: 'Time has transfigured them into / Untruth.'

Many commentators upon the poem have failed to recognise that its speaker is robustly unpersuaded by everything that he apprehends, that the poem is in truth an affirmation of cynical disbelief, both in the significance of love as anything beyond the emblematic, and in the possibility of there being something after death. Such misreadings testify to the brilliance of Larkin's counterpointing of the respectful, deferential manner of the poem against what it actually says.

The closing stanza could make a claim to being the most calculated, beautifully misleading use of syntax in English verse:

> ... The stone fidelity
> They hardly meant has come to be
> Their final blazon, and to prove
> Our almost-instinct almost true:
> What will survive of us is love.

Read with emphasis upon the euphoric cascade of verbs and nouns – 'stone fidelity', 'has come to be', 'their final blazon', 'instinct', 'true' – the last line appears to be a triumphant celebration of what it says. But the deceptively innocuous modifiers 'hardly', and, twice, 'almost' assassinate this optimistic motif; and 'almost true' will always be a lie. He sent Monica an early draft and offered his own comments on what prompts our desire to be entombed near our loved ones: 'love being stronger than death' is, he concludes, a 'sentiment ... only justifiable if love can stop people dying', which, of course, it cannot.

On four occasions during the eight weeks following their trip to Chichester, Larkin sent Monica versions of these lines, and she would not have recognised that they were as much a comment on the two of them as a reflection of the monument to the earl and countess.

The words interact like notes in a finely crafted piece of music, and we have a record of how Larkin arrived at this wonderful act of synthesis. His letter to Monica of 26 February 1956 was the last in which he would consult her on the poem. He included the penultimate version of the closing stanza.

> Time has transfigured them into
> Untruth. The stone fidelity
> They hardly meant has come to be
> Their final blazon, fit to prove
> Our nearest instinct nearly true:
> All that survives of us is love.

He points out that 'the "almost" line wouldn't do if the last line was to start with All ... a "subtle" penult line would strengthen a "simple" last line.' Listening to him working towards the completed draft is fascinating enough, but so are the metaphysical speculations that accompany his stylistic tinkering. These might seem based on abstractions were it not for the fact that they tie directly into Larkin's more specific musings on his love for Monica, or to be more honest his confessions on being unable to particularise his feelings for her.

> This leads naturally onto love being stronger than death: I expect I'm being rather silly, but it is sentiment that does seem to me only justifiable if love *can* stop people dying, which I don't think it can, or not provably.

Amis and undergraduate friends in a quadrangle of St John's College, Oxford. Amis is fourth from right; sixth is Edward du Cann, seventh Norman Iles and ninth Nick Russel.

Patsy Strang in Belfast, 1951.

LEFT The Amis family in Swansea. 'Patsy says their house is *filthy*. I pressed her: "As filthy as Kingsley's?"' (Larkin to Monica, 16 October 1952)

BELOW The Amis family outside 24 The Grove, Swansea. From left: Philip (named after Larkin), Hilly holding Sally, Kingsley, Martin. 'It's the most beautiful personal poem I've ever read, and I've put it in my special box of letters and things, to keep for her.' (Hilly to Larkin, 26 January 1954, thanking him for 'Born Yesterday', written shortly after the birth of Sally)

The tomb of the Fitzalans in Chichester Cathedral, visited by Larkin and Monica in 1956.
'The stone fidelity / They hardly meant...' ('An Arundel Tomb')

Anthony Powell, Kingsley Amis, Philip Larkin and Hilly Amis, 1958. 'The lunch with Powell took place at the Ivy (K paid) and I was wondering what he'd be like ... I didn't *mind* him, but felt no tremendous admiration.' (Larkin to Monica, 10 October 1958)

Bruce Montgomery in the mid-1960s.

Amis in Cambridge, 1962. 'KINGSLEY AMIS TO QUIT STUFFY CAMBRIDGE', *Daily Telegraph*, 21 December 1962.

LEFT Maeve Brennan in 32 Pearson Park, Larkin's flat in Hull, 1961.

BELOW Larkin's mother, Eva, in the conservatory of 32 Pearson Park, Hull. 'Philip told me she liked me – even to the extent that she hoped he would marry me.' (Maeve Brennan)

Elizabeth Jane Howard and Kingsley Amis, 1970s. 'Have read [*One Fat Englishman*] myself ... it's not an especially good book to my mind ... "To Jane" E. J. Howard? ... How my friends outsoar the shadow of my night.' (Larkin to Monica, 12 November 1963)

LEFT Larkin at Coldstream, 1971, photographed by Monica shortly before he urinated over the sign.

RIGHT Monica at Coldstream, photographed by Larkin before she photographed him.

Kingsley Amis in London, early 1980s.

Of course love is not just a word: I don't mean to be 'cynical' about it. Nor do I want to enlist myself under it because, again, it isn't just a word, and I can see clearly that my life isn't governed by it. Some bright lad (E. M. F.?) said the opposite of love wasn't hate but individuality (personality, egotism) and I've been feeling increasingly that it is this that keeps me from love – I mean love isn't just something extra, it's a definite acceptance of the fact that you aren't the most important person in the world. Of course I'm not speaking of love as an emotion but as a *motive*, that leads to action, which seems to me the only real proof of a quality or feeling.

His comments are a distillation of the letter to her on 2 October 1955 in which he admits to emotional 'self-centred[ness]'.

It was during the mid-1950s that Larkin found his essential voice as a poet, and the part played in this by his relationships with Amis and Monica cannot be understated. Even before *Lucky Jim*, Amis inhibited him as a novelist. Larkin was intellectually far more adventurous than his friend but he preferred to remodel his opinions and tastes in accordance with Amis's view that he was his temperamental double. He was not, but in those early years he was prepared to make concessions to maintain a friendship he valued more than any other. Amis's early success eroded Larkin's affection for him, but envy was not the cause. Instead, he gradually became aware of the fact that he had become Amis's anonymous, unacknowledged co-author. The role he played in the writing and revisions of *Lucky Jim* is well documented, but there was a more insidious process at work whereby Larkin's double role as Amis's confessor and family friend, particularly his closeness with Hilly, had become the engine for Amis's signature method of layering his stories as secrets, sparingly disclosed and preserved during their telling and open only to the reader.

Many of Larkin's poems of the early 1950s – notably 'Poetry of Departures', 'Toads' and 'Success Story' – are self-interrogations, too well-written to be treated as solipsistic, but at the same time partial and questioning, as if he is unhappy not with who he is – pessimism was his creative treasury – but rather that some unnamed presence is forever frustrating his attempts to write about anything but his feelings of inadequacy.

His finest poems of the mid-1950s, particularly 'Church Going', 'An Arundel Tomb' and 'The Whitsun Weddings', owe much to the presence of Monica, in part because he valued her comments on them and they involved places and states of mind special to the two of them. And there is something less considered, and in that more compelling, about her effect on his maturing as a poet. His letters to her involve a special, and for her often painful, degree of candour and only in his finest verse from this period do we encounter a comparable gallery of diverse, sometimes incongruous, traits and disclosures. His relationship with her enabled him to procure for his poetry an ingenuous version of the real Philip Larkin. As we have seen, his letters to her from the beginning of 1953 onwards are like none of those he wrote to his closest friends, or lovers. In the latter one can always detect a choreographing of emotions along with a calculated rationing of facts. For Monica, typically, there is an overture involving mundane and unashamedly tedious details of his existence.

> I'm sitting in my, for once, overheated room, listening to *Porgy & Bess* from Brussels, but it's a hell of a bore except for the two famous tunes, neither of wch have been played yet. This is the only sheet of paper I have here – at least, I can't see any more, & I know I left a pad in my desk at the Library. Well, to give this place its due, the weather has been splendid yesterday & today. I have been quite transported by the sun, warm air, bees still burrowing into late flowers, the beautiful chill mauve blue of Michaelmas daisies in the churchyard; and in the villages, when I rode out this afternoon, the thick stacks behind the warm brick farmhouses. The sky was pale blue, with the immoveable small curly clouds of autumn in it. Yesterday – after a degree congregation and lunch-eon of *surpassing* foulness – the village seemed quite lovely.

Then there will be a shift to an acceptance of others as part of his world.

> I went to the local library and strolled very slowly back up the main street, pausing to buy two teaspoons and a root of celery, feeling contented with the content that comes from feeling that the world is all right, even if I am all wrong. The pavement outside the Union Hall (over the Cooperative Stores) was scattered with confetti, and inside they were dancing and drinking and singing *Let the rest of the world go by*.

He feels a sense of unaffiliated tenderness, not denying himself the 'contented' observation of moments of commitment, happiness, experienced by others.

Next he turns to a more recondite contemplative mood: 'as you know, or have guessed, I am always, emotionally, "on the hop"! by feeling bound to "explain" *why*, if you mean so much to me, I don't "prewve it". I always feel so defensive about this' (L to Monica, 9 October 1955). It sounds like a prose version of one of his poems.

When he wrote to her of Amis, that 'I've grown tired of all my friends except you ... I'm through with this. Basically. You have shown me better things!' (3 May 1955), his declaration was prophetic but not quite in the way that it seemed at the time. As far as Amis knew they would remain friends, but Monica had enabled Larkin to sideline his creative preoccupation with him.

In 1957 Amis had applied for the post of Visiting Fellow in Creative Writing at Princeton University in the United States, was accepted and arranged with Swansea to give up his lectureship for the forthcoming academic year.

By the end of the 1950s Swansea had become the fulcrum of Amis's personal, professional and creative life. It had provided him with his first full-time job, his and Hilly's first permanent home, their children had grown up there, *Lucky Jim* had been born there and without it Lewis and Bowen would not have existed. It enfolded and bespoke the tensions of his marriage, which had on several occasions almost ended there but had survived, precariously. Leaving it would not, he knew, miraculously transform his personality, habits and inclinations, but at the same time he suspected that a complete change of place and environment, a detachment from ever-present memories, would be at least a gesture towards optimism, alteration. He began to think seriously about leaving Wales for good during his academic year in the United States in 1958–9. Princeton had offered him a two-year extension of his contract, and he was tempted.

One Fat Englishman would be based on many of his experiences in the United States, but perversely. A more economical and honest account of the visit was written, to Larkin, shortly after his return to Swansea (30 July 1959). He had met and listened to a number of jazz players who had featured in his letters to Larkin over the previous fifteen years; the imagined presences behind the records had become real. Buster Bailey 'played far hotter and better than I've ever heard him on records, [and] yelled out during a

[Speedy] Jones drum solo: "Ain't he the most, Kingsley?"' Along with the
jazz Amis was impressed by the energy of the place:

> for the first half of my time there I was boozing and working harder than I
> have ever done since the Army ... for the second half I was boozing and fuck-
> ing harder than at any time at all. On the second count I found myself at it
> practically full time.

A year earlier, just before setting out for America, he had informed Larkin
(30 July 1958) of how, apart from Hilly not wanting him to 'make with the
old prok swrod [pork sword] very much', he had felt for the first time in his
life generally unenthused by the prospect of sex in general: obviously the
United States had re-energised him.

The Amises' permanent US base was in Edgerstoune Road, about two
miles from the Princeton Campus. The houses were 'ranch style', open plan,
post-war constructions with spacious gardens opening on to woodland
and meadows. The area was within commuting distance of New York, and
the lifestyle of most of its residents more than justified the evocations of
the period and region fifty years later in series such as *Mad Men*. In fact,
the Amis's closest neighbours, John and Jean McAndrew, could have featured
in the programme. He was a stylish, sophisticated advertising executive
and his wife matched him in her taste for drink-fuelled socialising. Compared
with the drab environs of Swansea – robustly provincial in its habits and,
physically, still carrying scars of the Blitz – the place seemed like nirvana.
The McAndrews had five children, all girls and close in age to Martin and
Philip, and the two families soon began to treat each other's homes as open
houses, so much so that within a month of their arrival Amis had begun an
affair with Jean, and Hilly, more seriously, with John. As with Henry Fairlie,
she came close to considering their relationship as a long-term alternative to
her marriage. Amis's fling with Jean was, characteristically, more casual; he
also had liaisons with graduate students in Princeton and Boston and with a
New York publisher.

In a 1959 letter to Larkin he is ambivalently resigned to not going back to
America, despite the attractions. 'They have more energy than we have, and
they are better at enjoying themselves. [We] both want to go there again ...
though not, I feel definitely at the moment, to stay' (30 July 1959). In fact,

Hilly had provided the common-sense arguments that financially he still needed tenure, and that three years abroad would disrupt their children's lives and education. He knew that his best option was another academic job in England. Along with its potentially beneficial effects upon his family life, a move would, Amis hoped, help him in his attempt to evolve a different method of writing novels.

Within two years of his return from the United States he would find a permanent job in Cambridge, but Princeton was important for other reasons. When he was there he continued with, indeed accelerated, his Swansea-regime of serial infidelity, but because he was now in an alien, if welcoming, environment he was granted the opportunity to step outside his life. Changed circumstances brought into sharper relief his own degree of hedonistic licence and as a result he wrote two novels about versions of himself that he found by degrees shameful, culpable and inescapable.

In *Take a Girl Like You* the principal male figure, Patrick Standish, is, like his predecessors, autobiographical, but while they variously improved upon their creator, Patrick is the first uncensored version of Amis. The 1950s men all had at least the potential for serial philandering, but, with the exception of Lewis's single act of infidelity, they restrained themselves. Patrick is a prodigious libertine. He inherits their sardonic view of the world and, like them, shares an extended version of this with his narrator, but while Amis in his 1950s writing had chosen targets who largely deserved ridicule, Patrick seems to enjoy the crueller aspects of making fun of people, irrespective of their hapless vulnerability. Sam Dawson, a colleague at Swansea, recalls that while Amis was celebrated as an entertainer, these same talents often hurt and offended his more sensitive victims. 'He would exaggerate the potentially absurd in people. He could make people very uncomfortable by playing upon their absurdities. But his mimicry was done so well that he made it difficult for people to take exception to it.' Patrick, too, exploits his acquaintances' fears of appearing to spoil the fun. Of the 1950s men, Lewis is the most candid regarding his own uncertainties and vulnerabilities, but in general Amis presents them as tough, transparent pragmatists. Patrick carries us into private states of disillusionment, weakness, almost depression, which were honest reflections of Amis's occasional states of mind.

By drawing upon aspects of himself that had not previously featured in his published work, Amis had gone some way towards a new mode of writing, but not far enough. He needed another character, and he invented Jenny Bunn.

She involved Amis for the first time in the creation of a mindset that was not his own, and one that evinced the experiences of a woman. In a 1974 interview Amis reflected on how difficult the novel had been, how he was 'so nervous' that he had 'made at least twelve drafts of the first chapter' (Dale Salwak, *Kingsley Amis: Modern Novelist*, p. 109); the first chapter is Jenny's. What he did not disclose was the exact nature of his difficulties and how he overcame them. Jenny is based essentially upon the one person whom Amis knew almost as well as himself: Hilly. This raised problems, the most straightforward being the prospect of a journalist suggesting that his new departure was actually a reworking of his earlier autobiographical enterprises, this time including his wife. The London media and literati had a basic knowledge of Amis's personal history, and if he were to retain his and Hilly's story at the core of the novel he would need enough camouflage to make comparisons tortuously difficult.

Hilly was neither working class nor from the north. She was certainly not a moralist, but nor is Jenny. Jenny might appear to embody outdated moral principles, yet she is as much a realist as an idealist; other people's lives are not her business. Her determination to preserve her virginity until marriage is pragmatic, a means of realising a personal objective. Hilly had sex with Amis before they married, but their married relationship became an extended version of the state of conflict that exists between Patrick and Jenny. For Hilly, like Jenny, marriage should involve monogamy, not because the institution enshrined a religious or abstract doctrine, but for the straightforward, practical reason that extramarital sex caused distress and unhappiness.

Martin Amis read the novel when he was about fourteen and, without discussing it with his father, he recognised his mother in Jenny. 'She [Hilly] was a paradox – yes, she was odd, rebellious, but she was also principled. She would never judge, but nor would she *fake* anything, *invent* anything. She was, is, an individual. Yes, Jenny was certainly a version of her.'

As well as being a slightly bizarre act of confession, the novel also enables Amis to rewrite his past as a sequence of events of which he is the principal cause but for which he is not entirely responsible. He recreates their relationship as something that involves a kind of fatalistic inevitability. The external forces favour his lifestyle and are marshalled against Hilly.

At the end of the novel, after Patrick has had sex with her against her will, Jenny arrives at the Thompsons', with whom she lodged, and finds waiting for her Miss Sinclair, her headmistress.

Miss Sinclair 'look[ed] her up and down from thatch hair to muddy shoes, with wine splashed dress paying an important part in between'. She is evidently hungover and besmeared with the debris of indulgence. There is a silent exchange of signals, and Miss Sinclair states, 'There's no need to put yourself out, Miss Bunn. I'm sure you have lots of things to do.' She gives Jenny the up-and-down treatment in shortened form, then finishes: 'Goodbye.' The immense significance of her closing word is evident to Jenny and the reader. She is now deemed to be part of the world she tried so honourably to resist. Soon after Miss Sinclair has left, there is a knock on the door, and it is Patrick. He had been sitting in his car round the corner, waiting. Suddenly and without explanation, she knows she must return to him.

'She knew more or less what the future would be like, and how different it would be from what she had hoped', recalling, perhaps, that Hilly's first discovery of Amis's infidelities would be repeated many times over the next thirteen years. But Jenny resigns herself to the inevitable:

> but she felt now that there had been something selfish in that hope, that a lot of time she had been pursuing not what was right but what she wanted. And she could hardly pretend that what she had got was not worth having at all. She must learn to take the rough with the smooth, just like everybody else. (Amis, *Take a Girl Like You*, p. 317)

Larkin does not feature as a character in the novel but obliquely he informs it. Amis kept carbons of most of his letters to his friend, and as a consequence he was able to conduct two dialogues, or to be more accurate he took charge of a triangle of communication involving the figures who occupied the two other points, Larkin and Hilly. In *Take a Girl Like You*, alternate chapters, albeit each in the third person, are dominated by the mindsets of Patrick and Jenny. Jenny is commendably transparent in that her private and public personae rarely clash, while Patrick sometimes tells blatant lies about his feelings and his activities.

For the reader the effect is frustrating and quite brilliantly executed. The characters are, like Amis's best, beautifully credible; within a few pages' acquaintance we feel as though we have met and got to know them. As their story unfolds, and as each hands over control chapter-by-chapter, we want to get into the narrative and, depending on our disposition, tell Patrick that he should deal more honestly with Jenny or warn her that despite her doubts about him he is much worse than she thinks. We cannot do either because it is a work of fiction, but the energy from this dynamic comes from real life. Larkin, who knew the true Amis, was also aware of Hilly's sense of distress, while knowing she was alert to only half the story, and was effectively turned into the mute witness to all this, despite his better instincts. When we read Amis's letters to Larkin, we feel the same sense of unease that arises from the juggling in the novel between subterfuge, disclosure and unknowing.

For example, Chapters 17 to 20 are Patrick's and involve his trip with Ormerod to London, where he has sex with Joan, a woman to whom his friend has introduced him in a Soho nightclub.

Jenny never learns of what happens in London. In fact, at the end of Chapter 16 – just as Patrick sets off – we find her musing on whether she should commit herself to their uncertain relationship, and on his return at the beginning of Chapter 21 he declares his love for her and she replies in kind. Certainly Jenny's thoughts about the future would have been altered if she had known of Joan, but she would not necessarily have been shocked – she is shrewd and perceptive enough. What would have stunned her was a knowledge of the cynical, almost nihilistic attitude that underpinned Patrick's lechery.

Amis began the novel before his departure for the US but Chapters 16 to 21 were written after his return and Patrick's excursion was based on fact. Amis wrote to Larkin on 15 December 1959, apologised for sending no letters at all during his time away, and as usual updated him on the state of his sex life. The only difference between this menu of boasts and disclosures, leavened with faux guilt, and the many others Larkin had received over the previous twelve years was that in this letter it is difficult to distinguish truth from fiction. Amis is not trying to deceive Larkin, at least not intentionally, but often he appears to find it difficult fully to distinguish the world of his ongoing novel from the one he inhabits.

Jenny caught by the back hair and pulled viciously downward. Anna cried out; Jenny sniggered and thrust her c – to encourage me while I do all manner of filthy articles for the money, like a fool ... Still haven't finished my adultery poem, but shall have a bash today before plugning on with Jenny ...

Were it not for the fact that Amis had already named for Larkin the personnel of his novel, he might easily have assumed that 'Jenny' and 'Anna' were two of his numerous sexual conquests. He continues the report as follows.

Tackling of adultery, my activities in this direction, which have ramified some in the last few months, received a severe check when Hilly found some letters I had received and initiated the most strenuous and painful row we have ever had. I am to give all that up, it appears, with an exemption clause covering my Yank girl when she turns up over here in the summer. Trouble is it's so hard to give all that up, habit of years and all that, and such bloody good fun too. Especially just after finding the most splendid busty redhead in an ideal location. But being walked out on by H. (and kids), the sure-fire consequence of any further discovery, is a rather unwelcome prospect too. You can't have it both ways, you see. Got to make up your mind which you want and stick to it.

The shift from the state of the novel to that of his marriage is so seamless that Jenny appears to belong in the same category as his 'Yank girl' – who had become sufficiently besotted with Amis in the States to have begun her graduate research in the UK – and the 'busty redhead'.

 Larkin had yet to see anything of *Take a Girl Like You*, but as Amis completed it he began to feel that as witness to Amis's life he was being offered a remarkably accurate foretaste. The letter, as he would find, closely resembles those parts of the book dominated by Patrick, involving private revelations of his shamelessly dissolute temperament, which we know he will reshape for the benefit of Jenny, aka Hilly.

Larkin regularly confided in Monica on Amis's apparent addiction to dissimulation, something that went beyond serial infidelity. In a letter of 12 May 1958 he commented on a recent radio broadcast in which the famous novelist had been invited to read and comment upon his favourite poems.

How curious Kingsley is, presenting all those quiet little poems! These rustic moralists! When he never puts his nose out of doors except to go to the boozer, *or meet his latest mistress*, and wouldn't get on a horse for a hatful of golden guineas. The opulence of his private life doesn't extend to his taste does it. I suppose he was tailoring a particular programme to this theme, but I think it was a bit silly as it was *personal* choice: they ought to have been as mixed up as possible, like his women. (L to Monica, 12 May 1958, Bod)

While he did not make the true cause of his offence explicit, Monica would surely have realised that he was embittered by yet another of appropriation by Amis of territory he thought was immune from their exchanges. It was to Monica alone that Larkin sent elegiac accounts of his love for the country-side and wildlife: now Amis was busily telling wireless listeners that he had a taste for rusticity which contrasted fascinatingly with his reputation as an urban, metropolitan presence.

The previous year Amis had reported that

Life continues to be blody hecktic ... I cut a recent dinner to take my young lady (ole Mavis) 8, cutting therefore a dinner of the Old Dyneforions, at which ... I learned later, I ... was scheduled as guest of honour, sitting between the Mare and the Director of Education and all that. Glad I didn't go but wish I'd devised a better excuse. 'Your absence was remarked upon' I was told. Ho hum. Mavis thought you were very attractive. Po bum. She is a dear little thing, that one. (A to L, 9 March 1957, Bod)

Amis had introduced him to Mavis at a party at his house, and the invitation to Swansea had come from Hilly. Amis in the letter exudes a sense of smug triumphalism. He clearly enjoys his regime of dishonesty, especially since it now also involves telling lies to local dignitaries – and in this he was rejoicing in becoming a version of Lewis in *That Uncertain Feeling*. Larkin, he knew, was existing in a realm of the mundane. Was he also aware of how his torrent of boasts would make his friend feel? His hint that Mavis's estimation of him as 'attractive' was a reflection of her charitable temperament suggests either that he was not aware, or that he did not care.

Patrick's excursion to London with Ormerod is based on a weekend in the city in August shortly after Amis's return from the States, involving Amis, Robert

Conquest and Larkin, without their various partners. Larkin sent a report to Monica.

> The weekend ... was two sauna-baths of train journeys enclosing a Saturday spent entirely with Bob and Kingsley ... on the whole enjoying myself, though acutely aware, once more, of the difference in the lives of us – their lives are to mine as mine is to yours, as regards incident and sensation. (L to Monica, 25 August 1959)

He feels like the reader of a novel; caught up in the lives of the characters but at the same time detached from them, watching from the outside. He continues: 'We spent most of the day drinking ... As usual everyone is having affairs with all the old people and lots of new ones.' Specifically, Amis was seeing his 'Yank girl' while reigniting his long-term affair with Mavis Nicholson. All of this, as with Patrick's trip to London, was conducted in private, well-appointed premises: 'He [Conquest] was in a flat in St George's Square, rented from 3 school mistresses.'

Hilly wrote to Larkin just before he received Amis's letter of 15 December in which he had told of his wife's discovery of incriminating letters. Some of these were from the Yank girl and referred to the weekend in London. Hilly's tone is generally resigned but sometimes she allows her anger to break through: 'the fucking bastard [Amis] deserves to be shot'. Her comments on John McAndrew are curious, as though their relationship is something she has to endure. 'I'm in love with a filthy yank, he's a Catholic with 5 girls and is 47 years. Oh well (secret).' One must assume that the secret involves her love for him, since Amis was fully aware of their affair. The weary mood is maintained in her report on what her existence actually involves, despite the affair. 'Life with Amis remains the same and I'm sure nothing will ever change much in this way – and I suppose I'm lucky in gleaning the droppings of his success' (December 1959; no specific date or postmark, Hull). The temper of this letter is strikingly different from the witty, sometimes comically heroic manner of virtually all her previous correspondence with Larkin, and given that it was written at the close of 1959 just as Amis was completing the final draft of *Take a Girl Like You*, one cannot help but note the similarities between it and the mindset of Jenny as the novel closes.

She shook her head again, but this time meaning that she agreed ...

'You know, Patrick Standish, I should really never have met you. Or I should have got rid of you while I still had the chance. But I couldn't think how to. And it's a bit late for that now, isn't it?' (Amis, *Take a Girl Like You*, p. 317)

That Amis and Larkin did not communicate directly on the novel is not surprising. Amis had long ceased to apologise or even acknowledge for Larkin the parallels between the world he constructed and his fiction and Larkin by now had reached the point of forgetting that what he was about to read was not something he had already encountered.

He wrote to Judy Egerton that he 'disliked' Patrick 'and K's coyly indulgent attitude to him, and found it all rather remote from what I think of as reality' (21 October 1960). One should not treat this as him regarding the novel as implausible; as he had commented to Monica, frequently, Amis's life defied credibility. It evoked the type of 'reality' experienced by Amis, and indeed Conquest, which others indeed regard as 'remote'. 'Julian [Ormerod] leant heavily on the Conquest *persona*, I thought,' he added.

His comments to Monica were equally telling. Following Amis's first reports on the invention of Jenny and Patrick, he writes, 'even discounting my envy-inspired rancour ... I'm not sure I find it all particularly sympathetic. I only wish I felt any confidence that I was the tortoise to his hare, but the way I feel now (about 9 months) I'm certainly not: I'm not anything to anybody's anything' (L to Monica, 11 August 1959).

Throughout the letter Larkin seems unsure of his frame of reference, shifting uneasily between his feelings regarding Amis himself and a more oblique sense of Amis being no longer distinguishable from the world he creates in his fiction. In a later letter: 'TAGLY [*Take a Girl Like You*] is hitting the jackpot – over 20,000, film rights gone. Can't stop him now. He's there. He's arrived. Not down here with me and John Holloway, but up there with Arnold Bennett' (L to Monica, 10 November 1960). 'Down here' and 'up there' seem to refer to their respective rankings in the literary establishment, but in the broader context of Larkin's knowledge that Amis has built his reputation as a novelist upon a life of subterfuge and indulgence, the phrase takes on a far more private nuance. Larkin, 'down here', recognises that his verse will forever involve a sanguine appreciation of failure.

He was running out of patience with Amis and soon he would put their friendship into a state of suspension.

7

The Third Man

Larkin's comment to Judy Egerton on Amis's having 'leant heavily on the Conquest persona' in his creation of Julian Ormerod is accurate enough, but its hint at censure requires comment. Robert Conquest had by 1960 become an enormously important figure for both of them.

Much has been written about the Movement, and as far as the undisputed facts are concerned little more needs to be said. The term was given its capital letter by J. D. Scott in an anonymous *Spectator* leader on 1 October 1954, but it had for several years been attached by reviewers, albeit tentatively, to a definite article. 'The' Movement referred to a group of writers – mostly but not exclusively poets – who had started to publish in the late 1940s. By the early 1950s reviewers were beginning to notice common features in their work. Most frequently they counterpointed informal, sometimes even demotic, contemporary locutions against traditional verse forms and throughout the poem maintained a prose-like coherence.

Donald Davie, himself deemed a Movement poet, argued that they had revived a Popian blend of accessibility, correctness and journalistic relevance; he called them 'the New Augustans'. The critic Anthony Hartley (1954) thought they had as much in common with the sardonic, conversational ironies of the School of Donne.

The 1953 PEN anthology contained verse by Larkin, Amis, Elizabeth Jennings and Robert Conquest, who edited the collection. The archetypal Movement collection, *New Lines* (1956), was also edited by Conquest and contained verse by himself, D. J. Enright, John Holloway, John Wain, Elizabeth Jennings, Donald Davie, Amis and Larkin. In the introduction, Conquest propounded a manifesto. Poetry, he wrote, should be 'empirical in its attitude to all that comes', should 'resist the agglomeration of unconscious commands' and 'maintain a rational structure and comprehensible language'.

Like practically all other literary groups the Movement has suffered from a general wish to dissociate expressed in varying degrees by its supposed members, which is, of course, understandable given that few if any literary artists are content to have their individuality compromised by collective association. At the same time, however, the Movement can make a minor claim to uniqueness as probably the only cultural enterprise which is disliked by virtually everyone who writes about it. It has earned little more than grudging tolerance from academics and routine helpings of opprobrium from assemblies of poets, novelists and dramatists who regard affiliation to conservative or traditional habits of composition as the equivalent of betrayal. Blake Morrison's book *The Movement* is acclaimed justifiably as the best scholarly account of the people involved and their work, yet throughout it Morrison's prose puts one in mind of a court pathologist's report upon a tragic accident. Due consideration is given to all involved, commendable acts are noted, but it would, of course, be unthinkable actually to celebrate the events.

The question of why attitudes to the Movement rarely shift outside a spectrum between stoic acceptance and distaste has not been fully addressed, but the answer is self-evident. Never before in literary history has there been a collection of writers who appear to deserve, indeed welcome, the epithet 'reactionary'. Even the Augustans, with whom Davie concedes tenuous association, can claim to be innovators. True, they venerated principles of order, symmetry and transparency in poetic writing, but they saw these as radical alternatives to the unlicensed indulgences of the Renaissance: something new was happening, the poetic equivalent of the sharp symmetries of Bauhaus. After modernism, however, nothing unprecedented could ever be done again. Certainly reworkings of modernist precedent offered, and still offer, virtually limitless possibilities to writers so disposed, but reworkings are all they can be – variations, improvements, sidelong glances upon or self-referring acknowledgements of the work of Pound, Eliot, Joyce, Woolf *et al.* In short, after modernism literary history came if not to an end then to an endless network of recirculations. Was the only alternative a return to the past?

Conquest in his introduction to *New Lines* does not bother even to mention modernism. Instead, he begins by examining how the poets of the previous three decades had failed to unshackle themselves from its influence. While not actually referring to the Auden group he accuses them of giving the 'Id ... too much of a say' and with similarly polite discretion he laments the more recent 'debilitating' obsession with metaphor, 'diffuse and sentimental verbiage, or hollow technical pirouettes' without naming Dylan Thomas as principal offender. Having pressed the point that the poets of the volume have successfully detached themselves from modernism and its aftermath, he raises the inevitable question of whether they are engaged in some kind of nostalgic atavism. 'Restorations are not repetitions. The atmosphere, the attack of these poets is as concentratedly contemporary as could be imagined.' Poetry informed by contemporaneity is, he argues, by its very nature new. Just as significantly, these poets are the first literary grouping whose unity is guaranteed by the fact that they neither share nor individually pay allegiance to 'great systems of theoretical constructs'; their work stands determinedly separate from anything resembling an aesthetic or intellectual formula.

In 1958 William Van O'Connor, an American academic, wrote to Larkin asking him if he had felt as though he was part of something that could be treated as a Movement, an assembly of writers with recognisably shared characteristics. Larkin replied that he had never even met Elizabeth Jennings, Thom Gunn, John Holloway or Iris Murdoch. He conceded a 'recent and intermittent acquaintance' (2 April 1958) with Donald Davie and a slightly closer one with John Wain. Amis, he stated, was the only alleged member of this nebulous formation whom he knew well. Larkin's impression of indifference might seem to imply that he thought the Movement a chimera, but at the same time one suspects that he is not so much denying its existence as reflecting his puzzlement at how such an enterprise could have been brought about without any kind of collaboration. In a slightly obtuse manner he is underlining Conquest's point that the Movement was born out of a reaction to recent literary history. Its members were escaping the net of modernism, and their similarities bore witness to the fact that this exodus could only lead them in one direction; as Conquest put it in the introduction to *New Lines*, 'to be empirical in [their] attitude to all that comes' and to 'maintain a rational structure and comprehensible language'.

The prevailing opinion is that by about 1957–8 most members of the Movement had already begun to disown it, which is not so much an untruth as a misinterpretation of the facts. Certainly during the couple of years following the appearance of Conquest's volume (1956), Enright's *Poets of the 1950s* (1955) and G. S. Fraser's *Poetry Now* (1956), those included in each were taking the opportunity to reflect upon what, if anything, had happened, and puzzlement rather than outright denial is the keynote. The factor that caused virtually all of the poets involved so much confusion was the Movement's unforeseen and unplanned advent. Apart from the disclosure by the likes of Conquest that they had participated in this broad, discernible transition and crystallisation of literary mores, none appeared to be aware that it was happening. The result was often ambivalence prompted by a conflict between opportunism and disbelief. In a letter to Patsy Strang in 1954, Larkin writes:

> People like Anthony Hartley and G. S. Fraser are very stupidly crying us all up these days: take my word for it, people will get very sick of us (or *them*; that is, Wain, Gunn, Davie, Amis) and then, UNLESS they produce some unassailably good work, I think the tide will turn rapidly and they will rapidly be discredited. I'm sure I don't care. (9 October 1954)

The last sentence is disingenuous to say the least. He certainly did care, and although he refers to reviews by Fraser and Hartley that contributed to a sense that something was indeed happening, he would also have recalled a letter from Amis earlier that year that reads like a celebration of fantasy made real. Along with reports on sales of the film rights for *Lucky Jim* and his daily baskets of fan mail, he tells of a recent trip to Oxford and London where, of course, he was celebrated as the most outstanding new arrival, a poet who could also write hilarious fiction. Along the way he had met Hartley, J. D. Scott, C. P. Snow, G. S. Fraser, Harry Hoff and Ken Tynan, all keen to offer him unstinting praise. 'I feel in a sense that "they can't stop me now" ... There's no doubt, you know, but we are getting to be a movement, even if the only people in it we like apart from ourselves are each other' (A to L, 14 March 1954). In 1960 Amis would dismiss the Movement as a 'phantom', but in truth what he meant was that it was real enough to have served a purpose in 1954–5, when Amis rode its tide of publicity, but that by 1960, when he had published three more novels, it could conveniently disappear. He wrote: 'the less appealing side of the Angry Young Men business was that it embodied and encouraged a Philistine, paraphrasing, digest-compiling attitude to literature, one which was favoured not only outside the phantom 'movement' (on the daily's book pages) but 'inside it as well' (Kingsley Amis, 'Lone Voices', *Encounter* (1960), vol. XV, no. 1, reprinted in Kingsley Amis, *What Became of Jane Austen? and Other Questions*, p. 163).

Amis was irritated by the critical and journalistic inclination to treat literature like politics, to subsume individual writers within a broader doctrine that might attract the person who 'would rather read a book as a purée of trends and attitudes than as a work of art having its own unique, unparaphrasable qualities' (ibid.).

Larkin in 1954 was beginning to feel left out, hence his only partially successful attempt in the letter to Patsy to disguise envy as indifference and scepticism, but within six months he, too, was moving closer towards the centre of things and his mood changed accordingly. To Enright he wrote (26 April 1955) with enthusiasm regarding his selections for the forthcoming volume – in which not only his own verse but his 'Statement' on contemporaneous poetry would be included. He comments on Enright's choices as 'well balanced' and, significantly, 'representative' – from which one might infer that there was something which the volume would represent. A month later he asked Conquest if he could look at a pre-proof copy of the introduction to *New Lines*, indicating that he was aware that it would be treated as a kind of manifesto. Larkin offered sceptical comments on some points – particularly Conquest's contention that the new writers had completely detached themselves from self-conscious literariness; not all of them, averred Larkin – but his most telling sentence is:

> For my part I feel that we have got the method right – plain language, absence of posturings, sense of proportion, humour, abandonment of the dithyrambic ideal – and are waiting for the matter: a fuller and more sensitive response to life as it appears from day to day, and not only on Mediterranean holidays financed by the British Council. (28 May 1955)

A year before this he had no concept of a 'we' with whose 'method' he might concede affinity, and his description of them as 'waiting for the matter' subscribes exactly to Conquest's 'empirical in our attitude to all that comes'.

Two weeks later he wrote again stating that he was 'glad' Conquest had found his comments 'useful' – he had made some slight alterations following

Larkin's letter – and offered further reflections on the nature of this curious community of writers having suddenly discovered themselves. 'I certainly don't think attacks on other people help a "movement": the way to attack bad work is to produce good yourself: that's about all you can do' (10 June 1955). Larkin is referring here to Conquest's distancing of the new writing from any given aesthetic or theoretical confederation, and surmising that in abjuring the support of association they are guaranteeing themselves a form of courageous unity; they will each be judged purely by the quality of their work.

Larkin felt that he was participating in a moment of recognition, that the features which in his view made poetry important were gradually regaining a just and natural ascendancy after approximately four decades of marginalisation. The poets who appeared in *New Lines*, and indeed in the Enright and Fraser volumes, were joined by a thread of affinity made all the more evident by their differences. They had without planning or consultation all been drawn to those mainstays of traditional verse, regular metre and the stanza. These had not, of course, been abandoned in previous decades, but what made the Movement poets recognisably new was that each was prepared to test his or her own temperamental presence, voice, idiom against an abstract structure to see if the former could be at once sustained, sharpened and certainly not obscured by the latter. As a consequence the Movement reminds one of a room of people painted by an exemplary representational artist – a sense of separateness and individualism within and almost in spite of a shared fabric is palpable.

Conquest had begun to discover the existence of the Movement approximately three years earlier. Donald Davie's *Purity of Diction in English Poetry*, published in 1952, proposes a model of literary history involving regular, periodic tensions between radicalism and established convention. He argues that the latter will always eventually restore poetry to an affinity with the reading public, that 'pure' rather than arbitrarily distorted or obscure diction will ultimately triumph. Most significantly Davie claims that the poetry of the mid-twentieth century has faced a greater threat than ever before from the forces of impurity and that there is evidence of an accordingly decisive return to transparency.

Conquest agreed, and found within the work of many of his contemporaries what amounted to a backlash against the pre-war elitism of the avant-garde. What cannot be overstated is his influence upon the period as a back-room choreographer, a man who saw similarities in writers, created channels of communication between them but in no way indicated that what they shared compromised them as unaffiliated figures. He is acclaimed as much for his writings and opinions on modern politics as for his literary endeavours, but there are parallels: he believed that communism and modernism were united in the elevation of the abstract, all-inclusive idea above the private voice.

In June 1952 Kingsley Amis was invited to a party in Chelsea at which the first PEN anthology of verse would be launched (PEN being an organisation founded in the 1920s to promote international freedom of expression). He was a contributor, along with Conquest, with whom he had previously only communicated briefly by letter. Their first meeting in person began formally enough with the discovery that they had each read Davie's book and found it to be both prescient and encouraging. Quite soon and after a few more drinks their focus shifted to other fields of shared interest – particularly caricature, parody and women – involving appropriately enough a recitation by Conquest of 'Mexican Pete', his own sequel to 'Eskimo Nell'. Conquest suggested that they go on for a late dinner, but Amis, already drunk, had to be back in Swansea the following day and regretfully declined the offer.

It was the beginning of a friendship that lasted until Amis's death, and when the latter learned about a year later of Conquest's plans for a collection that would embody Davie's diagnosis he made sure that Conquest was aware of Larkin. *The North Ship* had faded into obscurity by then, but during 1954–5 *The Spectator* had begun to publish several new poems a week, which in various ways gave witness to J. D. Scott's polemical leader article, including four by Larkin, fruits of his discovery of a more confident lyric voice during the last years in Belfast. Amis had encouraged Larkin to approach *The Spectator*, with whose editors and regular contributors he had become well acquainted since the success *of Lucky Jim*. Amis and Wain, already friends of Conquest, were by the end of 1954 involved with plans for *New Lines* and, prompted by Amis, Conquest wrote to Larkin in January 1955 asking him if he would be willing to participate. It was the beginning of their correspondence, and by midsummer they had arranged to meet. Larkin and Monica were to take their summer holiday late that year, in September. They were going to Sark, the smallest and most unusual of the Channel Islands, owned and governed by an aristocrat and having no motor vehicles. It would be another in their by now regular excursions to parts of the UK which satisfied their mutual taste for places remote, mildly idiosyncratic and unfashionable. First, though, they would stay over in London at the Strand Palace Hotel where, Larkin wrote to Conquest, 'I look forward to meeting you ... I don't know the place at all, but I expect we shall be where drinking takes place. I am tall, bespectacled, balding (sounds like Time), probably wearing a sea-water coloured suit' (7 September 1955).

In their letters each had gradually discovered reciprocal opinions on poetry and during the same period learned, vicariously through Amis, something of their respective temperaments and dispositions. In the hotel bar drinks were bought, jovial informality replaced polite curiosity and both soon became aware of why Amis had encouraged them to meet. The Amis–Larkin partnership had found a new member, which meant that subsequently confidentiality would play some part in their exchanges. Monica was present at the Strand Palace, but in October Larkin spent a weekend unaccompanied at the Conquests' house in Hampstead. Larkin had previously informed Conquest of how six of his nine pieces for *New Lines* were due to appear around the same time in a collection of his own, *The Less Deceived*, but that the publisher was a somewhat obscure, provincial organisation, based, coincidentally, in Hull, run by, owned and indeed comprised entirely of a married couple, Jean and George Hartley. Conquest was intrigued and promised to include some reference to 'the Marvell Press' in the introduction to *New Lines*, partly to illustrate his point that the new writers were as yet unrecognised, even snubbed, by the major houses and partly as a promotional boost for Larkin's forthcoming volume.

Following the visit Larkin wrote to him with details of the Marvell Press, congratulated him also on an essay of his recently accepted by *Essays in Criticism*, suggested a meeting with Amis in London in early January 1956 and concluded, 'Glad about the Bizarre – pabulum is very thin these days. "Modèles academiques" – crikey' (9 November 1955). *Bizarre* was a pornographic magazine whose most recent special feature involved what it claimed were French female undergraduates engaged in demonstrably unacademic pursuits. Throughout the next two decades Conquest regularly supplied his friend with magazines and other material that were well before their time with regard to the complexity and sophistication of acts depicted. Nothing particularly perverted would be involved, and it was almost entirely aimed at a composite heterosexual readership, but Larkin remained impressed by its vivid, imaginative spirit. His letters to Conquest are littered with expressions of sincere admiration, such as

> I got the pictures – whacko. I admired the painstaking realism of it – I mean, the teacher did really look like a teacher, and I greatly appreciated the school-like electric bell on the wall. The action and standard of definition left something to be desired – I'll leave you to guess what. (4 July 1959)

The rest of the letter concerns a Donald Davie piece in *The Listener* on the Movement, specifically its most pronounced antagonist, Charles Tomlinson, plus a modest tribute to Conquest for spotting an autobiographical essay by Larkin in the Coventry arts magazine *Umbrella*. It ends, '*Silky* is not v. good: try *The Fabulous Rosina* 216. Most extraordinary tits, like saucers – Areolae, that is, as opposed to breasts'. The detailed close reading that Larkin brings to erotica betrays the temperamental trademark of a New Critic, but what is most remarkable about the letters to Conquest is their likeness to the Amis correspondence. Both resemble surrealist paintings of the mildly farcical Magritte type, where each image is familiar but not quite where it ought to be. The most noticeable difference involves the function and status of women, with the likes of Patsy, Winifred and Ruth featuring in the Amis letters while for Conquest he is mostly preoccupied by their unnamed, glossy counterparts.

It was not that Conquest replaced Amis, but from *Lucky Jim* onwards there was a subtle but discernible change in Larkin's relationship with the latter. Before that, the Larkin–Amis interchanges had been for each of them unique. For everyone else in their respective lives, from closest family through friends to colleagues, a judicious process of editing and selection would come into play, but with each other they shared everything. Once Conquest had joined this exclusive club Larkin gradually began to redistribute his confidences, including in letters remarks which, though certainly not vindictive, carry a hint of envy and resentment. 'I haven't had a letter from Kingsley for ages, despite letters of condolences [on the death of Amis's mother], cheerings up etc. is he cross or just lazy? Of course, now term's started he's got 6 hours work to do every week, mustn't forget that's pretty tough going' (7 May 1957). 'Yes, Swansea's secret weapon screeded me at last, with *some* information regarding his year's experiences [as Writer in Residence at Princeton] but not much. He seems to have spent his time drinking and fucking, as if this should surprise me' (13 August 1959).

Conquest himself has been given due credit as one of the most effective polemicists for the sub-genre of tough, unpretentious writing associated with the Movement, but his role in the lives and work of Amis and Larkin is both engrossing and largely unrecognised. He functioned for both as a strange combination of provocateur and wise uncle.

Born in Great Malvern in 1917, he retained dual US/UK citizenship, and after education at Winchester and Magdalen College, Oxford, and war service in the infantry and intelligence corps, he joined the diplomatic service. He was working in Whitehall and environs when he met Larkin and Amis, but to both, at least in the early years of their acquaintance, he remained coyly evasive about what exactly he did there. Larkin was caused to enquire about why, for instance, he had 'chucked up [his] job', which he did in 1956 to become a research fellow at the London School of Economics. 'I can't imagine what you are doing,' pondered Larkin; 'is it research?' (5 October 1956). Yes, but not quite the kind that Larkin envisaged. Along with his literary involvements Conquest's principal claim to fame is as a political historian, specifically a Sovietologist. During the 1950s and 1960s he regularly produced articles that chipped away at the established middle ground and leftist consensus that the Soviet Union was flawed but profoundly well intentioned, and in 1968 he published *The Great Terror*, a book which showed that the Soviet state had evolved a machinery just as efficient and relentlessly evil as that of its Nazi counterpart. His knowledge of Soviet affairs went beyond that of a standard home-based Foreign Office officer and academic.

Also, as described, he provided Amis with alibis and sometimes the use of his flat for adulterous liaisons with women in London, one of which was memorably alluded to in the poem 'Nothing to Fear'. Their relationship had a subtle effect on the development of Amis's novels after *Lucky Jim*. Conquest appeared only once in the books but his actual presence provided Amis with a supplement to the interchange with Larkin that had fed *Lucky Jim*. Virtually all of the novels up to the early 1960s engage with the themes of domestic contentment, monogamy, mature and loving commitment and the factors that make each of these variously absurd or impossible. Conquest joined Larkin as Amis's intimate and supplemented this as a magician of promiscuity. Just as significant was Conquest's influence upon Amis's political opinions.

Amis first met Anthony Powell after praising his *Music of Time* sequence in a *Spectator* article in 1953. Powell wrote him a letter, partly of thanks; they met for lunch, got on well and remained close friends until Amis's death. At first, Amis felt slightly uneasy about Powell's upper-class background and lifestyle – he tells of how, when the Powells stayed with them in Swansea, Lady Violet, a minor aristocrat, would leave a ten-shilling note in the bedroom for 'the cleaner', which Hilly, the cleaner, much appreciated. But it soon became evident to each of them that they shared the opinion that class only really mattered to people with social ambitions or left-leaning obsessions.

In late 1955 the BBC invited Amis to interview Powell on the *Third Programme*, and it became clear that the producer knew nothing of their friendship. The interview had been planned as a nasty encounter between a new novelist with apparently radical ideas on society and an established figure who had more in common with the Bloomsbury Group. It would go out live, and during the rehearsal the producer became annoyed, first because Amis seemed to respect Powell's work and, even worse, because he was talking about books as books rather than as instruments of unrest.

Amis certainly did not hold the view that literature could or should separate itself from its political, historical context; his own novels offer us commentaries on British life since the 1950s that are perceptive without being explanatory or analytical. What he did reject was the treatment of literature by its practitioners as a vehicle for political opinions and by its theorists as evidence of trends and states of mind that have little to do with the quality of the writing.

In 1956 Amis reviewed Richard Hoggart's study of working-class life and culture, *The Uses of Literacy*. He liked the book, but he qualified his praise by inferring that Hoggart had come close to sentimentalising his own experience of northern working-class life: 'if a structure is propped up by unemployment, bad housing and an agonising fear of debt, then we must kick the prop away' (Amis, *What Became of Jane Austen?*, p. 86). By 'structure' Amis means the culture and social fabric of working-class life, and he is uneasy with Hoggart's implied celebration of art as a compensation for poverty. Hoggart's study is rooted in the 1930s, and the 'prop', as

Amis put it, was now being dismantled by the legacy of the 1945 Labour government – nationalisation, living wages, the National Health Service and the welfare state. The review reflects the tensions and inconsistencies of Amis's own political outlook. His enduring approval of the 1945 reforms was at odds with a more recent, more assertive, one might almost say pre-Thatcherite, inclination towards individualism. He would attempt to reconcile these oppositions in his 1957 pamphlet *Socialism and the Intellectuals*.

He begins with a candid biographical profile of himself: lower middle-class suburban background, father a clerk, scholarship boy to a not-quite-public school and Oxford. He confesses that at Oxford he had gone through 'that callow, Marxist phase that seemed almost compulsory for my generation'. This opening is a calculated gesture: he has confessed his own, earlier inclinations and, as the title suggests, the rest of the pamphlet will be about other people and their beliefs. Some of it is, but each point is attached to an autobiographical, self-scrutinising subtext.

A recurrent theme is the Auden generation of the 1930s, which in Amis's view was comprised of hypocrites and charlatans: figures whose leftish leanings were partly a guilty compensation for their privileged backgrounds and, even worse, a calculatedly fashionable supplement to their writing.

He goes on to claim that the hypocrisies and self-deluding inconsistencies of the 1930s have in the 1950s been refashioned by a much broader network of thinkers and political activists, some of whom now hold positions of power. He states that the 'condemnation' of the invasion of Suez by the Labour opposition was shifting, qualified and probably a concession to the nationalistic tendencies of its working-class electorate. (Decades later he would tell of how, when attending an anti-Suez demonstration in Swansea, he was recognised and chased down the road by an old lady who brandished a sharp umbrella and accused him of treachery.) For Amis, it was the Russian invasion of Hungary that effectively exposed the inconsistencies of British socialists, many of whom still refused to recognise that the Soviet Union was an aggressive, totalitarian inversion of the socialist idyll. He asks if there is an alternative to socialism as an all-embracing philosophical–political formula. A few, he claims, have returned to the fascism of Mosley, others find solace in religion, and some, encouraged by the likes of F. R. Leavis and J. B. Priestley, promote a brand of clubbish intellectualism. The unifying feature of these diatribes, more implied than explicitly stated, is Amis's loathing for systems, irrespective of their ideological fabric. What he is really attacking is the precondition that if you hold any opinion you must belong to a group that shares and validates it, that a particular attitude is inevitably part of a general ideology. He gives examples of how important and very specific issues – racism, capital punishment, divorce laws, homosexuality – have been marginalised by political opportunism, 'I cannot see myself explaining, to an audience of dockers, say, just why homosexual relations between consenting adults should be freed from legal penalty' (ibid., p. 10), by which he means that the social radicalism of Labour will provide a badge for its sophisticated middle-class adherents but will, in pragmatic terms, always attend to the illiberal bigotries of the electorate.

The pamphlet attracted a good deal of public interest. Profiles of Amis the novelist had speculated on the leftish, anti-establishment drift of his fiction as a reflection of the man, but this was the first time that Amis himself had said anything at length about his beliefs and opinions. In a review of the pamphlet in the *Daily Worker* on 12 February 1957, the Marxist critic Arnold Kettle offered a patronising explanation for Amis's brand of political cynicism. He was, argued Kettle, a socialist at heart, but his involvement in literature was very bourgeois, and had caused his sympathies to become eclectic and disorganised. Amis, provoked, wrote a letter of reply in which the feelings that inspired the pamphlet are much less understated.

> I have … utterly rejected [Marxism]. No world view, it seems to me, comes within light years of being adequate to the world it professes to categorise. Each fact, each entity, each event is unique. To pretend otherwise is mere Victorian system building. Marxism, I think, does just that. It repels me also by offering certainty instead of truth. (14 February 1957)

He continues: 'He also denies that the Communist Party goes in for violence. What really happened in Hungary then? Wasn't there any violence? Or was it all inter-Hungarian violence, with Russian troops acting as umpires. Or were they acting against Russian orders?' These seemingly exaggerated hypotheses were, in fact, based on speculations made by left-leaning British journalists. He could, if challenged, have pointed out specific articles in which these apologies for Russian intervention were made: they had been supplied to him by Conquest.

It is certainly true that Amis's temperamental desire to dissociate played a part in his abandonment of standard left-wing ideas, but Conquest himself was immensely influential in this process. When they first met, Conquest was employed at the Foreign Office, specifically in the Information Research Department (IRD), a unit whose very existence was not acknowledged until it was disbanded in 1977. The IRD was responsible primarily for the covert distribution of 'propaganda', mainly among journalists, trades unionists and academics. I make use of inverted commas because while the primary function of this material was to counterbalance the indulgent coverage in much of the media of the Soviet bloc and the spread of communism in the Third World, it was comprised entirely of fact.

The problem was that most of this had been gleaned via the British intelligence services, which also, officially, did not exist, and was therefore unverifiable. Conquest's access to the truth about the Soviet Union during the 1950s and earlier would prove invaluable for his work as an academic and later as a freelance writer on politics, but he also disclosed it to Amis. It is no coincidence that Amis's drift away from the left began within months of his night with Conquest at the PEN party. It was not that Conquest indoctrinated Amis – he was far too contemptuous of dogma to attempt to impose his opinions on someone else – but he did provide a rare source of alternative evidence when virtually all others in the literary intelligentsia treated anything other than leftism as vulgar and jaundiced.

Larkin was politically apathetic and while he was intrigued by what Conquest got up to at the Foreign Office and later in the LSE, he remained largely indifferent to his unique knowledge of world affairs. If he had needed alibis for clandestine liaisons Conquest would no doubt have provided them, but it soon became evident that Larkin's requirements were of a slightly more introversive, voyeuristic character. 'I greatly enjoyed our tour of the dens,' he wrote (26 June 1957), 'and reckon that place in Greek Street is as good as any.' This one apparently allowed customers to take photographs: 'my 2 sets were very mixed – one bloody awful and I enclose it, you can have it (hope the letter doesn't go astray!).' Approximately three months after this, Conquest played a practical joke upon Larkin which, although in the same vein as his tape-recordings for Amis, proved to be far more unnerving for its victim.

One morning in October 1957 Larkin opened a Scotland Yard-embossed envelope to find a letter from the Vice Squad detailing proceedings already being undertaken under the Obscene Publications Act of 1921 and informing him that as yet no decisions had been made regarding the involvement of Philip Arthur Larkin as a witness. He should, however, make himself ready to attend court proceedings if summoned. Larkin telephoned the library apologising for an unforeseen bout of illness and spent the rest of the day with his solicitor who eventually advised him that they were unable to offer him proper assistance unless or until a prosecution or warrant for his arrest was actually issued (without noticing that the 1921 Act was an invention by Conquest). Eventually, Conquest confessed to the ruse and took care of the solicitor's expenses; after he had informed Amis, the latter wrote to commiserate. 'What a day for you ... The bloody fool [Conquest]. And in his letter to me he seems to think it a bit farcical on your part not to have smelt a rat straightaway. God if it had happened to me I should have been suicidal' (15 March 1958). There is a hint, just a hint, of disingenuous sympathy here, combined with the typescript equivalent of a straight face.

Suspicion that Amis and Conquest would always in some way be the wags and himself the stooge in such manoeuvres is likely to have prompted Larkin's letter to Conquest stating that it all

> left a frightful scar on my sensibility, which will probably mean that nude pics will act as a detumescent in future, not that I shall ever have the courage to buy any. You've probably turned me homo, come to think of it. Perhaps you'll be the first to suffer the fearful consequences of this. What? (9 September 1958)

His readiness to take the joke is as convincing as Amis's commiserations. Larkin's role in the threesome with Amis and Conquest involved a blend of stoical acquiescence and masochistic enthusiasm.

For Larkin, the friendship between Patrick and Julian in *Take a Girl Like You* was clearly based on that between Amis and Conquest, but what, he asked himself, was envisaged in the parallel? Conquest was five years older than both Amis and Larkin, an insignificance these day perhaps, but for those who reached early adulthood at the beginning of the Second World War the difference could be that of a generation. Patrick was too young for war service, but even though Amis served in the Signals, Conquest's distinguished and sometimes mysterious activities from 1939–45, both in the regular infantry and in the murkier realms of military intelligence, made it seem as though Amis's time in uniform was a token gesture. In the book Julian's record as a pilot with bomber command – by 1960 recognised as the service with least chance of survival – causes Patrick to feel embarrassed about his gallery of neuroses, based apparently on nothing but his own innate sense of anxiety. Similarly, Amis treated Conquest with a degree of awe, as a man who seemed to have dealt with the most terrifying aspects of life in an insouciant, casual manner. By 1955 Amis's letters to Conquest seemed very similar to his correspondence with Larkin, a blend of scurrilous disclosure and exchanges in ongoing work. Yet some differences are discernible. He seems to take it for granted in his letters to Larkin that the latter will not be offended by snide comments on his sex life, his mundane job and unostentatious lifestyle; Larkin, he assumes, is always willing to laugh at jokes in which he features. By contrast, Conquest is addressed with a blend of familiarity and deference. Certainly, he and Amis share a taste for obscene limericks and other lewd poetic inventions. However, Amis never treats his new friend's creations as he once did Larkin's pseudo-pornographic novels (that is, as both risible and indicative of his sense of sexual frustration), but rather as confirmation of Conquest's magnetic personality. Mavis Nicholson:

> I met Bob when he visited Kings and Hilly in Swansea. We remained in touch when everyone, apart from Philip, had moved to London. I found it hard to hear him. He'd mumble and mutter, but this suited Kingsley because when they were together they always seemed to be whispering confidences to each other. Eventually though they'd begin to snigger and this would break into a guffaw, which would subside and the whole thing would begin again. Mostly they shared private jokes or Bob would come out with his latest limerick. They were very schoolboyish when together. Very irritating. We used to think 'grow up!' I'd say that Bob and Philip didn't really get on, at least in the way Kingsley and Bob did. I think Philip was more vulnerable, even more thoughtful, than the other two.

After a visit to Conquest in London in 1954 Amis wrote to him for a full draft of 'Please don't burn the shithouse down', one of his many recitations that had reduced the London party to tears of laughter. For others, such performances might be treated as boorish philistinism, but Conquest had earned himself a special kind of immunity. His taste for obscene hudisbrastic verse was a foil to his modestly concealed attainments as a Renaissance man. At Oxford in 1937 he had reduced his tutor to silence when he told him that Dante's *Inferno* could only be properly appreciated if heard in medieval Italian, a language he had acquired aged thirteen when one summer his family was forced by bailiffs to flee to southern France.

Conquest had divorced his first wife, Joan, and married Tatiana Mihailova in 1948. Amis and Larkin got on well with her. For all three monogamy was something of a burden, but Conquest's personal life was by far the most glamorous and exhilarating. He had first met Mihailova in Bulgaria in 1944 when he was acting as liaison officer with the advancing Soviet forces and working clandestinely with the anti-German Bulgarian resistance. Later in 1948 he returned to Sofia under diplomatic cover, contacted Mihailova again and arranged for her to be smuggled to the West via routes then used by defectors. Back in London he left his wife, and then moved in with and married Tatiana. Julian Ormerod epitomises this same quixotic blend of kindness and irresponsibility. Conquest, like Julian, is an enigma. He eventually disclosed both to Amis and to Larkin, albeit in confidence, aspects of his work at the IRD. The department was run by John Rennie who would later become head of MI6.

The fact that a figure from the world associated with espionage and counter-propaganda was also responsible for a one-man attempt to marshal the disparate talents of 1950s literature into a recognisable alternative to the intellectually fashionable legacies of modernism lent Conquest a special sheen of glamour and authority. For Amis, the already peculiar relationship between life and fiction had taken on a new twist: Conquest was too fantastic for this world; he could have walked out of a novel. In Amis's recreation of his own friendship with Conquest in Patrick and Julian there is a certain amount of obeisance, virtually hero-worship, involved. Patrick is, like his creator, an accomplished seducer, but his looks and talents are compromised by private uncertainties. Julian, while retaining a complex, humane persona, has no time for anxiety. In fact, he comes close to being Patrick's sexual tutor, ensuring that he meets the right women in unproblematic circumstances. Amis wrote to Conquest on 16 October 1956, 'Haven't seen a women for weeks, except in college, and you can't count that. Can't count college cunt,

I should say. Hope you can fix me up with fornicatorium, even fornicatee, some time.' As indeed does Julian for Patrick during their visit to London. Throughout the novel Julian appears as someone who, for no obvious reason, transcends the various states of subterfuge, pathos and absurdity that beset the rest of its characters. He is by no means perfect but his imperfections are sidelined by his air of mystery. He has a heroic past and powerful contacts, yet no one is certain about what he does for a living.

Larkin recognised Patrick as Amis and Julian as Conquest but there was one passage that would have struck him as an insult, a reminder by Amis that he was now something of an outsider. At the beginning of Chapter 17, shortly after Julian and Patrick arrive in London, Julian explains that the women they're about to meet are models. 'Oh I don't mean the 48-18-38 sort people always seem to be reading about in newsagents' windows. Nothing like that about them at all. They model clothes.' Or, as he might have put it, nothing like the sort who pose for the type of magazines Conquest supplied for Larkin. A little later Patrick and Julian are passing a shop with a neon sign announcing 'Books and Magazines', the latter being made up of *Kamera*, *QT*, *Model* and other leading works in that field. Julian pauses, opens the door and shouts inside to the dozen or so browsers, 'Ah you dirty lot, you dirty lot', the kind of joke to which he seems addicted and which by parts unsettles and fascinates Patrick (Amis, *Take a Girl Like You*, pp. 205–7).

It is not difficult to imagine how Larkin would have responded to this passage, so shortly after Conquest's Obscene Publications jest. Jokes are one thing, but this cut a little deeper. It was a reminder that Conquest, as sexual impresario, provided magazines for Larkin, while for Amis, like Patrick, a high grade of the real thing was made available.

8

The Split

Within a two-year period, between 1961 and 1963, Amis exchanged his Swansea job for a Cambridge fellowship, moved there with his family, became disenchanted with academia in general and made arrangements to emigrate to Majorca (where the Amises planned to live as well-heeled bohemians), caused his marriage to break up irretrievably, and moved in permanently with the novelist Elizabeth Jane Howard. Hilly had a nervous breakdown and attempted suicide, and all three of the children underwent experiences variously unfathomable and traumatising. For all involved this would mark a crossroads in their lives, yet the events eclipse an occurrence just as extraordinary and less explicable. During the same period, communications between two men who were each other's oldest, and arguably closest, friends ceased almost completely.

Correspondence drew to a close in early 1961 and the most obvious reason for this seems to be the onset of Larkin's mysterious illness involving a blackout in March of that year. There is, however, circumstantial evidence to suggest a rather more curious, even ominous cause: Larkin appeared to have entered a period of fastidiously self-inflicted lunacy.

In 1959 Amis, having resumed contact after his return from America, began to send him reports on his ongoing novel and poems and, perhaps unwittingly, disclosed to him once more the porous borders between his life and work. It seemed as though he could overcome the troubling disappointments and uncertainties of existence in the same way that a novelist or poet can remake the world according to their inclinations. Certainly, Larkin had come across this before from his friend, but there is a limit to anyone's level of endurance and it appears that Larkin had reached his.

It is surely no coincidence that at this point he returned to the draft of a poem that he had left untouched since he had sent it to Amis more than two years earlier, 'Letter to a Friend about Girls'. He worked on it constantly from October to mid-December 1959. He wrote to Monica (1 December 1959, Bod) that he had recently been 'hacking at a satirical poem called *Letter to a friend about girls*, wch has been in my mind for some time'. The version received by Amis carries the same air of droll resignation as Larkin's letters but his reference to the new revised draft as a satire is significant. In this he would withdraw from their fraternal bond and treat their history far more dispassionately. He produced fifteen tortuously revised draft pages – as he put it to Monica, 'It's not going very brilliantly' – each involving passages that would not feature in the final copy (all of the unpublished passages quoted below are from the Hull archive).

The various transcriptions of the poem made during the closing months of the decade tell a fascinating story. In the parts that Larkin would cut completely, Amis is ever-present. One sequence of stanzas refers to the weekend in London he spent with Amis and Conquest where, as he reported to Monica, 'Everyone is having affairs' (25 August 1959). Larkin even considers this as a new opening for the poem:

Back once again in that north-eastern port
Where no one comes except on business
The ['soaring' crossed-out] weekend settles in my mind and I sort
My recollections, note them ....

His reference to Hull as a place not visited by those with any other choice is consistent with his general sense of disenchantment with the town, but we should remember that this piece was written with a particular individual in mind. Only once had Amis made specific plans to visit Larkin there, roughly three years earlier and as a way of finding a brief period of relief from the pressures of imminent marriage break-up when Hilly threatened to leave him for Fairlie (A to L, 20 November 1956). He cancelled not because of his reconciliation with her. His 'young lady' who had previously distracted him from the crisis 'has just decided to give me up... So I couldn't face a 12 and a half hour journey on top of it' (A to L, 22 November 1956). In the light of what follows it would not be too cynical to treat Larkin's 'except on business' as an allusion to his friend's rather callous dealings with sincerity. He continues,

I write to say what fun I found our short
Extravagent encounter – just the sort
Of session one can do with, working here;
And let me make it clear; I wasn't tight
Or sulking in that basement when you turned
And lectured me on women – I was quite
Aware you meant it kindly, and I might
have said so, I suppose

If we are to believe that this is what happened it seems that Larkin could not
think of a reply:

... and you scored
So many points, I was completely floored
And gave up answering. What you said was right,
I suppose, in that you'd found it so, but quite
Four fifths I couldn't swallow, even then ...

Five crossed-out stanzas later, he is still searching for a reply:

And even now the least I can retort
Much less negotiate an answer to:
Is that if girls decoy you round to show
Their morals off like poultry, if it's true
They lob themselves like quoits towards your bed
Then something is up, and ...
Why do I meet a wholly different sort?

Leaving aside the occasional moment of stylistic clumsiness ('lob themselves
like quoits'), Larkin's main problem is finding an honest response to Amis's
lecture. The question of why he meets a 'wholly different sort' seems to
perplex him particularly:

We're clearly much alike in what we want, I'd say:
Clean breath, firm breasts, big bottom for a start,
A friendly unpossessive sensual way

That doesn't sulk or tease or try to play
A game of race-me-to-the-altar-rails.

Larkin had already secured a partner who met these criteria. Monica was 'sensual' and 'unpossessive' in that she was well attuned to his preference for a compromise in their relationship: availability without commitment. And as far as the infuriating 'game of race-me-to-the-altar-rails' was concerned Larkin appeared to have settled this issue as early as 1955, much in the manner of a senior negotiator drawing up an agreement for possible later consultation.

I would sooner marry you than anyone else I know, and in any case I don't want to lose you. The sort of thing that gives me pause (paws) is wondering whether I do more than just like you very, very much and find it flattering and easy to stay with you ... Is it right to marry without feeling 'quite sure'? But am I the kind of person ever to feel 'quite sure'? (29 January 1955)

Monica was happy to accept this, which might indicate that he did not have her in mind when he pondered the nature of the 'wholly different sort' who would involve him in a race to the altar rails, but as we shall see, in December 1959, when he wrote these lines, he had reason to be rather more anxious about Monica's compliant state of mind.

After this stanza he continues with his somewhat masochistic ruminations on how Amis's lifestyle almost defies credibility.

And no one gets upset or seems to mind
At what you say to them, or what you don't
I disbelieved it once, but now its unfurled.

Amis is, Larkin realises, treating real life in a way that a novelist deals its imagined version: in whatever way he wishes. He is a world unto himself, so much so that he is probably immune to the feelings and lives of those beyond his private realm of gratification.

I see your sort all over the place,
Pushing the glass doors open with their breasts
(Forty one, twenty two, thirty nine),

Though you probably don't see mine:
Only cameras memorise her face
Her clothes would never hang among your interests

These alluringly specified measurements of 'your sort' were surely prompted by the '48-18-38 sort' contemplated by Julian (Conquest) and Patrick (Amis) in *Take A Girl Like You*. Amis had never queried the physical attractiveness of Monica, Patsy or Ruth Bowman, and again this notion of a woman so unprepossessing as an individual, and unattractive, that Amis wouldn't even notice her raises the question of who specifically Larkin has in mind.

The sprawling drafts were more than an address to Amis. Larkin was exploring the possibility of reinventing himself. He was saying goodbye to the decade that would end two weeks after he laid down his pen, and while his relationship with Monica played a part in this self-directed epitaph, Amis dominates it. The 1950s began with him and Amis as genuine, intimate friends, confident in what their own and each other's abilities would enable them to achieve as writers. Ten years later Larkin wanted rid of what these years had brought him. Often in the drafts he seems to be responding to letters that Amis wrote to him long before. The lecture given to him by Amis on women in general in 1959 might have prompted him to look again at a letter from two years earlier, when Larkin himself was considering a brief affair with a woman in London, unnamed in the correspondence. 'As I said,' writes Amis,

I found her very attractive in that funny way, with nice posture, all hips and parted feet, and clearly a ravening cock hound ... Can't understand why you didn't say, well I'm not in love with you, of course, but perhaps if you let me whip you and bugger you, I might sort of learn to love you. Something along those lines anyway. What seemed to be the trouble? I mean why didn't you say something along those general lines? Mm? (8 March 1957, Bod)

One can almost detect a condescending smile forming on Amis's face as he opens with 'I found her attractive in that funny way', the subtext being: 'not top class but acceptable enough, given your limited expectations'. In a 1954 letter, Amis tries to recall a girl who Larkin had attempted to seduce and about whom Larkin had sought his advice. 'She had a biggish, rather sullen, podgy sort of face, and a striding, leaning-forward gait... And lank hair?'

(A to L, 20 December 1954, Bod) There is an abandoned passage in the drafts of the poem that could be Larkin's reply: 'You and your girls that I have never known: / Their different faces so enhanced with hair ...'

It was not quite that Larkin had 'never known' Amis's particular girlfriends or encountered their like; more that Amis, by capturing them so alluringly in prose as well as seducing them, confers upon each an exclusivity verging upon the fantastic: 'Their muslins coming over a dark lawn / Like music on calm air ...'

Larkin also writes of:

And girls deflowered at twelve wait by white phones
And crimson table lamps in cobbled mews
For you ...

The image of twelve-year-old girls is derived from the sequence of letters Amis wrote to him during 1946–7, involving his encounters with at least four school-girls aged between twelve and thirteen. There is no reason to assume that Larkin's emphasis upon the slightly younger ladies implies censure on his part. It was a matter of stylistic necessity: 'thirteen' did not scan. Nonetheless, the letters that Larkin consulted indicated that his friend was equitable in his preferences.

I have always dreamed of doing it with the maximum degree of degradation ... During the past week I have been trying very carefully and slowly to work out what I would really like to happen to me with sex. I have got as far as deciding on the preliminaries: a girl of 13, starting with her school hat and raincoat, takes off all her clothes while I sit and watch. She is rather shy, and blushes and looks down a good deal, but she is also glad to be doing it and smiles and looks slyly at me. When she is naked, she comes and stands over me, her hands behind her back, very red but still smiling faintly. (A to L, 6 February 1947, Bod)

The girls of 1946–7 would by 1959 be in their twenties, the same age as many of those who wait in classy mews flats, usually provided by Conquest. Larkin seems particularly preoccupied with these elegant sites of Amis's liaisons, rewriting the stanza several times, sometimes involving 'top floor flatlets with white phones', sometimes having the women 'throw down their keys'; 'and none defrays / How much commits to what'.

His dating of the final page, '15, xii, 59' is significant for reasons other than the imminent close of the decade. Two days earlier he had received a postcard from Monica informing him that her father had died.

In early October 1959 Monica's mother died unexpectedly of a heart attack, an occurrence that accelerated her father's decline. It was at this point that Larkin began his extensive rewritings of the poem. Monica's father had been ill with cancer for more than a year and effectively gave up resistance following his wife's death. Following her mother's death Larkin wrote her a letter incorporating standard platitudes on 'how thin the surface of life is' (13 October 1959). He attended neither of their funerals, nor did he offer any assistance with the at once distressing and practical problems that awaited Monica in Stourport-on-Severn where she had to deal with solicitors, disposal of house and contents and all the other tasks faced by the only living relatives of the recently deceased. Monica was disappointed but not particularly surprised by this. She had gradually come to recognise in Larkin a trait he shared with his mother: a tendency to observe the formalities of concern for other people's distress while reserving virtually all of one's emotional and indeed physical resources for matters much closer to home.

Larkin's concern for Monica was genuine in the sense that only the vilest hypocrite would dissemble when enquiring of their lover, 'How is your father this weekend?', and empathising with the 'awful mixture of regret and sorrow' (26 November 1959) that attended her time with a man recently widowed and terminally ill. Monica's father had, as Larkin suspected, little more than a week to live when he wrote this, and if one were to harbour any doubts regarding his sincerity then a reading of the rest of the letter would invalidate them. As is his habit he shifts focus and mood continuously, but on this occasion one can discern a desperate though unstated subtext. He piles in information regarding 'your rolls of pink toilet paper at my elbow ... their only significance is that I've been too lazy to put them away'. He even included the name of their manufacturer – 'only just discovered Bronco' – and adds that 'well it's curious to begin a letter in this way'. Indeed it is, and even more curious to leave a sentence such as that as it stands and then launch into a manic display of randomness incorporating, breathlessly, his experience of a recent Italian film, battered pikelets with two glasses of milk, the problem of obtaining screws for his particularly heavy bedroom mirror, the SCR Kitchen Committee, Geoffrey Grigson, Richard Hoggart, Auden and the satiating effects of Chinese food. This is the unmistakable sign of someone shy of disclosing genuine emotion. Panic has set in, verbal rambling has taken over, and the fact that Larkin exhibits this in a letter testifies to the intensity of his feelings. Normally such disordered prolixity would only affect speech, but for Larkin letters had become so closely interwoven with his emotional and mental fabric that he is typing without control, filling the page with anything that comes to mind to put off for as long as possible his engagement with Monica's ongoing state of distress. This veers between the embarrassing and the endearing – given that his pain, though differently founded, seems almost equal to hers – but it is not quite hypocritical.

It is a transparent reflection of his private sense of terror. He had already on several occasions made clear to her his somewhat bizarre notion of love without commitment, but it would have been heartless to maintain this if Monica, after such a loss, required more of him. This was another reason why he returned to 'Letter to a Friend about Girls' at this point and with such intensity. The final version, the one that went into print, was pared down to an address to Amis on their respective sex lives, but the more extensive drafts reveal that Larkin was wrestling with a more complex, existential problem. Essentially, he regarded himself as a figure defined by his relationships with others, notably Amis and Monica, a state that had intensified over the previous decade. The poem enabled him to consider how, by reinventing himself, he might escape it.

The sense of hysteria that slips between the expressions of condolence in his letters to Monica reflected his fear of change and his knowledge that change might be unavoidable. He had, years earlier, made his position clear on matters such as marriage but now that Monica was alone and vulnerable a 'game of race-me-to-the-altar-rails' might become a distinct possibility.

The hypothetical woman who Amis wouldn't see, whose face 'only cameras memorise', would become more crisply defined in the penultimate stanza.

It is here that he gives a detailed account of the 'different gauge of girl' that makes up his and certainly not Amis's experiences. She is apparently 'unattractive', 'too shy', possessed of 'morals', reluctant to 'give in' and would in any event 'go quite rigid with disgust / At anything but marriage'. This is certainly not a description of Monica or Patsy Strang, and few if any would find a convincing resemblance between the figure in the poem and Ruth Bowman or Winifred Arnott, despite Larkin's persistent lack of success with the latter. So is this person an assembly of the characteristics he most dislikes but feels, masochistically, that he probably deserves? Perhaps, but one cannot help but give attention to the chronology of events that attends this poem.

As he took the poem in a variety of directions during the closing months of 1959, the woman he had in mind certainly existed, if only on the margins of his private life. She was called Maeve Brennan and she worked in the library.

In the summer of 1959 Larkin enhanced his reputation as a thoughtful, benevolent boss by starting classes for those members of his staff who wanted to take the Library Association Registration examination as the foundation for a long-term career. Seven signed up by the end of the year, but by midsummer 1960 all but one had dropped out: Maeve Brennan. She had spoken only occasionally to Larkin before enrolling for his classes, but as the numbers declined he began to suggest that they meet informally, and by late summer 1960 she, Larkin and the Rexes, a young couple then occupying the ground floor of 32 Pearson Park, regularly made up a 'foursome' for films, drinks, parties and, on one occasion, an Acker Bilk concert.

Maeve, as she herself accepted, was not a classically handsome woman, her physiognomy incorporating some of the combative, well-defined features that we more readily associate with maleness. She was not only a practising Roman Catholic but one who regarded her Church's regulations, particularly regarding sex, as more than arbitrarily imposed rules, as necessary adjuncts to a faith that underpinned any proper understanding of the world and the human condition. Larkin, when he finished stanzas three and four of 'Letter to a Friend', knew of Maeve and knew that she would be likely to enrol for his classes. Orwell and Huxley are traditionally cited as the chief twentieth-century journeymen of prophetic literature, but perhaps Larkin in 'Letter to a Friend' was staking his claim as practitioner of a very private, self-fulfilling offshoot of the genre.

Maeve states that during 1960 her 'friendship with Philip Larkin was still entirely Platonic' (Maeve Brennan, *The Philip Larkin I Knew*, p. 38). In formal terms this is true, but the fact that Larkin was self-consciously honest about his ongoing relationship with Monica, and Maeve similarly candid about her steady boyfriend (only ever referred to since as 'Philip C'), suggests that a rehearsal for something potentially more than platonic was taking place, particularly given that neither introduced the other to their respective partners. Larkin first made his intentions explicit in February 1961. Maeve had just passed her Library Association examination, and they had gone out for a celebratory meal in the Beverley Arms, in the agreeably antique town of that name some seven miles north of Hull city. Afterwards icy pavements provided the opportunity for gentlemanly supportive contact, which Larkin translated to an unambiguous embrace in the taxi home. Maeve: 'from that evening our friendship entered a new and headier phase which was to have greater significance than either of us could have envisaged then' (*The Philip Larkin I Knew*, pp. 38–9). This new and headier phase involved Larkin, while remaining respectful of her religious convictions, attempting to persuade Maeve to have sex with him, and for those with whom they worked and socialised it became evident that theirs was now more than a friendship. Foursomes became twosomes, and in the library an unspoken convention was observed that when Larkin entered Maeve's office towards the end of the working day everyone else would leave it. He was bringing to life the hypothesis of the poem.

Gradually he began to replicate, with appropriate adjustments, aspects of his relationship with Monica. They would read literature together – Sassoon, Owen, Betjeman, Hardy, Yeats – and as a potential bridge between their differences Larkin avowed a particular, though utterly false, enthusiasm for Evelyn Waugh as one who combined devoutness with cynicism. While Monica was Bunny or Bun and regularly in receipt of gifts from Larkin that maintained the rabbit theme – tea cosies, wooden models and orna-ments, etc. – Maeve became Miss Mouse or simply Mouse. From 1961 to 1972 they would read and read to each other ongoing novels, six in total, by Margery Sharp. These were intended for children and involved principally Miss Bianca, a rodent of almost aristocratic bearing who lived in a Porcelain Pagoda and was the favourite of the Ambassador's son. She was the Embassy mouse, Secretary and later President of the Mouse Prisoners' Aid Society and attended regularly by a rather dim mouse-slave called Bernard.

The fact that Larkin had begun to lead a double life is beyond dispute, but the fascinating question of why exactly he chose to do so still awaits a satisfactory answer. His relationship with Monica was unconventional, a curious amalgam of the clandestine and the predictable, and even though he might have feared further demands for security on her part following her parents' deaths, a tentative relationship with another woman for whom sex, marriage, fidelity and permanence were virtually synonymous would seem an unwise alternative, let alone an escape route. His most telling comment on Maeve is in a letter to his mother: 'I have built her in my own image and made her dependent on me' (1 January 1961). This is an explicit admission of what is persistently implied in 'Letter to a Friend about Girls'. He had imagined what this woman would be like and once he encountered someone who seemed to meet these requirements he transferred the process of invention from the poem to real life.

In Maeve he encountered a version of himself, or at least the parts of his temperament that he had managed over the previous two decades to subdue or conceal: anxiety, insularity, shyness. He had since his teens been unhappy with his ungainly stature, his baldness, his stammer, his sense of never being quite at comfort in the presence of strangers. He saw in Maeve a figure similarly inhibited, but his attraction to her was not sympathetic. She would, as 'Letters to a Friend' has it, be his appropriate and deserved girl. Just as Amis had seemingly discovered a limitless number of women who were as attractive and recklessly licentious as him, so Larkin felt that fate, or to be more accurate his pen, should find him a woman who was his depressing mirror image.

How exactly Monica became aware that Larkin was seeing someone else on more than friendly terms is unclear – although given that she visited Hull virtually every month and was on good terms with most of Larkin's acquaintances some kind of deliberate or accidental disclosure was inevitable. He certainly gave nothing away, and it was during early 1961 that Monica first began asking him if it was true that he was indeed pursuing an interest in another woman. He could do no other than admit the existence of Maeve and concede that he was seeing her regularly, but he assured Monica that the arrangement was more social than sexual and that even if he were tempted to take things further – not that he would, of course – Maeve's religious convictions would rule out congress. She did not believe him. One is struck most of all in his letters to Monica during this period not so much by Larkin's tendency towards dissimulation as by his curious manner. He is sincere, even repentant, but all the time he gives the impression that his feelings are generated by matters beyond the control of either of them. Typically: 'I'm terribly sorry you feel so miserable these days, though not surprised – it is a most trying position to be in, and I should hate it and feel utterly down and out, hopeless, scared to death, just as you do' (1 January 1961).

He seems to have taken a step back, sympathising with her feelings of distress and confusion while implying that he is neither their cause nor capable of remedying them. Monica had during the 1950s become resigned to Larkin's emotional self-protectionism, his refusal to commit, but now he seemed, at least in his letters, to be showing symptoms of mental imbalance. There is, however, evidence that his denial of involvement was based more upon calculation than confusion. 'None of the Books Have Time' was never published in his lifetime, but it was the first poem he wrote after setting aside the various drafts of 'Letter to a Friend about Girls'. The interim period of a week involved the New Year of 1960, which Larkin spent with his mother, and while the process of moving directly from one work to the next does not necessarily involve the perpetuation of themes there is a case for treating 'None of the Books Have Time' as a private reflection on some of the points addressed to '*Horatio*' (i.e. Amis).

> None of the books have time
> To say how being selfless feels,
> They make it sound a superior way
> Of getting what you want. It isn't at all.
>
> Selflessness is like waiting in a hospital
> In a badly-fitting suit on a cold wet morning.
> Selfishness is like listening to good jazz
> With drinks for further orders and a huge fire.

One's first assumption might be that the 'books' are works on morality or ethics, but given that Larkin states they do not 'have time' to consider how being selfless feels, this seems misplaced. These books work by implication. They 'make it sound'; a tendency exhibited in novels where the specifics of feeling and principle are exchanged for nuance and suggestion. The first stanza dwells upon, as Larkin sees it, the inherent hypocrisy of fiction writing – and we should note that Amis was particularly skilled in allow-ing his male heroes to get 'what they want' without causing them to seem distasteful – while in the second he shifts the perspective to his own life and state of mind, in which selflessness is the unnervingly dreadful borne with insouciance and selfishness is defined as the indulgence of private pleasures, aspects of his life that he does not share but which, equally, are not denied to others. The poem is his mantra for change. In 'Letter to a Friend about Girls' he tried to make sense of, and to an extent say goodbye to, his life of the

1940s and 1950s. Now he is looking at how he might make himself immune from the more distressing aspects of these years. His solution is to become emotionally unaccountable, a strategy that he displays in his curious letters to Monica about Maeve. This short poem was a rehearsal for one he wrote almost two years later, drolly entitled 'Love'.

> The difficult part of love
> Is being selfish enough,
> Is having the blind persistence
> To upset an existence
> Just for your own sake.
> What cheek it must take.
>
> And then the unselfish side –
> How can you be satisfied,
> Putting someone else first
> So that you come off worst?
> My life is for me.
> As well ignore gravity.

'Love' would not be published until 1966 but it was written in 1962, and by this point he had manufactured an emotional strategy that corresponded closely with the mood of the poem and which some might see as sadistic.

His poem 'Broadcast' offers an account of an actual event in 1961. On 5 November that year Maeve attended a concert of various pieces by Elgar at Hull City Hall that was broadcast live on the radio, and the poem involves Larkin listening to the concert at home in Pearson Park and imagining Maeve in the audience.

We cannot be certain of when exactly Monica realised that it was addressed to Maeve but a reasonable guess would be shortly after 25 January 1962, when it appeared in *The Listener*. She had certainly not attended such a concert. In a letter to her barely two weeks later Larkin apologises for 'causing embarrassment *vis à vis* old Charity Boots' (a nickname for Maeve, ridiculing her humble piety, invented by him for Monica). He goes on the dismiss 'Broadcast' as 'the first "love" poem I've written since *Maiden Name* ... I think both are pretty tenuous, pretty remote, as far as general approach goes. In fact I think this one just a shade ludicrous!' (L to Monica, 8 February 1962) By way of an explanation this is not even disingenuous. He knew exactly how she would feel when she read the poem. He had intended to cause distress.

As we have seen, his letters to Monica during the 1950s worked almost as templates for his evolving verse technique. Listening to concerts or other radio programmes simultaneously, imagining the other's response and then exchanging recollections, had become a trademark of their relationship, special because it indicated, particularly for Monica, that there would always be something they shared despite their lengthy separations. They began this when Larkin was in Belfast. He would offer her impressionistic sketches of the day, what he had done in the library, his lunch, maybe a drink in the Senior Common Room, the weather, and gradually the letter would move towards the present. The wireless is on: 'Whoops just heard that Princess M [Margaret] isn't going to marry Group Captain Fiddlesticks – well, what a frost' (26 October 1955). Eventually they agreed in advance on points of vicarious contact (including episodes of *The Archers*) that they would talk about later. Now she found that not only was he involving someone else in an idiosyncrasy she thought exclusive to them, but he had made a poem out of it. He describes the preliminaries of the concert, the 'whispering and coughing', the 'drum' roll and then, 'I think of your face among all those faces, / Beautiful and devout'; or as Monica would have read it, 'her face'. He imagines 'One of your gloves unnoticed on the floor / Beside those new, slightly-outmoded shoes', and the last lines have him 'desperate to pick out / Your hands, tiny in all that air, applauding'.

This was the equivalent of inviting her to listen into his endearments to his other girlfriends meticulously tailored to echo the world she thought was theirs alone. It was almost as though he was at once replicating yet distancing himself from the Amis of the 1950s, with the latter's desperate, often incompetent, attempts at deception exchanged for acts of calculated disclosure that verged on the malevolent.

Within a month of this he completed the first draft of 'Dockery and Son', occasioned by his visit to Oxford in March 1962 to attend the funeral of Agnes Cuming, his predecessor at Hull. Its true inspiration was deeper and more personal.

While there he also visited St John's, and Dockery and his son are not so much inventions as distillations of the fact that many of his college contemporaries – Iles, Hughes, Wain and particularly Amis – now had children. 'I try the door of where I used to live: / Locked.'

His awareness that those days are now distant and irretrievable is supplemented by his sense that he, despite appearances, has changed very little.

To have no son, no wife,
No house or land still seemed quite natural.
Only a numbness registered the shock
Of finding out how much had gone of life,
How widely from the others.

He goes on to consider why others want or need children – 'Why did he think adding meant increase?' and why he, Larkin, did not and never would – 'To me it was dilution', and the poem concludes with his particular vision of life, stripped as it is of those supports, such as children, which for others grant it significance.

The most engrossing lines are hardly ever commented upon. He is changing trains at Sheffield, has eaten 'an awful pie' and walked to the end of the platform

                    ... to see the ranged
Joining and parting lines reflect a strong

Unhindered moon.

No figurative import is apparent, but the tone indicates a moment when he is, if not exactly content, then at least without complaint. The contrast between the lines 'joining and parting' and the moon 'unhindered' by their different directions is a fitting depiction of Larkin's double life with Monica and Maeve. It is a terrible moment. He is not absolving himself from responsibility in causing these lines to cross, merely ceasing to care.

During the next two years Larkin's letters to Monica became even more peculiar, verging upon the bizarre. For example, he opens one letter: 'Cry all you need. It is not right to think you have to spare me the pain of remorse caused by injury to you is it?', and having dealt with their mutual distress, in the manner of one who had ruined his friend's dinner party, he moves on to a hypothesis, an endearingly honest admission of uncertainty. 'But then I wonder if there is a "situation" – do I *really* want an RC wedding with Maeve and a "reception somewhere in Hull" etc.' (31 July 1964), at which point one begins to wonder if he has experienced the epistolary equivalent of the poem's crossed lines, forgotten that he is writing to Monica and temporarily replaced her with his mother. No, of course not: 'Anyway, dear, I wish I were with you now, especially if you are wearing your mauve dress.'

Five days later:

> I was terribly hot last night. I lay thinking how nice it would be to have you beside (or under!) me ... just gathering your great smooth hips under me and shoving into you as I felt inclined ... It didn't happen last night ... At least not for me and I hope not for you – I'm not thinking of your friend Bill as much as someone who might invite you out to dinner. (5 August 1964)

'Bill' is Bill Ruddick, who was reading English at Leicester. There is no evidence that they had a relationship, but he was one of many male undergraduates who was attracted to Monica; she looked glamorous and unlike her colleagues was happy to socialise with students. Larkin, however, cultivated an image of him as a somewhat rakish foil for Maeve, part of a game that he appeared to be playing with the lives and emotions of those closest to him.

Earlier that year he had virtually admitted to this: 'as I say, I think sometimes I am ultimately an auto-erotic writer case incapable of love for anyone but himself' (10 May 1964). Elsewhere in the same letter he writes that 'I'm very depressed to hear you had such a sad birthday, but surprised too, as I left feeling that I had really assured you that I liked you better than Maeve and that if I felt I was cheating anyone it was *her!*' He is referring here to a traumatic weekend in April when whatever he told Monica about Maeve could hardly have been reassuring. It caused her to be physically sick.

Any attempt to explain Larkin's behaviour through these years must take us back to 'Letter to a Friend about Girls' and ultimately to his relationship with Amis.

Often in his letters to both women he comes close to providing a clue to what has made him act as he does. To Maeve in 1962:

Looking back on my first 40 years, I think what strikes me most is that hardly
any of the things that are supposed to happen or be so do in fact happen or are
so. What little happens or is so isn't at all expected or agreeable. And I don't
feel that everything could have been different if only I'd acted differently – to
have acted differently I shd have needed to have *felt* differently, to have *been*
different, wch means going back years and years, out of my lifetime. (L to
Maeve, 7 August 1962)

Later, to Monica, he was more blunt: 'I have never in my life felt I had
free will, have you?' He added, 'I could never see why anyone should ever
imagined for a moment that it existed, except because they wanted to. Then
you see people like Kingsley!' (L to Monica, 18 September 1966, Bod).

Throughout 'Letter to a Friend about Girls', he complains that fate has
treated him unfairly, albeit conceding that Amis's combination of charm
and less respectable gifts meant that he was less dependent on good fortune.
Although he admits to a similar sense of weary resignation in these letters
to Maeve and Monica there is a suspicion that after setting the poem aside
he did indeed do his best to impose his will upon events, in a grotesque
performance seemingly designed to visit various forms of misery upon all
involved, himself included. To Monica he almost admits this: 'In a way you
reflect what I am, she [Maeve] what I might have been – manager of a local
insurance branch, I should guess. But you know how potent what one isn't
can become!' (L to Monica, 29 April 1964). This echoes those passages in
'Letter to a Friend about Girls' that dwell upon the kind of girl he deserved
but which, when he wrote the piece, did not exist. As he confides to Monica,
she soon would: 'Sometimes I think Maeve is a kind of 40-ish.'

Only one exchange of correspondence between Amis and Larkin survives
from 1960. On 24 September, Amis returned to Larkin a Society of College,
National and University Libraries (SCONUL) questionnaire. Librarians were
forwarding these to established authors in an attempt to gauge the extent to
which British literary manuscripts were being poached by more generously
financed US libraries. Amis filled it in, making it clear that he would sell to
the highest bidder. In an accompanying personal letter he reported on an
evening in a London nightclub during which a girl with 'the gig frig biggest
tits I've ever seen' brought out and played a '"PIANO ACCORDIAN" ...
an action that nearly caused me to send our table flying over my shoulder'.

There is no record of a reply from Larkin and indeed only one letter from Larkin to Amis exists in the various archives from the period following the latter's departure to America in 1958. It is possible that some or all were lost, but circumstantial evidence suggests that none were written or sent. By this time Larkin had evolved a habit of gossipy letter-writing, of confiding in his various correspondents snippets of what he had recently received or posted to others. Rarely did he fail to comment to Monica or Conquest on his dealings with Amis, and the eighteen months between summer 1959 and the end of 1960 are notable for the complete absence of these. It was not that Larkin was doing what he had half-promised Monica three years earlier, cutting himself off from Amis. A more accurate pointer to what was happening can be found in the already quoted 1957 remark to Judy Egerton: 'Kingsley has less and less conception of talking *to* you: you are simply an audience' (4 August 1957). The letter in which Amis describes his experience in the nightclub was as usual a crisply executed piece of entertainment, but it was written as if to 'an audience', members of which are expected to listen, not take part. It should be noted that the letter contains not even a cursory enquiry as to Larkin's work or life. Perhaps it occurred to Larkin to see what would happen if he behaved according to Amis's expectations, as a non-participant, and did not bother to answer. The result was much as he no doubt expected: Amis appeared not to notice.

Larkin continued to be fascinated, transfixed, by Amis's activities, but he decided to observe them from a distance, using Conquest both as his source for information and adviser for speculations on what will happen next. For example, following the, unanswered, report on the nightclub, Conquest kept Larkin up-to-date on Amis's activities with almost one letter per week. He was, reported Conquest on 2 November 1960, finishing a volume of 'Short Stories' before beginning *The Egyptologists*, which Conquest would co-author. A few days later Amis visited London for a party with Conquest and George Gale, at which there was a 'fantastic racket ... denunciations, rows, booze etc (scenes too)'. Amis was in London, ostensibly, to give evidence on behalf of Penguin Books. It was the beginning of the court case that would eventually free Lawrence's *Lady Chatterley's Lover* from a ban under the Obscenities Act, and one has to wonder if Conquest's account of Amis's part in this caused Larkin to cite it, drolly, in his much quoted 'Annus Mirabilis' as the moment when 'Sexual intercourse began'. Amis failed to appear because, according to Conquest, 'he was at the time participating in an adulterous rendezvous. Pity he didn't just make it, breathing heavily, smeared with lipstick and fly buttons mostly undone to testify that Lady C was a sacred monogamous work.'

Six weeks later Conquest wrote to tell Larkin that he had rented yet another flat in West London (13 January 1961, Bod). He does not bother to explain why he needed a second address but implies that he and Amis would make use of it for the same purpose. He offered Larkin the spare room and added that if the two of them found themselves present when Amis was entertaining one of his girlfriends 'we could pretend to be mutes couldn't we? Trusty blind eunuchs, I mean. Who are they? Oh they're quite safe darling: Mustapha, say something to the lady? Glubashlubaslubablublamammum. You see dear?' Clearly Conquest shared Larkin's impression of having become a bystander, a hapless witness to Amis's unrestrained pursuit of gratification. Conquest evidently treated this as wryly amusing and one has to wonder if his presentation of both of them as walk-ons in a running comedy was tinged, just slightly, with cruelty, given his knowledge that Larkin resented this role.

From autumn 1960 onwards, the first full academic year since Amis's return from the United States, there is evidence that he was considering a permanent move from Swansea. Conquest wrote to Larkin on 13 September (Bod) that 'KingKongsley seemed in fine fettle', after a visit by Amis to London, but that 'Hillie still regrets USA'. This last comment is ambiguous: does she regret the loss of it or regret her actions there, specifically her affair with John McAndrew? In November Amis had written to Curtis Brown, his American agent, ostensibly about a planned 'novel about the US' (which would eventually become *One Fat Englishman*) and to ask them to enquire of their academic contacts to see if further appointments would be available. He did not state whether he was looking for something permanent but his note to Cindy Dyner of Curtis Brown suggests that he might have been: 'For an extended period'(23 November 1960). His contacts at Curtis Brown were involved in tentative negotiations with Williams College, Massachusetts, San Francisco State University and the University of Chicago when in December 1960 a different route of escape from Swansea was suggested to Amis, to somewhere closer to London.

Amis had got to know George Gale in the mid-1950s. Gale, briefly Labour correspondent of the *Manchester Guardian* and later in editorial roles at

The Spectator and the *Daily Express*, the latter much more sympathetic to his Conservative inclinations, was part of the pub-based culture of Fleet Street that Amis enjoyed so much during his frequent flights from Swansea to the capital. Gale and his wife Pat became family friends with Kingsley and Hilly and in December 1960, knowing that Amis was contemplating a move, Gale informed him, unofficially, that Peterhouse, Cambridge, was considering the creation of a new post of Official Fellow and Tutor in English, and later orchestrated contacts between Amis and Herbert Butterfield, Master of Peterhouse.

Butterfield was fully aware of Peterhouse's reputation as the most conservative, anachronistic of the Cambridge colleges – Tom Sharpe's *Porterhouse Blue* was comprised partly of stories, many accurate, of the bizarre, ritualistic archaisms of the place – and he relished the prospect of a new don who embodied the world beyond academe. Amis was interviewed for the fellowship in March 1961. Some fellows had never previously heard of him, and others were unsettled by the prospect of bringing in someone who was as much a celebrity as a scholar. But Butterfield wanted to modernise the college, and his preference for Amis held sway. He was elected and would take up the appointment in October 1961. Amis resigned from Swansea and Peterhouse provided the family with a quaint converted mill cottage in West Wratting. Soon after that they purchased a spacious, mid-Victorian house, No. 9 Madingley Road, Cambridge. Kingsley and Hilly would turn this into a version of their Swansea houses, with regular, now more convenient visits from friends in London.

One must assume that Larkin learned of Amis's appointment either via the press or, more likely, from Conquest. There is no record of a letter from Amis and nowhere does Larkin mention that his friend had written to him on the matter. He commented to Monica on 2 March 1961: 'Isn't it a scream about Kingsley, a scream of laughter or rage as the case may be?' He informs her that two academics at Hull are 'white with fury', presumably at the vulgar notion of an Oxbridge college appointing a novelist. He expresses some relief that at least John Wain, D. J. Enright, John Press or Charles Tomlinson weren't similarly honoured, but he evades the disclosure of whether it is laughter or rage that consumes him most. One suspects the latter since he adds, without explanation that 'I must say I'm glad it's Cambridge and not Oxford who have done it'. Monica was fully aware of his sense of Amis as always being ahead of him, through a combination of good fortune and nefariousness. This went back to when they first met and discussed their respective literary ambitions in Oxford. The image of him returning there in triumph, as novelist become don, would have been difficult to bear.

In the same letter Larkin reports that he had intended to write to her the previous night but that something awfully disturbing 'had prevented him from doing so: my eyes went peculiar at about 4 p.m. and I couldn't see to write or type'. He adds that he was effectively incapacitated and able only to lie in bed. Three days later, on 5 March, Larkin suffered what appeared to be a seizure during a meeting at the university. He remained unconscious for more than half an hour before an ambulance was called and he was not properly coherent until the following day, which he spent in Kingston General Hospital. He was sent home but there was sufficient concern among Kingston medical staff to have him referred to a specialist neurological unit at Fieldon House, London. No evidence of a serious neurological problem, such as a tumour, was found and he was advised it was probably an epileptic seizure. The true cause of his blackout remains a mystery – he certainly never experienced the like again – but it is impossible to ignore the fact that shortly after learning of Amis's seemingly limitless capacity to make life comply with his appetites and aspirations Larkin had succumbed to a form of oblivion. While in hospital in London he was visited briefly by Amis and Hilly and he later commented to Maeve Brennan that 'I envied them as they walked away into the evening sunshine' (8 April 1961). It would be two years before he saw Amis again. He wrote to Conquest on 5 August 1961, 'His joy at learning I was discharged without any discoverable defect must have rendered his right hand useless: give him my sympathy. It must be hell not being able to toss off.'

If Swansea had seemed charmingly dissolute Cambridge had an air of self-destructive decadence about it. Hilly maintained her tenderness for stray dogs and these were now supplemented by Debbie the donkey who lived in a shed outside the back door. Guests would be encouraged to ride her around the lawn or the kitchen and sitting room. The house had eight bedrooms, one bathroom and three reception rooms, each the size of the ground floor at Swansea. The only other permanent resident was Nicky de Peche Craddock who, recalls Martin Amis, was a non-paying guest originally brought in to deal with the forbidding proportions of the house. 'She was the daughter-in-law of Fanny Craddock.'

She was, by consensus, very attractive, seemingly in her early thirties with a young child 'being looked after' by unspecified benefactors, and if her accent, manner and general demeanour were anything to go by, insouciantly upper class. Philip Amis, with a hint of pity and unease, casts her as 'a sort of posh slave' (Leader, 2006, p. 462) while Martin's recollection differs somewhat.

> She seemed to spend most of her time as a louche social secretary, telephoning those coming up for weekend parties, fixing cocktails at dos, chatting to everyone without actually doing anything. My mother would be responsible for most of the day-to-day jobs, cooking, cleaning and clearing up the after-party debris.

Nicky also felt it her responsibility to set the moral tone for life at No. 9. She had sex with Bill Rukeyser, a Princeton student now in Cambridge at whose recent wedding Amis had been best man, several of Amis's friends and the occasional undergraduate reading English at Peterhouse. Showing no bias for age or experience she also slept with Amis himself and relieved Philip, aged fourteen, of his virginity. Nicky's long-term admirer was 'Bummer' Scott, who would arrive regularly in a decrepit saloon, perhaps take part in whatever jollities might be occurring at the time or disappear with Nicky for no more than an evening. He appeared at least three decades older than his paramour and, by the way he spoke and disported himself, of the same quintessentially English class. Amis recommended Bummer to his sons as an exemplar of good spoken English, even when drunk, which he seemed to be for most of his waking existence. The battered saloon acquired fresh dents after his every departure.

On the margins of the household was the part-time barmaid at the nearby Merton Arms, to which the Amises and guests would repair for a hair of the dog, following an arduous evening at home; the landlord, an indulgent sort, observed no regulated opening hours for thirsty regulars. Amis began a daylight-only affair with the barmaid, conducted in one of the empty back rooms of the pub. Rarely was she admitted to Madingley Road, despite her habit, in drink, of standing beneath what she believed to be the

Amises' bedroom window and keening for another encounter with 'Billy'. Apparently she never learned his other name and was happily indifferent to his eminence.

It is difficult to conceive of a more dissipated milieu than Madingley Road, but such imaginings are superfluous thanks to George and Pat Gale, occasional visitors at Swansea and now regulars at Cambridge. Gale, then editor of the *Daily Express*, lived in Staines. Despite being extremely well paid, his baronial ambitions were constrained by the then-punitive tax regime and he had to make do with one half of a gigantic Victorian-Gothic pile, albeit the part which, to his great satisfaction, included an absurdly vast ballroom. There was a regular, indeed incessant, counterflow of revellers between Staines and Cambridge, attendant guests at both locations playing the double role of participant and scrutineer, assessing the relative levels of excess achieved by each. In truth there was no competition, with Gale able to outdo the Amises financially and offer a limitless supply of expensive drink and food. The Gale's house also had three more bedrooms, the ballroom was frequently the site of hand-to-hand combat – males only – and the Gale's non-paying guest, Ronnie, was the equal of Nicky as the house's faintly debauched social secretary.

Larkin knew from Conquest that Madingley Road was even more raucous than Swansea, but the decision to distance himself from the new regime had nothing to do with self-righteousness. As early as October 1960 he confided in Monica, 'The very existence of people like Stevens, Pound, Eliot and Yeats seems to fill [Conquest] with dancing fury: he has written denouncing them all in the Obs.' This might seem to be a complaint against Conquest's dogmatic anti-modernist stance but as the rest of the letter reveals, Larkin perceives his inflexible approach as symptomatic of temperamental indifference to the feelings of others, a characteristic which in Larkin's view he shares with Amis.

Larkin continues: 'He [Conquest] is going to Swansea with a girl this weekend: that's what I mean about people like him … always being on the lookout for flats etc.' Conquest was at the time still married to his second wife. The most revealing passage is his statement that 'I congratulated [Conquest] on replacing me as chief unpaid acknowledged gagman to Amis Inc. Trust the shaft goes home' (L to Monica, 11 October 1960).

Larkin might sometimes have been disillusioned with Conquest, but he retained him as a source for information. Typically, 'Kingsley is in fine form, and entering a new sex life ... He explains that he needs a new girl to take his mind off the one that's just gone' (Conquest to L, 2 October 1961, Bod). Amis visited London from Cambridge once a week, ostensibly for meetings with publishers, literary journalists, *et al.* In truth he was meeting women in flats borrowed from Conquest. All the time Conquest kept Larkin up to date on the minutiae, such as the fact that Amis's two girls had left the flat littered with earrings, perfume, compacts 'which my girls take offence at' (12 December 1961).

By far the most vivid depiction of the mood of 9 Madingley Road can be found in a work of fiction. Reviewing Martin Amis's *Dead Babies* (1975) more than a decade later, Elaine Feinstein remarked that 'I hope for society that this is no true prophecy, I hope for Martin Amis that the nightmare of this vision will rapidly become part of his past.' Unintended irony can be the most arresting and in this instance Martin Amis was darkly amused. When he put it into words, the 'vision' was already part of his past.

> Everyone is always blacking out ... and they can't remember farther back than a few days ... Everything is out of whack ... Appleseed Rectory is a place of shifting outlines and imploding vacuums; it is a place of lagging time and false memory, a place of street sadness, night fatigue and cancelled sex. (Martin Amis, *Dead Babies* [Jonathan Cape, London, 1975], p. 31)

There are, of course, obvious differences between the Rectory and Cambridge: heroin and other hard drugs were not part of the latter and no one was ever 'fist fucked' by one of the athletic undergraduates who treated the house as a licence for unrestraint. Yet the feature of the novel, indeed the engine of its narrative – that would, one assumes, disqualify it completely as a personal allegory – is also that which binds it to Martin Amis's unique, very private experience of the excesses of adult behaviour. The Appleseeders are, one by one, murdered – or at least their demise is meticulously assisted – by an undisclosed presence who eventually turns out to be their aloof, dispassionate host, the Hon. Quentin Villiers. No motive is ever indicated, but throughout the book Martin Amis sews into the dialogue and third-person narrative moments that blend resignation and disquiet. Everyone is at some point alert to a premonitory feeling of grim and ineluctable closure. They know it will end, in all likelihood unpleasantly, but none seems inclined to arrest this descent to oblivion.

The disintegration of Madingley Road was brought about initially because Kingsley Amis became disenchanted with his working life in the university. Ultimately, however, the end would be caused by something almost as shocking as Villiers's actions and it can surely be no accident that Villiers's aristocratic status is mirrored by Amis's ascent to the gentry, if only by association, after his break-up with Hilly.

For Amis the attractions of Cambridge were various and speculative. He later disclosed in his *Memoirs* that he hoped for 'a kind of displaced return to Oxford, and echo of the romantic view of it which intervening time had enhanced' (p. 217). Within his first year at Peterhouse he had begun to regret the move. Along with teaching, Oxbridge fellows effectively owned and ran their colleges, and Amis found that even less time was available for writing than in Swansea. In 1961 the vast majority of Cambridge undergraduates, particularly at Peterhouse, were upper middle class and public-school educated, and the college was all male. Undergraduates late with essays or absent from tutorials would offer excuses that were variously insouciant, pretentious or arrogant, and Amis would recall those of their Swansea counterparts with nostalgic affection. 'Sorry Mr Amis, but I left my essay on *King Lear* on the bus, see, coming down from Fforestfach' (ibid., p. 224). Frequent attendance at high table was expected, followed by port in the Common Room. Amis loathed having to talk about academic and intellectual matters outside working hours, but his new colleagues seemed unwilling or incapable of doing anything else. After an evening during which a fellow, whose universe seemed to comprise nineteenth-century French painting exclusively, had refused to leave him alone, he found himself wishing 'for perhaps the hundredth time since arriving in Cambridge, that I were back in the Bryn-y-Mor with David, Jo and Willie Smyth' (ibid., p. 219). In truth, he had soon decided on a means of dealing with the social obligations of college life by ignoring them. It is likely that his evening with the art historian was memorable as much for its rarity as its boredom. Despite reminders from Butterfield about the conventions of college life, Amis rarely entered the buildings for anything other than tutorials.

During the 1962 summer vacation Amis took the family on holiday to Majorca, a trip funded by a commission from the US magazine *Show* to do an interview with Robert Graves, who had lived on the island since before the war. Amis admired Graves's poetry and fiction and had been in occasional contact with him by letter since 1954. Graves, although generally suspicious of prying journalists, welcomed this exchange with a fellow writer and put up the Amis family for ten days in August on his property in Deya, a fishing village then, like the rest of the island, unmolested by the tourist boom of a decade later. Amis and Graves got on well. Amis liked the area, and when he returned to Cambridge in late August he made a decision. He would resign from Peterhouse and follow Graves's example. He tendered his resignation to Herbert Butterfield in September. The terms of his fellowship obliged him to give three months' notice, and he decided to stay for the rest of the forthcoming year. This would allow him and Hilly to arrange the rental of a property in Majorca and deal in advance with potential problems of residence there, particularly the education of the children, all now in their early teens. He planned to stay for at least a year, beginning in the summer of 1963. The budget would be tight, but he calculated that his accumulated royalties, his regular payments for articles and reviews and the island's low cost of living would enable them to exist comfortably enough.

Larkin knew from Conquest that Amis intended to leave Cambridge but the advance press interest in his decision to go took him by surprise. On 21 December 1962, the *Daily Telegraph*, still a reserved, conservative paper, devoted the front-page headline to an event seemingly as significant as the recent Cuban Missile Crisis: 'KINGSLEY AMIS TO QUIT STUFFY CAMBRIDGE'. In the interview that accompanied the report Amis declared that he 'dislike[d] the formality of College life; too much dressing up and respectability ... Dining out in other colleges as a guest seems to invite an excessive amount of protocol.' For those who knew of Amis's life in Cambridge this would have seemed extraordinarily and characteristically disingenuous. His contempt for such formalities as dining in the old universities was sincere, except that it was based mostly upon hypothesis. Most of his social life revolved around Madingley Road, the Gales's house and his weekly excursions to Conquest in London. He continued: 'The academic time taken up at Peterhouse is substantially more than I had expected, and so much of my time and energy go into teaching that I have no time to write in the evenings.' Larkin's letter to Conquest of 30 December 1962 is a commentary on how Amis had reinvented himself for the *Telegraph*.

I think it would have been more graceful of K. to glide out of Cambridge without all this public posturing. If he made a mistake in thinking he could write there that's his fault, not anyone else's: no need to put them in the wrong. I can't imagine Majorca will be any better. Whose flat will he borrow there? Who'll he screw?

Conquest replied, 'He'll get screws from a dozen or so expatriate wives, and EVERYONE WILL KNOW ALL ABOUT IT. And where will he do it?' he asks, invoking Larkin's reference to borrowed flats and, famously, his own back garden: 'In cactus groves, with a dozens of sniffling local kids sniggering away behind covers' (Conquest to L, 4 January 1963, Bod). But Amis's plan to shift his regime of deceit and fabrication to the Mediterranean would end within six months, when he left Hilly for Elizabeth Jane Howard.

In early October 1962, a month after tendering his resignation, Amis attended the Cheltenham Literature Festival. He had been invited to take part in a panel discussion on the subject of 'Sex in Literature'. The other panellists were Joseph Heller, who had recently published *Catch 22*, a surreal and candid picture of the lives of US airmen during the last war, not least their enthusiastic pursuit of sex; Carson McCullers, author of *The Heart Is a Lonely Hunter*, whom Amis had met in New York; and Romain Gary, writer and diplomat, who had presumably been brought in to offer a stereotypically exciting French perspective. F. R. Leavis's description of Amis as a 'pornographer' had already reached the broadsheet gossip columns and *Take a Girl Like You*, published eighteen months earlier, was his most explicit examination of sexuality.

In his presentation at the festival Amis argued that sex, being part of life, had to be part of fiction but that descriptions of physical minutiae betrayed the author's downmarket inclinations and their readers' less-than-literary interests. Amis always believed that the immediately enjoyable aspects of sex were something that should be had rather than represented and, living up to his axiom, his concern with the debate was exceeded by his interest in the festival's director, Elizabeth Jane Howard. Hilly had gone with him to Cheltenham and his exchanges with Elizabeth, known to her friends as Jane, amounted only to flirtation, with the potential for more. The attraction was mutual. Jane Howard recalls that they had met before, briefly, on a couple of occasions. They had appeared together on two television arts programmes.

She remembered one, he the other. Amis offered an amusing comment on this and she sensed that something else was happening. Nothing specific was agreed at Cheltenham, but they exchanged telephone numbers and she suspected that he would phone 'quite soon'. He did. They arranged to meet in London and she remembers that they 'sat up and talked nearly all night.'

Elizabeth Jane Howard was a successful novelist. Her first book, *The Beautiful Visit*, published four years before *Lucky Jim* in 1950, was set during the First World War and its aftermath and had won her a prestigious John Llewellyn Rhys Memorial Prize. It combined well-crafted and evocative prose with a strong absorption in time and place. Her later novels of the 1950s, *The Long View* (1956) and *The Sea Change* (1959), brought her fictional settings closer to the present day. When they met at Cheltenham, Amis had not read any of her work, but he knew that she, like him, was regarded as a serious writer with popular appeal. Moreover, they shared the image of figures who had walked out of their own fictions; eight years after *Lucky Jim* Amis was still represented in the popular press as a version of Jim Dixon and Jane's chronicles of the Cazalet family were regarded as semi-autobiographical. Jane Howard's fictional world was a class above that of Amis; it reflected her background and, indeed, her presence. Her family had, since the mid-nineteenth century, owned a successful timber firm and were a classic, very English combination of unobtrusive wealth, sophistication and business acumen. She had received no formal education in school or university but had been taught philosophy, mathematics, Greek and Latin by her slightly eccentric governess, a Miss Cobhan. *The Beautiful Visit* evokes a world in which personal crisis is borne with a quiet dignity, and involves individuals who seem capable of transcending matters such as moneyed privilege; Jane's own life had offered her plenty of material for the project.

Aged nineteen, she had married Peter Scott, son of the Antarctic explorer, and he had spent most of their first three years on destroyers protecting the Atlantic convoys against U-boats. In 1945 he returned as a hero, having twice won the Distinguished Service Cross, and their marriage lasted less than two years after that. They were, they found, incompatible. During the mid-1940s Jane had, in any event, established her own sense of independence, working variously as a model, a publisher's copy-editor, a minor civil servant and a BBC newsreader. When she met Amis she had recently ended her second marriage to James Douglas-Henry, an Australian journalist and broadcaster.

She was also, by anyone's standards, a very attractive woman. She looked like a model, with long blonde hair and high cheekbones, but she combined this glamorous physical presence with an unshowy command of language and an equally restrained intellectual adroitness. She was a year younger than Amis.

During the next six months Amis's life progressed much as it had done for the previous fifteen years. He taught, got on with *One Fat Englishman*, did reviews and articles and existed, on the face of things, as a family man. As usual, he made regular trips to London, where he would meet Jane. A number of male friends knew of this and, viewed from the outside, there seemed to be few differences between this particular extramarital excursion and its predecessors. Obviously he planned to stay with Hilly. Why else would he continue, as he did, to make arrangements for their move to Majorca? Indeed, Jane recalls that Amis had stated, regarding Majorca, that he '*might* be able to get back to England, perhaps twice a year', indication enough that his affair with her, while serious, was likely to remain an affair.

However, Amis's still very new relationship with Jane was affecting him in ways that were unprecedented. The figure of the traveller in 'Song of Experience' had been a candid exploration of his tendency to report to his male friends, Larkin and Conquest particularly, on his sex life: the states of play with Hilly had been covered with the same laddish incaution as his adulterous triumphs. Now he only wrote of his experiences with and feelings for Jane in letters to her, and these – always in longhand, given that the home-based typewriter might involve disclosure – reveal a dimension of Amis that few would ever encounter. Some extracts: 'Never been so knocked over by love' (22 January 1963); 'I love you, everything about you, especially everything' (23 January 1963); 'You're on the edge of my thoughts all the time ... I don't really see how you could give me more pleasure than you do already ...' (10 February 1963); 'I do enjoy life more because of you ... And I have nothing to bear except not being with you when I want to, which is all the time' (25 February 1963); 'I miss your mouth and your breath and your skin and your left eyelid and your right breast and right collarbone ... And your voice. And eyes' (4 April 1963); 'I worship you' (26 May 1963). Hyperbole? Or the discovery by an over forty-year-old cynic that love is not an abstraction? Also in these letters he tells Jane, confesses to her, of how he is fully aware of a peculiar, almost ironic, change in his personality. He states, on several occasions, that she has dispelled his previous certainty that monogamy is part-myth, part-imposition. Now, for the first time in his life, he has no interest in other women as potential sexual conquests. 'My lack of interest in other women is beginning to get me down rather. The *real* reason is, I think ... that I know it wouldn't be nearly as good ... I love you all the time' (29 April 1963). He writes to Jane of how simply thinking of her presence causes him to be more polite, less brittle, with people who would previously have made him angry and impatient.

The contrast between these gushing, oleaginous declarations to Jane and his treatment of Hilly barely three years earlier is stunning. In a letter to Larkin on what seemed yet another marital crisis, Conquest observed, 'What Hilly really minds, I always think, is K's unromantic attitude to her – "You are looking sweet and marvellous" is better than "What about a screw, old tart", I always feel' (27 March 1959). This brings to mind Patrick Standish who in Chapter 13 of *Take a Girl Like You* demolished all of Jenny's illusions about men, with a short lecture that was by parts an apology and justification for Amis's extramarital recidivism. Her ideal man 'died in 1914 or thereabouts. He isn't ever going to turn up, Jenny, that bloke with the honour and bunches of flowers and the attraction' (p. 160). Cruelly, Amis made sure he wouldn't turn up for Jenny/Hilly, but for Jane he seemed to have applied inventive skills to an act of reincarnation. The man of 1914 had risen again in the form of a slavishly besotted Kingsley Amis. All of which opens the question of whether he was to some degree involved in an exercise in self-delusion.

He distilled the emotional energy of the letters into two poems, 'Waking Beauty' and 'An Attempt at Time Travel'. In the latter he imagines both of them, she aged nine, he ten, on a horse-drawn buggy with her father and grandfather. She had, as she told him, done this with her family – who had residences outside London – in the 1930s: she had shown him a photograph. Amis had come from a family that was a little further down the social order, but he imagines himself there. Why, one might ask? Because she is the woman he has been waiting for; he has always been there.

'Waking Beauty' is a compressed version of Keats's 'Eve of St Agnes'. He, Amis the speaker, gets to her by cutting through thick briars 'neatly tagged by Freud the gardener', implying that Freudian notions of love and sexuality are just obfuscations, unnecessary barriers. They leave, with her 'eyes cleared and steadied': 'Side by side we advanced'; the 'briars' that had previously kept him from her have now 'all withered'. (And one hopes that when writing this he had not consulted his undergraduate edition of Keats's poems, where twenty years earlier Larkin had inserted a marginal note at the corresponding moment in 'The Eve of St Agnes': 'You mean he fucked her.')

In August 1963 Amis finally tested Hilly's endurance of their semi-open marriage beyond its acceptable limits. Despite his attempts to keep things secret she had become aware by early summer that he was having an affair and with whom. Jane recalls Amis telling her later that Hilly first confronted him with her knowledge on the train back from their visit to Yugoslavia and that they had 'the most frightful row which lasted till they got home'. (This was the holiday during which Hilly had written on Amis's back in lipstick 'I FAT ENGLISHMAN. I FUCK ANYONE'.) At the beginning of August, Amis and Jane went to Sitges in Spain for a two-week holiday. Hilly was aware that they were together and by various means found out where they were. One day, on answering their hotel room doorbell, they were confronted by a journalist from the *Daily Express*. They fielded such questions as 'Are you in love?' with standard 'no comments' and then suggested that since he had blown their cover he might want to do a full story, with photographs. They would, they promised, do a full interview after he returned to the hotel with a professional photographer, the best available being in the next town. They then fled, leaving a trail of false clues that eventually took the hack to Barcelona – they, meanwhile, had gone in the other direction.

Had Hilly informed the *Express*? It is possible, given that she had also been making other plans. When Amis returned to Cambridge, the Madingley Road house was empty. A note from Hilly informed him that she had gone with the children to Majorca and that he should not follow them. Their marriage was, it seemed, finally over. The next day Amis packed what he could carry, caught the train to London and moved into Jane's flat in Maida Vale. Hilly and the children stayed in Majorca. Amis next saw his children, or at least two of them, the boys, when Hilly sent them back to London to see their father in late November 1963. He was still living with Jane, and it was evident to all concerned that this situation was not going to change.

Amis and Jane spent their first month in the maisonette that she shared with her brother Colin, known to friends and family as Monkey, in Blomfield Road, Maida Vale, and then decided that if they were starting a proper relationship they should do so on their own. They moved to a more prestigious location, a flat in Basil Street, Knightsbridge, near Harrods. Amis's calculation that Majorca would have allowed him to live solely from his earnings as a writer was not irrelevant. He now had to both provide for his own needs and support his distant family, and for the first few years Jane took care of their major expenses. She paid for the Knightsbridge flat, which itself proved to be too expensive, and before Christmas 1963, after six weeks in Majorca, they moved back to Maida Vale and Monkey, who would continue to live with them in various residences until shortly before their relationship ended. The flat was small, and eventually they acquired a ten-year lease for a house, 108 Maida Vale, paid for by Jane, and moved into it in 1965.

The Anti-Death League was the first of Amis's novels to be planned and completed after the beginning of his relationship with Jane, and these years had a major influence upon it. It would be radically different from anything he had written before, but first he had to complete a number of projects that were transitional yet reflected his lack of certainty regarding his new direction. In 1960, when Amis and Conquest started to edit *Spectrum: A Science Fiction Anthology*, five volumes of which would appear over the next six years, they were also making plans to co-author a novel. *The Egyptologists* would eventually be published in 1965, and like many shared works of fiction it is suspended somewhere between the original idea and the completed project. The Egyptologists are a group of middle-class, married professional men who lease a building in West London for the pursuit of their amateur but fiercely enthusiastic interests in ancient Egypt. They hold regular meetings and seminars, invite esteemed scholars to give lectures and use the building at other times for individual study. It is also equipped with private suites of rooms that serve the society's actual function, as an ongoing, reliable alibi for regular acts of adultery. The plot clearly originated in its creators' own experiences together in London during the 1950s, particularly Conquest's provision of excuses and locations for Amis's infidelities.

Amis wrote the closing chapters in late 1964. In these, the general mood of lechery, deceit, cynicism and polite misogyny lifts briefly. The Treasurer has an affair with Lee Elliot Swarz, an American research student and real Egyptologist, who has become aware of what the society actually involves. He tells her that he will leave his wife and marry her and that, for once, his commitment is genuine. She declines his offer, explaining that the state of mind which first caused him to abandon monogamy is probably irreversible. As usual, this episode involves a blurred reconfiguration of various aspects of Amis's life. He wrote it when he was on holiday with Jane in Majorca. Their relationship was little more than a year old, and Jane was aware that his new, and on his part genuine, state of commitment to one woman was at odds with his past. It is thus appropriate that the Treasurer should become the only member of the society to revoke its code of infidelity and, for no apparent reason, unsettle the prevailing tone of the earlier chapters. Lee's scepticism could well be an acceptance on Amis's part that Jane herself would have occasional doubts.

She later wrote in her memoir, *Slipstream*, that in the early months of their relationship Amis had insisted on discretion, adding, 'If it came out, I will blacken you – I want you to know that' (Elizabeth Jane Howard, *Slipstream: A Memoir*, p. 340).

Larkin, who could at the time claim to know Amis better than Jane did, wrote to Conquest shortly after the book came out: 'I still see Kingsley as the Treasurer and you as the Secretary: wrong, perhaps, but it "helps me to imagine it"' (1 January 1966).

Hilly and the children's journey to Majorca was a curious experience. Hilly drove, as she always did, and Martin and Philip exchanged roles as front-seat passenger, where Kingsley should have been. Aged only eight, Sally remained largely immune to the strangeness of these events and indeed the atmosphere. 'It is difficult to remember exactly what happened,' Martin Amis told me. 'Hilly was calm but it was as though she had no idea what to do without him.'

In other circumstances Majorca would have been an idyll. Their house was in Soller, the island's second-largest town. Philip and Martin would take a daily train from Soller to the International School in Palma. 'It was a 40–50 minute journey, twice a day. It was a beautiful little train, lovely countryside,' Martin recalls.

Looking back Hilly was in a state of limbo. Nicky Craddock [of Madingley Road] had come over too. She lived with us, and she and Phil had a kind of affair. I was very shocked and very envious. We didn't talk about what had happened but it was becoming clear, to us, that we were deluding ourselves. It was wonderful, yet it was also, we knew, temporary and pointless.

Hilly returned with the children to London in January 1964, having arranged to rent a flat in Ovington Gardens, Knightsbridge. Conquest updated Larkin: 'I have to give a reference for Mr W. Kingsley Amis's ability to pay for a flat for Hilly' (7 May 1964). They stayed there for only a month and then moved on to a rented house, 128 Fulham Road, Chelsea. Accounts of what occurred there vary, but only in terms of the specifics of the indulgences allowed and practised. Martin enrolled at Battersea Grammar School – and immediately began a regime of truancy. Philip had returned to his boarding school and although Sally was now the only one of the children who needed her mother's help and attention – Martin having opted for feckless independence – Hilly seemed to lapse into a state of depressed inertia. 'The only time she seemed to revive,' recalls Martin,

> was after she got in touch with Henry Fairlie again. He became a regular visitor for maybe a month to six weeks – at Ovington Gardens – and they restarted their relationship. I don't know why it cooled off but it did, and soon after that Mum went even further downhill. I'd been out but I saw her being taken away, to hospital.

He refers to a night in June 1964 when she telephoned her friend Mavis Nicholson, repeating the phrase 'we're all disposable darling', and sounded to Mavis close to collapse. Everything else she said was slurred and incoherent. Mavis called back and was eventually answered by a hysterical Sally. Her mother, she screamed, would not wake up.

After summoning an ambulance Mavis telephoned Amis, who had spent most of the evening with Jane's brother Colin, drinking. Although unsettled by the news he seemed infuriated by Mavis's implication that he should go immediately to the hospital: 'Why do I have to?' he repeated, as much to himself as to Mavis. But he did so the next morning and visited upon the semi-comatose Hilly an outpouring of invective for what she had done. Whether he was genuinely angry with Hilly or whether he was turning his own feelings of guilt and distress against her is unclear.

Towards the end of 1963, when the publicity surrounding his relationship with Jane began to die down, Amis re-established contact with Larkin, or to be more accurate Jane orchestrated a meeting. He had told her of their friendship and without stating that it had now come to an impasse he was honest enough about the cessation in communication. Jane, with commendable tact, wrote to Larkin, in part to introduce herself, and to suggest that, if it were convenient, he might be her guest at a function of the Society of Authors in London where she was due to give a talk. She would, she added, apparently superfluously but by way of a prompt, be accompanied by Kingsley. Larkin accepted her invitation and the only record of what occurred is his letter to Conquest of 31 December 1963. 'I met Kingsley before Christmas through the good offices of EJH ... Amiable relations were established, or re-established. She seemed nice.' His comment on the 're-establishment' of 'amiable relations' is curious since nowhere else in Larkin's correspondence with Conquest is there any specific reference to their having fallen out. Conquest was aware that he had been acting as Larkin's informer on their mutual friend's activities but throughout he never enquired about why he was expected to do so and Larkin never volunteered an explanation. Amis himself was too busy with the whirlwind of catastrophe he had reaped to keep in regular contact with his friend in Hull, and Conquest's role as reliable witness to events in Cambridge and London seemed to him a matter of convenience.

Earlier in the month Larkin had written to the novelist Barbara Pym, with whom over the previous two years he had established a form of friendship by correspondence, that he had just received the revised proofs for a reissue of *Jill*. The introduction 'turned out mostly to be about K. Amis: funnily enough I met him in London last week for the first time in two years, and was able, as they say, to get it cleared' (7 December 1963). The clearance for 'it' was, one assumes, Amis's approval for the introduction, which was the first account for the reading public of how they met in Oxford and became friends. But one wonders why he is informing Pym of this. Never before had he mentioned his friendship with Amis in their correspondence. He seems here to be exhibiting a tendency that was becoming more frequent in his letters, a kind of epistolary thinking out loud, where he allows his private reflections to intrude upon his notion of addressing someone else. On this occasion his subliminal musings on Amis's and Jane's attempt at reconciliation – 'was able, as they say, to get it cleared' – appear to blend with an innocuous comment on editorial niceties.

The recipients of these involuntary asides, always involving Amis, even included Monica. The following year he wrote to her of a good review of the reissue that had appeared in *The Observer*, and seemed unable to prevent himself from dissociating the novel from another feature of his past. 'See K. [Kingsley] is reduced to fill-in for Pen Gilliatt [Penelope Gilliatt was the regular film reviewer for *The Observer*] – twenty years ago he was borrowing from me – well, fifteen, – fifteen years hence he'll be borrowing again, poor old hack' (L to Monica, 29 March 1964). The passage appears riddled with discontinuities. There is some circumstantial connection between the favourable review of *Jill* in *The Observer* and Amis's temporary appearance in the same paper as fill-in reviewer, but then we find the curious leap from the notion of Amis having 'borrowed' something from Gilliatt and his having done the same with Larkin. One should note that the letter was written ten years almost to the month after *Lucky Jim* had piloted Amis from academic obscurity to nationwide fame. Five years before that – 'fifteen years ago' – Larkin had begun helping him with the early drafts of 'Dixon and Christine', and it was roughly twenty years since they had started to exchange ideas on their respective works in progress. It is almost as though certain triggers, such as the reissue of *Jill*, ignited a chain reaction of half formulated but generally bitter thoughts on Amis.

In early 1965 Larkin, in London on SCONUL business, had lunch with Amis and Jane and reported to Conquest, in a rather cool dispassionate manner: 'Had lunch with KWA and EJH almost a week or so ago – they seem to be settling down to a house in Edgware Road and to be happy as usual' (L to Conquest, 1 February 1965). It would be three years before they met again. While his comments to Conquest on Jane are measured and uncensorious he sometimes, for Monica, allows the mask to slip. In 1964 Larkin first met John Betjeman in preparation for their co-appearance in an edition of the BBC arts series, *Monitor*. The implication was that Larkin would be, indeed was becoming, successor to Betjeman as the poet who appealed to the ordinary reader, an impression borne out by his own recent experiences. On 3 March 1964 he wrote to Monica of his train journey from London; 'Had a good journey back – 2 people asked me to autograph *TWW*'s in the train – the Ringo Starr of contemporary verse'. On 9 June he reported that he had met Betjeman's wife, Lady Elizabeth. 'She is a friend of Eliz. J. Howard, so my image of the English aristocracy is somewhat tarnished.' Conquest, the previous year, had sown the image for him of Amis as energised by the combination of sex and social climbing: 'Kingsley once told me that he quite appreciated the hypergamy feeling ... [Dr Johnson] said sir a duchess makes a thrilling screw ... Still there are other thrills, doubtless; and K speaks very highly of them' (29 June 1964). Conquest's comments are rather more cynical, at least regarding Amis's motives, than those of Larkin a few months earlier: 'He always had ideas about marrying, or what have you, a writer ... Shall I get in touch with E. Jennings? Another Ted Sylvia team?' (24 November 1963). Beneath the flippancy lies, for both, a knowledge of Amis's record of emotional mendacity. Clearly Amis had been discreet to Conquest regarding the transformation of his personality, seemingly evident in his early letters to Jane: either that or the new Amis involved a compound of fraudulence and wishful thinking. Larkin wrote to Monica of a 'double spread in the *Evening Standard* with pictures of KA and EJH. Pity I missed it... K is apparently still decanting on the virtues of monogamy, faithfulness etc. You can't win, can you?' (11 March 1964, Bod)

Amis and Hilly were divorced in June 1965 and he married Jane three weeks later on 29 June at Marylebone Register Office. As usual Conquest reported events to Larkin: 'reception at the *bride's* publisher, as convention demands' (Conquest to L, 2–3 August 1965, Bod). The party was at the office of Jonathan Cape, which would within a year become Amis's publisher too. Both events were orchestrated by Tom Maschler, Jane's editor at Cape and friend of Amis since the beginning of his relationship with her. Maschler also ensured that the event was well publicised, with their train journey on 30 June and two-day holiday in Brighton covered in the news and gossip columns of all the major newspapers.

Hilly had last seen Larkin three years earlier when she and Amis were still married. She had written to him regularly during the 1950s but her letters stopped after the revelation of Amis's affair with Jane. Now, unprompted, she wrote again. The letter is not dated yet it is postmarked as 4 June 1965 (archived at Hull): the same day as the decree absolute came through. She opens by congratulating him. 'You are a clever beast getting the Queen's medal and I bet you are chuffed – nice that you always like the Queen so much too.' A month earlier he had been awarded the Queen's Gold Medal for poetry, and Hilly's comment on his affection for the monarch is quaint. He was disappointed that the award arrived by post, having hoped for an invitation to Buckingham Palace, but the medal further testified to his elevation to public prominence: in 1964 he was elected Fellow of the Royal Society of Literature.

Hilly continues: 'Things were *very nasty* for a couple of years for me but now things have got much better and I think everyone is better off.' The sense of acquiescent resignation carried into the end of the sentence might be genuine but, given the facts, self-evidently misplaced. Throughout, she appears to present herself as much the cause of the break-up as its victim. She tells Larkin of how 'the boys' are 'at K and J's place now'; that she and Sally have a house 'filled to the brim with lodgers'; of how much she had enjoyed her time working at London Zoo – including an account of squirrels that want to 'mate' with 'your head' – and as the rather chaotic, though endearing, report continues it betrays a forced sense of cheer and resolution, as if she is crowding the letter with random events to avoid or postpone the topic that really prompted her to write to Larkin. Eventually, she arrives at it.

> I think he is really much better off with someone like Jane – he can really be King and she is very Queenly. Anyway, I'm very glad I had those years with K because I can't imagine anyone else teaching me so much and making me laugh as much and parts of it were wonderful.

She was fully aware of Amis's and Jane's plans for their imminent wedding and of the press coverage that would surround it. It was, officially and publically, the end of the only life she had known since her late teens and it would have seemed appropriate to write of it, artlessly but elegiacally, to the man who had shared so much of 'those years with K'.

She tells Larkin of how she hopes soon to spend some time in Africa and perhaps look for work in the United States, a place she enjoyed. Within two months, however, she had abandoned such ambitions and moved with Sally to a cottage in Sussex. There, before the end of the year, she would meet David Roy Shackleton Bailey, a Cambridge don who could have walked out of the previous century. Martin Amis believes that her eventual marriage to him was a desperate attempt to obliterate her past. He was the complete antithesis of the anarchic, high-spirited, mischievous qualities that attracted her to Kingsley, and indeed to Fairlie. The marriage lasted three years.

9

Worlds Apart

Aside from the hyperbole-ridden letters to Jane, there is very little on record about how Amis really felt during the turbulent opening years of the 1960s. Indications can, however, be gleaned from a novel begun while he was with Hilly and completed after he moved in with Jane.

Roger Micheldene, the eponymous *One Fat Englishman*, published in 1963, inherits all of Patrick Standish's lecherous proclivities, supplemented by a limitless desire for drink, food, money and the comfortable observation of other people's distress. He is ugly, balding, massively overweight and candidly unpleasant to all people with whom he is not attempting to effect sexual intercourse or professional advancement. He is a snob; Englishness at its worst. His card offers his full nomenclature as Roger H. St. John W. Micheldene MA (Cantab). Amis's paperback illustrators faced grave problems with Micheldene, because it was difficult to offer a visual exaggeration of someone so loathsome and excessive as the man between the covers.

Amis's initial reason for the creation of so horrible an individual was that Micheldene and the novel were intended as a ceremony of expulsion that would be irreversible. He was attempting to unshackle himself from his 1950s legacy. Micheldene distilled all of the worst aspects of his previous figures into something so unforgivably foul that, thereafter, new directions were inevitable. But what Amis did not, could not, foresee was that halfway through writing the book, his own world would alter irrevocably.

Micheldene is a publisher's agent who is visiting the United States on the lookout for new writers. Much of the novel occurs in a place called Budweisser College, a somewhat downmarket version of Amis's Ivy League location in Princeton, and many of its incidents are based upon things that happened to Amis in America. Apart from being much more unpleasant than any of Amis's previous creations, Micheldene is the first without a sense of humour. A thread of comedy runs through the novel, but it is not the type that would provoke laughter and much of it is directed against Micheldene himself.

For example, Chapter 11 begins with a silent recitation of Latin poetry, including brief comments on how difficult it is to recognise line endings in time-based classical metres. It becomes apparent that this rehearsal of Micheldene's high-cultural reference points – extending to a survey of Evelyn Waugh's celebration of Pre-Raphaelite aesthetics – has a single functional purpose: it is his only reliable method of preventing premature ejaculation. The playful device of reader-orientation had become Amis's authorial signature, beginning with Jim Dixon apparently delivering his Merrie England lecture before doing an ape impression in what turns out to be his empty bedroom. With Micheldene, however, the method is not designed to disclose his taste for self-parody; more to extend his range of shallow, mechanical responses to events that we might expect to be attended by emotion.

Appropriately, it opens a chapter in which his state of pragmatic, guiltless hypocrisy is fully explored. He is in bed with Helene Bang, the wife of a Budweisser College academic. Helene is fascinated by Micheldene's apparently limitless nastiness, and after they have had sex she tries to see if there is anything beneath the surface. She asks him if he feels the need to have sex with every attractive woman he meets. 'That's who you really want, isn't it? Everybody?' (*One Fat Englishman*, 1963, pp. 135–6). He wishes to maintain Helene's interest in him, and his answer is an ingenious lie. He calculatedly becomes uncertain, even vulnerable, and responds to her question with a self-directed enquiry. Sex: 'A way of getting to know someone better than you can in any other way? That sort of thing?' But the narrator discloses to the reader what is actually going through his mind. Sex: 'To convert a creature who is cool, dry, calm, articulate, independent, purposeful into a creature which is the opposite of these; to demonstrate to an animal that is pretending not to be an animal that it is an animal.' Apart from the satisfaction of lust, his desire for sex seems to involve the proof-positive confirmation that all human beings share his brutal, nihilistic state of mind, despite their frequent claims to be better than that.

Micheldene is, by a combination of inclination and circumstance, on his own. He is the first of Amis's principal characters to be and remain in this state. He has been married twice, and we are caused to suspect that his relationship with his second wife, who remains in England, is entirely over. Amis had always dreaded being left by Hilly, and *One Fat Englishman* began partly as a projection, a hypothetical exploration of his worst fears. Detached from Hilly and his family, Amis suspected that he might become more like his loathsome creation than he cared to imagine. He had tempted fate, and fate with apposite swiftness had responded. He did not, like Micheldene, end up on his own: he moved in with Jane. At the same time, a sense of shock and disorientation attended these events. When Hilly left him he had not been planning anything permanent with Jane. Indeed, he had resigned from Cambridge and was intending to move with Hilly and family to Majorca and to live there entirely from his writing. But circumstances that he had created had altered his life in a manner that was far beyond his control, and something similar happens to Micheldene.

At the end of the novel he has boarded the liner for England. Helene has seen him off on the quay and insisted that further encounters are unlikely and unwanted, and soon afterwards,

> He looked out of his porthole and saw the quay sliding slowly past. Then he wanted very much to cry and started to do so. This was unusual for him when sober and he tried to work out why he was doing it. It was obviously a lot to do with Helene, but he had said good-bye to her and to plenty of other girls in the past without even considering crying. What was so special? (pp. 212–3).

When he wrote this Amis had already begun another relationship, but one suspects that it involves some recollection of the experience of becoming detached from the woman with whom he had lived for almost twenty years, albeit turbulent ones. The transposition of other memories with this one added to its poignancy. Four years earlier he and Hilly had left the United States together on a liner like the one on which Micheldene finds himself alone and distressed. Helene's closing words had been brief and unambiguous – 'Goodbye, Roger' – and he had watched as she 'reached the customs shed and disappeared from sight' (p. 212).

Amis had always been aware of the curious relationship between the way in which he orchestrated the experiences of his characters and the way he ran his life, and to a large extent the former had been an improvement upon the latter. With *One Fat Englishman* it must have seemed as though fiction had taken control of reality. Half-finished, the novel of departure and change had borne witness to an experience of this that its author had certainly not envisaged. Larkin was fascinated.

Via regular reports from Conquest, Larkin was fully aware of the cataclysmic events that Amis had visited upon his family, and now this story was supplemented by another. Larkin was, as always, sent a complimentary copy of Amis's new novel just before the official publication date and once more he found himself struggling to disentangle the images conjured by the words on the page from his knowledge of the man who had written them. The parallels between Micheldene and Amis would have been clear enough but why, he would have asked, was he recreating himself as someone so loathsome? The only record of how he felt about it is in a letter to Monica: 'it had a fulsome review in the *TLS* – have read it myself ... it's not an especially good book to my mind ... "To Jane" E. J. Howard? Well, warrior, no. How my friends outsoar the shadow of my night. I mean how they change, get around' (L to Monica, 12 November 1963, Bod). He clearly did not like the novel but, uncharacteristically, he did not say why. Perhaps he was unsettled by the similarities between Micheldene – by parts pathetic and vindictive – and the way he often behaved towards Monica.

Even before the novel was published, his references to Maeve, sometimes apologetic but not always, carried an air of the dispassionate and impersonal, as though she were someone not quite present or even a figure from his very distant past. After he read it, however, this tendency veers toward the disturbing.

Dear, don't, please be miserable over this Maeve business. You've been extremely tolerant all the time, and I shall be glad to have your sympathy, but I think we both feel this is the best thing at present – she is perhaps more upset than I, because it is she who has been rebuffed. I felt bound to say that I had not finished with you, nor did I seem likely to, & she just said, Well that doesn't give me much alternative, does it, & I couldn't honestly think of one. We are quite friendly & have to see each other daily – the *real* breach & dismay is yet to come, I feel. And I suppose it will come. This is like the interval between Sept 3 1939 & the first air raids. (14 September 1964)

To discuss one's occasional lover with one's long-term partner is unusual enough but to take for granted either the latter's emotional disinterestedness or immunity from distress is bizarre. Micheldene is an appalling embodiment of hypocrisy, able to disguise his true ghastly nature via a regime of dissimulation that dominates the entirety of his conscious existence. Larkin appears to have reversed this formula and forced his private and public personae into a grotesque state of coexistence. Earlier that year he had reported to Monica on Conquest's forthcoming marriage. 'He sounded in fine fettle ... What I wonder is what will happen when they're unfaithful as I feel sure they will be. And if they think they won't, they'd echo GBS "To be so greedy for a woman that you deceive yourself in the process of deceiving her"' (L to Monica, 4 January 1964, Bod). Reflecting upon the moral shortcomings of others – and he saw Conquest as a version of Amis – so dispassionately with the victim of one's own self-same misdemeanours defies comment, and is only explicable in terms of Larkin's choice to behave like his friends, but without any trace of apology or dissimulation.

The passage in Chapter 11 where Micheldene's account to Helene of the meaning of sex and love is contrasted with the narrator's disclosure of what he actually feels is pre-empted almost verbatim in a letter from Larkin to Monica, as though he had a copy of the novel to hand as he composed it, except that Larkin dispenses completely with the boundary between his inner and outer worlds.

> I'm sorry that our love-making fizzled out in Devon, as you rightly noticed ... I am not a highly sexed person, or, if I am, it's not in a way that demands constant physical intercourse with other people ... I think sex is a curious thing ... A kind of double symbol that we aren't alone and that we aren't selfish whereas of course we are alone and we are selfish ... Anyway, I'm sorry to have failed with you! (9 August 1958)

Having witnessed Amis's lifelong career of mendacity, echoed continuously in his fiction, perhaps Larkin had decided to test a thesis: is unbridled honesty more or less harmful or morally unsound than endless deceit? Significantly, one should note that during this period the peculiarities of his letter writing began to find parallels in his verse. Since the mid-1950s he had maintained the kind of emotional detachment from the topics of his poems that bespoke a sense of humility and puzzlement: he observed, was often confounded, but never really ventured to understand. Now, however, he dared to move much closer to the subjects of his verse. He did not pretend to care too much about what he dealt with; but nor did he exempt himself from a kind of self-lacerating involvement. This is evident in the brutally honest 'Love' and we find it too in a poem he began in 1962 and returned to and completed in 1964 after reading *One Fat Englishman*. His description of the 'girl on the poster' in the opening stanza of 'Sunny Prestatyn' is an almost elegiac celebration of lust:

> Kneeling up on the sand
> In tautened white satin.
> Behind her, a hunk of coast, a
> Hotel with palms
> Seemed to expand from her thighs and
> Spread breast-lifting arms.

The poster existed, certainly, and Larkin's verbalisation of it makes one wonder if its creator was attempting to transplant a jollier version of Edvard Munch's *The Madonna* to the Welsh seaside. Larkin is honest enough in his admiration for the way in which pure sexuality has blended so well with provincial cosiness, and in this respect the poster would have brought to mind his holidays with Monica, as they took their happily decadent sexual practices to nowhere more exotic than, say, Guernsey.

Within 'A couple of weeks', however, the girl has been visited by graffiti artists who disfigure her face, embolden the rest of her with 'Huge tits and a fissured crotch', 'set her fairly astride / A tuberous cock and balls' and eventually ruin her completely with a knife stab through her already 'moustached lips'. 'She was,' concludes Larkin with a pitiless irony that would have made Swift wince,

> ... too good for this life.
> Very soon, a great transverse tear
> Left only a hand and some blue.
> Now *Fight Cancer* is there.

The most troubling aspect of the poem is not so much its mood of quiet indifference as an implied sense of approval. The original image of the girl 'In tautened white satin' was visited by what it provoked, aggressive male sexuality. While Larkin never displayed any inclination toward sexual violence, his treatment of Monica during this period involved something close to cruelty, and again we find that his life comes to resemble a grotesque caricature of the figure of Amis who stalks the sprawling unpublished version of 'Letter to a Friend about Girls'. They are men who treat women much as the girl on the poster is treated, with a mixture of desire, concern and disassociation. As art, 'Sunny Prestatyn' is excellent. It combines a superb control of language with an incautious demonstration of male uncontrol, and it involves the same degree of unapologetic candour as the more disturbing letters to Monica. This sense of affiliation to events and experiences that for most would prompt denial or revulsion, despite how we might actually feel, would become a feature of the most important and widely quoted poems written during the period of his dissociation from Amis.

Maeve Brennan stated that the background to 'The Dance' involved Larkin going 'against his better judgement in following me to a Senior Common Room dance' (Brennan, *The Philip Larkin I Knew*, p. 58) that took place in late spring 1963. His better judgement told him that on this occasion Maeve would be accompanied by her, as she put it, 'jolly, lively group' of friends, who are referred to in the poem as 'her sad set'.

Throughout the poem Larkin is confronted with decisions he is reluctant to make and encounters with people that generate immediate feelings of envy, boredom and undisguised contempt. He offers us each of these in an unnervingly direct manner, as if he is participating in the poem involuntarily yet doing his best either to stay in control or find release. For example:

> ... Chuckles from the drains
> Decide me suddenly:
> *Ring for a car right now*. But doing so
>
> Needs pennies, and in making for the bar
> For change I see your lot are waving, till
> I have to cross and smile and stay and share
> Instead of walking out, and so from there
> The evening starts again ...

The piece is informed by a blend of impressionism and determinism, as if the language of the poem is continually attempting to accommodate and mediate factors that the speaker cannot foresee. Larkin had never attempted anything like it before, and the opening stanza involves his self-conscious acknowledgement of this.

> 'Drink, sex and jazz – all sweet things, brother: far
> Too sweet to be diluted to "a dance",
> That muddled middle-class pretence at each
> No one who really ...' But contemptuous speech
> Fades at my equally-contemptuous glance,
> That in the darkening mirror sees
> The shame of evening trousers, evening tie.

The first three-and-a-half lines carry inverted commas not as a disclaimer – quite the opposite. They incorporate the trademark tension between colloquial informality and arrogant control of the idiom that Larkin had perfected since the early 1950s.

Maeve's account of it is fascinating because it is often impossible to make a clear distinction between her references to the poem and her recollections of the evening. For example: 'The events and emotions that followed [Larkin's late arrival] were every bit as intense as he describes them in the poem which, for the next year, not only arrested his poetic output but also created a significant watershed in his emotional life' (ibid., p. 58). She argues that Larkin's alleged feelings of anxiety and uncertainty are re-enacted submissively in the poem, that the frantic state of mind caused by the event re-emerges as stylistic clumsiness. I would contend that quite the opposite occurs. He might well have felt temperamentally unsettled by these events but in the poem he relishes the opportunity to revenge himself against his memories. He does not attempt to disguise the truth but his unsurpassed skill as a poet enables him to impose his authority upon it. The poem presages a radical shift in Larkin's temper and manner that would manifest itself in some of the more controversial poems of *High Windows*. His verse became an enactment of the brief unapologetic mantra of 'Love', 'My life is for me'. Other people, other lives and moments of private experience would all feature but Larkin would treat them with a mixture of technical genius and casual disdain, a procedure he rehearsed during these years with those closest to him. He had watched with a mixture of amusement, disbelief and eventually envy as Amis had caused his private world of hide-and-seek to become the engine for his fiction. By contrast Larkin evolved a fascinating technique of oblique, misleading candour. He told Maeve and Monica the truth about each other, including just enough confessional material to create an authenticating blend of guilt on his part and hurt on theirs. When pressed he would also disclose to one of them characteristics of the other that were veracious – Monica's retentiveness and Maeve's unswerving religious commitment, for example – but in a double-edged way: he would subtly present them as features that despite himself he had to endure when in fact they made up the essential differences between the two women that fuelled his attraction to each. There is calculation here, certainly, but tinged with a scent of the ghoulish, which strengthens when we consider the identity of the third woman involved in this clandestine fabric of truth-telling and evasion: Eva, Larkin's mother.

Maeve had got to know Larkin's mother on an irregular, informal basis as his junior colleague during Eva's occasional visits to Hull and in 1960 it was Eva who introduced Maeve to Monica when all three were assembled to watch Philip officiate at the Queen Mother's opening of the new library. When exactly Eva was informed of Maeve's new status is not known, but she soon became her son's confidante in this, offering opinions to him on both of them while disclosing little or nothing to either of what she knew of Larkin's divided feelings.

When Eva first met Monica in the early 1950s they got on well enough, but the latter detected a reluctance to accept anyone into the Larkin clan who might not attend to its established conventions of how the women should behave with regard to the men; that is, as subservient. Eva's anxiety about Monica's confidence and independence was gradually dispersed by her recognition that while the relationship was serious and long-term it would not actually involve marriage and its expectations. Things were different with Maeve.

I liked Mrs Larkin. Although initially she seemed of a somewhat nervous disposition, she was friendly and I found her easy to talk to. Philip told me she liked me – even to the extent that she hoped he would marry me. She talked a good deal about Kitty, her daughter, and Rosemary, her granddaughter, and was obviously immensely proud of Philip. (ibid., p. 26)

Maeve's account tells us as much about her as it does about Eva. Philip and indeed Monica regarded Eva's commitment to family as inhibiting and stifling; Maeve's report on the same without comment – seamlessly attached to her disclosure that Eva saw her as a suitable daughter-in-law – indicates a special degree of fellow feeling. But before one gives in to the onrush of that debilitating interpretive virus, the Oedipus complex, one should note that, rather than treating Maeve as a substitute for something he may or may not have felt about Eva, he kept his mother informed in a rather dry, sometimes ironic way of her and Maeve's similarities. He reported on how Maeve in spring 1966 had persuaded him to donate a bottle of sherry and to attend an Oxfam party on the following Saturday, providing a detailed description of her dedication to the event and its charitable objectives, and communicating a feeling of indulgent, genial boredom: 'You see how different she is from Monica – or from me, for that matter' (13 March 1966), and, there was no reason to add, how like you.

Eva, born and brought up in the reign of Victoria, was old-fashioned, but she was not naively credulous or incognisant of the world around her. She was aware that after staying in each other's flats and holidaying together for more than fifteen years Larkin and Monica were on more than platonic terms. Indeed, while she made demands upon Larkin's time and affections that he resented, she indulged him in a way that no doubt deferred to the memory of Sydney. Larkin encouraged his mother to remain on friendly terms with two women with whom, simultaneously, he was having relationships, confident that his subtle games of deceit would not be disclosed by her to either of them and that she would talk with him confidentially about each – an unusual arrangement for middle-class, provincial England of the mid-twentieth century. Had it not been true it might have been written by Joe Orton, despite each character seeming, superficially at least, to have more in common with figures from the work of Barbara Pym.

Larkin's admiration for and eventual friendship with Pym is well recorded by Motion and in *The Selected Letters*. Her novels of the 1940s and 1950s were perhaps the only literary enthusiasm that he shared with his mother and sister Kitty. Monica enjoyed them, too, and in 1961 Maeve, following Larkin's advice, read *A Glass of Blessings* and *Less than Angels* and became a convert. The feature of Pym's work that ensured interest among this otherwise disparate network of fans was her ability to blend realism with something that appeared anachronistically at odds with post-war British society. Her novels are generally set in the quiet backwaters of middle-class Englishness where spinsters, curates and junior academics pursue routines of professional and intellectual contentment shot through with celibate flirtation.

There are, of course, parallels between this version of Barbara Pym's fictional world and Philip Larkin's poetic counterpart, but just as intriguing is the hint of personal empathy that underpins his praise for the former. In his letters to Pym, Larkin created yet another hybrid reshaping of his various foibles and idiosyncrasies, but this one was different from the others because for most of its existence, from 1961 until they met in 1975, it comprised only words on the page. By 1963 Larkin in his letters to Pym was beginning to sound like a character from one of her novels. For example, he asks without a hint of self-caricature, 'Do you know any librarians who want to come north? They are in terribly short supply these days' (13 January 1967), and when telling of his recent 'pleasant few days in Shropshire and Herefordshire, looking at eccentric decaying churches', he informed her of how 'consoled' he had felt by 'passing Michael Cantuar in a narrow lane one day' (3 October 1967; this being Michael Ramsey, Archbishop of Canterbury). Significantly, his mother features regularly – Larkin painting verbal pictures of the two of them on holiday in run-down East Anglian resorts, for example – but he cautiously avoids reference to anyone else. 'As a librarian I'm remote from teaching, examining and research; as a bachelor I'm remote from the Wives' Club or the Ups and Downs of Entertaining; as an introvert I hardly notice anything anyway' (18 July 1971). His claim to bachelordom was, of course, true but only in legal terms. Elsewhere he would report to Pym on his excursions through the picturesque regions of Britain without ever mentioning that he was accompanied by Monica. Along with his cultivated self-image as the retiring librarian his style of writing takes on the air of the cynical and certainly not unworldly Edwardian marooned six decades hence. Amis knew something of Larkin's admiration for Pym's writing but nothing of the persona he cultivated for his exchanges with her. He would have treated it as a ludicrous inversion of the man to whom he assumed he had exclusive access, which is why Larkin reinvented himself. It was one more stage in his process of distancing himself from Amis.

For some this might seem freakish, but it was consistent with Larkin's treatment of particular friendships and indeed relationships throughout the 1960s, his period of detachment from his friend. His sincerity was beyond question, yet all else was malleable to the extent that it could be shaped to accommodate another's apparent expectations of him. His concerns were as much for the other person as himself; he might argue, disagree, even appear obtuse, but within the controlling ground rules of a game played only by the two of them, if knowingly only by him. In his poetry, however, he was able to borrow features from the separate dimensions of his protean, real exist-ence and reposition them as a hybrid, recognisably Larkin to all who knew him but not exactly the one they knew. Larkin addresses Maeve, Monica, Eva and Barbara Pym with confident foreknowledge of their responses. Their expectations of him are, albeit in different ways, conditioned by what he has caused each of them to expect. Sex is the predominant issue only for two of them, but all four have become part of a fabric, constructed by Larkin, where sex, even by its absence, is whisperingly apparent. His versatil-ity is immense. He controls a web in which Edwardian hypocrisies, indeed locutions (Eva and Pym), exist alongside fetishism (Monica) and pietistic morality (Maeve). The exercise is the deliberately contrived antithesis of his friendship with Amis where the latter seemed always to have the controlling hand while Larkin felt his sense of autonomy was compromised, felt indeed like a character in one of his erstwhile friend's novels.

In the light of this, 'High Windows', 'Annus Mirabilis' and 'This Be The Verse' should be seen as pure distillations of irony. Each addresses the theme of sex, and each ridicules its own candour. Larkin writes of 'kids ... fuck-ing', of 'sexual intercourse' as now being virtually an obligation and of being fucked up by his parents. But he does so as one contemplating a society in which the new opportunity to talk about all this seems a collective delusion. He had seen it all before: the inherent tensions between public morality and private inclination, lecherous predilection and conformity, libidinous excess and monogamy had been what made sex interesting, albeit vicariously. Amis had performed for twenty years as the energetic showman. Now, apparently little is forbidden and all can be said. He joined these exchanges, in his poems, as someone who could not quite make up his mind about whether he regretted the past, envied the present or was too disappointed by both to make up his mind.

Jean Hartley tells of how during the 1960s he would comment upon the apparent changes in the moral climate in a way that combined envy with cynicism. Frequently he 'would have a good moan about his sex life, and [then] ... mention, enviously, how he had seen so-and-so coming out of a tutorial room with his arm round some toothsome undergraduate. "He's no doubt having it off with her. Lucky sod"' (Hartley, *Philip Larkin*, p. 95), which could have been a rehearsal of the famous opening of 'High Windows':

When I see a couple of kids
And guess he's fucking her and she's
Taking pills or wearing a diaphragm,
I know this is paradise

Everyone old has dreamed of all their lives

Hartley's observations are revealing but slightly misleading regarding the true inspiration for the poem. In a letter to Monica written seven years before the poem was drafted, he tells of an experience in London when he was doing a recording for the British Council. The producer was 'a dwarfish sallow ... Welshwoman so reminiscent of Mrs W John Morgan and Mrs Geoffrey Nicholson [each now married but previously Amis's mistresses, simultaneously] that I felt Kingsley would be returning from the Garden at any moment' (L to Monica, 12 May 1958, Bod). (He alludes here to the dinner party when Amis busily retired to the garden with three female guests, albeit separately.) It seemed to him, throughout the 1950s, that virtually everyone he knew – particularly if they were connected with the Amises – was likely to be involved in some kind of illicit sexual congress with someone else of his acquaintance. The mid-1960s sense of the country having suddenly discovered promiscuity seemed to him preposterous, hence the embittered irony of 'I know this is paradise / Everyone old has dreamed of all their lives'. He felt as though he'd been excluded from the excesses of the previous two decades. He had 'dreamed' of this 'paradise' knowing that it was being enjoyed by others.

Jean's shrewd depiction of him as caught between frustration and a kind of apathetic resignation corresponds closely with the voice of the poem, but in the poem he takes this a stage further to an image that is at once beautiful and outstandingly depressing. The 'deep blue air' that is 'nothing', 'nowhere', 'endless' is the most impersonal yet deeply felt conclusion to any English language poem about human relationships. The puzzle of how it can be offered 'Rather than words', given that it comprises words, provides a link between 'High Windows' and its twin, 'Annus Mirabilis', because the latter demonstrates how words can cause candour and sanguine falsehood to coexist happily.

Larkin's declaration that sexual intercourse began in 1963 carries an absurdist echo of previous attempts to rewrite history and common sense – most obviously that of the French Revolutionaries who decided that nothing worth mentioning had happened before 1789. It is also a mercilessly jargon-free anticipation of the writings of cultural theorists who would come to perceive the 1960s as a kind of fantasy via public discourse; in his opening stanza he implies – and by implication ridicules – a symbiotic link between the legalisation of Lawrence's allegedly corrupting novel, the unchaste potentiality of rock-and-roll now made socially acceptable and the sudden discovery of sex. Next he rehearses the 1960s mantras on how, prior to 'sexual liberation', all human beings existed in a state of crippling self-denial beset by the twin evils of ritual and guilt.

> Up till then there'd only been
> A sort of bargaining,
> A wrangle for a ring,
> A shame that started at sixteen
> And spread to everything.

Larkin's cold glance upon contemporaneity should not be written off as that of the standard reactionary. It was far more personal. The year when sexual intercourse 'began' was his first without any communication at all with Amis. He would have recalled Conquest's wry account of how Amis failed to appear at his appointed time at the early stage of the Chatterley trial; he was making use of the visit to London to see his current mistress and could not drag himself from their bedroom. Sexual intercourse did not, he knew, begin in 1963. Over two decades he had witnessed a sexual extravaganza that would have dumbfounded the newly 'liberated' generation.

'Annus Mirabilis' involves the same arch, ironic tone that Larkin employed when writing to his mother about Maeve and Monica, but in 'This Be The

Verse' – a poem which maintains the theme of generations present and past – the parent is shifted from addressee to subject. Some critics have attempted to read a deeper, secondary significance into the words of this poem; gratuitously, because it needs no explication. It is a witheringly transparent text. The idiom of the famous opening ('They fuck you up, your mum and dad') gives a slight nod towards fashionable, contemporaneous ideas that respect for preceding generations should be replaced by radical contempt, but Larkin rapidly undermines this: we shall inherit the worst characteristics of our forebears, irrespective of us and them being guiltless in this spiral of decline. Procreation guarantees the perpetuation of the foulest aspects of humanity and the only way to prevent this is to remain childless.

One wonders if Larkin had a quiet regard for Milton because, as with 'Dockery and Son', *Paradise Lost*, Book X, is brought to mind. Eve suggests to Adam that their dreadful condition should not be visited upon their successors: 'Childless thou art; Childless remain'. True, Larkin's circumstances differed in that he was not the potential originator of the human race, but there were parallels. He had throughout his life regarded having children as a forbidding, menacing prospect. Now, alongside this inclination, he had the opportunity to reflect upon the long-term consequences of having parents. He was becoming more and more like Sydney; for both, their job and their shared inclination towards rigour and efficiency had become, in part, a release from other aspects of life, particularly those that involved emotional commitment. Eva had become retentive and demanding to the extent that Larkin had entered a cycle of finding it difficult to distinguish between regretful, tedious duty, genuine feeling and the kind of loathing in which one sees the other party as a mirror image of oneself.

While he would offer Eva a deadpan account of the state of play with Maeve and Monica, the latter received more complex reflections upon his feelings about his mother. In August 1968 he wrote Monica a long letter that strings anecdotes on his miserable times in Loughborough between more fundamental questions on why exactly he experiences such levels of contempt for Eva. Typically:

> I wish I could avoid being so cross and irritable at home. I wish I knew what caused it. It's probably a stock psychological trait ... Or is it just that I resent the slightest demand on my self consciousness? ... really my anger is a fight for

emotional freedom against its enemy ... I suppose it links with my unhappiness at ties of all sorts, or not so much at them, but at having to do anything
to honour them.

He confesses to finding Eva 'irritating *and* boring' and then corrects himself:
'hasn't one a right to be boring at eighty?' (4 August 1968). In truth, what
irritated Larkin most were the interdependencies that come with being
alive. Parents were of course a necessary condition of existing at all, but
the concomitant responsibility of giving up elements of one's own world to
them seemed an unfair aspect of this arrangement. Or, as he put it in a more
blunt report to Monica a week later, 'God, what hell ... they [parents] *bugger
you up*, then, then *hang around your neck* and stop you ever curing yourself.
To escape from home is a life's work ...' (10 August 1968). He was working
on 'This Be The Verse' at the same time that he wrote this, and the parallels
are obvious, except that in the poem he takes the circle of questions and
complaints of the letters to an unerring conclusion:

> Man hands on misery to man.
> It deepens like a coastal shelf.
> Get out as early as you can,
> And don't have any kids yourself.

At the end of April 1971 he sent Monica the typescript, calling it 'A Little
Easter Poem' and commenting that 'I never remember my parents making a
single spontaneous gesture of affection towards each other'.

It would be absurd to argue that Larkin was able to predict exactly the
consequences of his self-willed alienation of Amis. Nevertheless he knew
that once his erstwhile friend was only a distant presence, discernible via
the media and contrived reports from Conquest, some alteration in his own
state of mind as a writer would follow. Since the age of nineteen Amis had
been part of his life. Close friendships can endure the test of time and behaviour but when this also involves a commitment by both parties to success
in a shared vocation major tensions are inevitable, especially if one of them
feels unfairly overlooked. So Larkin made a decision: 'My life is for me'. The
effect of this upon Amis was, it must be said, negligible.

The Anti-Death League explores in detail themes that Amis had only touched upon in his 1950s writing: death, absolute commitment to other human beings, our role in a world upon whose future we seem to have no influence. Its inspiration was his relationship with Jane.

The novel begins in what seem to be the grounds of a country house. Two women, unnamed, are watching an exercise in animal intrigue. A black cat is crouched in a shadow, while a bird, aware of the cat's presence, wheels in the air in an attempt to protect her nest from the hostile carnivore. Another group, 'three men in uniform', arrive and one comments: 'Look at this,' he says. 'Did you ever see anything like it?' He is referring not to the cat and the bird but to a water tower built in the same sinister, gothic style as the house. A low-flying aircraft draws the attention of both groups. It also startles the cat, whose flight across the grass causes one of the women and one of the men to glance at each other. 'Just when the girl turned and looked at the tall young man it was as if the sun went out for an instant. He flinched and drew in his breath almost with a cry' (Kingsley Amis, *The Anti-Death League*, p. 10).

The young officer and the girl are eventually disclosed as James Churchill and Catherine Casement, whose love affair is a central feature of the narrative. James is an officer involved with Operation Apollo, and Catherine is recovering from a nervous breakdown. As a means of reintroducing herself to normal life, she takes a part-time job at the village pub, where, eighty pages later, they meet again.

> 'I knew you straight away.'
> She could not stop herself saying, 'And I knew you straight away.'
> 'I know.' (p. 86)

Their encounter seems to both of them inevitable, predetermined, and their relationship begins almost immediately. Amis had never written anything like this before. The exchanges between the men sometimes involve the banter of kinship, but apart from this there is no comedy. Humour in all of Amis's previous fiction had operated partly as a support mechanism against the more unwelcome aspects of harsh reality, a tendency that reached its peak with John Lewis and its nadir in Roger Micheldene. This episode, involving the first encounters between James and Catherine, was based entirely on the opening months of the relationship between Amis and Jane.

The brief moment of eye contact in the grounds of the house is intended to capture the resonances of the Cheltenham Festival. In the novel James and Catherine seem briefly to stand outside the fabric of their respective worlds, and their companions remain largely unaware of the feeling of recognition that they share. So it was at Cheltenham, in an albeit more mundane way, that Amis and Jane secretly made each other aware of the mutual attraction. Their subsequent meetings, unlike those of their fictional counterparts, were planned, but fate seemed to have taken a hand when Hilly and the family disappeared without explanation and Amis found himself back in London with Jane, apparently for good. Amis imbues these events with echoes of the supernatural, but he integrates this with parallels drawn from actual experience.

Also, there are clues which, privately for Amis and Jane, enshrine the episode as a version of their recent, shared past. When he and Jane were conducting their secret, extramarital affair he always in his letters addressed her as 'bird'. Both knew that the word's use as a demotic term for a young, potentially seducible and unsophisticated woman was the antithesis of their exclusive understanding of it. As Amis explained in the letters his 'bird' was a creature of beauty, perceived from a distance as invulnerable and mysterious but known to him as something more. The bird of the novel threatened by the cat is wonderfully symbolic of their first encounters. Jane was fully aware of Amis's predatory, catlike reputation as a successful seducer. Conscious of this, Amis frequently signed his letters to Jane as Major Hunter, another name that would resurface in the book. In the novel the cat–bird encounter is brief and delicately ambiguous. It is the beginning of a series of accidents that bring James and Catherine together; it causes them to look at each other, yet its more ominous significance becomes part of the past.

He told Jane that the central relationship of the novel would be based on theirs, he read extracts to her and invited her to name the fictional character who was, in effect, herself. She chose Catherine Casement, he James Churchill. Catherine, like Jane, was first married at the age of nineteen. Both discovered that their husbands, while decent and affectionate enough, had married them because this was what men of their age and class were expected to do. Sex was more a part of the established ritual than a reflection of intense and mutual attraction. Both married again, and disappointment was replaced by distress. Catherine's second husband became a self-obsessed bully and would beat her when she refused to conform to his expectations of what a wife should be and do. Jane's experiences with James Douglas-Henry were not quite so unpleasant, but he did turn out to be a man whose thoughtless, selfish habits became unendurable. Catherine's second marriage has caused the nervous breakdown for which she is receiving treatment in the house that provides the setting for the opening episode, and here we begin to wonder about the motivation for Amis's distortions of actuality. James becomes the man Catherine has always been looking for, the resolution of her previous experiences of discontent and maltreatment. Jane had far more strength and confidence than her fictional counterpart; she and Amis came together on equal terms, and it is evident that in his recreation of their relationship Amis was involved in the massaging of his ego.

The name Max Hunter, borrowed by Amis from his letters to Jane, is appended in the novel to a friend of James, another officer involved in Operation Apollo, and the first of Amis's principal characters who is homosexual. He reflects Amis's liberal but not condescending opinions on homosexuality, and he catches the mood of the period. At one point James suggests to him that, while his enforced lifestyle denies him even the option of continued emotional involvement with one person, it also licenses uncommitted sexual activity, a state that many heterosexual men would, if they were honest, envy. Hunter answers that 'Yes it ought' and adds, enigmatically, that 'it didn't work like that. I was still finding my way in those days. I'm in no such danger now' (p. 91). Hunter seems to be saying that age and endurance have immunised him from the need for emotional commitment, but the reader knows that he is lying, that James has reminded him of the cruel irony of their respective roles. James has fallen in love and has chosen fidelity, and Hunter envies James.

As he prepared the exchange between James and Hunter, Amis would have been transcribing and rewriting conversations with himself. His own libidinous career was not, like that of Hunter, a legal necessity, but there were many similarities. His habit of having sex with practically every attractive woman who was similarly inclined was, as he often conceded to the likes of Larkin and Conquest, as much a condition as an option. Moreover, he shared with Hunter an ongoing mixture of fear, conspiratorial excitement and clubbish falsehood. All of his pre-*Anti-Death League* novels had drawn upon and made use of the divided, multi-faceted nature of his world. The most productive parallel between his world and his writing was his life of deception with Hilly, and suddenly all of this had changed completely and apparently irreversibly.

Hilly had admired, read and enjoyed his work, but she was not a conscious participant in it. Jane was a writer. She joined in with what had now become Amis's only professional activity. Assisted by Monkey, she tried the experiment of imitating his style, and parts of *One Fat Englishman* were written by her, although to this day she refuses to identify them. In effect, the Amis who had previously been the private point of intersection between his various personae had become part of an open exchange with someone else. His keeping of secrets from Hilly, which involved the interspersing of displaced guilt with the pleasures of calculated invention, was the perfect foundation for a fictional mode that was at once candid and evasive. *The Anti-Death League* obliged him to try something different.

What happens in *The Anti-Death League* is that truth becomes part of the book's fabric, something that its characters have to confront and not just enact. For the first time Amis obliges us to wonder if there are forces at work in the narrative and, by implication, in the real world, that are not grounded only in choice and circumstance.

Soon after James and Catherine begin their relationship we find them strolling through the countryside. James

> looked at her and past her together, so that girl, trees and stream formed a unity. She turned her head and looked at him. He knew for certain that in some way this moment had become inevitable ever since that other moment the afternoon he first saw her when he had looked at a patch of country similar to this one and thought of her. He felt his heart lift. This had never happened to him before, and he was surprised at how physical the sensation was. He was filled with joy. (ibid., p. 198)

The style of this passage and its implied message are so different from anything that Amis had written before as to beggar belief. It is elegant enough and while it stops short of being mawkishly overwritten one suspects that Amis is not quite certain of how much further it is safe to venture. He was in unfamiliar territory and the novel provides a fascinating index to a writer caught between resolution and perplexity. It resonates with eagerness for life and an almost evangelistic appetite for candour that belies everything known about its cynically guileful middle-aged author.

It was his first post-Larkin novel and while the energy of the narrative derives from his relationship with Jane it must be said that if he were still in close contact with his friend it probably would not have been written, or at least not in anything like the way that it was. Even though there were periods such as the year in Princeton when Amis became lazily distant from Larkin he always did his best to make up for lost time, keeping him informed on everything from his affairs to his by parts hilarious and cruel portraits of mutual acquaintances. It was Larkin who ceased communications in 1960 and we can never know for certain what would have happened had he not done so. It is, however, more than probable that Larkin's silence reinforced Amis's sense of having alighted upon a world exclusive to himself and Jane. For the first time in his adult life he found himself without the necessities and pleasures of duplicity. Even though he committed himself to a monogamous relationship with Jane this did not mean that he would have undergone a comparably radical change in his friendship with Larkin, had correspondence and meetings continued on a regular basis. Certainly, he would no longer have used him as a counsel for his infidelities and correlate attacks of insecurity, but it is impossible to imagine that their habit of sharing intimate aspects of their lives and thoughts denied to all others would not have continued. It was the unique, defining feature of their friendship. It caused Larkin to bring it to a close, feeling as he did variously stifled and manipulated by the experience, and its cessation, ironically, enabled Amis to write a novel unlike any other he had so far produced or would venture to write in the future. Truth, and its corresponding qualities – candour, principle, commitment, resolution *et al.* – are distributed through it as tributes to the equally guileless, faithful state of mind that its author had engineered for himself. The continued presence of Larkin would have undermined both, albeit involuntarily on his part.

Ten years before, such a passage as that quoted above, by some other writer, would for the amusement of Larkin have been subjected by Amis to merciless ridicule. But Larkin was no longer around.

The first two years of Amis's relationship with Jane were unimprovably idyllic, at least in Amis's view. Soon, however, shadows began to spread across his image of perfection and signs of doubt are evident in his next novel,

I Want It Now. Ronnie Appleyard, the principal male character, has a background in journalism and, as the novel begins, is enjoying the high salary, fame and hedonistic lifestyle of a TV current-affairs programme presenter. He secures his own popularity by exposing politicians as self-serving hypocrites and by comparison presenting himself as a caring radical whose leftish opinions nonetheless transcend the careerist motives of politics. Ronnie is symptomatic of what in Amis's view is the almost obligatory attachment to fashionable left-wing causes by writers, journalists and all persons associated with the arts and the media. In the year the novel came out Amis wrote a pamphlet called *Lucky Jim's Politics*, which was published by the Conservative Political Centre. As he had done in its predecessor, *Socialism and the Intellectuals*, he made provocative use of his opinion that political allegiance by its very nature involves simplifications and falsifications of the contemporary world. For Amis the Conservative Party was now the only political grouping without an all-inclusive ideology, and in Jane's view even this grudging attachment was disingenuous – his apparent interest in any kind of politics was, according to her, 'a complete façade'. The novel would supplement the Catherine/James creation as an evocation of the uniqueness of Amis's still new relationship with Jane, and their trip to America would provide him with useful material for this enterprise.

Amis had made and maintained a large number of friends and contacts during his year in Princeton. One, Russell Fraser, had become head of the English Department at Vanderbilt University, Nashville, an Ivy League-style institution as old as the Confederacy. Fraser contacted Amis at the end of 1966 and suggested that he spend the first part of the following academic year there, partly as writer-in-residence and partly as a replacement for an academic on sabbatical, the latter providing him with a decent salary plus expenses. Amis in his *Memoirs* wrote that he had enjoyed his first American experience so much that he accepted the invitation almost immediately and 'failed to do what I soon discovered I should have done and drop it like a hot potato' (*Memoirs*, p. 279). He knew about the American South, but until he arrived in Nashville he was not aware that most of it had hardly changed at all since before the Civil War. Amis and Howard boarded the *Queen Mary* in October 1967 for what would be the liner's final transatlantic voyage. They went on their own, leaving his children, now all in their mid- to late teens, with various relatives, Hilly included.

There is a joke about a man being shown the various rooms available in Hell. The best seems to involve a group of condemned souls chatting agreeably and drinking cocktails, albeit while standing knee deep in something resembling faeces. The man chooses this one only to be told that the weekly break is now over: 'Back on your heads.' An experience not unlike this was visited upon Kingsley and Jane when they arrived in the United States. They first spent a week with his old friends in Princeton, where the people were much as he remembered them from a decade before, while the place had become victim to the ongoing state of 'modernisation' that characterised American town planning and architecture. Things got much worse. During his previous trip Amis had visited only the northeastern states, but during this one, as the train rolled south, he began to notice not just a change in the climate and scenery but in time. This suspicion was confirmed by a number of his experiences in Nashville. Despite attempts by Washington governments from the Kennedy years onwards to drag the South out of its racist practices, still frequently enshrined in state legislation, racism was in 1967 very much the uncontested state of mind of the majority of its white population. Worse than that, Amis found that the university itself, which he expected to be an enlightened retreat from a world involving the Klan and the legendary 'separate-seats' policy of public transport and bars, contained a large number of educated people who regarded 'nigas' as sub-humans. Walter Sullivan, the academic and novelist on sabbatical, was an unashamed proponent of the maxim that black students could never receive A grades since they were, in his view, mentally deficient. His thesis was hypothetical, because he had never had to mark the work of black students. Amis, soon after his arrival, asked a colleague if Vanderbilt had started to admit blacks. 'Yes, of course,' he was told. 'He's called Mr Moore... when he first came here a couple of years ago he seemed to enjoy it, but now, he doesn't seem to like it so well' (*Memoirs*, p. 282). Amis treated the 'Moore' pun as a case of unintended and ominous irony.

Racism operated in Nashville and the surrounding area as a remarkably classless doctrine, unaffected by matters such as wealth, position or intellectual acumen. Amis was introduced to the director of the Jack Daniel's distillery in neighbouring Lynchburg, who told of how they all still revered the memory of old Jack whose statue stood prominently in the town square. The director recalled an incident in which a group of blacks, who had been trimming trees around the statue, had carelessly allowed a falling branch to take a chip out of Jack's hat. The director's predecessor, a Mr Motlow, felt they should be disciplined, and he shot them. When was this? enquired Amis. Back in 1890; 1910? No; 1952. Then there was the wife of a Professor of Iberian Languages who was appalled at how 'Surr Lawrence Oh-livayay' had to endure in the filming of '*Oh-thello*' the humiliating experience of being forced to 'look', 'woke' and 'toke' 'like a black mayon' (*Memoirs*, p. 286).

For Amis, Nashville was a distorted mirror image of Czechoslovakia, which he and Jane had visited in 1965. In Prague people had to endure an ideology that was forced upon them and which, in their own best interests, they reluctantly endorsed. In Nashville one half of the population imposed upon the other an evil ideology that the former regarded as fact and the latter as something they could do little about.

The Nashville experience presented Amis with a problem that went beyond his loathing for the place. He had now become an eccentric Tory. He had publicly announced his support for the US policy in Vietnam – against virtually all other writers in Britain – even suggesting that Britain should join in. As he saw it, the totalitarian and overtly Maoist regime of North Vietnam would be much worse than the alleged corruption of the South.

Amis's rightward drift prompted the only exchange of letters between him and Larkin of the late 1960s. Conquest had alerted the latter to Amis's imminent emergence as a spokesman on Vietnam. 'KA has got very active politically, and just organised a letter to *The Times* saying balls to the Vietcong from all of us' (15 January 1967). The 'us' were mainly those connected with the so-called 'fascist' lunches at Bertorelli's restaurant near the offices of *The Spectator*, notably Amis, Conquest, John Braine, Peregrine Worsthorne and Bernard Levin. Three weeks later, Conquest sent Larkin an enthusiastic report on the impact of *The Times* letter, which provoked outrage among all shades of the media. 'Good stuff. You should have joined in – old KA was the moving spirit, getting the signatures, taking them in etc., etc.' (9 February 1967). Larkin wrote to Amis in March expressing his support and suggesting, rather bizarrely, that they should both attend a forthcoming anti-Vietnam demonstration in London as vocal supporters of US intervention. The letter no longer exists and there is therefore no concrete evidence to support the suspicion that the proposal was intentionally farcical. Amis, however, appears to have taken him seriously, replying, 'I can't, of course, come to the

Communist demonstration ... because I shall be in America then. Not that I would even if I'd been able to. It's no use trying to argue with anti-British fanatics' (A to L, 21 May 1967). Larkin's reply indicates, contra Amis's rant, that the idea of them attending the march had been put very much in the spirit of the men they used to be in the 1950s, writers for whom politics was more a subject for caricature than serious involvement: 'Delighted to hear from you. Don't worry about the red lads: I'll fix'm' (L to A, 3 June 1967). This instance of crossed lines probably confirmed for Larkin that Amis was still an individual whose world and life were largely self-contained. The brief correspondence ceased thereafter but Larkin remained faintly intrigued by how Amis would distil his newfound political idealism and his forthcoming, second, visit to the US into his new novel.

In America in 1967 the anti-war movement was finding a voice, particularly among students and younger academics. Although Vanderbilt was in general more conservative than its northern counterparts, it was not immune to the growing mood of protest, and Amis faced, had indeed become, an example of his thesis that all-inclusive political doctrines involved innate contradictions. He frequently found himself having to explain how someone who supported the war could at the same time feel so disturbed and unsettled by the time-honoured version of apartheid still practised in the American South and publicly defended by the kind of politicians who were also enthusiastic cold warriors. This would eventually become an irritating chore, but it would also play an important part in the reinvention of himself as Ronnie Appleyard in *I Want It Now*.

Ronnie is a successful and comfortably uncommitted seducer, at least until he meets Simona Quick at a London party. The event is another reworking of Amis's and Jane's meeting at the Cheltenham Festival, with the initial mood of mutual attraction and sexual potential being gradually replaced by something more unique and enduring. Amis changes a large number of things, partly to hide the personal element from reviewers and journalists and partly to mount an assault upon what he regarded as the more disagreeable aspects of late 1960s society. Simona is nineteen, much younger than Catherine, and has personal characteristics so completely different from Jane's as to virtually announce themselves as covering devices. Her verbal habits involve the use of main clauses rather than sentences or, if she is feeling particularly bored or indifferent, monosyllables, a feature of contemporary 'youth culture' offered to Amis by his children and their friends. She is spoilt and selfish, she takes drugs and she began her sexual career aged fourteen. She has, she tells Ronnie, since then had sex with forty-two men, none of which she has enjoyed and none of whom she has even liked. The title of the novel is her response to Ronnie's unnecessarily sophisticated opening chat-up. These characteristics are, however, interweaved with a love story that is an indulgently romanticised version of the one Amis was in, so much so as to suggest parallels between himself and Ronnie as the Prince and Jane/Simona as the Sleeping Beauty.

Simona belongs to a very wealthy family. Her mother, Lady Baldock, is a successful social climber, whose first marriage to a hereditary peer, resulting in Simona, has piloted her into a career involving even richer partners. Lady Baldock and her minions profess concern with Simona's unhealthy, self-destructive lifestyle, but Amis makes it clear that their own state of indifferent greed is actually its cause. The model for the hideous Lady Baldock was provided by Jane's friend Dolly Burns, a wealthy self-indulgent socialite and daughter of the hereditary peer Lord Duveen. Dolly was seventy when Amis first met her and he was caused on one occasion to comment to Jane that it was fortunate for any putative human being not to have become her son or daughter. The Burnses had houses in Mayfair and Jamaica and maintained the lifestyle of millionaire aristocrats seemingly unaffected by the levelling policies of the post-war Labour administration. Amis and Jane dined regularly at Chesterfield Hall, their Mayfair mansion, once, memorably, sharing the fourteen-seat table with the American Secretary of State for Defense, three hereditary peers – one a duke – and the two most senior remaining members of the Habsburg dynasty, and in late summer 1965 spent a week with them, at the Burnses' expense, at the most expensive hotel in Cap d'Antibes. Dolly would spend afternoons with her lover, a Russian composer, chauffeured back and forth to his flat in the Rolls-Royce that had been driven from London by the chauffeur for their use in the south of France. Amis, for a while, assumed the demeanour of the amused but indulgent spectator, but gradually he began to feel less comfortable with the fact that Jane moved among these types with artless insouciance; she obviously already belonged. He did not envy her background. Indeed, her sense of being from a class he had known only vicariously was part of her attraction. But as he became more acquainted with the Burnses and their like, he found that his disavowal of everything leftish was slightly contrary to something still deeply embedded in his temperament.

In 1966 when he and Jane accompanied the Burnses on a trip to the West Indies, his mask of indulgence slipped. Ostentatious lives of luxury were one thing but he found himself appalled by the way that the indigenous population, the Afro-Caribbeans, were treated by the rich whites as though slavery were still in place. He wrote to Colin, Jane's brother, of

> the rather horrible rich white people and the rather miserable resentful black people. My old lefty-wing, or just humanitarian, feelings came back with a rush. I wouldn't argue that they ought not to have been given their independence but they bloody well ought to have been given some means of livelihood. (3 February 1966)

Amis's reversion to his old sympathies was compounded by his experience in Nashville, and out of this Ronnie Appleyard was born. Ronnie's patience is tested beyond endurance by the Baldocks, and after insulting one of their blatantly racist guests he is expelled from their house. But he went further than using Ronnie as a convenient salve to his conscience. He rescues Simona from the family and the milieu that have caused her egregious narcissism. As a consequence, Simona emerges as an individual with intelligence, self-esteem and a genuine capacity to fall in love. In between the fictional refashionings of their situation, Amis's perception of himself as a class below Jane, and as someone who can transcend the privileged features of her lifestyle, shines through. The novel ends with Ronnie and Simona in London and, in effect, an exchange between Amis and Jane. He confesses that 'I was a shit when I met you. I still am in lots of ways. But because of you I've had to give up trying to be a dedicated full-time shit.' She, too, admits that she has often 'been a terrible fool' and that 'we'll have to work on each other'. The closing image is of them leaving the novel: 'they went out and in a diagonal shuffle, arms about shoulders, made their ways across the road' (*I Want It Now*, p. 204).

The recreation of himself as Ronnie, a figure who becomes a better man and a point of stability for his more vulnerable partner, carried much more than a trace of egotism. He is reverting to a habit that marked all of his 1950s fiction. This was far more subtle and complex than self-delusion, but it involved the same technique of overriding those aspects of lived existence that proved unsuitable with versions that were virtually identical but for the fact that Amis takes over from intractable circumstance and fate. To an extent Ronnie and Simona's relationship closely resembled that of Amis and Jane, in that Amis sows into the former a commendable thread of doubt and on his/Ronnie's part a remorseful disclosure of his imperfections. With Jane/Simona, however, it involves a far more manipulative reshaping of truth for his own ends. In simple terms Amis was becoming intolerant of the kind of society that came as part of the package of their relationship, so in the novel he rescues her from it, improves her as an individual and ensures that the two of them can exist undisturbed by its influences. Larkin spotted the author in the fiction. To Conquest he expresses admiration for the craftsmanship, particularly the 'lean foul mouthed prose', but qualifies this:

> as usual ... he betrays his hero. Having chosen a 'bad' man as his central character, K. puts so much of himself into him that ¾ of the way through the book he has to slap him down, he's too attractive (like Milton and Satan) – and of course the slapping is terribly artificial, and one hates it, and ends the book in a bad temper. (L to Conquest, 2 November 1968)

Even though he did not know of the background to Amis's recreation of himself as Ronnie – particularly the private dilemma caused by Jane's class and background – Larkin was familiar enough with Amis's use of fiction as a vehicle for self-exculpation to be able to read through the novel. He continues. It 'reminded me ... of *LJ* where a nasty character (Bertram, Lady What'sit [Baldock]) has to be defeated and a ludicrous scene has to be engineered for this purpose, quite unconvincing'. In *Lucky Jim*, the target for Amis's revenge was by parts his in-laws and Monica, and his means was the 'ludicrous' fist fight with Bertrand, the drunken lecture and the triumphant railway station departure with Christine. Despite his ignorance of the Burnses, the trips to the West Indies and Nashville, he knew Amis well enough to detect another case of truth 'engineered' according to preference.

10

Reconciliation

After the cursory exchange of letters in 1966 silence reigned during the subsequent eighteen months, which included Amis's and Jane's visit to the US and Mexico. In early March 1968, Conquest tried to persuade Larkin to come to a 'Welcome Home Kingers' lunch at Bertorelli's restaurant on the twenty-first of that month. Larkin declined, but wrote to Amis in early April to apologise for his absence and to suggest, if it were convenient for the latter, lunch in London on 8 May when Larkin would be in the city on university business. Amis enthusiastically agreed, but in his reply Larkin, for the first time ever in correspondence, admonished him without even a hint of clubbish banter. As if to warn him of what he expected at their meeting he reminded him of their last lunch, three years before, when Amis's drunkenness, 'insane cackling and truculent conduct' had drawn 'many curious looks' (22 April 1968, Hunt). Larkin reported to Conquest on 12 May that he had endured the more recent meeting while not greatly enjoying it. Amis constantly 'talked of £50,000 houses in Barnet'. The 'houses' were actually one residence already looked at by Jane, which they would purchase by auction on 25 May. Lemmons was a late-Georgian mansion with eight bedrooms, extensive ancient outbuildings including a guest cottage and two acres of mature gardens. It was, just, a country house, but within walking distance of the underground's Northern Line, and thereafter only half an hour away from central London. Larkin had commented that 'this must be by the saying of Crazy Jane mustn't it?' Not quite. Since before their departure for the US, Amis was showing further signs of a temperamental reflex that first manifested itself a decade earlier when he left for Princeton, and soon after that decided on a permanent move to Cambridge and then to Majorca. He seemed to think that alterations in his outward life, his environment, might remedy more deep-rooted problems. Colin 'Monkey' Howard: 'Nashville was supposed to revive the honeymoon period. Well no, Kingsley thought that it would. And it seemed to work. The time away was I think cementing for them, they spent a lot of time in each other's company.' Lemmons seems to have been the next stage in this process of transformative 'cementing'. The house would be a middle-class commune, comprising the owners, Kingsley and Jane, Monkey, his friend the artist Sargy Mann, Martin when he was down from Oxford, where he had just secured a place to read English, and various other friends and disparate family members. Conquest, replying to Larkin, was fascinated. 'The theory of Barnet it seems is that anyone going there for dinner stays the night ... Christ knows what K is up to' (21 May 1968, Bod). *A Look Round the Estate*, Amis's most recent volume of verse, was published six months before they purchased Lemmons, but its title drew on what inspired Amis's search, before they left for the US, for a house rather like Ormerod's in *Take a Girl Like You*. Ormerod is a man with no illusions, sagacious, wry but not unkind in his dealings with others. His demeanour is conferred upon him, in part, by his patrician status and Patrick, like his creator, views him with jaundiced admiration. Amis now found himself pretending to features of his persona, though these competed unequally with those of a more recent invention. When they purchased the house Amis was two-thirds of his way through *The Green Man* (1969).

Maurice Allington owns a hotel and restaurant called the Green Man, forty miles from London and within easy reach for the culinary sophisticates of Cambridge. We know the location of the Green Man, the price of its eel soup and the unsound quality of its white Burgundies before we encounter Maurice: an excerpt from *The Good Food Guide* precedes the narrative.

This mixture of candour and detail sets the standard for Maurice's account. In the next five pages he tells of his family: his wife Joyce; Amy, his thirteen-year-old daughter from his first marriage; and his eighty-year-old father. He confides in the reader: he drinks a bottle of whisky a day and he intends to have sex with 'tall, blonde and full-breasted Diana', the wife of his closest friend (Kingsley Amis, *The Green Man*, p. 14). All of this is shot through with asides on the varying qualities of his pork and salmon dishes, the gullish philistinism of his clientele and the 'hypocrisy' of having *sauce vinaigrette* with avocado pears. We might not like Maurice Allington, but he is disarmingly honest.

Why, we wonder, does Maurice feel the need to confess, albeit unapologetically, while embedding these confidences in meticulous detail? He leaves nothing out of his account, partly because he needs to reassure himself that his story is true. Maurice is given to entertaining his guests, particularly Americans, with the tale of Thomas Underhill, who owned the inn in the seventeenth century, made a pact with the devil, sacrificed his wife and monitored the murderous activities of a wood creature from whom the inn takes its name. Maurice's tale to the reader involves his discovery that the legend is true and that Underhill has returned.

For the first half of the narrative Maurice allows us to share his initial scepticism. He has seen figures, shapes, oddly coloured birds. But he is in a peculiar condition. His father has just died, his domestic life is a mess and he drinks too much. Soon after he has seduced Diana she, too, sees a terrifying, not-quite human figure in the lane; but so what? This is an exciting element of their shared deception: 'she had demonstrated a fresh superiority by seeing a ghost when I had not. Did she now think she had really seen a ghost?'(ibid., p. 123).

In Chapter 4 any ambiguities are removed. From his sitting-room Maurice witnesses the freezing of time and space. 'Down to the left, forty or fifty yards away across the grass, a couple of waxworks cast their shadows, the seated one with a hand stuck out in the direction of something, probably a cup of tea, that the standing one was offering it, and were Lucy and Nick', his daughter-in-law and son (ibid., p. 137). In his sitting-room is a young man, whom Maurice describes with customary attention to detail: about twenty-eight, clean-shaven, good teeth, silver-grey suit, black knitted tie, humorous but not very trustworthy face. The young man is God. Michael Radcliffe in *The Times* argued that 'In relating supernatural hallucinations to the psychology of a selfish and unhappy man [Amis] has moved towards the tough metaphor of disintegration.' In short, Maurice, throughout his account, is mad. Amis, in a 1975 interview, disagreed. 'It all really happens ... none of what is recounted happens only in the hero's mind' (*Contemporary Literature*, 16 January 1975). In an interview with Clive James (*New Review*, July 1974, pp. 21–8), Amis told of how, when planning the book, he had posed a question: 'What happens when the man who sees ghosts is an alcoholic?' In the interview this figure is treated as an invention, a hypothesis, but in fact Amis was talking about himself. Jane Howard testifies to the fact that by the end of the 1960s he would often match the bottle-a-day intake of Maurice. The bouts of anxiety attacks that in the late 1940s he had feared were symptoms of mental disorder returned with a vengeance. Maurice suffers from 'jactitations', an uncontrollable twitching of limbs frequently accompanied by 'hypnogogic hallucinations', and so did Amis. For both, the condition was exacerbated by excessive boozing. Jane claims that Amis would sometimes hallucinate, alleging that on several occasions he became incapable of distinguishing between actual and imagined events. Once he spent a day arguing with her about who exactly had attended the previous evening's dinner party, when no such gathering had actually taken place.

Conquest kept Larkin up to date, reporting on 15 January 1970 (Bod) on their mutual friend's periods of alcohol-fuelled amnesia, notably 'an increasingly common experience of not remembering how he got home'. No one present at the time would deny that Amis was drinking a lot but opinions differ on the true extent of the effects. Colin Howard states that 'yes, he would "forget things" from the night before but only to the extent that after drink none of us can claim to have an accurate recollection of exactly what we did or said'. He continues. 'The house was stocked with every brand of malt whisky, and many other types of spirit. There were crates of beer and a full wine cellar. It seemed as though the place was being prepared for a siege. But Kingsley was not a private drinker. He enjoyed playing host.' A host not unlike the landlord of the Green Man. The parallels between Maurice's regime at his hostelry and Amis's at Lemmons are clear enough. Certainly, the latter did not claim to have encountered an agent of Satan in the spacious grounds or entertained God in the well-appointed sitting room but each figure divided opinion on whether drink had begun to loosen their grip upon reality. It could be contended that his ability to write such a book as *The Green Man*, where a beguiling game of truth and delusion is offset by beautifully engineered prose, testified to Kingsley's claim, endorsed by Colin Howard, that throughout those years he remained balanced and rational.

But the significance of the book, for Amis, ran much deeper than the issue of his drinking habits and their effects. The opinions of members of Allington's family and his circle of friends on the kind of man that he is, and in particular on the sincerity of his commitment to Joyce, differ considerably, which is a fair reflection of the varying perceptions of Amis himself and the state of his marriage. Amis had encountered this before when he was married to Hilly. Then, in his fiction, he refashioned, often sanitised, the truth. Now, however, he has Allington summon the truth for his own private contemplation. That others might treat his story as absurdly implausible secures it as a condition that he alone can no longer avoid.

When Maurice first has sex with Diana he chooses to do so in a wooded vale, a peculiar choice given that the Green Man is a hotel with plenty of empty rooms and beds. Diana comments on this, and asks him if he has visited this location before for the same purpose. He admits that he has, and so had Amis in *The Anti-Death League* when he used an almost identical situation to cement the relationship between Catherine and James (Jane and himself). In the earlier novel he had qualified the blissful optimism of the moment with the discovery of Catherine's cancer. In *The Green Man* Maurice has chosen the site for adultery not because he has used it before – he lies about this – but because it is close to the churchyard in which Underhill the Satanist is buried.

Jane Howard states that during their marriage Amis had 'at least two' brief affairs and that by the end of the 1960s his previous commitment to monogamy and fidelity was beginning to disintegrate. It thus seems appropriate that Maurice should have decided to indulge his lustful impulses in a place that is adjacent to the grave of the most horrible fictional presence that he has ever created. When he first meets the resurrected Satanist, Maurice asks Underhill why exactly he has been selected as his contact in the mortal world. Underhill answers, 'How have I chosen you, when it is you that have each time come in search of me?' (p. 153).

Maurice, like his author, is despite himself in search of disagreeable truths, and the most significant of these was Amis's recreation of Jane as two women, Joyce and Diana. Joyce embodies Jane's combination of tolerance and endurance. Both worry about their husband's state of mind, health and self-destructive habits, take care of the mundane day-to-day chores that existed outside his selfish solipsistic lifestyle, and both do their best, with some success, as replacement mother figures for his children. Diana is Maurice's exciting excursion from monogamy and domesticity, much as Jane had been five years before, and there are more ingrained similarities. Joyce is offered Jane's more endearing qualities, while Diana is provided with those that had begun to irritate Amis. Diana is egotistical, her linguistic mannerisms are at once intrusive and theatrical, and she is intrigued by Maurice's inner turmoil in a way which, to Amis, seemed pretentious and hypocritical. Four years after their final break-up, Amis openly based Nowell Hutchinson of *Stanley and the Women* (1984) on Jane, and Nowell is Diana reborn. Significantly, he confided to his official biographer, Eric Jacobs, that they should have broken up earlier than they did; 'about 1970 would be right', a year after *The Green Man* was published. Maurice attempts to persuade Joyce and Diana that a sexual threesome would for each of them be exciting and, in a perverse way, honest. This happens, with the result that the two women are far more attracted to and interested in each other than in Maurice, and soon afterwards he loses both of them.

The marriage would endure but for each of them unalloyed infatuation and devotion was replaced by a confrontation with fact. Each was coming to terms with what the other was really like. Could this have prompted Amis to renew communications with his oldest friend, the man in whom he had once confided his true and often disgraceful habits and state of mind? Colin Howard offers an insight:

> Most of us knew about his friendship with Larkin and it did seem odd, that since he'd married Jane he was never a guest at the house, and he hardly ever came up in conversation. But at the end of the 1960s Kingsley began to talk more often about 'Philip'. Anecdotes and so on. It did seem strange, the contrast between the mood of Kingsley's recollections – nostalgic, as if there was no going back – and the fact that Philip was still very much alive, a public figure.

Amis's eventual overture to Larkin might have come from Allington. At the beginning of the novel he disabuses the reader of his claims to connoisseurship regarding drink, wine in particular.

> The point about white Burgundies is that I hate them myself ... I enjoyed seeing those glasses of Chablis or Pouilly Fuissé, so closely resembling a blend of cold chalk soup and alum cordial with an additive or two to bring it to the colour of child's pee, being peered and sniffed at, rolled around the shrinking tongue and forced down somehow by parties of young technology dons from Cambridge or junior television producers and their girls. Minor compensations of this sort are all too rare in a modern innkeeper's day. (Amis, *The Green Man*, p. 7)

The mood of this – let's play a joke on the intelligentsia of drink – informs Amis's letter to Larkin of 11 August 1970. He had, he reported, recently secured a contract to do a series of articles on drink and drinking for the *Daily Telegraph*, which he wishes to supplement with observations on the subject from 'distinguished shags of my acquaintance'. Would Larkin, he asks, care to participate in this collective practical joke?

The manner of Larkin's reply can best be described as overwrought courtesy. He opens: 'Many thanks for your letter – what a pleasant surprise – and for thinking of me in connection with your article' (L to A, 14 August 1970, Hunt). As the letter proceeds Amis might have been forgiven for suspecting that his erstwhile friend had been stricken by mild amnesia. There are touches of the old raillery: 'Of course I agree to cooperate in principle, as long as you're not letting me in for anything derogatory ("After Dylan Who?" "Alcoholics Of the Seventies") … I don't have any "favourite drinking places" in Hull, except my own flat.' But these are brief remissions from a mood of leaden formality.

> Arranging it, I am afraid, will be rather difficult. Next week (say 17th–24th) I am taking my mother to Cheltenham for a holiday, and after that I shall be very busy here until I go to Oxford in the middle of September. In consequence, I shan't be able to accept your very kind invitation to the party – wish I could – so that most obvious opportunity is no good.

Amis had suggested that he might interview Larkin, even that 'I could come to Hull, if need sodding be' (11 August 1970). Since Larkin's time in Belfast it had been a point of good-natured complaint from Larkin that Amis was never willing to visit him. It had at least begun as good-natured but by the late 1950s, in Hull, Larkin was allowing a hint of genuine rancour into such comments, and Amis now appeared to show a degree of supplication. The 'party' to which Larkin refers was an event to which in the same letter Amis had invited him, proposing that 'Bob and C' [Conquest and his third wife Caroleen] would collect him from King's Cross. The *Telegraph* piece was clearly a pretext for suggestions that they might begin to renew something that, inexplicably, they had lost almost ten years before. Without turning him down completely, Larkin indicated that this was not quite good enough. His reply was professionally typed on a University of Hull,

Brynmor Jones Library letterhead ('Librarian: P. A. Larkin, MA') and just
to ensure that Amis had no doubts that the piece had indeed been dictated
to Larkin's secretary, in the manner of a formal if politely relaxed letter to
a fellow librarian, he added the token endnote in longhand: 'Conor Cruise
O'Brien bum.' Amis didn't give up, apologising in his next letter (3 August
1970) for the deadline being shortened by the *Telegraph*, which meant that
the interview would be imminent. Larkin replied on 1 September that the
interview was not possible and that since 'I'm not going to have the pleasure
of seeing you – and sharing gin and jocosity' he would have to 'open my
bloody old typewriter and *think* ... aren't I practically writing for the DT
Colour Mag? Shouldn't they slip me ten guineas at the least?' Then, antagonism is replaced by the Larkin-to-Amis of old, in the form of what he would
write if Amis insisted:

> My general thoughts are along the lines of the job of drink is to make you
> drunk ('He remembered reading somewhere–') and tasting so horrible that
> no one would drink it if it didn't; how it ought to be taxed less and things like
> tea and ice-cream and sweets taxed more; how frightful pubs are becoming IN
> ALL WAYS – that kind of thing you want? And how fat it makes you how fat
> it m.' (1 September 1970, Hunt)

Both seemed capable of making tentative gestures towards renewal, but
something of their respective temperaments would hinder this. Amis had
already stated, in a jokey manner but founded on fact, that the *Telegraph*
series would secure for him virtually limitless supplies of expensive alcohol,
either free or tax-deductable, and when he returned to Larkin a version of
his 'drink is to make you drunk' passage, roughened with observations of his
own disguised as those of Larkin, for approval before going to press Larkin
ordered him to withdraw the piece and refused to take any further part.

> I'm afraid this idea is getting beyond me. The first suggestion was for an inter-
> view, and I agreed. Then this turned into a request for 250 words for nothing,
> which I wasn't so keen on. Now you suggest you make up 100 words from
> about 50 of mine not chosen for publication at all. No, it might turn out all
> right, but chances are that I should feel I'd been misrepresented, and I shall
> only have myself to blame so let's scrub it. (4 September 1970, Hunt)

One feels that beneath the nominal subject, the article, runs a thread of bitterness at being the also-ran stretching back to *Lucky Jim*. The indignation is palpable but he cannot sustain it. It lifts in the closing paragraph.

> I'd love it if you could visit Oxford for a day. I get there on 6 September, and my address is Set 3, Beechwood House, Iffley Turn, Oxford. It has a telephone number which I don't know. When I know what the form is better about guests at All Souls perhaps you could manage a visit overnight.

The references by Larkin to Oxford in these exchanges and to his imminent move there are insistent, to the point that he seems to be almost imploring Amis to enquire about the reason for his temporary change of address. He never did. How exactly Amis learned that Larkin was to become a visiting fellow at All Souls is not clear but he obviously did not during summer 1970 seem disposed to give even cursory attention to Larkin's remarks, which confirmed for the latter that his old friend was as solipsistic as ever. Yet again correspondence between them ceased, but only for two months.

Aside from his imminent period in Oxford Larkin had littered his correspondence, amounting to four letters in total, with seemingly perfunctory reference to his busy work schedule in Hull and on two occasions to his mother, the kind of things that Amis once asked about during the 1940s and early 1950s when their exchanges were less one-sided. He was, tentatively, offering Amis openings for enquiry and there was much to tell.

By early spring 1969, stage two of the library at Hull was close to completion. Its official title was something of a misnomer; its sheer size and architectural presence made stage one seem insignificant. It stood, indeed stands, as a seven-storey rebuke to the modest pseudo-Classical and Renaissance frontages of the original university buildings. Larkin, despite his loathing for modernism, was proud of this statement in white tile, glass and provincialist Le Corbusier. He had been the intermediary between the different bodies, listened to the requests of the academic community, stood between what the Hull University management team said it wanted and what the University Grants Committee said it could have, and balanced the sometimes impractical suggestions of the architects against his knowledge of what a library is and how it works. The building won the 1970 Civic Trust Award and in 1971 the Yorkshire Region Architecture Award from the Royal Institute of British Architects. Larkin was quietly content to be celebrated as major-domo in this claim by Hull to first-division status among the redbrick universities. A great deal had changed since the 1950s when Larkin would comment persistently on how the irredeemable dreariness of his job seemed appropriate to his temperament, and Amis would drolly support his view. But despite the grand letterhead of his replies Amis seemed interested only in the *Telegraph* article.

In August 1971 it was evident to Larkin and his sister that Eva, even with daily assistance, was incapable of living in her own house. Physically she found it difficult to walk from room to room, and her mental condition was in rapid decline, with her memory and frame of reference displaying unsettling levels of unreliability and arbitrariness. They found her a place in Abbeyfield House, an old people's home in Loughborough. In practical terms this appeared a reasonable, inevitable solution, although a year later it was decided by Larkin and Kitty to move Eva to the Berrystead Nursing Home, better equipped, private and consequently very expensive. Aside from the fact that Larkin experienced the standard levels of distress at watching his widowed elderly mother enter the final stages of existence, he pretended in all communications with Eva, by letter or in person, that little had changed. In his first letter to Amis (14 August 1970), he refers to the week in Cheltenham he was about to spend with his mother, an annual event, a filial duty undertaken every August since his father's death. By 1970 Eva was suffering manifestly from Alzheimer's disease. No record exists of what happened at Cheltenham but it would be the last holiday they would spend together. Amis did not enquire as to her health.

Larkin had secured the visiting fellowship at All Souls College, Oxford, in 1969 and would begin in October 1970. Four years earlier he had been approached by Oxford University Press to become editor of a collection of twentieth-century English verse. It would, they informed him, supplant Yeats's *Oxford Book of Modern Verse* (1936) by covering the next third of the ongoing century. Yeats's editorship had reflected the general perception of him as guardian of the genre. Larkin was flattered and, although the contract had been signed in 1967, he had had little time to even think about the project. The All Souls fellowship, secured with the assistance of his Faber editor, Charles Monteith, who was himself a fellow, would enable him to spend two terms working in the Bodleian Library, which as a copyright institution contained editions of all poems published since 1900.

He had been back for short visits before, but this was the first time since the completion of his degree that he had lived in Oxford. The blackened stonework had mostly been cleaned up, but little else had changed. He had an office in All Souls, but he lived in a set of rooms in a college-owned house just off the Iffley Road, overlooking the Thames. He would take lunch in the King's Arms, next to the Bodleian, and most evenings dine in college. His companions, such as the eminent historian A. L. Rowse and warden of the college John Sparrow, found his habits and demeanour unsettling. He drank enthusiastically and was unguarded in his opinions on the condition of the arts, academia and public life in general, to the extent that Rowse thought that he was 'Falling over backwards to be philistine ... an undergraduate attitude perpetuated into adult life' (Motion, *Philip Larkin*, p. 404). The stern pomposity of Rowse's account is appropriate in that it was exactly the response that Larkin wanted to provoke. The one poem that he addressed directly to Monica ('Poem about Oxford') was written during his time in Oxford. It is the 'City we shared without knowing'.

> Till we left, and were glad to be going
> (Unlike the arselicker who stays),
> Does it stick in our minds as a touchstone
> Of learning and *la politesse?*
> For while the old place hadn't much tone,
> Two others we know have got less.

The ambivalent tone of the poems reflects mixed feelings of irritation and fascination regarding the place where, three decades earlier, he had begun his adult life. Now he was back and was expected to behave like the dons ('the arselicker who stays') that he, Amis and the rest of 'The Seven' had regarded with amused contempt; Larkin, to Rowse's humourless gall, was behaving as if he had never left, too. He wrote to Anthony Thwaite in April 1971, 'I'm through with All Souls now: Cinderella is back in the kitchen ... Rowse and Sparrow as the ugly sisters.'

Amis did not even respond to Larkin's September invitation to Oxford, but in late October when he was installed at All Souls, Larkin wrote to him again. 'There is a Guest Night here on 21 November ... would it "amuse" you to be my guest? Naturally I'd be delighted.' He apologises: 'I know how you feel about candles and nuts and wine and all that ... if you feel it would be a bore then have no scruples, lad, in demurring. But it would be splendid to see you' (23 October 1970, Hunt). Amis declined the invitation but they continued to write: 'Sorry you won't be coming to Guest Night. I'd like you to meet my pal Leslie Rowowow*wow* beggar my carnal shillelagh. I'll come to your lunch instead' (3 November 1970, Hunt). Amis's lunch was more a convenience than an invitation. He had been asked to give a reading at Balliol, and Amis, Jane and Martin (now beginning his third year) met for lunch at the Randolph. He reported it to Monica, evasively – 'it wd take far too long to describe it all' – allowing himself some space to disparage Amis's performance. 'Kingsley's reading was very poor, I thought: got hardly any laughs, wch was absurd, but it was his own fault. He adopts an absurd AEH [Housman] manner, wch as you may imagine didn't commend itself to the audience' (L to Monica, 19 November 1970). At lunch, however, he was charmed by Martin: 'he looked and behaved like Mick Jagger, but was curiously good about offering his cigarettes round and standing up when EJ joined/rejoined the company so there may be some good in the lad. Am wondering whether to have him in to All Souls: stiff cocks wd upset the table.' He went with his mischievous inclinations and invited Martin, whom he had not seen since the latter was ten years old, to dinner at All Souls, twice. Martin enjoyed his encounters with his father's old friend, recalling Larkin's nod towards Rowse and Sparrow and his comment that high academia reminded him of the clergy of the eighteenth century, the refuge of second sons of the gentry: not eligible to inherit and too thick to do anything else.

Martin helped to sustain contact between his father and Larkin while the latter was in Oxford but it was a woeful accident of fate that brought them back together. Larkin had been exchanging letters with Cecil Day-Lewis since the mid-1960s. He admired his work, thought him a suitable incumbent as Poet Laureate and invited him to Hull as the first writer-in-residence to preside over the Poetry Room, newly established by Larkin in the Library. At Day-Lewis's instalment in 1970 no students attended the event, and Larkin was impressed by Day-Lewis's polite unconcern. In his letter to Amis of 23 October 1970 (Hunt), Larkin reported that 'I'm having old Cecil [Day-Lewis] to the second one [Guest Evening] in Dec. If he can do it I'm sure you could.' Amis couldn't but two years later the knowledge that Day-Lewis and Larkin were friends prompted him to proffer another invitation. For a brief period in 1958, Day-Lewis and Jane had been lovers. Day-Lewis's wife,

Jill, knew of this but the three of them remained friends, and in spring 1972 Jane visited the couple at their home in Greenwich to interview the poet for a newspaper article. She knew he was ill but was shocked to find his cancer so advanced that the two of them, unable to cope in their large house, were reluctantly contemplating a hospice. Amis agreed that the Day-Lewises should move to Lemmons, and a week later wrote to Larkin telling him that Day-Lewis 'would love to see you. If you're in London, you could pop up here without much difficulty, and we could easily, indeed would love to put you up for the night. He's very weak but totally compus and cheerful (Christ)' (A to L, 28 April 1972). 'Don't care for the prospect much,' Larkin wrote to Monica (30 April 1972, Bod).

Larkin reported on the visit to Conquest, dwelling mostly on Day-Lewis and his maintenance of a 'cool and cheerful demeanour' despite his having little more than a few months to live (L to Conquest, 31 May 1972). His letter to Amis of a fortnight earlier, despatched immediately after his return to Hull, is more revealing. It was as though the previous ten years of inexplicable silence had been erased.

> Shall I never learn not to drink to excess? But many thanks all the same. Your house is v. Impressive ('I'll impress a branding iron on you'). I must say our old friend Al Cohol has wiped away the memory of what I said I'd do about July 1936. (L to A, 18 May 1972, Hunt)

Amis had written, 'By the living God, cully, that was a fine old time, as far as I remember ... I found that *Men Only* on my desk under a copy of *The Times*, I mean *The Times*. Who put it there hey?' (A to L, 7 May 1972). The jovial intimacy is back, as are the less amusing confidences: 'My mother is,' writes Larkin, 'in a Nursing Home, not very well, wch is a worry and v. Time consuming: also starts up chain-reaction of gloomy reflections on one's own account' (18 May 1972). All seemed to go well with Amis but Larkin still had reservations, as he wrote to Monica: 'the visit, though good, not v. Good. In practice – K turns it into a drink/jazz old pal visit, whereas I can't help feeling a lower key would have been kinder' (L to Monica, 4 May 1972, Bod). Amis had almost completed *The Riverside Villas Murder* (1973), an elegy to his father disguised as a piece of 1930s detective fiction, but he spent their first proper meeting since 1959 telling Larkin about his ideas for his next novel, *Ending Up*.

Lemmons was now occupied by Amis, Jane, Jane's brother Colin, Colin's friend Sargy Mann and, until her death in 1975, Jane's mother Kit. Amis was content enough with this arrangement, but at the same time it seemed rather dull compared with the clandestine, romantic mood of their early years, and there appeared to be no reason now why things should change. So he imagined what such a gathering would involve for a similar group of people twenty years hence, when they were in their seventies. Out of this would evolve *Ending Up*, published in 1974. Larkin was intrigued, mainly because he and Amis had been born in the same year and had reached the point at which old age was still something to be contemplated but only just; its beginnings were imminent. A gloomy subtext to these exchanges was provided by Day-Lewis, who would die within a week of Larkin's departure, aged sixty-eight.

As Amis's notebook shows, the novel at planning stage drew heavily upon his life at Lemmons. From the nature of this material one might have suspected that the completed work would become a vehicle for its author's prejudices regarding his co-residents, an act of vengeance upon unhappy circumstances, but quite the opposite occurred. Bernard emerges as the most prominent of the five characters, in the sense that his acts have more effect upon the eventual direction of the narrative than anything else. Each of the other four involves a blend of personal flaws and more endearing elements of decency and kindness, combinations that age has cemented. Bernard appears to be the only one who is still subject to change. He is the most bitter and the only comprehensively unpleasant member of the cast, and as the story progresses he gets even worse.

Bernard hated his co-residents.

There was still a little satisfaction to be had out of scoring off them in talk, but it did seem to be on the decrease. He must see if he could not come up with some less subtle means of venting on the four of them his lack of respect and affection. What had happened, what was the change in his circumstances that had led him to this decision? Well, anyhow, such a project would help to pass the time (Kingsley Amis, *Ending Up*, pp. 74–5).

Bernard sidesteps the self-addressed question of why he feels and acts in the way that he does, but the answer is there for the reader. Bernard, when younger, had thrived upon the interconnected tensions and deceits that had made up his life.

As a vision of life at Lemmons, albeit some time in the early 1990s, it is depressing, but it is clear also that Amis has based Bernard, effectively the cause of the collective distress, upon the very worst aspects of himself. The other characters are, by comparison, blameless victims. Jane recalls that alongside their marital problems, Amis by the 1970s had begun to think that 'life was passing him by', in that the complexities and excitements of pre-middle age – the affairs, the ambition, the juggling between job and writing, the periodic desire to start again somewhere else – were what had made his life worthwhile, and they were all now largely in the past. She says that he constantly seemed to be looking for replacements and that even the purchase of and move to Lemmons was partly a means by which he could get involved in something new and unusual, but that once they were established there the excitement wore off. He enjoyed the idea of a country residence – hence his 'look round the estate' joke – but he had not thought about its practical consequences such as travelling between Barnet and central London.

All of which take us back to Bernard's question regarding his malevolent state. He was now too old to rectify even the most mundane causes of his daily sense of disappointment. Amis did not turn his frustrations into a vicious campaign against his co-residents, but he clearly wondered whether if he were still in the same place with the same people in twenty years time – with everything that had once engaged him just a memory – would he become as evil as Bernard?

Within a couple of months Larkin began drafts for a poem that he would complete in January 1973. A comparison of 'The Old Fools' with Amis's *Ending Up* provides us with an insight into the different ways in which the personal characteristics of each man inform their writings. Amis's narrative moves with alarming speed. The chapters are short, and in each one there is an almost manic, kaleidoscopic blending of different foci, all of which contrasts in a darkly amusing manner with the fact that in real terms the characters' lives are slowing down. Everyone dies in the concluding chapter, alone and in a variety of sordid, uncomfortable ways, each departure linked to the residue of practical jokes set in chain by the malicious central character, Bernard. Larkin had been amused by Amis's plan, particularly the modelling of Bernard around his friend's role at Lemmons. It was also evident to Larkin that, although they were both contemplating the notion of ageing, Amis's projection of this into his writing reminded him of *Lucky Jim*; Amis had made fantasy seem realistic and now he was turning black comedy into a substitute for a very humourless prospect.

'The Old Fools' was Larkin's response to this. At first it appears to treat its apparent subjects in a brutally uncompassionate manner:

> ... Do they somehow suppose
> It's more grown-up when your mouth hangs open and drools,
> And you keep on pissing yourself, and can't remember
> Who called this morning?

Gradually it becomes clear that the dreadful states that accompany ageing are not so much reflections upon what Larkin has witnessed as a myriad contemplation of everything he fears. At one point he imagines

> ... being old is having lighted rooms
> Inside your head, and people in them, acting.
> People you know, yet can't quite name; each looms
> Like a deep loss restored ...

In August 1972 he received a birthday card from Winifred Arnott, now Bradshaw, prompted by a radio programme called *Larkin at Fifty* which included Roy Fuller reading, as Larkin put it in his reply, 'your poem', 'A Few Lines on a Young Lady's Photograph Album'. All of this might appear innocuous enough, even gratifying – for some – but in a letter to Amis he moves seamlessly from reporting on his renewed contact with Winifred to 'Funny being fifty isn't it ... add ten years on, what's ten years? Compared with eternity ... ah gets tuft. No doesn't bear thinking about ...' (11 August 1972). But in the poem he does force himself to think about it, of 'never perceiving/How near it is ... how it will end'.

In November he received a letter from Patsy, not entirely coherent but informing him that she had been admitted to a nursing home that dealt with mental illness and specifically with the psychological effects of alcoholism. She would not have found his reply particularly cheering: 'I don't expect to write any more. As for being 50 that hasn't cheered me either – to think that even if I attain 3 score years and 10 I've only as long forwards as arriving in Belfast was backwards' (25 November 1972). Belfast, where everything had been so different for each of them. Patsy would be dead in less than four years. As in the poem, the 'lighted rooms' of Larkin's own head were becoming crowded with presences from his past who in different ways insisted to him that memories carry a dreadful message that the past is irrecoverable.

... they give

An air of baffled absence, trying to be there
Yet being here. For the rooms grow farther, leaving
Incompetent cold ...

As if by some conspiracy of fate he received, two days after his reply to Patsy, a letter from Barry Bloomfield asking if he would approve his editorship of a bibliography of all Larkin's writings and related published material. Bibliographies, while very flattering, were generally regarded as monuments to death and completion. After its publication in 1979 Larkin recalled that his first hearing of it felt 'like a tombstone being gently lowered over me' (L to Winifred Bradshaw, 23 August 1979).

For both Amis and Larkin their half-century prompted them to take stock of the state of their lives, but while Amis, looking forward, decided that some sort of peremptory action was necessary, irrespective of its exact consequences, Larkin, as was evidenced in his verse of the 1970s and elsewhere, felt trapped in an existential limbo. The past to a large extent depressed him and, increasingly, the future seemed to beckon him to only one certainty: oblivion.

The most predictable consequence of Amis's belief that something new, a radical change of place and circumstance, would improve his marriage and refresh his work was that his initial enthusiasm would rapidly be dispersed by a blend of disinterest and disappointment. Something similar happened with Lemmons.

The idea of moving out of central London, beyond the suburbs, had been a collective one, but once it had been mooted and Lemmons viewed as the potential location, Amis was visited by an almost adolescent excitement.

As usual, the image of something unprecedented and untried, in his case playing lord of the manor, displaced considerations of its practical consequences, which would be more problematical for Amis than for the others.

As already mentioned, during the 1960s he had, virtually every week, met up with a group of close friends and other acquaintances for lunch, often in Bertorelli's in Charlotte Street, and these would be frequently extended to day-long drinking sessions. Along with Conquest, Braine and Worsthorne, Tibor Szamuely and Anthony Powell were now regular attendees. They were not, despite Amis's self-mocking description of them as 'Fascist lunches', serious political gatherings, but there was a feeling of collective dislocation from a political and cultural milieu that seemed to demand left-of-centre sympathies. Nicholas Ridley MP, later to be Mrs Thatcher's aide-de-camp, sometimes called in. Amis and Conquest often attended similar gatherings in the Marlborough Arms in Torrington Place, the so-called '*Spectator* pub'. *The Spectator* has always been a magazine with conservative associations but which has prided itself on its political independence; and in the 1960s and 1970s this involved practically any state of mind that was not left-leaning. Amis was a regular contributor and reviewer.

It obviously did not occur to him that aspects of his 1960s life that he took for granted would be seriously affected by the move to Lemmons, but they certainly were. The seeming convenience of the tube journey soon began to test Amis's patience. Routine and impromptu activities such as going to the pub for a drink, visiting the shop for cigarettes, a typewriter ribbon or a loaf of bread required the use of the car and the cooperation of Jane. Soon Amis's enthusiasm for the move began to be replaced by disillusionment and a litany of complaints. In order for him to exercise his independence, particularly regarding his circle of friends and acquaintances in London, he was dependent on Jane.

Jane recalls that in 1975 Amis, after a couple of drinks, had slipped on the stairs and injured his shoulder but not seriously enough to require immediate medical assistance. Next morning, however, the pain had increased. He wondered if something might be broken, and they arranged an appointment with the local GP for later that day, when Jane was due to be in Broadcasting House discussing material for a radio play. Amis

was enraged because, in Jane's view, he was obliged to confront a number
of what were for him incompatible yet equally irritating sets of circumstances. He was reminded of how much he relied upon her, which in itself
embittered him, while at the same time he was faced with the fact that the
woman on whom he depended but no longer loved had a career and a life
that were independent of his own.

In late 1975 Lemmons was put on the market, and Amis and Jane began
looking for somewhere closer to central London. By the end of the year they
had found a detached eighteenth-century property called Gardnor House
in Flask Walk, Hampstead, and a buyer who was seriously interested in
Lemmons. Amis wanted to move back towards the centre of town, but just
as significantly they were, at his instigation, engaging in a familiar ritual of
desperation: a change of place might encourage a change of mood and state.
They moved to Gardnor House with Monkey and Sargy in May 1976, but
the condition of their marriage did not improve.

Larkin became an occasional visitor. Jane was expected and was indeed
willing to play hostess to Amis's circle of acquaintances, irrespective of
what she thought of them. Most, such as Conquest, Gale, Montgomery
and Szamuely, she found agreeable, and she had enjoyed the company of
Betjeman for as long as Amis. She tried to get on with Larkin but she found
this more difficult. They treated each other with mutual courtesy. They
never actually argued or displayed manifest animosity but it was clear to all
involved that she was not particularly happy with the return of this figure
from her husband's past, his life before her. He was, as she put it, 'snarled up
about women', though it should be pointed out that she remarked on this
to me some time after the publication of Larkin's *Letters*. During Larkin's
visits she would 'leave them alone to play their games'. 'When Philip visited
they seemed like adolescents, spending hours secreted in his study on their
own, talking. About what, I do not know, Kingsley never told me.' Jane
knew that until the late 1950s Larkin had been the only person with whom
Amis had discussed his ongoing work, a role that she had adopted in 1963.
He genuinely valued her opinion as a critic and fellow novelist, and their
sense of humour was similarly attuned to the dry and sardonic. Now,
however, her predecessor was back, and his return seemed symptomatic
of a broader sense of upheaval. As early as 1972 when Larkin first began
to visit Lemmons, Jane expressed to Amis her feelings about him. Jane's

ambivalence regarding Larkin was reciprocated by him for her. Although Larkin never showed any intrinsic discomfort with what remained of the British class system, he was irritated when cliquish entitlement encroached on literary matters. Six years before his reconciliation with Amis he wrote to Monica:

> I had a letter from Betjeman, acknowledging the picture [of the two of them on the BBC *Monitor* set] and very kind about it. He says that he and Elizabeth (Cavendish) met Kingsley and EJH and had a long chat or some such nonsense. Grr, brr. They're all the same really. The only good life is to live in some sodding seedy city and work and keep yr gob shut and be unhappy. (L to Monica, 16 January 1966)

After Day-Lewis's death he was enraged by what he saw as the clubbish hyperbole of Jane's obituary.

> My sense of nausea wasn't diminished by EJH's stuff in the *S. Times* – God they wring every little drop out of it don't they? ... and how vulgar ... And her description of his work as Laureate didn't go unnoticed – no a fearful life. Mr Poesy. The Frankie Vaughan of Verse. The Elvis Presley of English Poets. (L to Monica, 30 July 1972)

The other residents of Lemmons greeted his visits with amused curiosity. 'We thought we'd lay on a bit of a show for you since you don't come to London all that often ...' wrote Kingsley to his friend on 28 October 1976, 'with some of your admirers', including Arnold Wesker, George Steiner, Ian Hamilton, Al Alvarez and A. L. Rowse. This retinue of Larkin's enemies was a transparent spoof, but a modest get-together did take place. During a later visit, Christopher Hitchens, fascinated, watched from a distance as Larkin illustrated his discourse with impassioned hand gestures. Later he asked Kingsley what the subject of this had been; perhaps something about contemporary writing and politics, which he could himself, as an ambitious young man of letters, add to his stockpile of anecdotes. 'Oh not quite,' said Kingsley, 'light bulbs – difficult to find the 40 watt type these days apparently – the inflated price of train tickets from Hull, the cost of new shirts, the usual stuff ...'

Colin Howard adds:

I can't say I really knew him. Only Kingsley did. But his visits were fascinating spectacles. I've never seen anyone invest so much energy in saying so little, but listening was worth the effort. I don't think he spoke much about life and literature. He seemed fascinated with the mundane and without ever seeming to make it funny he'd succeed in doing so. It's odd. Kingsley was amusing, garrulous, but when his friend was there he appeared to hold back a little, slip into Philip's tempo.

From 1970 onwards virtually all of Larkin's poems involve what can only be described as a reluctant presence. Read as a sequence they are informed by a temper that has no exact precedent. Literature is replete with figures beset by various conditions – mental, emotional and physical – from which they seek release, but none comes close to the effect created by Larkin in these pieces where a mood of claustrophobic unease seems to surround each word or phrase, irrespective of its meaning.

'Vers de Société' reads almost as their manifesto. He is pithily contemptuous of another evening with 'a crowd of craps', including the 'bitch/Who's read nothing but *Which*' and the 'ass' with his 'fool research', but the alternative involves something that he cannot quite bring himself to describe. He circles it, using such phrases as 'Funny how hard it is to be alone', and comes closest to disclosure with:

    ... sitting by a lamp more often brings
    Not peace, but other things.
    Beyond the light stand failure and remorse
    Whispering *Dear Warlock-Williams: Why, of course* –

He splits the semantics of the two words 'failure' and 'remorse' so that we are never certain if they refer to the grim social obligations that irritate him, but from which he cannot fully disengage, or whether they carry traces of those 'other things' that haunt his solitariness.

'Forget What Did' is, as he stated in a 1980 interview, 'about a time when I stopped keeping a diary because I couldn't bear to record what was going on' (Philip Larkin, *Further Requirements: Interviews, Broadcasts, Statements*

and Book Reviews, ed. A. Thwaite, p. 60). His diary was his informal poem
manquée, not simply a 'record' of things and feelings but a process by which
words gave some shape to life. Now,

Stopping the diary
Was a stun to memory,
Was a blank starting,

One no longer cicatrized
By such words, such actions
As bleakened waking.

The syntax itself seems crippled by the pain of putting the words on the page,
and while the ostensible subject is the cessation of his diary entries, his fear of
'words' as prolonging a 'bleakened' state of mind is brilliantly, grievously enacted
in the poem itself. It was completed three weeks before he informed Monica
that 'I don't really want to write [poems] about myself' (26 September 1971).

Two poems, 'I have started to say' and 'The View', were written within a
year of 'Forget What Did' and in both he gives voice to some of the thoughts
about himself that distressed him:

All that's left to happen
Is some deaths (my own included).
Their order, and their manner,
Remain to be learnt.

As he put it in a letter to Amis, 'I keep seeing obits of chaps who've passed over
"suddenly, aged 55", "after a short illness", "after a long illness bravely borne,
and 57" ... No it doesn't bear thinking about' (11 August 1972). Thinking about
it was bad enough, but putting it into words was worse. In 'The View' he tried:

Where has it gone, the lifetime?
        Search me. What's left is drear.
Unchilded and unwifed, I'm
        Able to view that clear:
        So final. And so near.

In 'Dockery and Son' he had contemplated this same state of unwifed child-lessness as a token of life without significance, and had done so with clinical indifference. Now, fear seemed to play a part. He left both pieces out of *High Windows*, and they remained unpublished during his life. Stylistically they meet the standard set by other pieces in the volume, but Larkin's problem was that unlike 'Vers de Société' or 'Forget What Did', in which his depressive, nihilistic condition is made enigmatic, or even 'This Be The Verse' and 'Annus Mirabilis', where it is protected by a hint of self-caricature, they are unambiguously reflections of a state of mind that he loathed, could not escape from or even properly comprehend. They were the poems that he 'did not want to write about himself'.

His sense of discomfort with his state of mind registers too in his newly begun correspondence with Amis. In January 1974, Hull University informed Larkin that it had decided to sell off a number of the non-academic and administrative properties that it owned in the city. Pearson Park would go on the market later that year, and he would have to find somewhere else to live. Larkin had, since Oxford, been an obsessive upper-storey-flat renter. The notion of being physically detached from while able to observe the rest of the world, along with the welcome absence of responsibility, suited his temperament.

He wrote to Amis (30 January 1974, Hunt): 'I'm using this paper because I'm negotiating to buy a house – agh HAGHhagh – stamp duty bum, Conveyancing bum, asking price bum, Caveat Emptor bum – especially *that*. It's not as nice as your's – not nice at all actually. A modern kennel, hideous to behold. Oh fuck.' There was no reason why he could not have rented another flat, or purchased one for that matter, and although Hull did not have an abundance of charming, antiquated properties there was a sufficient number of Victorian and Edwardian houses on the market to have suited his politely reclusive sensibility. Instead, and for no obvious reason, he responded to the suggestion of a fellow member of one of his university dining clubs, went to see 105 Newland Park and then, with suicidal abruptness, decided to buy it. It was the kind of house owned by Arnold of 'Self's the Man' (1958) or similarly ensnared wife-and-two-kids characters who feature regularly in his verse, like demonic reminders of what he would always avoid.

By all accounts, his own included, Larkin hated virtually every minute that he spent in the house, where he would live until his death just over a decade later. Architecturally it was a perfect example of the kind of nullity-by-compromise that was only properly achieved in Britain in the 1950s and 1960s, in that while it disclaimed all reference to earlier styles it also cautiously avoided anything even mildly radical. Larkin soon made matters worse by redecorating with William Morris wallpaper, 1970s vintage, and sympathetically patterned carpets.

Many of his most pessimistic poems appeared able to set in train actual events and occurrences that had first been imagined illustrations of mood – the most obvious being 'Ambulances', written approximately six months prior to the seizure or blackout that caused him to spend lengthy periods being treated and speculatively diagnosed. His decision to purchase the Newland Park house, the 'kennel' he loathed even before he signed the first documents, seems to reverse this procedure; it was as though he was determined to visit upon his private life the almost palpable sense of unease that informed his poems. Along with his catalogue of complaints to Amis about the house, he adds, 'God my writing's not up to much'. Larkin had in letters and elsewhere fashioned the complaint into something like a literary sub-genre. There was always a hint of self-assured masochism, and he took perverse pleasure in turning his misery into a good read. But his reports on the house that litter his correspondence with Amis throughout the 1970s carry a note of genuine hopelessness, as if he can't make sense of why he has burdened himself with a place and a way of life he loathed. Always, his lament on the particulars of his life would be appended to something more private and intractable. 'Has it a "mature garden"?' he asks Amis and Jane after they had moved to Flask Walk closer to central London. 'You can have mine. I have a gardener now: he spends ¾ hour taking tools out (now, now), ¾ hr bringing them back, and half an hour in the middle wondering wch one to use, if by any chance he were to be seized by such a reckless notion.' This comes close to sustaining itself with droll energy but the momentum is curbed when Larkin turns his gaze inward: 'I find *any* visitor a strain, except Monica. Comes of being a lonely artist-man, I suppose, except that I'm no longer even that. Well, I'm lonely, annyhway' (20 July 1976, Hunt).

The Whitsun Weddings had involved the poetic equivalent of someone you thought you had known for years disclosing new dimensions of their personality; now more than a decade later there was much speculation over how *High Windows* might further compound the paradox of this withdrawn, enigmatic figure who spoke so candidly to his readers.

The reviews were generally favourable, with the notable exception of Robert Nye in *The Times*, but each reflected the difficulty of writing a 500–1,000 words piece on a collection which, while short, compelled fascination and confusion. The admiration for the volume was genuine for most reviewers, but one also senses anxiety in their prose, particularly on how to describe the individual genius at work in poems such as 'Annus Mirabilis', 'The Explosion' and 'The Building' and at the same time explain why each is so radically different. Nye overcomes this problem by treating the differences as ineffective masks for a consistently nasty presence. Conversely, John Bayley in the *Times Literary Supplement* offered a thumbnail monograph on Larkin's entire literary career, including comparisons with Shakespeare, Keats, Owen, Hardy and Yeats, which prompted Amis (whose own *Observer* piece was unreserved and unspecific in its praise) to comment, 'What does he *mean*? (Bayley) Throughout. Eh?' (A to L, 31 July 1974).

It was the most popular volume of previously uncollected verse to go into print since the war, with over 20,000 copies sold in the twelve months following the publication date. Since *Lucky Jim*, and as their friendship became interwoven with their literary careers, Larkin had accepted the role of sanguine junior partner to Amis; gradually he had earned respect in his second-choice genre while Amis had rarely been out of the spotlight as the celebrity novelist. Now, briefly, their roles were reversed. *Ending Up*, published a few months after *High Windows*, was shortlisted for the Booker Prize, but it did not sell as many copies as its poetic counterpart, and nor did its author attract so much popular fascination. Christopher Hitchens:

> We, friends of Martin [Amis], were mostly leftish politically, and as writers thought ourselves the coming generation ... Martin, James [Fenton], Julian Barnes, Ian McEwan, all wanted to put a distance between ourselves and the post-war set. Through Martin we got to know Kingsley and Bob Conquest and there was a lot of banter, argument, good natured caricature, left versus right. But oddly Larkin stood above all of it, closed the gap. After *High Windows* everyone saw him as the finest poet writing in English. Even James, proselytising Trotskyite, thought him unimprovable. You could sense in Kingsley a feeling of unselfish pride, simply that they were friends.

In March 1974, three months before the publication of *High Windows*, he
began work on what would be his last major poem, and by the end of that
year the first three stanzas of 'Aubade' were in draft form. Among the dozens
of significant poems on death in English this one can claim uniqueness
not entirely because of what it says but through its sinister emulation of
its theme. From *The North Ship* onwards, the image of time as a dreadful,
threatening presence, forcing us to accompany it to an even more terrifying
state of nothingness, seems never far from the core of Larkin's verse, while
never quite the comprehensive, inescapable theme of the poem. In 'Aubade'
it becomes just that. His choice of sub-genre, the poem that, traditionally,
laments the dawn as the moment that lovers must separate, involves a dark
inversion of expectations. He spends nights alone, 'half-drunk' following the
day's work, and 'Waking at four' he stares past the 'curtain-edges',

> Till then I see what's really always there:
> Unresting death, a whole day nearer now,
> Making all thought impossible but how
> And where and when I shall myself die.

The sense of death as informing 'all thought' resonates through the poem. It
is a brilliant, exquisitely crafted piece of work in that he proves able to write
continuously about the same theme, never releasing the texture of the verse
from a sense of dread and hopelessness, but at the same time lending this
horrible process an equal dimension of beauty.

The experience of writing the poem would have involved for Larkin something close to what Motion calls 'creative suicide'. After 'Aubade' it would
have been impossible for him to write another poem that addressed itself
to his particular conception of death, and while it would, hypothetically,
have been possible to write about other things Larkin was aware that doing
so involved at the very least the adoption of a false persona. Thoughts of
death, as he made clear in 'Aubade', pervaded every element of his conscious
existence. It had become evident to him that the changes in his lifestyle that
had occurred during 1973–4 – specifically the purchase of Newland Park and
the monogamous relationship with Monica – bespoke feelings of occlusion
and cessation that were demonstrably counterproductive for his poetry: he
was in the midst of writing a poem with an insistent subtext; 'beyond this

there is little, if anything, to be said'. So in November 1974 he set the poem aside. He knew that eventually he would finish it, but for the time being its progress could be suspended because he had decided to alter yet again, and this time more radically, the mode of existence for which it seemed to be a self-composed obituary.

Sixteen months earlier he had split up with Maeve. They saw each other regularly in the library and exchanged occasional letters of the friendly, uncomfortably reserved kind – 'I hope the book [*High Windows*] will receive as happy a reception with your reading public as its presentation means to me,' she had written in May 1974 – and in mid-November they found themselves at a Friday afternoon drinks party organised by a colleague in the Senior Common Room. Early that evening when other guests were dispersing Larkin suggested that she might come with him and look at his new residence in Newland Park, which she had never seen, and both knew that the invitation was politely spurious, that he wanted them to begin again. They did and with a more passionate intensity than before. Absence had made much grow stronger and her reservations regarding sex considerably less so.

Little more than three weeks later, in March 1974, he began an affair with his then secretary, Betty Mackereth. Apart from Conquest, Amis and Monica, no one knew more about the real Larkin than Betty. As his personal assistant she was fully acquainted with the pragmatics of deceit that enabled him to conduct a dual affair with Monica and Maeve; on those rare occasions that he took the latter for holidays, Betty would assist with his 'official business' cover stories. When his fame as a writer increased she devised a full recipe of responses to protect him from unwanted enquiries, and she was the one who knew which of the office cupboards contained his impressive collection of pornography. From the late 1960s onwards, Larkin had become notorious for the ways in which he would indicate various levels of indifference and contempt for senior members of the university – academics and administrators alike – whose bickering and insistence on this or that policy for the library encroached on his way of doing things. At meetings of the Senate he would often contrive to fall asleep in the chair, only to revive himself miraculously and pour scorn on an outstandingly pointless contribution from a fellow member. With mischievous skill he would make sure that the secretary of a professor to whom he was conveying a telephone message would have to edit out comments such as 'tell the old windbag' or 'inform the pompous arsehole', in the full knowledge that the windbag or arsehole concerned could hear him in the background. Through all of this Betty became the sanguine, pragmatic half of a kind of double act, and, when from the mid-1970s onwards his feigned periods of somnolence were frequently exchanged for more genuine drink-fuelled versions, Betty made sure that he would be able to sleep them off in his office without disturbance. 'I was like a wife really. I knew everything a wife knows, more than some wives know, probably' (Motion, *Philip Larkin*, p. 282).

What he did not tell her was that while his attraction was very real it involved a supplementary agenda of motives. His renewed affair with Maeve, in terms of sex and his personal attachment to her, was fulfilling enough, but at the same time the blend of falsehood and uncertainty, even perhaps guilt, that accompanied it during the 1960s and helped infuse his poetry with its characteristic dimorphism had been replaced by a tiresome predictability. It was certain that Monica would find out, he knew that her response would be less than cordial, but he knew also that they were now too set in their ways for her to be bothered even with an implied threat of separation. With Betty there could be a brief period of treble deception, involving an exhausting but, for Larkin, perversely satisfying exercise in emotional gymnastics. Although Betty seemed to be the only one of his three lovers with comprehensive knowledge of what was happening, even she was sometimes obliged to play an involuntary, unwitting role, as the poem 'When first we faced, and touching showed' testifies. It was begun soon after the start of his affair with Betty and completed in December 1975.

It stops just short of the rhapsodic, hinting at the affected in its description of a first kiss. The moment itself compels a reflection upon how the past, with its private commitments and demands, will always compete against a moment of intimacy, raising the question of whether two people can ever really know each other, irrespective of the apparent depth of their immediate feelings.

> But when did love not try to change
> The world back to itself – no cost,
> No past, no people else at all –
> Only what meeting made us feel,
> So new, and gentle-sharp, and strange?

This question is rhetorical – love has always tried to reclaim everything for itself – but he leaves unresolved the attendant issue of whether it might ever succeed.

Maeve was not aware of the existence of the poem until Anthony Thwaite showed it to her when he was scrutinising unpublished material in preparation for the *Collected Poems*. Her first response was recognition. The final stanza, quoted above, 'sharply resembled Philip's actual words to me on that February evening in 1961 when we embraced for the first time' (Brennan, *The Philip Larkin I Knew*, p. 66), but taking into account its date of composition she conceded that it could have been written to 'celebrate his mature affair with Betty Mackereth' (ibid., p. 67). In truth it could only have been written because Larkin was having a relationship with both of them. He sent Betty a copy of 'When first we faced' ten days after completing it, knowing that she would experience the gratifying sensation of having been selected for special treatment in a poetic memento; she knew, of course, of his affair with Maeve, but the poem was hers. Or was it? On the same day that he sent the poem to Betty, 31 December 1975, he wrote to Maeve, 'I am very close to Monica and very fond of her ... But it's you I *love*; you're the one I want.' He was lying. Within three years their relationship would be over, forever.

Poetic inspiration has through literary history laid claim to many grounding impulses – moments of spiritual revelation, opium, nightingales and so on – but Larkin is probably unique in his (albeit late) addiction to multiple infidelity. The moment in the poem where the sense of 'other meetings, other loves' seems to threaten their moment of togetherness is also that which enables Larkin to write it. One can only guess at the motive for Larkin's exercise in middle-aged saturnalia. The most obvious explanation would be that a man who had never been particularly successful as a womaniser was now, desperately, savouring his remaining opportunities before sex became a matter only for recollection. There is, however, evidence to suggest another point of inspiration. Amis had not been guarded to Larkin about the occasionally unsettled state of his marriage with Jane, and Conquest had continued to update him on the principal cause of their difficulties: Amis was becoming uninterested in sex. On 3 October 1973, for instance, Conquest tells Larkin of how they were 'just back from, evidently, a weekend *together* at Tony Powell's but there you get separate rooms. All the same, perhaps a sign of one more shot at the problem' (Conquest to L, 3 October 1973, Bod). Larkin and Amis talked regularly of the latter's mid-1970s novel *The Alteration* (1976), and long before publication Larkin knew of the oblique and very grim autobiographical resonances of the plot. It is set in England in 1976, but this is 1976 as it would have been if Henry VIII's elder brother Arthur had lived to become king, married Catherine of Aragon and sired a line of alternative Tudors. England and the parts of Europe uncolonised by the Islamic enemy have remained Catholic, and the religious institution has effectively replaced secular power. It tells the story of Hubert Anvil, ten years old and the best boy soprano in living memory. The alteration of the title is the planned surgical castration of Hubert, which will preserve his magnificent voice and secure for him respect and position in the world where the arts are the esteemed preserve of the Vatican hierarchy.

By the time that he completed *The Alteration*, Amis's lack of interest in sex was becoming the most persistent feature of the variously troubled state of his marriage – so much so that Jane had begun to suggest that he see a therapist, despite her knowledge of his visceral contempt for psychoanalysis. The novel involved the projection of his feelings of unease on to its central character, with a number of typically ironic distortions. For Hubert, sex, let alone the ways in which sex influences other parts of life, is a hypothesis. It is an activity confined exclusively to language and the operations of the mind. It is something that potentially he will never experience, and one can imagine Amis considering the bizarre possibility that he might someday undergo a version of Hubert's state in reverse; that sex might become a remembrance, a disembodied memory recorded in his novels. All of Amis's novels were linked, some obliquely, others more directly, with his sex life, which had now entered a state of atrophy. Hubert is castrated and continues to sing beautifully and one must wonder if Amis was offering himself some kind of compensatory hypothesis: even if I become a version of Hubert I might still be a good novelist. This seems unlikely if we are to believe his account of how in 1973 he had listened to a scratchy 1909 recording of the last known castrato, Alessandro Moreschi. He recognised that the performance was 'very fine'; Moreschi, then aged forty-six, had retained the unique skills of the prepubescent vocalist. But for other reasons Amis found that the experience was 'intolerable';

it caused him to endure for several days a state of 'jittery depression'. Moreschi's 'decision brings out everything of importance in human life. Your arguments for and against, your duty to God, to sing his music. Your duty to art, sex. Love. Marriage. Children. Fame. Money. Security' (*New Review* [1974], vol. I, no. 4, pp. 21–8). The consiliences between these units of lived existence were what made the whole experience worthwhile. So although Moreschi, and Hubert, are great artists their skills have cost them fundamental aspects of their humanity. Larkin praised the novel as 'a remarkable imaginative feat' (L to A, 4 November 1976, Hunt).

In the same letter he thanks Amis for his hospitality during the previous weekend, and without giving a full account of what they talked about it is clear that their renewed friendship involved a return for Larkin to the role as audience for Amis's disclosures of his lurid fantasies. 'I can't rid myself of the notion of this dark-haired girl in knee stockings carrying a violin-case whom you meet when the lamps in Flask Walk are throwing leaf-patterns on the dry (or indeed wet) pavements ... yow, leggo.' Despite the fact that his sex life with Jane was problematic, Amis was still capable of treating the subject as something more than an abstraction. As a consequence Larkin is puzzled by the novel's conclusion, which he had read on his return to Hull. 'The only thing I didn't "get", and I suppose it's a pretty big thing ("do you mean –"), is why Hubert loses his balls in the end. The happy ending had been set up suitably enough; it came as a shock.' Larkin was aware of the parallels between what might happen to Hubert and Amis's troubles, and was unsettled by the fate that Amis visited upon his creation. Throughout their friendship Larkin had always been the quintessential pessimist, both as an individual and in his work, in contrast to Amis's apparent ability as a magician of good fortune. Now, it seemed, Amis had joined him in the defeatist camp.

The fact that, while he witnessed Amis's private crisis unfold as a grisly allegory of emasculation, he embarked upon a faintly bizarre enactment of the kind of triangle of infidelity that the former had once practised with such aplomb is surely something more than a coincidence.

'Aubade' was Larkin's final statement, in poetry, on death. He knew there was no more to be said, and 'Love Again' took care of everything else.

He had completed the latter's first stanza and the opening four lines of the second in August 1975, shortly after rekindling his relationship with Maeve.

Love again: wanking at ten past three
(Surely he's taken her home by now?) ...

Someone else feeling her breasts and cunt,
Someone else drowned in that lash-wide stare ...

Motion proposed that the poem was evidence of his 'discovery that beneath the calm surface of his affair lurked feelings as turbulent as those he had known as a young man' (Motion, *Philip Larkin*, p. 454). This is by parts an understatement and a misinterpretation. Maeve, in her interviews with Motion and her subsequent memoir, insisted that she was the 'her', and the fact that Larkin began the poem when he restarted their relationship and completed it in 1979 when they finally parted has discouraged those who might doubt her assumption. But also in 1974 he stated to Conquest that he had taken to 'boiling down my diaries', meaning that he hoped to find enough in the voluminous notebooks and diaries of the early 1940s to the 1960s to provide the raw material for something autobiographical. What kind of generic shape would be given to this – poems, fiction, memoirs – was not clear, but his desperation was evident. His life and his writing were coterminous. The present offered nothing for either, so he attempted to ransack the past.

'Aubade' often reads like a versified distillation of Larkin's morbid reflections on the meaning of life over the previous thirty years: 'death is the most important thing about life (because it puts an end to life and extinguishes further hope of restitution or recompense, as well as any more experience)' (L to Monica, 8 November 1952, Bod); 'I can't imagine how people can say "no use worrying about it, it's inevitable". That's *exactly why* I worry about it' (L. to Monica, 19 February 1955, Bod). He was finding no consolation in looking back and certainly no inspiration for poetry, apart from the poem he was reluctant to finish, it being a verbal enactment of what he feared most of all, oblivion. Halfway through the poem he wrote a letter to Amis that comes close to being an annulment of his career as a poet. He does not mention 'Aubade' – indeed, at the time Amis knew nothing of the poem – but read alongside it the latter is the most eloquent testimony in existence of Larkin's state of mind: he was immured in a poem about oblivion, after which he would have little to say, as a poet, about anything. He begins with a report on their mutual friend, Bruce Montgomery: 'The doctors say that if he can live a year he may well live five or six. He's been on the drink again and back in a nursing home. The sodding *fool*. I don't know how this makes you feel: it makes me feel frightened and angry and sad.' Montgomery would die almost exactly a year after the letter was despatched. Larkin continues:

> Not that I can talk. Poetry, that rare bird, has flown out of the window and now sings on some alien shore. In other words I just drink these days ... Why didn't you come to me before? I wake at four and lie worrying till seven. Loneliness. Death. Law suits. Talent gone. Law suits. Loneliness. Talent gone. Death. I really am not happy these days. (L to A, 12 August 1977, Hunt)

Poetry had not quite 'flown', but its continued presence involved him in two pieces he both loathed and was reluctant to complete: one, 'Aubade', was his persistently deferred last word on the last moment, and the other was revisitation of a past that offered neither nostalgia nor hope. When he returned to 'Love Again' he shifted the focus away from 'her' to himself and asked 'but why put it into words?' The succeeding six lines, the last he would produce before becoming in verse a shadow of himself, have of course been subject to considerable scrutiny; attempts to explain the 'element' which 'spreads through others lives like a tree' but which 'never worked for me', and the latent, suggestive,

> Something to do with violence
> A long way back, and wrong rewards,
> And arrogant eternity.

Given a sufficient degree of application and cunning it is possible to fashion an ill-fitting biographical frame for those lines – a residual sense of envy for what others achieved and enjoyed and he did not, a memory of the fractious, bitter mood of the Larkin household – not literal 'violence', of course – and the arrogance of something that is at once limitless, pointless and unavoidable. But in doing so, one also becomes aware of Larkin's dejected anticipation of such a procedure, his offering to the credulous reader of obvious clues, and then of a more pervasive condition that drains the lines of any significant meaning at all – a mixture of resignation and weariness that informs the tired syntax. The passage answers its prefatory question of 'why put it into words?' with a dispirited demonstration of what it is to be unwilling and unable to write the kind of poetry that was inimitably his own.

The years between late 1974 and mid-1979 saw the decline and death of Larkin as a poet. The best explanation for this is offered, obliquely of course, by the man himself. As chairman of the Booker Prize selection committee he gave an address in November 1977 on the award of that year's prize at a dinner held in Claridge's. He states that he considers 'the novel at its best to be the maturest of our literary forms'.

> The poem ... is a single emotional spear point, a concentrated effect that is achieved by leaving everything out but the emotion itself ... In the novel, the emotion has to be attached to a human being, and the human being has to be attached to a particular time and a particular place, and has to do with other human beings and be involved with them. (Larkin, *Required Writing*, pp. 95–6)

If we accept his thesis, or even if we accept it as tenable for particular poets, then what happens if the poet reaches the point at which he feels that nothing unprecedented will ever happen to him and that everything else is already addressed in his writings? According to Larkin's model of poetic creativity the answer would be straightforward: he ceases to be able to write anything.

Larkin had reached that point. His experiment with Maeve and Betty was consistent with his conception of life and poetry. It was not that he was using these women as inspirational devices; not quite. His failure to produce anything but extensions of themes addressed in *High Windows* was symptomatic of his general condition of torpidity and stagnation. There might perhaps be uncharted emotional and indeed sexual territories to explore, an enterprise that would enrich the lives of those involved (assuming that Maeve remained ignorant of Betty, of course) and cause a concomitant reanimation of his verse. It did not work. Around the same time that he gave the Booker address, he returned to and completed 'Aubade', fully aware that it was only a matter of time before his relationship with Maeve would end for good.

One other event drew him back to the unfinished poem: on 17 November, Eva died in her sleep. Larkin's relationship with her was unusual, to say the least. After Sydney's death she became her husband's passive, and adhesive, replacement. Her personality comprised all that his was not: his drive and

energy were matched by her enervating anxiety, his combative certainties
equalled by her cloying vacuousness. But despite their differences she became
a kind of living monument to him, her presence demanding surrogate
respect and attention. Larkin obliged, gradually recognising the bifurcation
of his inherited personality. The more the memories of Sydney, good and
bad, receded the more Larkin began to recognise those features of his mother
that were now his own, particularly an inclination towards lethargic fatalism.
His response to her death – somewhere between respect and supine quiescence – was thus appropriate. When her ashes were interred next to those of
Sydney he remarked to his sister Kitty that at last 'they are together again',
which from a confirmed agnostic could have been faux-Christian sentiment
displacing morbid humour, or the other way around. He had helped Kitty
with the funeral arrangements and subsequent legal matters, but beyond
that he remained for those who knew him best predictably saddened and
no more. For someone like Larkin, however, such apparent insouciance was
deceptive; death was part of life, its presence continually anticipated and
pondered so that when it actually occurred it was as much a confirmation
as a calamity. Or as he put it in 'Aubade', 'Death is no different whined at
than withstood'.

   He was running out of things to say about death, at least in poetry, but
it seemed to be pursuing him with a vengeful assiduousness. Inevitably
many of his friends and acquaintances had literary connections, but it
is striking how their deaths seemed to suggest for him that oblivion was
making amends for his poetic treatment of it. David Williams, one of
'The Seven', had died in March 1976. Larkin wrote to Amis, 'Bad news
about David, Christ. The first of "The Seven" to go.' For Larkin there
was an essential if illogical connection between being of an age when,
for all seven, death was more than a hypothesis and another kind of loss.
He continues, 'I am more or less all right except that I never put pen
to paper' (13 April 1976). Two years later, following the death of their
mutual friend Bruce Montgomery, he appears, again in a letter to Amis,
unable to separate the man from the writer. 'Whatever one thought of
his books, and his sense (sometimes) of what was funny or desirable, he
was an original nobody else was the least like, don't you think ... as well
as introducing us to things like Dickson Carr and "At Swim Two Birds"'
(19 September 1978). He had learned of Montgomery's demise when,

returning from his summer holiday, he had found three familiar-looking envelopes with Devon postmarks on his mat. The first was from the man himself, confirming that they would meet two weeks hence; the next, from Montgomery's wife, told him that this might have to be cancelled because of his illness; 'then another from Annie [his wife] saying you know what'. Amis did not need Larkin to comment on how much this resembled life in a gloomy epistolary novel.

'Last year I came back from holiday and found [via a letter] Patsy was dead,' he informed Amis on 19 September 1978. A week later W. G. Runciman, the eminent Cambridge sociologist, sent him copies of pieces by psychologists and anthropological theorists that attempted to isolate, by various empiricist strategies, the cause of our fear of death. Larkin wrote back to him, politely commentating upon the scientific modelling, but throughout the letter his subtext is clear enough: fear – the personal, irreducible fear of death – cannot be allayed by cold logic. He concludes by recommending some books to Runciman, literary treatments of the topic, particularly 'Llewelyn Powys's *Love and Death*, an autobiographical novel that ends with death in the first person, quite a *tour de force*'. Quite, given that, as Larkin was well aware that Powys's experiment played a tantalising game with the relationship between literature and life, his autobiographical first-person novel coming as close as was possible to death by writing. Larkin himself knew there were parallels with 'Aubade', and in reply to Runciman's rationalist comment on fear of death as a neurotic condition he replied that 'nothing really expunges the terror ... something one is *always* afraid of ... It certainly doesn't feel like egocentricity' (26 November 1978).

'Aubade' and 'Love Again' reflect a poet, and a man, caught between memories of a life that seemed a mixture of pointlessness and unrealised fantasy and a future that comprised little more than an endurance of the same until death intervened. Amis during the same period experienced a similar feeling of teetering between retrospection and prognosis, and the literary consequences seemed just as laden with melancholic resig- nation, ostensibly at least. Look closely at *Jake's Thing* (1979), however, and differences are discernible. While Amis shared with Larkin a general dissatisfaction with the way his life had turned out he found also that its disappointments had furnished him with an abundance of opportunities as a writer.

Jake Richardson's 'thing' is his lack of desire to have sex with women. He is still, physically, able to, but he does not want to and he cannot remember why he ever did. For Jake, this condition is made worse by the fact that his prolific libidinous career was always a substantial part of everything else: his interest in sex was coterminous with his interest in life. By the time they moved to Hampstead, Amis was going through an experience not unlike that of Jake. There was a slight difference in that while Jake's physical capabilities are overruled by a general and unexplained disinclination Amis's ability to have sex and his desire for it seemed equally dormant. Amis altered things slightly for the novel, because by making Jake's problem more a mental than a physical one he could better target those individuals for whom he had a comprehensive loathing: psychologists and psychoanalysts. In his *Memoirs*, Amis refers obliquely to having during the 1970s consulted two therapists; one, a Dr Cobb, 'called himself a psychologist', and another, unnamed, was an upmarket marriage guidance counsellor (*Memoirs*, p. 118). In truth, the Amises, mostly at Jane's instigation, had involved themselves in a more extensive schedule of consultation and group therapy than disclosed in the *Memoirs*. Amis, owing to his periodic bouts of depression and panic attacks, had consulted experts in mental–physical imbalances on a number of occasions before this, and he had debunked their pretensions in *The Anti-Death League*, but the two individuals who claimed to be able to provide remedies for his lack of interest in sex and the state of his marriage were almost beyond parody. None of them told Amis and Jane any more than they already knew, and their solutions seemed more like exercises in humiliation.

All of this is reworked in *Jake's Thing* and, while it is intriguing enough to find Amis writing a novel about his own sexual problems, he supplements this with an even more curious autobiographical parallel. Jake Richardson is about ten years older than Amis, but he is also Jim Dixon thirty-five years after *Lucky Jim*. There are plenty of intertextual clues. Jake's given name is James, and Richard is of course the formal version of Dick: Richardson? Dickson? Dixon? Jim left the academic profession. Jake has stayed in it, but he testifies to the three decades of cynicism that would have attended Jim's career had he not abandoned it. Jake's specialisation, classics, is, appropriately, more ancient than Jim's, and his interest in it has become, as Jim's already was in his, little more than a dutiful habit.

Jim, or rather the legend of Jim, was interwoven with Amis's memories of his career as a successful sexual predator, and by the late 1970s that was all they were: memories. In the opening chapter, Jake's journey home to his wife Brenda shows us just what effect his yet-to-be-specified problem has had upon him.

The plenitude of detail is obsessive, randomised and chaotic. We consider the practical and financial differences between taking a 127 bus or a taxi to Warren Street. We encounter pedestrian lights, the Orris Park National Westminster Bank, double-parked cars with CD plates, a person who Jake thinks could well be the chap who played the superintendent in 'that police series' and roadworks with no one working on them. Jake is enticed by the cut-price offers of Winesteads Ltd and is delayed at the check-out by a man in 'dirty whitish overalls smoking a cigar and chatting to the senior of the two shopmen' (*Jake's Thing*, p. 13). The exchange is relayed in meticulous detail, with the customer revealing himself to be a verbose bore who will not stop going on about his recently acquired expertise in very expensive malt whiskies.

It is as though Amis is inviting us to compare what happens here with what would have happened if a younger Jake – or rather, Jim – had found himself in similar circumstances. Then the alliance between character and narrator would have got to work on the drab mundanities of London street life and have taken crisply sardonic vengeance upon the whisky bore. But the alliance has been broken. We know that Jake witnesses all of this, but we are not told of what he thinks. He endures it, but he evidently no longer has either the energy or the inclination to make fun of it: 'Jake paid, picked up his goods and left, remembering he should have said Cheers as the exit door shut after him. Out on the street he noticed that away from the sunlight the air was chilly' (p. 14). Only the brief reference to 'cheers', used by the bore and the shopman as part of their exchange of fashionable, late 1970s demotic, indicates on Jake's part a slight residue of satirical angst.

As the story unfolds, it becomes clear that Jake is as much the hapless victim of the darkly comic mood of this novel as he is a contributor to it. Jake's encounters with the psycho-sexual specialists Professor Trefusis and Dr Rosenburg involve some of the most brilliant comedy that Amis ever produced, but it is also the blackest.

In Chapter 4 Jake is referred to Proinsias Rosenburg, MD MA (Dip. Psych.), of 878 Harley Street.

Jake found himself closeted with a person he took to be a boy of about seventeen, most likely a servant of some kind, in a stooped position doing something with an electric fire. 'I'm looking for Dr Rosenburg,' he said.

It was never to cut the least ice with him that the other did not reply, 'Ah now me tharlun man, de thop a de mornun thoo yiz' – he might fully as well have done by the effect ('Good morning' was what he did say). (p. 36)

The following ten pages are crowded with references to Rosenburg's Irishness. After Rosenburg asks him when he last masturbated, the narrator tells us that 'It took Jake a little while to get the final participle because the Irishman had stressed it on the third syllable'. Rosenburg explains the Germanic origin of his surname and fails to understand Jake's reference to Austria as a more appropriate location. The narrator discloses Jake's unease at 'being asked to believe in a student of the mind who didn't know where Freud had come from' (p. 37).

Rosenburg's most bizarre characteristic is his habit of switching idioms and frames of reference without warning. He shifts seamlessly from his explanation of his surname to his rate of £17.50 a session, and from an apparent interest in Jake's profession to the weight of his wife. Worst of all, he does this without any awareness of its darkly comic effect. At the end of their session he introduces Jake to the nocturnal mensurator which, he explains, will measure the frequency, duration and size of Jake's night-time erections. He tells him how to fit the plastic loop to his penis, how an erection is registered on the disc and circuit breaker and that he should not forget to turn off *both* switches when he gets out of bed. All this delivered by someone who, as the narrator reminds us, 'didn't really talk like an O'Casey peasant, his articulation was too precise for that, but he did talk like a real Irishman with a largely unreconstructed accent' (p. 36).

The creeping sensation of Rosenburg as a figure beyond parody is given a crisp finale when he hands Jake his visiting card.

'Proinsias. Is that a German name?'
'Irish. It's pronounced Francis. The correct Gaelic spelling. I take it you've no objections to exposing your genitals in public.' (p. 47)

The last sentence refers to Jake's forthcoming appointment with Dr Trefusis, but read it with a particular emphasis on 'your', and its potential as the punchline to the running Irish joke becomes apparent. The speech acquires a degree of continuity, with an implied sub-clause: 'as I do, habitually, being Irish and given to talking bollocks'.

The comedic fabric of this passage is tinged with a feeling of hostility never before apparent in Amis's work. Jake has been reduced to the condition of the participant in a farce which, for him, is humiliating and over which he seems to have no control. His mildly racist reflections, deftly orchestrated by the narrator, indicate a blend of malice and hopelessness, and the whole passage reflects Amis's feelings about what he had to go through with the likes of Dr Cobb.

Things get even worse when in Chapter 8 Jake undergoes an 'experimental session' at the hands of Professor Rowena Trefusis, attended by Dr Rosenburg, and assisted by the appropriately named Miss Newman and a Ghanaian whose function is not explained. The event is witnessed by eight medical students. Jake is seated on a straight-backed chair, formally dressed in grey suit jacket, regimental tie, grey socks and polished black shoes but without his trousers and underpants. This mildly surreal juxtaposition of public and intimate presentation is echoed throughout the episode.

Jake is asked to read passages from the flattest and most abstract philosophical tracts, alternated with photographs of naked women undergoing a variety of bizarre and physically strenuous sexual acts.

The crescendo of this bizarre double-parody of a real and a clinically engineered sexual encounter occurs when Professor Trefusis offers to conclude the session with an instrument called the 'artificial stimulator'. Their exchange shifts brilliantly between an implied memory of Jake's previous experience of intimate contact and the standardised and innocently ambiguous mannerisms of an air stewardess.

Professor Trefusis came and muttered in his ear, 'Would you like a climax? We can give you one, not out here of course, or we can arrange for you to give yourself one in private.'

'I don't think I will, thanks very much all the same.'

When they parted a few minutes later she said to him, 'I hope to see you again soon.'

'Again? Soon?'

'After the successful completion of Dr Rosenburg's treatment.' (p. 88)

Martin Amis gives an account of how, after reading *Jake's Thing*, he asked his father if it was true, 'that genital focusing stuff and going to bed with a ring around your cock?' 'Yes,' he answered, 'some of it'; adding that 'in a case like this you have to show willing.' Martin commented enigmatically that 'the *novel* didn't show willing, did it?' (Martin Amis, *Experience*, p. 230), suggesting that its style evinced an uncharacteristic mood of detachment, as if the events described did not merit comment. Indeed, Jake does not, via his narrator, reflect on the episode with Professor Trefusis.

The reader, if he or she is so inclined, is left to assemble an exercise in black comedy from the components of a largely objective report. In the majority of Amis's other third-person novels there is a cooperative alliance between the heterosexual character and the narrator. Sexuality, predominantly male sexuality, is always there, and the text will provide routes between this instinct and practically all other idioms and experiences. Jake's own condition, in which sex is something simultaneously remembered and absent, insinuates itself into the structure of the novel. If any of Amis's other male characters had been substituted for Jake, the parallels between the experimental session and the real world of mild flirtation, suggestive discourse and sexual intimacy would have become a running joke shared, implicitly, by character, narrator and reader. Jake's loss of sexual desire detaches him from four decades of familiar emotional, intellectual and verbal operations, and it has a concomitant effect upon the relationship between character, narrator and reader that in Amis's novels had lasted almost as long as Jake's sexual career.

Amis is forcing a middle-aged version of Jim Dixon to undergo a kind of humiliating, penitential exercise. The writing is just as sharp, beautifully timed, but it has also, deliberately, changed. Jim Dixon and his many reinventions formed an axis between their books' parodic atmosphere and an equally pervasive sense of tolerance: situations and people might be irritating, but if they could be made funny they were also endurable. But not now. Jim in his sixties is no longer particularly biddable or indulgent yet he remains the engine for quite brilliant fiction.

Larkin's letters to Amis during 1979–80 mark something of a nadir in his own well-rehearsed exercise in pessimism and self-loathing. They read like a prose annotation to 'Aubade'. Typically (on 18 September 1979, Hunt), he begins with unillusioned banter, this time on the forthcoming third marriage of Conquest: '– glutton for punishment. No doubt she will drag him back to her transatlantic lair, as all Yank bags do'. He adds that he 'can think of worse fates, with NUPE [National Union of Public Employees] shadowboxing for another winter of pisscontentment or whatever'. The characteristic sprayshot of impatience with the rest of humanity and its activities would have been familiar to Amis, even reassuring: they were back playing the same roles they'd adopted in the mid-1940s. Now, though, the deft choreography of misery might suddenly be sidelined by unfiltered desperation. The ritual of complaint was no longer a performance: 'I really dread falling ill (I dread lots of other things *to do with* falling ill, as well, but never mind that for the moment); visited a member of staff in two hospitals recently, and shuddered ... My mind has stopped at 1945, like some cheap wartime clock.'

The following weekend they met for a brief lunch in London.

Yes, funny we crossed ... Sorry about the self-pity. I've felt sodding awful this last week, as if I've reached some kind of am-pass (y tvwk) when I can't be alone, can't stand company, can't work, can't do nothing, can't think of the present, past or future, and am crucified every ten minutes or so by hideous memories ... Feel my mind's NOT ON MY SIDE any more. (23 September 1979, Hunt)

'Aubade' was his heroic imposition of eloquence and coherence upon despair, but even there the strain was beginning to show, and a mind 'NOT ON MY SIDE' and 'hideous memories' featured more conspicuously in 'Love Again'.

A month later: 'I write at 4.30 on a Sunday – well, this one, to be precise – what you might call the arsehole of the week. Lunchtime drink dead, not time for six o'clock gin ... Sorry you are feeling low down; I sympathise.' Amis was having further troubles with his marriage. Larkin's sympathy was authentic enough but in the next sentence he returns to his own sense of hopelessness. 'I don't know that I ever expected much of life, but it terrifies me to think that it's nearly over' (28 October 1979, Hunt). He goes on to report that his doctor, aged fifty-one, had just died from leukaemia. He was medical officer at the university. 'Pretty good, knowing you have leukaemia and listening to "Like, I get these depressions, man" all the time.' He finds the image horribly magnetic and is only able to exchange it for what was once his refuge and is now as depressing as the fate of his doctor. 'I've really given up jazz ... I don't even like *good* jazz any more.' He tells of how he tries to listen to Lyttelton, Clayton, Bechet, Sonny Price and their other shared favourites 'and then you remember you've got to take those papers to work tomorrow and by the time you've found them it's all over because you somehow haven't noticed it'. For the first time the plangent drift between terror and resignation that characterised the finest poems fully informs the letters. It is an unfair exchange; the pain is persistent but the beauty is lost. They are back as closest friends but the reconciliation is informed by tragedy. Larkin's terrible candour in the letters is an index to his sense of loss as a writer. Even at his darkest moments when feelings of dread, hopelessness and anger dogged him relentlessly, poems always provided, if not a solution, then a form of displacement. He may have felt defeated by every temperamental condition but making superb poems out of them was a form of triumph. This resource was no longer available and in his letters to Amis the overspill is abundant. The New Year saw no respite: 'undergoing vertiginous waves of realisation every so often i.e. about every three hours when not drunk that during this decade we i.e. MEEEE are quite likely to be dead ...' (10 January 1980, Hunt). The ominous prescience of this requires no comment.

From mid-1980, however, one detects a gradual change in mood. The feelings and events that depressed him were still present, but since his youth he had treated much of existence as a woeful disappointment. During the 1980s he seemed to rediscover something of the early years of his friendship with Amis. The latter could not change anything but he seemed to prompt in Larkin a brand of self-lacerating black comedy that offered a tangible sense of release.

11

'And age, and then the only end of age'

Jane left Amis in November 1980. She arranged to spend ten days at a health farm and while there she got her solicitors to deliver a letter to Gardnor House informing Amis that she did not intend to return and that divorce proceedings would follow. He wrote to Larkin in early December informing him of what had happened and how he felt about it. In his view, she had gone partly because of his lack of interest in sex with her and partly because he did not like her any more. In truth, she left him because she could no longer tolerate the effects of his drinking. In September they had gone to the Edinburgh Festival. Amis, with gleefully masochistic expectations, attended a performance-art exercise and a play by Lillian Hellman. 'Frightful piss,' he told Conquest (10 September 1980). He did not go to anything else, drank a lot and, according to Jane, spent an evening being incessantly abusive and insulting to the conductor Claudio Abbado.

The effect of Jane's departure upon Amis can only be described as shock. Throughout his life he had dealt with his various fears, weaknesses and unangelic predispositions by preparing himself for their likely consequences. This was different in that while he was fully aware that continued life with Jane would be far from easy, he had not envisioned its sudden termination. Philip Amis, then living at Flask Walk, provided his father with immediate support, soon to be followed by Martin. For the next year the brothers would coordinate 'dadsitting' sessions involving mostly the generation of writers who had begun their careers at the same time as Martin in London during the 1970s. Christopher Hitchens was the most frequent visitor, sometimes accompanied by James Fenton and Julian Barnes, all laden with bulging carrier bags from nearby off-licences.

It was significant that the first person to whom Amis sent a detailed account of Jane's departure, and his feelings about her, was Larkin.

> I'm sorry I've been so long but I haven't written any letters to anyone or done much of anything else since my wife left me 23 days ago. Not with anyone, just buggered off. She did it partly to punish me for stopping wanting to fuck her and partly because she realised I didn't like her much. Well, I liked her about as much as you could like anyone totally wrapped up in themselves and unable to tolerate the slightest competition or anything a raving lunatic could see as opposition and having to have their own way in everything all the time. Well, I expect reading between the lines there you can sense that we hadn't been getting on too well of late. Yeah, but not having her around and trying to take in the fact that she never will be around is immeasurably more crappy than having her around. I've had a wife for 32 years. One consolation: with any luck selling the house and dividing everything up and finding somewhere else and moving there will be so overmasteringly crappy that I won't be able to think of anything else. Your godson [Philip] is providentially around, having left his intolerable wife and been sacked from his job. I think he's the nicest fellow I've ever met. (A to L, 5 December 1980)

In late December he resumed regular communication with Jane, and they began to make a number of tentative attempts to repair the break-up. Jane eventually agreed to return to him but only on the condition that he gave up drink, completely. He attempted to negotiate a number of compromises – wine only with meals, a modest intake of spirits just at weekends, occasional and regular days of total abstinence and so on – but Jane's terms were final and absolute. He turned her down. By late January of 1981, communication between them had ceased and just prior to this he wrote to Larkin.

> Glad to hear you're not entirely off the drink for ever. Looks as if I shall be just that myself before long. Jane mentions that as her first condition or coming back to me, the second being presumably that I saw off my head and serve it up to her with a little hollandaise sauce. I don't know what's going to happen. The fuck I mean the mere thought of the future terrifies me.
>
> This sort of thing slows your work down because you can't bloody concentrate. (A to L, 14 January 1981)

Later in the letter he asks,

> I don't know if the enclosed is any good at all. Not being allowed to use IWDAFY ['I Would Do Anything for You'] and the rest of it cramped my style too. (What were those girls called? Marsha was one, right?) Give it a quick flip through and let me know as quick.

He is referring to a draft of his chapter for a Festschrift initiated by Anthony Thwaite in 1979 to mark Larkin's sixtieth birthday in 1982. Larkin was not pleased, commenting in February 1980 to Amis, 'Have you heard that this imbecile Thwaite is plotting some *festschrift*?' (L to A, 3 February 1980, Hunt), and his unease had two causes. The book seemed like yet another sign that his life and career as a writer were coming to a close and he feared also that aspects of his past life would be exposed to public scrutiny. It confirmed his sense of being caught between recollections that he would prefer to avoid and an unencouraging, and as he often feared brief, future. He was particularly concerned when he found that Anthony Thwaite had commissioned Noel Hughes to do a piece. Hughes had known Larkin both in Coventry and Oxford and was familiar with his father's political sympathies. It was for the same reason that he had asked Amis to avoid references to their more unusual collaborations at Oxford, specifically 'IWDAFY'. Larkin felt that his biographer-in-caricature, 'Jake Balokowsky', had reformed as a squadron of very real old pals.

Yet the volume would draw Larkin and Amis closer together and offer an unexpected source of relief from their respective moods of dejection. Amis had begun the January 1981 letter with a bitter account of Jane's terms for reconciliation but by the end his sense of gloom had lifted.

> I had a great time, dorling, going through your poetry-words. 'Dockery' reminded me I had a day in Oxford recently and went up to where I used to live – you remember, that bloody awful little pair of rooms on staircase 3 was it, looking out on to the public bogs in the Giler – and found that *each* of them was now occupied by a *different* undergraduate. The room you shared with Josh has probably got half the rugger xv in it. 'D' made me think of other things too, thanks very much. *LJ* was published almost exactly 27 years ago, the same as 1918 was in 1945. Where's it all gone?

Looking through your letters I came across the bit about Norman [Iles] thinking himself as important as Darwin, Marx and Freud. Yes, but in what field? And is he going to be famous any minute, or are envious shags conspiring to hush him up till after his death?

Amis had, when writing the chapter, been looking through Larkin's letters to him from the time when they were students together, an exercise that gathered momentum beyond its purpose. For much of 1980 Larkin had responded to Amis's enquiries about their time in Oxford, and despite the fact that he had spent much of the previous year attempting to eradicate the past from his state of mind, he now appeared to be amused, even energised by the experience of going back, probably because he was doing so in the company of the man who then meant more to him than anyone.

Can't tell you anything about Oxford really. Keep a-Knockin'. My wife revolves a barrel. Aarrghghmm the queen of averything. 'The piano pub' (didn't Philip Green used to call it that?) was the Victoria Arms, now converted to the base uses of the O.U.P. in Walton Street. There was a place up the Botley Road where you pretended to be blind. Don't recall half the things you mention. If TWWLN is 'I left a fart' God, deviating into sense. Eyelet a fart. Anyway, if it is, keep it under hatches. I am obscurely ashamed of it. Corrupt without being charming. As for IWDAFY, if you can say anything about that without arraigning us as pornophiliael ponces I mean you can't. So bedda not try, fella. (L to A, 20 March 1980, Hunt)

The sharing of remembrances continued even beyond Amis's completion of the draft in 1981, every enquiry and reply triggering another excursion along paths previously closed by forgetfulness. In the same letter,

Clare Allen my oath. I remember Bruce saying with some wonder that what he liked about her was that she was so entirely complaisant, it was ? compliant – probably not that word, but ykwin (shatto ykwin). She used to say she was the original of Katherine in AGIW, which was not very true. Fancy P. Green being fat. That slender gazelle-like waaooouughghgh Bet he isn't as fat as I am. Sounds like a put-off – the sort of reason 'a woman' would 'understand'. Fffffrrrrttttt

Despite Larkin's reservations about the Festschrift itself, his delight when Amis sent him the final draft of his piece contrasts strikingly with the predominantly gloomy mood of his letters of a year before.

> Well, dalling, I cried at the end, 'cos that's just how I feel about you and your letters; the obsessively neatly typed address and Hampstead postmark sets me chuckling in advance ... It was a strange experience, reading [your essay]. A bit like looking at yourself in a distorting mirror. My principal impression is that the character you have described is more like you than me! Surely you hated literature more than I did? How about 'I have gathered up six slender basketfuls OF HORSEPISS? 'I hope alwey behinde' TRYING TO BUGGER HIM, EH? Still, I'm not the chap to quibble about little things. I deny that I was going bald at Oxford, or that my nose is big. (L to A, 16 January 1981)

It was for both a form of escapism, but within a year of his break with Jane, Amis's indulgent recollections took on an unexpectedly tactile form. In early 1982 he was joined in Gardnor House by two people with whom he would share his domestic life for the rest of his natural one, Hilly and her third husband Alastair Boyd, Lord Kilmarnock. This somewhat unusual threesome sounds, as Amis would later reflect, like something from an Iris Murdoch novel, but it was the very real and pragmatic idea of Amis's sons, Philip and Martin. In July 1981, Philip took on the role of principal negotiator and spelt out the benefits of the plan to the three potential participants. Hilly and Boyd were short of cash, and a home close to central London would help out with Boyd's regular attendance at the House of Lords. They had a teenage son, Jaime. At the time they were living in a modest cottage in Buckinghamshire, and the Lords provided a minor source of income. The arrangement would remedy Amis's fear of being alone at night, and Hilly would take charge of day-to-day domestic practicalities. Moreover, Amis would have a housekeeper he knew very well indeed, and one who had a comprehensive knowledge of his largely unchanged habits and preferences. He and Boyd had never met, but during their first encounters to discuss the set-up they seemed to get on well enough.

Larkin was the first of his friends to whom Amis addressed his feelings about the new arrangement in a letter written the day after his cohabitants moved in.

The potential buyers and their surveyors have been and gone, and a great silence reigns. I think they've found some terrible defect that'll cost £249,995 to put right, and are about to offer me the odd £5 for the place. That will make ole Jane jolly sick, means she won't be able to afford her delightful little William and Mary house with its tiny unexpected patch of vivid garden. But my morale is much improved, in fact today I felt *all right* for about 20 mins, because I've found, and yesterday installed here, the couple who'll look after me. They are Hilly and her 3rd husband, Lord Kilmarnock. Nay, stare not so. Well, you'd be justified in staring a bit, but it was their suggestion, the boys are much in favour, it's the only way for me to have a bit of family, all that. Anyhow, the day this was decided on I started a new novel, and the day they came, yesterday as I said, I got the plot of same sorted out. They have a little boy of 9. Yes, but he's very nice. No, but there it is. (A to L, 27 August 1981)

The passage neatly captures Amis's mixed emotions. Whatever he once felt about Jane has been distilled into pure bitterness, with him finding delight in her being unable to afford her 'delightful little William and Mary house' if the Flask Walk property did not reach its asking price. The 'new novel' would be called 'Difficulties with Girls', a title he would later give to a very different book. The first he abandoned because the residual loathing for his recently departed wife that informed it sidelined its claims to literary quality. Regarding Hilly, Boyd and their son, he appears uncertain of how to articulate his feelings. His lie that it was 'their suggestion' is probably an attempt to disguise his sense of relief tinged with embarrassment. Despite the fact that the letter comprises half truths, confidences and partial disclosures, it signals something of a return to his perception of Larkin as the man to whom he can entrust his flawed personality: the subject might be very different but the mood recaptures the hide-and-seek confessional letters of the 1950s.

Apart from practical and terse exchanges during the 1960s, involving their divorce and their children's future, Hilly and Amis had remained largely out of contact since he left her for Jane. Indeed, she had spent most of this time outside England.

The first meeting of the eventual threesome was arranged by Philip Amis and took place in a West London restaurant. Amis, once his relationship with Jane had started to go wrong, had begun to recall his years with Hilly with a mixture of fondness and regret, some of which registers in the exchanges with

Larkin where they ponder their respective pasts. Now they were discussing a most unconventional reunion, along with their two sons and her husband. The scenario was too implausible for fiction, even in a reworked form, and it would be twelve years before Amis fully recreated Hilly in a novel, *You Can't Do Both*, published in 1994, a year before his death.

After the sale of Gardnor House in 1982 they moved first to a flat in Hampstead and then to a house in Leighton Road, Kentish Town. This proved to be too small to accommodate regular visitors, mostly Amis's friends, and in 1984 they purchased a more spacious Edwardian house, 194 Regent's Park Road, Primrose Hill, which would be Amis's house for the rest of his life. Boyd and Hilly stayed on until 1998.

The house had four storeys. Boyd and Hilly lived in a virtually self-contained basement flat; Amis occupied a study, bedroom and bathroom on the ground floor; the first floor was a communal collection of sitting-room, dining-room and kitchen, and upstairs there were bedrooms and a bathroom for guests. The arrangement was perfect for Amis. He could spend the morning writing, undisturbed, but when he was not out at his club or elsewhere he was never on his own. A more cramped version of this had operated in Leighton Road, and it was during the two years there that he wrote *Stanley and the Women*.

The Festschrift, *Larkin at Sixty*, was launched in London in June 1982 alongside a number of interviews and a BBC documentary, presented by Roy Hattersley, the latter an exemplary case of bipolar literary assessment. While acknowledging the immense popularity and quality of Larkin's verse, even betraying a genuine admiration for it himself, Hattersley struggled with little success to conceal his loathing for his opinions on culture, society and politics. Larkin wrote to Amis: 'The Hattersley one was extraordinary. Not a smile from him, not a titter from the audience. Made me realise what it's like to be a Russian writer and fall foul of the government. Great menacing slob'. He added, 'Andrew Motion [who also appeared] looked like someone let out of Borstal for the occasion' (26 June 1982, Hunt). In the same letter, the mood lifts as he thanks Amis for attending the launch of the book. Amis had brought with him individuals now in London whom Larkin had not met since the 1950s, including Mavis Nicholson, by then a well-known BBC presenter. Most of all he was delighted to find himself talking to someone he had liked so much and not seen for twenty years: Hilly. 'I'd have liked to have talked to her a bit longer, say nine hours. She's just the same, isn't she? I didn't believe you when you said that. M. [Monica] was pleased to see her too ... Takes you back.' It seemed that even the coldness that had once accompanied Monica's visits to the Amises of old had now been despatched as false memory.

Mavis Nicholson detected an incongruous hue of mellowing, even content-ment, among Larkin's routine spectrum of misanthropy and pessimism.

> Shortly after the launch I was asked to write a piece on Philip. He was back in London, and I said 'Philip, don't worry, the magazine will pay for everything, all courses of our meal and your taxi.' He paused, and sighed. 'No,' he said, 'I'll pay for the drinks, wine. Yes, I will.' I said, 'But Philip there's no need, they'll take care of it all.' He took a deep breath. 'I insist. I'll pay for the drinks. Mavis,' and he paused again, 'do you think I'm foolish? With money? I'm careful, I know, but I'm not really mean and I'm paying for the drink. Really, I must. It's a big day for me.' I thought, what does he mean? Is he due for an award? Decided to retire? Then I realised. It was all part of the performance. He was making fun of himself. The 'big day' was him putting his hand in his pocket. Really it was a prelude to a very relaxing lunch. I'd met him a number of times since the '50s but now he wasn't shy. He was funny – well he was always funny – but he was tender too.

There is something in Larkin's letters to Amis from 1980 onwards that bears out Mavis Nicholson's impression of him. Wry acceptance appears to have suddenly replaced the note of dread and hopelessness that marks the letters to Amis of the late 1970s. Certainly he never lacks subjects for complaint, but there is also a comic edge, variously dry and surreal, that surpasses even the heyday of their correspondence in the 1950s. A key element of the code that was exclusive to their letters was a tendency to allow the possible, sometimes preposterous, subtext of a passage to take flight as an absurdist digression. Often you feel that not only was Larkin 'making fun of himself', as Nicholson put it, but laughing as he typed, imagining the guffaw it would prompt for Amis.

> Well, I would say you are the *best* living poet, in that Betjemen and Larkin have had it, and you're better than Roy Fuller. Of course there's Gavin Ewart

awh yawh leggo my no seriously I know seriously I know he's barmy, and writes too much, and is a lefty, and ADOLESCENT ABOUT SEX herkherm but just sometimes *bum*times *come*times yerno?? Oh all right then. (L to A, 3 February 1980, Hunt)

[AWA] writes to me now and I don't answer. Funny business, life, eh? De Groet knocked out his pipe and poured himself another Hollands gin. 'Funnier than death, mynheer,' he acknowledged with a wry grin. Yes, all right. No, I find the populairy hairy popularity of Peter Porter inexplicable. Can't understand what he's on about ninety-nine HUNDREDTHS of the time. And I think one should be able to do that, don't you, my dear? ... I get more letters from strangers, saying they worked in B'ham Public Libraries or stammer or are called Larkin and have named their son Philip and will I Will I fuck. Funny how little it means. And dozens of schoolgirls of course. My God. Where were they when I needed them? (L to A, 29 January 1984, Hunt)

In all probability he did feel that 'it all' meant very little, but comedy is the last refuge of sanity and one detects the relish, indeed the pride, that accompanied the preparation of these outstandingly funny passages. On Amis's recent letters to *The Listener* regarding the dire quality of much modern music:

I once heard a bit of joke music on the car radio that I took to be the musical rendition of a drunk man falling about in a kitchen, bringing down a shelf-ful of pans, treading on the cat, getting growled at by the dog, etc. At the end they said it was Concerto for something by Boulez. I was wiping tears of laughter from my eyes, no mean feat in the middle lane of the M1. (L to A, 26 June 1982, Hunt)

After Amis had become temporarily incapacitated:

How *can* you have broken your leg *standing up*? ... Were you drinking standing up? In a bar? Dylan Marlais sure has nothing on you. How are you managing without drink in hospital? Maybe the start of a new life. 'It was then I realised that it was just a vicious circle – break it, and you were free. No, I've no desire to drink now – God, well, that's an old-fashioned word of course, but whatever we mean by what isn't us, has given me streeeeooooowwwwghghgh whooogh whooogh leggo my yowowowow.' (L to A, 25 March 1982, Hunt)

The way he teases nuances of irony and absurdity from an otherwise genuine note of commiseration belies the image of a literary genius no longer able to write.

Social occasions are a trial to me now because I can't hear what anyone says ... I often wonder if they're saying 'My youngest, she's fourteen and quite absurdly struck on your poems – but then she's advanced in all ways – refuses to wear a –' or 'I happen to know that HM wants someone to look after a little library of hers down at Windsor – apparently old Edward VII collected the most amazing hot stuff, and it all needs –' You know. (L to A, 26 June 1982, Hunt)

Christopher Hitchens was a regular 'dadsitter' during Amis's period of limbo after Jane left him. On politics and related matters they were poles apart – 'I was a zealous Trotskyist,' he stated – but temperamentally they were well-suited. 'Later', recalled Hitchens,

he said to me that during the early eighties one thing in particular would cheer him up. An envelope with the Hull postmark. He knew what would follow; friendship, hilarity. Sometimes during those years he could be vindictively morose, difficult to be with, but he admitted that if he'd had a letter from Philip he would try not to recall it later in the day. Otherwise he might begin to giggle at lunch or in the middle of a conversation.

After 1980 Larkin's poetic output amounted to brief cursory pieces that for various reasons he felt difficult to avoid. The poems that followed 'Love Again' are a small, desultory crew, each reflective of distracted quiescence. He had not completely given up verse, but he was no longer attempting to write poems that tested his virtuosity or said anything beyond their self-confirming subjects.

'The Mower' is a poeticised version of his account to Judy Egerton of finding 'a hedgehog cruising about my garden, clearly just woken up' (20 May 1979), and a couple of weeks later: 'killed a hedgehog when mowing the lawn, by accident of course. It's upset me rather' (10 June 1979). The poem clothes this in unmetrical pentameters, which he cannot even be bothered to rhyme, and the reflective coda reminds one of a priest who no longer believes in God reciting a litany:

... we should be careful

Of each other, we should be kind
While there is still time.

Larkin still carried a special affection for animals, but it is revealing to compare 'The Mower' with 'Take One Home for the Kiddies', written two decades earlier. The latter creates an unnerving dynamic between two supposed states of innocence and vulnerability, in animals and children, and more than hints at the human version as a mask for innate malevolence. Larkin's feelings had not changed, but they no longer energised his verse.

His two pieces honouring, respectively, the birthdays of Gavin Ewart and Charles Causley, are tortuously respectful and amiable, and while he certainly admired the work of both men and liked each of them, the poems are shot through with the difficulty of writing about age and verse without lapsing into self-pity or offsetting this with cloying banality, or as he puts it in 'Dear CHARLES, My Muse, asleep or dead':

One of the sadder things, I think,
Is how our birthdays slowly sink ...

Although, I'm trying very hard
To sound unlike a birthday card ...

Larkin's lifetime comprised events or experiences that not even the most languorous person would treat as exciting, but after 1979 dullness acquired an almost rampant trajectory. Things happened, of course, but they did so either as an involuntary consequence of fame or because life in general becomes for those approaching and overtaking sixty beset by unwonted difficulties. Amis, however, was bitterly inspired. *Russian Hide and Seek* came out in 1980 and he began his next novel within a month of his break-up with Jane.

For much of his life Amis had depended upon, sometimes enjoyed, the predictability of a routine. His childhood at home and at school, Oxford, the army, academia and eventually the exclusive profession of writing had provided him with a timetable of objectives and obligations. These organised the components of his life and they also licensed various degrees of rebellion, excursion and imaginative reinvention. In practically all of his fiction there is a tension between two states of mind. One involves performance, responsibility and a foreseeable future, while the other incorporates factors that might threaten or seem preferable to these.

Since he had married Hilly in 1947 he had never been without a permanent partner, an anchor, and frequently, with Hilly, a counterpoint for whatever he did in his spare time; adultery included. When Jane left him he was fifty-eight; hardly the age to go out in search of a replacement, especially since he was no longer interested in sex. For the best part of a year and a half he was, apart from Ms Uniacke the housekeeper and visits from his sons and 'dadsitters', on his own in Gardnor House.

The only time in which he had experienced anything similar to this was when he returned to Oxford after the war. This, too, was like finding himself in a familiar but empty house. Larkin and his other close friends from the pre-army period had all gone. It was during this time that he produced 'The Legacy' and his poetry collection, *Bright November*, the first unpublishable and the second published with a mixture of desperation and retrospective regret. Both were second-rate because Amis addressed them as much to himself as to the reader, and something similar happened with the unfinished novel of three decades later. Its central character is a homosexual, and, the period being *c.* 1962, he keeps his sexual inclination to himself. Even the wife of his closest friend presumes that he is heterosexual. She wants an affair with him, takes his rejection of her advances as an insult and seeks revenge by accusing him of interfering with her children. This might not sound like an account of Amis's recent experience, but boil down my summary into its most powerful constituents and the parallels are clear enough. There is a man who does not wish to have sex with women. There is a woman who wants him to have sex with her and, because of his disinclination to do so, seeks a malicious, ruinous form of revenge. This is, of course, a rather prejudiced, perverse version of his break-up with Jane, but it was written immediately after their attempts to achieve some kind of reconciliation had failed, in

Amis's view because of her unreasonable demands and conditions. His early feelings of loss were being overtaken by a compensatory sense of loathing. He gave it up because it involved a spiral of insularity and retribution that caused him both to disregard the reader and for related reasons made the novel impossible for him to complete. The main character's forthcoming trial would find him caught between the disclosure of his real inclinations, themselves illegal, or some other defence against heterosexual paedophilia. What had begun as a purgation of Amis's unsettled feelings now appeared to demand an intense exploration of sexuality, law, prejudice and perversion. His first inclinations had run out of control.

Its provisional title, 'Difficulties with Girls', was appended, with characteristic Amisian irony, to a later novel that addresses the shortcomings of manic heterosexuality. Its motive, however – his act of vengeance against Jane – did not disappear and after abandoning the first attempt in 1982 he turned it into readable copy for what would be his most controversial, provocative novel, *Stanley and the Women* (1984).

Amis abandoned his first attempt to fictionalise his break with Jane because he knew that anger had displaced the modulating prescriptions of writing. But it was as much a change in environment as a self-critical instinct that enabled him to redress the balance. He gave up on it soon after Hilly moved in.

Just as significantly, the only person in whom he confided his reasons for abandoning it was Larkin.

> I'll tell you a bit about that novel but you must promise to keep it to yourself. The Lie [*Private Eye*] got it wrong as always. I did 130 pp v. slowly and unenjoyably, then shelved it. Thing was, it was supposed to be going to be an account of two marriages, i.e. the hetero world, seen by a 1st-person queer – for distancing, unexpectedness etc., plus him being talked in front of and confided in in a way not open to a hetero? But it turned out, as you'd expect from a queer, to be all about him and being queer, which doesn't sort of appeal to me enough. (A to L, 1982)

He is offering Larkin a carefully tailored version of the truth. It was not the character's sexual orientation that bothered him; rather, that he too had found himself becoming a figure warped by his sense of bitterness, fear and uncertainty.

He would eventually devise a more complex Machiavellian scheme of revenge-by-fiction and it was to Larkin, exclusively, that he announced his intentions:

> The new one is about a chap with a nasty wife. At the beginning he thinks she's a nice wife, but then he finds out she's really a nasty wife all the time. She's a writer but *he's not* you see. Ha ha ha ha ha ha. Of course it's not thinking of the characters but thinking of what they do in their lives, as you said. (A to L, 3 August 1982)

The principal characters are Stanley Duke and his wife Susan. The Susan whom Stanley thought he knew, but discovered he did not, is Jane. Amis compresses eighteen years into about three months. His falling out of love with Jane was gradual, occasionally retrievable but effectively irreversible. Stanley's experience with Susan is much worse, far more accelerated, but involves a bizarre pattern of similarities and, for Jane at least, recognisable distortions.

Amis complained, after their break-up, that one of Jane's more irritating habits was her tendency to complicate apparently straightforward verbal exchanges. She would, according to him, turn ordinary factual statements into elaborate disquisitions and rather than answer a question directly she would speculate and enquire about why it had been asked in the first place. Evidence that Jane's linguistic idiosyncrasies were certainly in Amis's thoughts as he planned *Stanley* can be found in a letter to Larkin (2 March 1982), where he imagines and recreates an exchange between Jane and 'her-girl-chum' on how she had recently sent him the proofs of her forthcoming novel. His version of Jane responds to her friend's question on whether Amis had taken an interest in her work with:

> 'Oh yes' – a lot of work with eyes and hands here, 'things could be ... quite good even ... late on. He isn't the most ... outgoing of men but he ... really cares about ... art. That's one of the things I've always respected about him,' eyelids batting fast here – 'and I hope he knows it. Because if he doesn't it's too late to ...'

This digressive, thoughtfully hesitant style of address first surfaced in Amis's fiction with Diana in *The Green Man* (an unflattering version of Jane), but with Susan it becomes more polished and, particularly in her exchanges with Stanley, an indication of a slightly sinister aspect of her personality. At the beginning of the novel, following the departure of their dinner guests, the conversation between Stanley and Susan is a masterpiece of verbal shadow-boxing, engineered with seamless charm and subtlety by Susan. Everything Stanley says becomes for her not quite what it appears to be. Stanley half suspects that his wife does this kind of thing to remind him of her social and linguistic superiority, but he dismisses such thoughts as unjust – it is not personal, just an idiosyncrasy. At the end of the book, when she leaves him, his charitable assumptions are overturned. She drops her cosmopolitan, classless facade and tells him what she really thinks. 'You little bastard. Swine. Filth.' To emphasise the class of filth to which, in her view, he belongs, she shifts into a subcultural London accent and then elaborates.

> ... you lower-class turd ... with your gross table manners and your bloody little car and your frightful *mates* and your whole ghastly south-of-the-river man's world. You've no breeding and you've no respect for women. They're there to cook your breakfast and be fucked and that's it. So of course nothing they say's worth taking seriously. (Amis, *Stanley and the Women*, pp. 268–9)

When Amis began his relationship with Jane, there were comments by some of his friends, and a few by the press, that, apart from being beautiful, intelligent and a fellow writer, her class was an element of her attraction. Her background, her previous marriages and her ongoing social network placed her at the opposite end of the middle-class spectrum from Amis, who during the 1950s had cultivated in his writing an image of himself as not quite working class but not far off it. Given that Jane never said anything like this to Amis it is intriguing that he meticulously reinvented her as Susan so that she could.

Throughout the novel Amis conducts a curious exercise in profiling, detailing aspects of Susan's character and personal history that Jane would recognise as her own, while paradoxically causing a number of these to remain recognisable by becoming their exact opposites. It is as though Amis is reinventing Jane as someone who is, for both of them, recognisably herself while at the same time exaggerating and distorting features of her personality, so that she becomes a monster capable of virtually unlimited and calculated acts of malice.

At the beginning of the novel, immediately after the dinner party and their conversation, Stanley and Susan are visited by Steve, Stanley's son from his previous marriage. It becomes rapidly evident that Steve is mentally ill, and a considerable amount of the novel involves his visits, accompanied by Stanley, to a number of variously incompetent and fanatical psycho-analysts – a rerun of *Jake's Thing* but with the counterbalance of black comedy removed. Susan plays the role of tolerant, helpful wife and stepmother. Steve during a period of derangement stabs her in the arm, but even then she is understanding. It is Stanley who insists on him being committed to a mental hospital. Prior to his conversation with Lindsay Lucas – who knew Susan at Oxford and discloses to him the deranged vindictive aspects of her personality – Stanley has chided himself for even suspecting that Susan had in some way engineered this sequence of events, perhaps even stabbed herself – she and Steve were alone when the incident occurred – as a means of removing Steve from their lives. Now this becomes more than a guilty suspicion. Her manic egotism has been unsettled by the presence of someone else to whom Stanley directs his love and attention. It becomes evident to him that she might indeed have wounded herself.

Nothing like this ever happened during Amis's relationship with Jane, but the fact that almost the exact opposite occurred would make Amis's vitriolic intent all the more evident to her. During the 1960s she had taken on, very effectively, the demanding role of caring stepmother. Amis's sons, Martin and Philip, were not mad, but they indulged themselves in irresponsible, potentially self-destructive lifestyles. Jane, particularly with Martin, did her best to improve matters, largely without the assistance of Amis.

As the title indicates, there is more than one woman in Stanley's tale. Nowell, his ex-wife and Steve's mother, joins him in his ultimately hopeless search for a cure for their son. Nowell is an actress and, as Stanley implies, she shares with many people in that profession a tendency to be always, perhaps even unwittingly, playing roles. Also she exhibits a more extreme version of Susan's conversational tendencies. Nowell, rather as if she is improvising on stage, will make things up and creatively misinterpret other people's statements, Stanley's in particular. Her presence is to an extent a further exaggeration of Amis's already distorted image of Jane, a private recollection perhaps of an incident in the late 1960s when at a party Victor Gollancz mistook her for an actress. Amis later reflected that Gollancz's error was probably caused because he thought Jane 'affected' (Jacobs, *Kingsley Amis*, p. 318). Nowell's more important function is that she enables Amis to invent Bert Hutchinson, her husband.

Bert begins by informing Stanley that 'It's not much fun ... living with somebody you don't like much.' Not only does he dislike Nowell; he no longer wishes to have sex with her. 'If you don't like 'em you don't want to fuck 'em' (*Stanley and the Women*, p. 209). He cannot of course tell her that he thinks 'she's such a bloody horrible creature' because her reaction and its consequences, divorce, which he's been through once before, are too nasty to contemplate. He is in his mid-fifties (Amis's age in the late 1970s, while Stanley, significantly, is ten years younger) and feels too tired to deal with such experiences. Instead, he takes refuge in drink, and even when he is not drunk he frequently pretends that he is as a desperate but effective means of avoiding sex. This is an account of the closing years of Amis's marriage to Jane, and it contains a number of defensive elaborations. Stanley recognises in Bert a man, not unlike himself, who when drunk 'had the power of drinking more, perhaps much more, without collapsing ... Also without losing hold of the conversation.' Bert reads his thoughts: 'It's a protection in a way that probably hasn't occurred to you, sonny ...' and, as he might have added, 'not yet'. 'She thinks I'm pissed all the time, right? ... But I'm not ... A piss artist couldn't do my job'. This could be Amis answering Jane's claims that all too often alcohol reduced him to various forms of dementia. 'It's a protection ... She thinks I'm pissed ... but I'm not' (ibid., p. 208). All of this is unnervingly similar to Amis's reports to Larkin on his relationship with Jane – firstly on the matter of drink – and his feelings for her after she left him.

The third insufferable woman of the novel is Dr Trish Collings, one of the psychologists who treat Steve. Collings is not based upon a particular individual, but she enables Amis to extend his feelings about Susan/Nowell/Jane to characteristics shared, it seems, by women in general. For Collings, Steve's madness is less a clinical condition and more the effect of living in a society populated by such people as his father. She appears to be a feminist devotee of R. D. Laing, and she insists that Steven's 'cure' must involve him in a regressive confrontation with the worst aspects of his past. What she also wants is the humiliation of Stanley: he must accept that he has ruined Steve, that he didn't really want the child, that his insistence that the teenage Steve should pass examinations, succeed and get a job was a projection of his own dependence upon male aggression. This thesis is propounded by Collings to Stanley and Nowell, and at the beginning of their meeting Stanley detects ominous signs: 'they made it clear enough that they got on famously together. They both turned and looked at me. I knew that look, I would have known it even if I had never seen it before – it was the look of two women getting together to sort a man out' (p. 151). To complicate matters, Collings sometimes peppers her private exchanges with Stanley with indications that she might actually be attracted to him, and after their meeting Nowell suggests to him that Collings hates him because she fancies him.

Stanley and the Women is a brilliant and horrible piece of writing. Stanley is without doubt a victim, the kind who demands the sympathy of the reader – easygoing, tolerant, without a shred of nastiness. Amis builds into the novel, if not entirely a justification, then an explanation of Stanley's closing outburst. A triumvirate of women, variously deranged, malevolent and compulsively vindictive, have attempted with a degree of success to dismantle his life. Larkin enjoyed it, though he was surprised that Amis still had enough energy to renew the assault of *Jake's Thing*. 'I thought you'd given women a pretty good going-over in JT; still got more to say, eh? I've never met a woman who liked JT, except Monica. She loves it' (L to A, 29 January 1984, Hunt).

After the move to Primrose Hill with Hilly and Boyd, Amis settled into a daily routine which remained largely unchanged for the rest of his life. If not pre-empted by insomnia, his alarm clock would wake him at about 7.45. Following a shave and a shower, he would go upstairs to the communal part of the house and take a modest breakfast provided by Hilly, usually consisting of grapefruit juice, cereal and fruit. He would read *The Times* and the *Daily Mail* and by 9.30 at the latest be back downstairs in his study, writing. In the late 1960s he had bought an Adler typewriter, which he never exchanged for a more sophisticated machine. Sentimental attachment perhaps, but one suspects that a word-processor, with its temptations seriously to alter and revise, went against his self-imposed regime. What went on to the page would, with the occasional addition of Tippex, stay there. If in the end it turned out to be unsatisfactory he would start again.

Around noon he would consider a reward for his morning's work, and by 12.30 have accepted it, a generous glass or two of Macallan malt whisky. Early afternoon would sometimes be spent in the Queen's pub, a short walk from the house. If he was not promoting a book or being interviewed he would next take a taxi to the Garrick Club for a late lunch, followed by more drinks, mainly whisky, and exchanges with fellow members of similar age and disposition. On 18 December 1984 he closed a letter to Larkin with 'OFF to the Garrick shortly for my Christmas drunk there. If nothing else kept me in London that place would. Somewhere to get pissed in jovial not very literary bright *all male* company. You haven't got a place like that, have you? Don't need one? Balls man you're dreaming.' A taxi would return him to Primrose Hill by early evening for supper, again prepared by Hilly. She might join him and so occasionally might Philip or Sally, both of whom lived nearby. By 7.30 on Mondays and Wednesdays he would be in front of the television set for *Coronation Street*. He might take in whatever was available thereafter, certainly *The Bill*. In a letter to Larkin (14 October 1985), Amis reflects on how self-evident intellectualism must involve all sorts of enthusiasms, mainly for European culture and postmodern indulgence, and only one exclusion: 'we haven't got a television set'. He had, and he listed his preferences for Larkin. Apart from the soaps he liked the 'Rons' and 'B. Hill' (*The Two Ronnies* and *Benny Hill*) along with a little 'wild life and crime'; 'cricket and snooker' he preferred to 'filthy soccer'; and, as for history, these programmes seemed to have two themes: 'How the British killed all the Irish' and 'How the British killed all the Indians'. He even joined a local video library to fill in those evenings when he was not going out, when no one else was in and there was nothing on the set. He would be in bed, most nights, by midnight, preceded by a few more drinks, beer and whisky, and perhaps a sleeping-pill.

The most radical alteration in Larkin's routine occurred in March 1983. He wrote to Amis later that summer:

The last four months have been fucked up by poor Monica getting shingles on Easter Saturday: ten ghastly days at her cottage in Numberland, then 14 days in hospital here, then the rest here, chez moi, till further notice. It is a particularly nasty sort ... has sodded up her left eye so she sees double ... Don't know what the future will be, short term, medium or long. (L to A, 31 July 1983, Hunt)

'[T]ill further notice' is a half truth and the closing sentence a lie. He had already made it clear to Monica that Newland Park would, apart from shared excursions to her cottage, be her permanent home. Perhaps he was reluctant to admit as much to Amis because, aged sixty-one, he had embarked on what he had always claimed he would never countenance. Their relationship had begun almost four decades before and at last they had moved in together, become a couple.

The satisfaction that he had once gained from his job was now in abeyance. There would be no further library expansions. All that his stewardship of the institution involved during the 1980s was making-do against the cuts to higher education wrought by the Thatcher administration. In 1982 he considered early retirement, but the prospect of a life with neither the, now albeit dispiriting, distractions of his office nor the compensating demands of writing verse were, as he described it to Amis, unappetising. The passage is revealing in that it is clear that he is merely contemplating the postponement of the inevitable. He knew that shortly retirement would be an obligation.

I go on wondering about whether to retire. I have a notion that it would be absolutely marvellous for about two days, then Christ the *boredom*, the *depression*. Listening to the morning service on the BBC. Counting the minutes till drink time. Going out to the shops and realising you are just one silly old sod among thousands. Not being able to afford more than one bottle of spirits a week. 'Home made wine' bum. Choral evensong bum. 'Dear Philip, it is good to know you are writing again, and kind of you to send me a selection, but frankly bum. Your own high standards bum'. (L to A, 18 April 1982, Hunt)

His bleak hypothesis of days made up of the BBC, shopping for drink and impatiently counting down the minutes to 'drink time' could be a prose synopsis for a poem like any one of those in which the ghastly mundaneness of existence is distilled in a short masterpiece. But fusing his life with his erstwhile craft was not something he would ever attempt again, and his image of the politely disappointed editor testifies once more to the renewal of his friendship with Amis. No one else received such disclosures.

Larkin's final poems carry with them the kind of quirky austerity one might associate with a prison cell that has become a home. '1982' ('Long lion days') is economically beautiful, each line not more than five syllables in length, with all ten of them combining to leave an image of summertime and little else. He appears to have worked hard at excluding anything resembling comment, even impression, as if allowing himself to discourse upon a summer's day might lead him along a track towards reflections upon time, transience, evanescence.

'Party Politics', his last written and published piece (it appeared in *Poetry Review*, January 1984), is a conceit of the fastidiously reclusive kind. The half-full glass, never topped up, the guest continually ignored by 'mine host' might have something to do with Larkin's habitual sense of life as a catalogue of failures, or they might be a complaint about there never being sufficient booze at parties. In the end it is impossible to decide whether it is a figurative recasting of insignificance or simply a poem about insignificance. Like 'Long lion days' it evinces a reluctance to say anything more than is absolutely necessary.

In July 1984 he and Monica attended John Betjeman's memorial service in Westminster Abbey. Larkin was photographed by several newspapers, principally because it was thought that he would soon be asked to become Poet Laureate. Much amused speculation centred upon how the man whose most famous line was 'They fuck you up, your mum and dad' would deal with votive pieces on royal births, marriages and deaths, but irrespective of this Mrs Thatcher offered him the post. He turned it down, but not because he was incapable of fulfilling its slightly farcical, anachronistic duties. He had proved in his poem defending the English countryside, 'Going, Going', his elegy to the Humber Bridge and most recently (October 1983) his quatrain-blazon for the university library that he could write occasional poems that were neither trite nor affected. He did not want the job because he knew that the routine, obligatory production of such pieces would remind him that they were now all that he could do. He wrote to Amis:

Sorry about letting Ted in. Mrs T was very nice about it. I just couldn't face the 50 letters a day, series of 24 programmes with live audiences on ITV, British representative at international poetry festival at Belgrade side of it, and indeed what other side is there? Answer me that. However, I agree that the thought of being the cause of Ted's being buried in Westminster Abbey is hard to live with 'There is regret. Always, there is regret.' (L to A, 26 December 1984, Hunt)

Although on affable terms with Hughes on the rare occasions they met him, Larkin and Amis were united in their dismissive attitude to his poetry.

Larkin had never enjoyed particularly good health, with various ailments of the peripheral, mysterious and self-inflicted kind attending him from his thirties onwards. Some had been standard irritations. His failing eyesight required him to be tested for new and thicker lenses virtually every year, and since the mid-1960s he had endured a progressive condition of deafness. By the end of the 1970s he had attained a weight of sixteen-and-a-half stone, which, even for a man of his height, brought with it high blood pressure and breathless exhaustion when more than standard physical effort was necessary. In March 1985 his weight and excessive drinking appeared to be taking their toll in the form of 'cardio-spasms', with his heartbeat making percipient hesitations before resuming at a compensatory but no less terrifying high speed. Despite his bulk his appetite was poor, he had difficulty swallowing, he could sleep no more than three to four hours per night and he was plagued by a regular pain in his lower abdomen. He had a number of preliminary tests of which the only clear diagnosis was an enlarged liver, but in April the results of a barium meal disclosed a potentially cancerous tumour in his oesophagus.

Throughout, he had kept Amis informed and his uncomplaining candour contrasts starkly with the bitterness that routinely accompanies his observations on such trivialities as noisy neighbours and the price of bread. He wrote in March 1984 to arrange lunch with him in London. It would be their penultimate meeting and it was already becoming clear to Larkin that this time his illness would amount to something more than his standard recipe of disorders. 'No news of any kind. Death approaches daily, but that's not new. Letters from loonies pour in, but neither is that' (L to A, 25 March 1984, Hunt). They would meet for the final time five months later and Larkin's letter of thanks for his friend's hospitality is heart-rending.

Many thanks for entertaining me so well last week. It took me about a couple of days to get over the visit, featuring times when you know it is only by remaining absolutely motionless that immediate and permanent extinction can be avoided ... It was nice seeing Hilly for a second. We must exchange more paunch talk. Do you get breathless, dear? Of course you don't have shoes to lace. (L to A, 22 October 1984, Hunt)

He never would exchange more talk with them on paunches, or anything else. During 1985 accounts of his health – 'blood tests, x-rays, liver scans, barium enemas (grand lads those) and the like' – are briskly despatched, to be followed by the usual gallery of observations on the likes of Ted Hughes. 'Was delighted that one contestant on Mastermind couldn't say who the Poet Laureate is. Ole Ted's making un vrai Charlois de lvieme, n'est-ce-pas? *Compelling* chaps to realise he's no bloody good' (L to A, 20 March 1985, Hunt).

On 11 June he was operated upon. The cancer was confirmed and his oesophagus removed, but it was found that cancerous growths had spread to other parts of his upper body.

Monica was informed that the cancer was inoperable. She decided not to tell him that his condition was terminal, but because no one was prepared to offer him guidance on the length of his recuperation period or what this would involve he knew by implication that he was going to die.

Even before the operation he had begun to make small preparations for the worst. The night before his admission he had telephoned Maeve to ask if she along with his friends from the university, Michael Bowen, Virginia Peace and Betty, would be prepared to give regular lifts to Monica to and from the hospital. This setting up of a rota of lifts was on the face of things an indication of pragmatic concern for his partner, but his choice of partici-pants indicates something else. He knew that, regardless of the success of the operation, he would be in hospital for some time and that along with Monica the car drivers would also see him during visiting hours. Maeve gives an account of how on one occasion she was 'surprised' at the 'emotional intensity of his response as he exclaimed: "You look absolutely lovely." It reminded me of the occasion when I had visited him in hospital in 1961 when our friendship ignited into love.' More uncomfortably, she visited him a few days later at the same time as Monica: 'Philip reached out to me in a passionate embrace. Deeply embarrassed I froze under the hostile stare of Monica, who was sitting on the opposite side of the bed' (Brennan, *The*

Philip Larkin I Knew, p. 92). Maeve might be forgiven for a certain degree of emotional licence, but her account nonetheless raises the question of whether Larkin was recreating in miniature a version of his emotional life of the previous two decades. Betty, too, was regularly at his bedside.

He left hospital after two weeks and spent the next three months in Newland Park doing little more than drafting letters to his regular correspondents and those who had written to him on literary or professional matters. Not once in the letters or in his exchanges with Monica or friends who called did he mention what most if not all knew, with one exception: Amis. On 4 October 1985 he sent him a letter that touched on virtually every topic of mutual interest: John Wain and his current work and marital problems; Iris Murdoch ('Ay, Merde, och', alluding to their joke of twenty-five years before, involving two literary Scotsmen) who 'IS UNREADABLE. *Why do people read her? They can't*'; *The Guardian*, 'a paper written *by* Comprehensive schoolteachers for Comprehensive schoolteachers'; an itinerary, with comments, on his average day-long menu of television programmes ('I flinch from fearful sitcoms'); and recent reprints of *The Less Deceived* and *Lucky Jim*. On these he pauses for reflection: 'I think we can say that we've done *something* of what we hoped when unknown lads'. The letter, at seven pages, is one of the longest he had ever written, and the fact that Amis was his correspondent is revealing. It is as though he was scouring his recollections for anything and everything that had united them in various states of amusement, rage and ambition. He knew that quite soon their unique, curious connection would be severed. In the midst of his sprawling but compellingly desperate list of reflections we come upon something apparently more incidental. 'It's very nice of you to offer to visit; having pondered, I think we had better leave it for a bit.' The old joke, that Amis never came to see *him*, had now acquired a darkly comic resonance. As Larkin knew, Amis and Hilly would come, for his funeral. 'I can't fuckin eat fuck fuck all. It really is scary (or scarifying, as everyone says these days). So please could we postpone it a bit. Three months ago my doctors said I am slowly getting better. To my mind I am slowly getting worse' (L to A, 4 October 1985, Hunt).

His final letter to Amis was dictated on to a tape recorder – with difficulty since he had almost lost the ability to speak – and transcribed and posted by his secretary. He concluded, 'You will excuse the absence of the usual valediction'. Causing 'bum' to curtail the encroaching pomposity of a sentence was their private joke. The letter ends very movingly. He asks him to thank Sally, his goddaughter, for her letter and photograph. 'I am so glad to see strong resemblances in her to Hilly, who is the most beautiful woman I have ever seen without being in the least pretty (I am sure you know what I mean, and I hope she will too)'.

The final paragraph finds him slipping back, almost, towards his deftly evocative poetic signature. 'Well, the tape draws to an end; think of me packing up my pyjamas and shaving things ... I suppose it's all come at once, stead of being spread out as with most people' (L to A, 21 November 1985). On 28 November he collapsed at home and was rushed to hospital, where he died in the early hours of 2 December.

The funeral was a curious affair. It was explained to all present that Monica, his partner of almost four decades, was too ill to be there, although it was assumed and accepted that she was simply unable to face the prospect. Betty and Maeve attended, as colleagues. Kitty and his niece Rosemary represented the family. Amis and Hilly travelled up from London by train with Andrew Motion and his wife, Charles Monteith and Blake Morrison.

Amis gave the funeral address, by equal degrees unflinchingly honest and moving, a tribute to 'the most private of men, one who found the universe a bleak and hostile place and recognised very clearly the disagreeable realities of human life ... But there was no malice in it, no venom. If he regarded the world severely or astringently, it was a jovial astringency.' For those present, 'We are lucky enough to have known him', and the 'thousands who didn't and more thousands in the future will be able to share those poems with us. They offer comfort and not cold comfort either. They are not dismal or pessimistic, but invigorating.' Privately, he confided in Conquest: 'I don't know; presence? Keep forgetting he's dead for a millisecond at a time: I must tell/ask etc. Philip – oh Christ I can't. I still read a few pages of the works before going to bed' (1 January 1986).

Mavis Nicholson recalls a conversation with Amis about Larkin soon after his death.

'Kings said to me, "*Jill* and *A Girl in Winter* inspired me. They were extraordinary and they encouraged me to become a novelist." Of course he didn't mean that he in any way imitated Philip. They were very different writers.' Did he, I ask her, say anything of Larkin's part in *Lucky Jim*? 'No, he didn't say anything of that.'

Amis had known him as well as anyone, which, as he was soon to learn, did not guarantee that he knew the same person as others did. On 7 June 1986 he wrote to Conquest expressing his shock at having learned that Larkin had instructed Monica to destroy his diaries. It is clear from the mood of the letter that Larkin's decision itself was less significant than its contribution to Amis's growing perception of another man with other lives, particularly the one he shared with Monica. 'His chosen companion, what? Makes you think of Mr Bleaney "... having no more to show than that grim old bag should make him pretty sure He warranted no better". As Mart [Amis] said, Christ, what a *life*.'

There is a bitterness here certainly, and in December 1986, following a Radio 4 documentary on the anniversary of his death, Amis continued:

> Everybody talked on the level of 'he perhaps had a forbidding exterior but really he was very warm with a word for everyone'. So that was the cosy little nest that he had up there. The only point of interest was that P had a telescope on his windowsill to get a better view of passing tits. (A to Conquest, 6 December 1986)

Maeve Brennan irritated Amis most of all. She wrote to ask for a draft of his funeral address to quote in her own contribution to a forthcoming Festschrift while arguing, contra Amis, that Larkin had indeed shown signs of an (albeit vague) acceptance of God and an afterlife. Amis was outraged. His image of his friend as faithless cynic until death was the more accurate version, but what unsettled him most was the apparently incessant disclosure of new dimensions of the man he thought he knew. He wrote to Conquest, 'I never heard a word about her except that solitary "Maeve wants to marry me" blurting; you too I think,' and added, 'He didn't half keep his life in compartments' (17 November 1986).

Conquest's letters to Amis during the 1970s and 1980s are revealing with regard to the nature of the tripartite friendship, often reflecting Mavis Nicholson's observation that 'Kingsley and Bob seemed like middle-aged schoolboys. Any kind of smuttiness or sarcasm would have them huddled together, chortling. Philip did have a similar sense of humour but often they seemed to crowd him out.' 'Tony P [Powell] writes that Philip and Monica did indeed drop in there for lunch. I don't think they'd met Monica before. Impressions should be interesting' (Conquest to A, 16 September 1976, Hunt). 'Monica as Lady Larkin yet? – reminds one of Gypsy Jones (doubtless a sister) as Lady Craggs [Gypsy Jones is a figure in an Anthony Powell novel, a promiscuous radical who turns out to be a social climber]. I bet you Philip buckles down to a Jubilee or Coronation Ode' (Conquest to A, 30 November 1976, Hunt). In his next comment on 'Philip's Ode on the next coronation', scorn is exchanged for caricature.

> You'll notice Charles the First and Second
> As tyrant and lecher reckoned.
> If as a Good King you'd be read of
> Don't lose your head, or fuck your head off.

This is slightly below Conquest's usual standards, but he finds his proper voice when contemplating Larkin's dilemma of being terrified of marriage yet seemingly attached for ever to Monica. Invoking 'The Whitsun Weddings',

> if I don't jot it down I never shall, and it'll be lost to posterity –

> As I chugged down to London last Whitsun
> I said 'See all these horrible shits on
> The train, pawing tarts.
> That's how married life starts?
> I can't say I like it a bit, son.'
> (Conquest to A, 1 September 1977, Hunt)

'Philip writes that "Aubade" has been set to music in the USA. Cole Porter's dead, though, isn't he? Fats Waller?' (Conquest to A, 13 April 1978, Hunt). On his own contribution to the Thwaite Festschrift, 'I think I must omit the bit where he sniggers at "Once I am sure there's nothing *going on*"' (Conquest to A, 5 February 1981, Hunt). On the Laureateship, 'If I were Philip, I would insist on the sack being reinstated – worth more than the cash equivalent these days, and he could commute it to scotch or whatever it is he soaks up like a sponge' (Conquest to A, 16 July 1984, Hunt). Even after Larkin's final illness had begun:

I wrote him a (fairly brief) letter ... I didn't like to put in the other herewith enclosure, the German painting of the devil lying in wait for chaps by a cunt, which may strike you as of interest in one way or another, but which somehow seemed too gloomy or sententious for a sickbed. Copies to Monica and Maeve? (Conquest to A, 10 July 1985, Hunt)

I had been just about to write to him ... with some such thing as all the top guys go to hospital at the same time; but postponed it and they found that R's [Ronald Reagan's] was cancer after all; it would have been a bit rocky to have sent such ... Though Reagan surely gets one's vote / He's not in Larkin's class. / They only went down Philip's throat / They went up Ronald's arse. (Conquest to A, 28 July 1985, Hunt)

When news of his death came, Conquest seemed to acknowledge that Amis would be more severely affected. 'Very sad loss on all possible counts, as you're the last person who needs to be told. Only consolation ... is that it was quick and unconscious: considerations not to be sniffed at' (Conquest to A, 2 December 1985, Hunt). Gradually ridicule is pushed aside, post mortem, by a combination of respect and puzzlement. 'Well, a happy new year to you, even if inevitably clouded by the absence of old Philip. As Xmas approaches, one thinks that at least he missed that – he says somewhere it's when his mild distaste for other people turns into active loathing.' He continues, 'Someone will no doubt do a bit on the sum of P. L. ... a scenario of doing things he wanted? – Apart from being headmaster of Roedean I mean ... Actually what I fear Jake B will miss ... which you caught in the *Obs* piece was P's jolly side' (Conquest to A, 24 December 1985).

As if to illustrate, he contributes, on behalf of their late friend, a piece on the service of remembrance at Westminster Abbey, attended by Amis, Hilly and Monica.

I can't help thinking: What would Philip have said?

The lesson being read by old Ted!
While the Dean tells the flock
'He'd have thought it all cock...'
Ain't it grand to be blooming well dead!
(Conquest to A, 20 January 1986, Hunt)

Opinions differ on the quality of Amis's *The Old Devils* (1986) but what has not been properly appreciated is the way in which his deeply unsettled feelings about his closest friend inform it. It was begun before Amis became aware of the severity of Larkin's illness yet his presence among the complex permutations upon each character's perceptions of themselves and their relationship with others is tangible from the start.

The novel carries us into the lives of four married couples. They are all about the same age as Amis, retired to semi-retired, have known each other since their university days and are spending their declining years in the town where most of them grew up. The town is unnamed but it is undoubtedly Swansea. There is Malcolm Cellan-Davies, ex-teacher and unsung local writer, who spends his spare time translating *Heledd Cariad*, a fourteenth-century Welsh epic. Malcolm gets on well enough with his wife Gwen, but their exchanges reflect a kind of loveless endurance, particularly on her part. They are, however, too old and tired to voice their true feelings or have a proper argument. Charlie Norris owns a local restaurant but leaves the running of it to a manager. Charlie is permanently, albeit to varying degrees, drunk. He has an impressive intellectual command of practically all topics, but most of these bore him and he has long since lost the inclination to impress other people. Sophie, his wife, puts up with him with a kind of grudging affection; 'I never realised how much he drank till the night he came home sober. A revelation, it was'. Peter Thomas is a semi-retired chemical engineer. In his twenties he briefly taught the subject at the local university, and he married Muriel because her father owned the company that enabled him to exchange academia for a better-paid life in industry. Peter and Muriel have not touched each other for ten years; 'separate rooms, no hugs, no endearments'. Their mutual loathing is evident, but, like the rest, they observe the rituals of enforced cohabitation.

Alun and Rhiannon Weaver had been friends with the rest during their youth and at university but have spent the previous three decades or so in London. Alun, who was once Alan, is a media Welshman; a television front man and writer whose professional success has been based upon his ruthless exploitation of other people's, particularly English people's, image of Wales. He has written about, made programmes on and publicly idolised the poet with no Christian name, Brydan, a thinly disguised version of Dylan Thomas. Indeed, his planned novel about Wales, his other writings and his media performances betray a calculated dependency upon Brydan's bardic persona and linguistic habits.

The Weavers are coming home, and the frisson of anxiety and aroused expectation that runs through the first chapter proves to be fully justified. The presence of Alun involves for the rest an almost compulsory revisitation of their pasts. He and Rhiannon are the same age as the others, but they are better preserved; they still have sex, they get on well together and, despite Rhiannon's awareness of his adulterous inclinations, they still seem to be in love.

Alun enters the lives of the other characters as rejuvenation personified. He arouses a mixture of feelings ranging through lust, jealousy, contempt, admiration and friendship, which before his arrival had been submerged beneath a weary catalogue of mutually agreed protocols. He even reintroduces the wives of the others to sex. He has had affairs with most of them before, contributing of course to their husbands' unease at his return, and he picks up where he had left off. Amis distributes aspects of himself and his habits among several of the male characters but for people who had known him for most of his adult life, Hilly in particular, Alun would be at once recognisable and, in a peculiar sense, unreal. He combines the most amusing, agreeable and regrettable features of practically all of the principal men of Amis's novels of the 1950s and early 1960s.

As an individual, Alun energises the lives of the other characters. He is a hyperactive embodiment of their pasts, and in various ways he causes them briefly to act as he does, as if they were still in their twenties or thirties; a kind of demonic rejuvenation. Amis was not the cause of anything like this, but the inspiration for it came from the renewal of his friendship with Larkin. Since the end of the 1970s their letters are engrossing examples of how recollection of things and feelings that are in themselves irrecoverable can revive the energy that once accompanied them. In this five-year period of correspondence they expend an enormous amount of effort on sharing memories, but it is not a mournful, regretful process. Instead, these revisitations of their shared pasts, particularly the 1940s and 1950s, reignite the energetic, reckless style of their letters from that time. This same sense of their defying *tempus fugit* by the sheer injection of gesture and style is a key to Alun's effect upon the book. In Chapter 3 Charlie looks on with grim admiration as Alun mocks, jokes and humiliates his way through a

series of social encounters. Alun has been asked to unveil a monument to
Brydan and Charlie observes how he deals with one Llywelyn Caswollen
Pugh, 'an official of the Cymric Companionship of the USA', by playing
off Pugh's tedious discourses on Pennsylvanian Welshness with slyly ironic
rejoinders and a final promise to visit him, perhaps in 1995, a decade hence.
Charlie reflects:

> The fluid, seamless way Alun converted his unthinking glance towards the
> waiting car into an urgent request for assistance for somebody to accompany
> his Mr Pugh, was something Charlie was quite sure he would never forget ...
> At the moment before he ducked his head under the car roof Charlie caught a
> last glimpse of Pugh, looking not totally unlike an inflated rubber figure out of
> whose base the stopper had been drawn an instant earlier. Charlie might have
> felt some pity if he had not been lost in admiration for Alun.
>
>   'Bloody marvellous bit of timing,' he told him when they were settled in
> the back seats. (p. 83)

Here, one is reminded of the beginning of Amis and Larkin's friendship, the
formation of their double act that would eventually enable Amis to write
Lucky Jim. The difference, however, is that now Alun is the sole performer
while Charlie attends merely as admiring spectator. It seems that Amis's
memory of their past, while vivid, was still somewhat selective. Amis wrote
to Larkin (17 November 1985) and asked him to 'run me up half a dozen
lines of sub-Thomas' for his ongoing novel. Amis had already done this
thirty years earlier with Gareth Probert's verse in *That Uncertain Feeling*,
but he tells Larkin that he wants something different from that, something
that blurs the line between parody and imitation so that the reader would
'wonder whether it was genius or piss'. Larkin had just over two weeks to
live, and a month after the death of his friend Amis killed Alun Weaver with
a heart attack. His gesture was elegiac, a quiet admission that the energy
generated seemingly by Alun himself was, in fact, a cooperative enterprise.
After his death, the infectious zest and dynamism diminishes and the other
characters return to their previous state of atrophy.

   The closing chapter involves Rhiannon and Peter, whose son and
daughter have decided to marry. They once had a relationship, she became
pregnant, had an abortion and they drifted apart, and just as the novel is

about to close we learn via Muriel that they have decided to share a house; not as a couple, but rather as companions. The autobiographical parallels are glaring. Aside from the abortion that Amis and Hilly decided against in the 1940s, he persuaded her to have a termination in 1960 just before the marriage began to fall apart. Now they are back together, like Peter and Rhiannon, as companions. But there is something else too. Malcolm had also loved Rhiannon but when he reminds her of his rather inept overtures she confesses that all she recalls is a kind of harmless sibling-like affection. This conversation between them takes place as they pass the same church where he had declared his feelings for her thirty years before and they walk on towards a beach and a headland.

Throughout, their exchange and the narrator's comments continually evoke moments from Larkin's poems of the 1950s, particularly 'Church Going', 'An Arundel Tomb' and 'To the Sea'. During the 1940s and 1950s Larkin was the only one of Amis's friends with whom Hilly formed a genuine personal affection, and the feeling was mutual. Malcolm, when he hears that Peter and Rhiannon have moved in together, comments: 'Good luck to them is what I say' (p. 293), much as Larkin had expressed his approval for Amis and Hilly's arrangement. This tribute to Larkin from Amis and, by implication, Hilly is sincere, moving and touchingly misguided. 'Church Going', 'An Arundel Tomb' and 'To the Sea' were born out of Larkin's and Monica's shared fondness for empty religious buildings and remote coastal regions. At this point Amis knew a little of the quiet enthusiasms that in truth he found slightly laughable, and he was certainly not aware of quite how much they cemented Larkin's relationship with Monica. More significantly the first two poems marked the point at which Larkin exchanged his friend for Monica as adviser on the mood and style of his verse.

Almost a decade later, with benefit of reflection and the disclosure of more of Larkin's correspondence, Amis shifted his perspective on his late friend. Robin Davies of *You Can't Do Both* (1994) is Amis's most transparently autobiographical appearance in fiction. The lack of disguise was in part an apology to Hilly; she, as Peggy, features as the kind, enduring victim of Robin's selfishness. Larkin also appears. No doubt as a gesture of respect to their friendship, he surrounded the character of Andrew Carpenter with enough evidential detail to distance him from Larkin (neither Jacobs nor any of Amis's reviewers noticed similarities), but all this is accompanied by private, resonant linkages.

Carpenter is the son of Robin's neighbours, his senior by a couple of years and an undergraduate at Cambridge. He becomes Robin's mentor, and this is a reasonably accurate version of how Amis felt about Larkin during his first period in Oxford. Carpenter takes Robin to his room in his parents' house, plays him some jazz records that he has never heard before and talks to him about literature. Robin notes on the bookshelves a copy of Huxley's *Point Counterpoint*. Larkin and Amis had shared an admiration for Huxley, but, more significantly, Carpenter introduces Robin to a piece by a poet, unnamed, whose style carries some echoes of Auden, again someone they both respected, and which is effectively a catalogue of Larkin's intellectual and literary heroes.

'You might anyway see different things in them from what I see. No, your immediate spontaneous reaction is what counts. But I'll be fascinated to hear. We'd better go down in a minute. God knows what your parents think we've been getting up to.'

Lawrence, Blake and Homer Lane,
    once healers in our English land,
These are dead as iron for ever;
    these can never hold our hand.
Lawrence was brought down by smut-hounds,
    Blake went dotty as he sang,
Homer Lane was killed in action by
    the Twickenham Baptist gang.
(*You Can't Do Both*, p. 36)

Then, and at later points in their friendship, Carpenter explains to Robin the attractions of Homer Lane and Lawrence. (And one should note also that Robin remarks that his very conventional parents would not have allowed Lawrence's 'obscene' works in the house, while Carpenter's father, like Larkin's, encouraged his son's admiration for him.) Lane was briefly Auden's lover, and his thesis that desire and instinct are the unacknowledged foundations for the intellect influenced Layard who, in the early 1940s, gave lectures at Oxford and for whom Larkin became an advocate. Lawrence, whom Larkin also admired, advanced a similar thesis in his literary and non-literary writings.

At the beginning Robin is fascinated by a man who has read so much radical, unorthodox material, but gradually respect is replaced by tolerance. Amis, too, moved beyond the feeling of awe and inferiority that had initially attended his friendship with Larkin to the extent that he forbade from their exchanges any mention of Lawrence, whose work he loathed because it broke his rule that literature should not be the vehicle for ideas.

At the same time Carpenter is a memorial to the closeness and sense of fun that Amis had shared with Larkin, particularly in their early years. Carpenter entertains Robin with imitations. 'He turned out to be a wonderful mimic, at least the voices and face he did were hilarious in themselves.' This is generous, given that Amis had held centre stage as the imitator-in-chief at St John's. Carpenter's imitation of a Cambridge don is actually a version of Amis's parody of Lord David Cecil: 'I want all to wemembah ... you owe a duty to your college ... not only to ush, your pahstorsh and mahshtorsh ... not only to this great university...' Robin is particularly impressed by 'something with no words to it, a killing upper-class-moron face with a lot of blinking and as many as possible of the lower teeth showing'. This, too, is an account of Amis himself, not his friend, but in an oblique manner it involves a note of gratitude. Jim Dixon could not have been invented without the blend of absurdity and anti-intellectualism that flavoured their exchanges. Larkin was the junior partner, but by reversing their roles, via Robin and Carpenter, Amis was finally acknowledging a debt; the irreverent dynamics of their times together and their letters were the foundation for Dixon's similarly energetic double-act with his narrator. Robin reflects that Carpenter 'was just about the most marvellous and amusing companion anyone could ever have wished for'.

Both *The Old Devils* and *You Can't Do Both* were covert ruminations on their friendship, and apart from the amusing chapter on Larkin in the *Memoirs* (1991), Amis seemed content to allow what they'd had to become an intimate memory. It is possible that he and Hilly sometimes spoke of him – they lived in the same house and he was part of their shared past – but after 1986 there are hardly any references to him in the correspondence between Amis and Conquest. Martin Amis writes that after 1985, 'the narrative of Kingsley's *Letters* takes on a stunned and deafened feel' (Martin Amis, *Experience*, p. 246). He adds that 'my sense of Philip comes mainly from my childhood in Swansea, though I had a few good times with him as an adult. After 1985 something in my father disappeared too. He rarely talked of Philip.' Mavis Nicholson: 'He [Amis] wasn't keeping secrets. It seemed to him pointless, even vulgar, to reminisce about Philip. It was a matter of respect. He wasn't coming back.' But he would.

When he penned his back-handed tribute to 'Jake Balokowsky, my biographer', Larkin captured accurately enough the standing of literary biography in the 1960s, as a rather dry adjunct to academia, and he, Conquest and Amis joked regularly in their letters about what their biographers would make of their correspondence. In 1984 when a literary biography of Barbara Pym was published, including some of her letters to Larkin, Conquest wonders disingenuously why there were none of his to her.

> I bet they were a bit different in tone from what he writes to you and me, eh? Though there is the possibility:
>
> Of the letters of Larkin and Pym
> There's only what she wrote to him,
> Because unlike hers,
> He so often refers
> To 'fuck', 'roger', 'arse', 'prick', and 'quim'.
> (Conquest to A, 8 August 1984, Hunt)

The hypothesis of a priggish scholar desperately attempting to salvage quotable passages from the reams of bawdiness was funny because it seemed also so unlikely and preposterous. In their experience, lives of writers involved stories of high-minded endeavour, not men who seemed unable to stop writing to each other about their sexual fantasies. Yet by the mid-1980s trade presses were finding that unabridged literary biographies were profitable, and by 1987 Anthony Thwaite had been commissioned to edit Larkin's letters and Andrew Motion to write his biography. Amis was their first point of contact and he cooperated without reservation. He got on well enough with Thwaite, whom he'd met several times before and who was, but for a decade, of his generation.

> He tells me Monica has found 'the missing final notebook' [January 1972 to November 1981] and he's got 8 more unpub'd poems out of it, including one beginning Love again: wanking at ten past three. As he quite funnily says, the reviewers will call it incompetent editing [Thwaite was also editing

the *Collected Poems*], letting through an obvious misprint for 'waking'. (A to Conquest, October–November 1987)

His account of his first meeting with Motion is more caustic. 'He's quite agreeable but he does wear half-a-dozen bangles on his arm. His thank-you card spoke of my giving him my time "so generously and *interestingly*". Well there it is' (A to Conquest, 6 December 1986). A year later, when Motion wrote a poem on Larkin ('This Is Your Subject Speaking'), Amis was not so accommodating. 'Christ, have you seen Motion's poem about Philip? I wrote to Thwaite, understating the case rather, that it was of horrendous banality and shapelessness' (A to Conquest, October–November 1987).

Amis's notion of reviewers treating 'wanking' as a misprint reflects his continued impression of the literati and the reading public as made up of a quiet minority of prudes and – in the majority – those who would treat Larkin as a humorous melancholic. Fans of Larkin were largely as Amis imagined them to be, people who enjoyed the wry, taciturn mood of his verse and who would not be at all surprised or disappointed by what the letters disclosed of the man behind the poems. But he seemed unaware of the fact that the literary establishment now included many who loathed the kind of poetry that ordinary readers might understand, and who were waiting for a pretext to demolish Larkin's reputation both as a writer and as an acceptable human being. As early as 1957 Charles Tomlinson had begun to lasso the unostentatious conservatism of Larkin's verse into the unedifying zone of chauvinism, writing that his 'narrowness suits the English perfectly'. 'They recognise their own abysmal suburban landscapes ... The stepped down version of human possibilities ... the joke that hesitates just on this side of nihilism, are national vices' (Charles Tomlinson, 'The Middlebrow Muse', *Essays in Criticism* [1957], 7, pp. 208–17). What Tomlinson and others implied was laid out comprehensively in Blake Morrison's informed but by no means impartial book on *The Movement* (1980): anti-modernism is complicit with political conservatism; the use of England as the locative fabric of writing is a version of colonialism; provincialism, and its handmaiden nostalgia, could at a stretch be associated with bigotry. After Larkin's death and following the publication of his *Collected Poems* (1988), the accusations became much less guarded. According to Tom Paulin, Larkin 'writhes with anxiety inside that sealed bunker which is the English ethic of privacy', a collective mood of loss and failure, the end of Empire. In Paulin's view even Larkin's reluctance to get married partakes of the psychological fear of losing sovereignty. His political counterpart, apparently, is Norman Tebbit. 'Larkin's snarl, his populism and his calculated philistinism all speak for Tebbit's England and for that gnarled and angry puritanism which is so deeply ingrained in the culture' (Tom Paulin, *Times Literary Supplement*, 20 July 1990).

If a commentator had proposed a similar interrelationship between a presumed, distasteful state of mind and a national shortcoming with regard to an Irish, Scottish or Welsh poet their reputation would soon be in shreds, and a day in court would surely await anyone who dared suggest the like for a writer of Asian or Caribbean ancestry, but for some time open season has been declared on the kind of Englishness that Larkin is supposed to represent, and once the *Letters* appeared in 1992 left-liberals began to foam at the mouth. Paulin found it to be 'a distressing and in many ways revolting compilation which imperfectly reveals and conceals the sewer under the national monument Larkin became' (Tom Paulin, *Times Literary Supplement*, 7 November 1992). For several months otherwise sane commentators formed a queue to pour unabridged contempt on the memory and literary reputation of Larkin. Peter Ackroyd, Bryan Appleyard and James Wood, among others, appeared to have decided virtually overnight that because Larkin had in a couple of letters transgressed the new dispensations of political correctness, his poetry – which they previously, though grudgingly, admired – was now worthless. Christopher Hitchens: 'Kingsley thought it all entirely predictable, and laughable. He guffawed at the news of the academic, a woman, which pleased him greatly, who'd proposed banning Philip's work from the degree course.' He refers to Professor Lisa Jardine, then of Queen Mary and Westfield College, London, who had not stated that she wished to ban Larkin completely. She had, however, urged that his poems should be allocated a special status, removed from the core curriculum and dealt with 'only to disclose the beliefs that lie behind them' (Lisa Jardine, *Guardian*, 8 December 1992), rather than as literary works in their own right – presumably according them a status similar, say, to *Mein Kampf* in a course on political philosophy. Hitchens says,

Yes, Kingsley loved that. It confirmed what he'd claimed for years, that the education system and much of the intelligentsia were riven with Marxists.

Their beliefs were, he thought, insidious and he felt grateful to Philip for, involuntarily, exposing them as preposterous too. But the following year when Motion's biography appeared he did become angry. He hated the book, saw it as condescending and insulting. He thought Motion the worst type of overreacher, a poet who was inferior to Larkin apologising for Philip's alleged defects as a human being.

Motion himself had virtually proclaimed the latter in the preface, writing of 'the beautiful flowers of his poetry ... growing on long stalks out of pretty dismal ground'. Hitchens's account of Amis's anger is borne out in the review of the biography he did for *The Spectator* (3 April 1993), in which he accuses Motion of lacking 'skill, dash, ability to select' and 'above all humour'. Amis presents Motion as a literary pathologist, respectful enough of the remains but indifferent to the real Philip Larkin. Amis takes issue with Motion's affected 'pious horror' at Larkin's taste for pornography. 'If he [Motion] has never leered, or even looked, at a photograph of a naked female, he is some kind of freak. If he has, he is no more than a medium-sized hypocrite.' Hitchens again: 'Kingsley was affronted, appalled that his closest friend had become the subject of a disdainful morality tale. He thought it was like some Stalinist rewriting of the truth.'

Amis died on 22 October 1995, in St Pancras Hospital, London. During the previous year he had suffered from a variety of undiagnosed conditions, causing him to behave erratically and sometimes to lose consciousness, and in August a mild stroke was recorded. Pneumonia was the official cause of death. Monica lived on in Newlands Park as a recluse. She died in 2001. In 1998 Hilly and Lord Kilmarnock sold the house in Primrose Hill and moved back to Spain to a small farmhouse outside Ronda, where Hilly tended animals. She died there in 2010.

The friendship between Amis and Larkin was by parts perverse, unique and deeply affectionate. It shaped the lives of each of them and more significantly, for us, left its imprint on some of the finest fiction and poetry of the twentieth century.

Select Bibliography

Philip Larkin

Novels

A Girl in Winter (Faber & Faber, London, 1947; Faber & Faber, London, 1975).

Jill (Fortune Press, London, 1946; Faber & Faber, London, 1964).

Trouble at Willow Gables and Other Fictions, ed. James Booth (Faber & Faber, London, 2002). (NB Page references for 'Trouble at Willow Gables', 'Michaelmas Term at St Bride's', 'What Are We Writing For? An Essay', 'Ante Meridian: The Autobiography of Brunette Coleman', 'No for an Answer' and 'A New World Symphony' are all from this work.)

Poetry

Collected Poems, ed. A. Thwaite (Marvell Press and Faber & Faber, London, 1988).

The Complete Poems of Philip Larkin, ed. A. Burnett (Faber & Faber, London, 2012).

Miscellaneous writings

All What Jazz: A Record Diary, 1961–68 (Faber & Faber, London, 1970).

Further Requirements: Interviews, Broadcasts, Statements and Book Reviews, ed. A. Thwaite (Faber & Faber, London, 2001).

Letters to Monica, ed. A. Thwaite (Faber & Faber and the Bodleian Library, London, 2010).

Required Writing: Miscellaneous Pieces, 1955–82 (Faber & Faber, London, 1983).

Selected Letters of Philip Larkin, 1940–1985, ed. A. Thwaite (Faber & Faber, London, 1992).

Secondary material

Peter Ackroyd, 'Poet Hands on Misery to Man', *The Times*, 1 April 1993.

A. Alvarez, *The New Poetry* (Penguin, Harmondsworth, 1962).

Alan Bennett, 'Alas! Deceived', *London Review of Books*, 25 March 1993.

B. C. Bloomfield, *Philip Larkin: A Bibliography 1933–76* (Faber & Faber, London, 1979).

Maeve Brennan, *The Philip Larkin I Knew* (Manchester University Press, Manchester, 2002).

R. L. Brett, 'Philip Larkin in Hull', in Jean Hartley, *Philip Larkin: The Marvell Press and Me* (Carcanet, Manchester, 1989).

Robert Conquest (ed.), *New Lines* (Macmillan, London, 1956).

George Hartley (ed.), *Philip Larkin 1922–1985: A Tribute* (Marvell Press, London, 1988).

Jean Hartley, *Philip Larkin: The Marvell Press and Me* (Carcanet, Manchester, 1989).

Noel Hughes, 'The Young Mr Larkin', in Anthony Thwaite, *Larkin at Sixty* (Faber & Faber, London, 1982).

Blake Morrison, *The Movement: English Poetry and Fiction of the 1950s* (Methuen, London, 1986).

Andrew Motion, *Philip Larkin: A Writer's Life* (Faber & Faber, London, 1993).

Anthony Thwaite (ed.), *Larkin at Sixty* (Faber & Faber, London, 1982).

Kingsley Amis

Novels

The Alteration (Jonathan Cape, London, 1976).

The Anti-Death League (Victor Gollancz, London, 1966).

The Biographer's Moustache (HarperCollins, London, 1995).

Colonel Sun (as Robert Markham) (Jonathan Cape, London, 1968).

The Crime of the Century (J. M. Dent, London, 1987).

Difficulties with Girls (Hutchinson, London, 1988).

The Egyptologists (with Robert Conquest) (Jonathan Cape, London, 1965).

Ending Up (Jonathan Cape, London, 1974).

The Folks that Live on the Hill (Hutchinson, London, 1990).

Girl, 20 (Jonathan Cape, London, 1971).

The Green Man (Jonathan Cape, London, 1969).
I Like It Here (Victor Gollancz, London, 1958).
I Want It Now (Jonathan Cape, London, 1968).
Jake's Thing (Hutchinson, London, 1978).
Lucky Jim (Victor Gollancz, London, 1954).
The Old Devils (Hutchinson, London, 1986).
One Fat Englishman (Victor Gollancz, London, 1963).
The Riverside Villas Murder (Jonathan Cape, London, 1973).
The Russian Girl (Hutchinson, London, 1992).
Russian Hide and Seek (Hutchinson, London, 1980).
Stanley and the Women (Hutchinson, London, 1984).
Take a Girl Like You (Victor Gollancz, London, 1960).
That Uncertain Feeling (Victor Gollancz, London, 1955).
You Can't Do Both (Hutchinson, London, 1994).

Poetry
Bright November (Fortune Press, London, 1947).
A Case of Samples: Poems 1946–1956 (Victor Gollancz, London, 1956).
Collected Poems 1944–1979 (Hutchinson, London, 1979).
The Evans Country (Fantasy Press, Oxford, 1962).
A Frame of Mind (School of Art, University of Reading, Reading, 1953).
Kingsley Amis: No. 22, The Fantasy Poets (Fantasy Press, Oxford, 1954).
A Look Round the Estate: Poems 1957–1967 (Jonathan Cape, London, 1967).

Short stories
Collected Short Stories (Hutchinson Press, London, 1980; Hutchinson Press, London, 1987, including 'Investing in Futures' and 'Affairs of Death').
The Darkwater Hall Mystery (Tragara Press, Edinburgh, 1978).
Dear Illusion (Covent Garden Press, London, 1972).
My Enemy's Enemy (Victor Gollancz, London, 1962).

Criticism
'Four Fluent Fellows: An Essay on Chesterton's Fiction', in *G. K. Chesterton: A Centenary Appraisal*, ed. J. Sullivan (Paul Elek, London, 1973).
New Maps of Hell: A Survey of Science Fiction (Victor Gollancz, London, 1961).

What Became of Jane Austen? and Other Questions (Jonathan Cape, London, 1970).

Works edited or with contributions by Amis
G. K. Chesterton: Selected Stories (Faber & Faber, London, 1972).
Introduction to G. K. Chesterton, *The Man Who Was Thursday* (Penguin, Harmondsworth, 1986).
Oxford Poetry 1949, with James Michie (Basil Blackwell, London, 1949).
Tennyson (Poet to Poet Series, Penguin, Harmondsworth, 1973).

Miscellaneous writings
The Amis Collection (Hutchinson, London, 1990).
An Arts Policy? (Centre for Policy Studies, London, 1979).
The King's English: A Guide to Modern Usage (HarperCollins, London, 1997).
The Letters of Kingsley Amis, ed. Zachary Leader (HarperCollins, London, 2000).
Lucky Jim's Politics (Conservative Political Centre, London, 1979).
Memoirs (Hutchinson, London, 1991).
Socialism and the Intellectuals (Fabian Society, London, 1957).

Secondary material
Al Alvarez, *Where Did It All Go Right?* (Bloomsbury, London, 1999).
Martin Amis, *Experience* (Jonathan Cape, London, 2000).
Paul Fussell, *The Anti-Egotist: Kingsley Amis, Man of Letters* (Oxford University Press, Oxford, 1994).
Elizabeth Jane Howard, *Slipstream: A Memoir* (Macmillan, Basingstoke, 2002).
Eric Jacobs, *Kingsley Amis: A Biography* (Hodder & Stoughton, London, 1995).
Zachary Leader, *The Life of Kingsley Amis* (Vintage, London, 2006).
Zachary Leader (ed.), *The Letters of Kingsley Amis* (HarperCollins, London, 2000).
David Lodge, 'The Modern, the Contemporary and the Importance of Being Amis', in *The Language of Fiction* (Routledge & Kegan Paul, London, 1966).
Dale Salwak, *Kingsley Amis: Modern Novelist* (Harvester, London, 1992).

Index